WITHDRAWN

## Goethe's Faust *and European Epic*

Goethe has long been enshrined as the greatest German poet, but his admirers have always been uneasy with the idea that he did not produce a great epic poem. A master in all the other genres and modes, it has been felt, should have done so. Arnd Bohm proposes that Goethe did compose an epic poem, which has been hidden in plain view: *Faust*. Goethe saw that the Faust legends provided the stuff for a national epic: a German hero, a villain (Mephistopheles), a quest (to know all things), a sublime conflict (good versus evil), a love story (via Helen of Troy), and elasticity (all human knowledge could be accommodated by the plot). Bohm reveals the care with which Goethe draws upon such sources as Tasso, Ariosto, Dante, and Vergil. In the microcosm of the "Auerbachs Keller" episode Faust has the opportunity to find "what holds the world together in its essence" and to end his quest happily, but he fails. He forgets the future because he cannot remember what epic teaches. His course ends tragically, bringing him back to the origin of epic, as he replicates the Trojans' mistake of presuming to cheat the gods.

Arnd Bohm is associate professor of English at Carleton University, Ottawa.

*Studies in German Literature, Linguistics, and Culture*

Men's Bath, *woodcut by Albrecht Dürer.*
*Reproduced by permission of Philadelphia Museum of Art:*
*SmithKline Beecham Corp. Fund for the Ars Medica Collection.*

# Goethe's *Faust* and European Epic

## Forgetting the Future

Arnd Bohm

CAMDEN HOUSE

First published 2007
by Camden House

Camden House is an imprint of Boydell & Brewer Inc.
668 Mt. Hope Avenue, Rochester, NY 14620, USA
www.camden-house.com
and of Boydell & Brewer Limited
PO Box 9, Woodbridge, Suffolk IP12 3DF, UK
www.boydellandbrewer.com

ISBN-13: 978–1–57113–344–1
ISBN-10: 1–57113–344–5

Library of Congress Cataloging-in-Publication Data

Bohm, Arnd, 1953–
    Goethe's Faust and European epic: forgetting the future / Arnd Bohm.
      p. cm.
    Includes bibliographical references and index.
    ISBN-13: 978–1–57113–344–1 (alk. paper)
    ISBN-10: 1–57113–344–5 (alk. paper)
      1. Goethe, Johann Wolfgang, 1749–1832. Faust.   2. Epic Poetry,
    European—History and criticism.   I. Title.

    PT1931.B64 2007
    831'.6—dc22
                                                          2006028323

Cover illustration: *Men's Bath,* woodcut by Albrecht Dürer. Reproduced by
permission of Philadelphia Museum of Art: SmithKline Beecham Corp. Fund for
the Ars Medica Collection.

A catalogue record for this title is available from the British Library.

This publication is printed on acid-free paper.
Printed in the United States of America.

Meinen Eltern

# Contents

# Acknowledgments

M<small>Y SINCERE THANKS</small> go to all those who, whether they knew it or not, whether they agree with the project or not, have contributed to the undertaking. Its flaws are mine; its strengths are ours. First I would like to acknowledge the support of colleagues from Carleton University: J. B. Dallett, M. J. Edwards, J. Goheen, R. Gould, B. Mogridge, and R. Herz-Fischler. The Department of German at Queen's University has provided a welcoming refuge from internal exile, for which I am truly grateful. The staff in Carleton's MacOdrum Library, especially the good folk at the circulation desk and the tireless team headed by Callista Kelly in inter-library loans, cannot be thanked enough. E. M. Oppenheimer shared his Goethe with me in conversation and generous gifts. Keith and Joan Neilson, Norman Gee and Moira Day, Christopher Head, Jennifer Head, Jean and Norman Strong, Richard Ruppel and Jutta Brendel, and Marc L. Harris have sustained me in countless ways. I am fortunate to have so many friends who gather under the auspices of the Canadian Association of University Teachers of German that listing them all is not possible here — Iris Bruce, Linda Feldman, Christa Fell, Hans Walter Frischkopf, Marianne Henn, Jean Snook, and Geoffrey Winthrop-Young come to mind immediately — but all of them are important to me. Thomas Klepper, magus of the south, has never given up hope. Of the many scholars who make the conferences of the American Society for Eighteenth-Century Studies a source of intellectual refreshment, I must single out Hans Adler, Charlotte Craig, Karl Fink, Wulf Koepke, Meredith Lee, Helga Madland, John McCarthy, Rudi Nollert, Hugh Ormsby-Lenon, J. G. A. Pocock and Karin Wurst for special thanks. I wish that Gloria Flaherty could read these pages and know she would have understood how they fit with her views on Goethe.

The first results of my investigations were presented in 1983 to a Department Colloquium at Bryn Mawr College, chaired by C. Stephen Jaeger; I would like to thank him at last for that opportunity and for his suggestion to look at D. P. Walker's book. Further findings were communicated to the 1994 annual meeting of the American Society for Eighteenth-Century Studies, in the Department of Germanic Languages, Literatures and Linguistics at the University of Alberta in 1996 and in the Department of German Studies at Michigan State University in 1999. The opportunity to present an analysis of "Gretchen am Spinnrad" at the Goethe Museum Düsseldorf in June, 2001 was most welcome; many thanks to the Director, Volkmar Hansen. The attentive reader will sense the Johns Hopkins *Geist* throughout; William McClain and Lieselotte Kurth inducted me into a select company, for which I will always be grateful.

Funds from the Social Sciences and Humanities Research Council of Canada have supported the research and the dissemination of results; I acknowledge the support with gratitude, knowing how limited the money is. And last but not least, I owe much to the students who have asked questions and encouraged me — figuratively, literally — to continue believing in the community of the mind. Without that first question, nothing happens.

A. B.
September, 2006

# Introduction

TWO IMMODEST AMBITIONS DRIVE THIS STUDY: to fill what has been perceived as a major gap in Goethe's œuvre and to initiate a radical new reading of *Faust*. The means to both ends is showing that *Faust* properly belongs in the sequence of works — including Homer's *Iliad* and *Odyssey*, Vergil's *Aeneid*, Dante's *Divine Comedy*, Ariosto's *Orlando Furioso*, Tasso's *Jerusalem Liberated*, and Milton's *Paradise Lost* — that together constitute the system of European epic. Attempts to define epic much more specifically than Aristotle did, who had described it as a long poem reporting the actions of "people who are to be taken seriously," quickly become exercises in the fallacy of begging the question.[1] A given work is an epic because it displays epic forms and features, but those are known from works considered to be epics. Trying to avoid the trap of logic, Franco Moretti opts for a deliberately vague definition of epic as "a hypothesis designed to introduce a little order into a question too important to remain so confused."[2] Well, perhaps too little order. More useful is the pragmatism of Brian Wilkie's solution when he proposes

> that we can best understand epic not as a genre governed by fixed rules, whether prescriptive or inductive, but as a tradition. It is a tradition, however, that operates in an unusual way, for although, like any tradition, it is rooted in the past, it typically rejects the past as well, sometimes vigorously and with strident contempt. The great paradox of the epic lies in the fact that the partial repudiation of earlier epic tradition is itself traditional.[3]

Because the root metaphor of "tradition" ("to hand over") is unidirectional, I refer instead to the epic system. System recognizes the possibility of mutual influences of the members of the system upon each other and of the parts upon the whole. Systems are dynamic and allow for expansion and transformation as new members are incorporated.[4]

---

[1] Aristotle, *Poetics*, trans. Gerald F. Else (Ann Arbor, MI: U of Michigan P, 1973), 24–25.

[2] Franco Moretti, *Modern Epic: The World-System from Goethe to García Márquez*, trans. Quintin Hoare (London and New York: Verso, 1996), 2.

[3] Brian Wilkie, *Romantic Poets and Epic Tradition* (Madison and Milwaukee: U of Wisconsin P, 1965), 10.

[4] Stimulating in this regard is Dieter Schaller, "Das mittelalterliche Epos im Gattungsystem," in *Kontinuität und Transformation der Antike im Mittelalter:*

Goethe scholars have been uneasy about the fact that the greatest German poet had not produced a great epic poem. A master in all the other genres and modes, one felt, should have done so. Neither *Hermann und Dorothea* nor *Reineke Fuchs*, while epics of a sort, could compete with the *Iliad* or Klopstock's *Messias* as major epics. Like the letter in Edgar Allan Poe's story, Goethe's epic had been purloined and yet was in plain view. Misdirected by presuppositions about genre categories, critics did not see that *Faust* was Goethe's great epic. Among the few to think outside the established categories was Lawrence Lipking, whose discussion was refreshingly open to the possibility that Goethe might have invented a new form: "Goethe's interest in distinguishing epic from tragedy seems to have prepared him above all to violate the distinction. He would protect himself from static Virgilian correctness by resorting to a form beyond all reason: epico-tragedy, tragedo-epic."[5] Perhaps even Lipking did not realize the implications of his thesis. If *Faust* belongs with the epics, then we have to investigate how Goethe related his work to his epic precursors and how he integrated it into the epic system.

My own route to the discovery of *Faust* as an epic was circuitous, proceeding bit by bit through empirical research. The project began with a student's half-jocular question put to me some twenty years ago in a seminar. "How does Mephistopheles get the wine from the table?" he wanted to know. "It would be a nice party trick." Without considering the risk, I replied confidently that I would have the answer for next class, once I had looked it up in the standard commentaries. Chastened and chagrined, I then had to admit at our next meeting that apparently no one knew. The notes to the various editions offered the unhelpful information that the wine trick was already found in Goethe's sources and that he had not added anything of his own. The student was willing to be let the matter drop, but I was not. There surely had to be some explanation, some underlying logic to the procedure carried out by Mephistopheles.

Very little had been written about "Auerbachs Keller," since most critics saw the scene as little more than as comic relief, a prelude to the high drama of Margarete's tragic affair with Faust and to the cosmic drama of *Faust II*. As for integrating the scene into the work as a whole, the lame consensus was that it was meant to show how bored Faust was by rowdy students and their carousing. Initially I thought that an intense close-reading could find a solution, but that approach yielded little. The breakthrough came via a recognition that canto 13 of Dante's *Divine Comedy* was thematically

---

*Veröffentlichung der Kongreßakten zum Freiburgr Symposion des Mediävistenverbandes,* ed. Willi Erzgräber (Sigmaringen: Jan Thorbecke, 1989), 355–71.

[5] Lawrence Lipking, *The Life of the Poet: Beginning and Ending Poetic Careers* (Chicago and London: U of Chicago P, 1981), 98.

and structurally related — somehow — to the wine trick. The grisly story about a bush that bleeds and talks was uncanny yet familiar; trees that bleed are an arresting and extraordinary image. Fortunately, Dante scholars have developed powerful tools for tracing the connections of his work to earlier as well as later texts. Through the intersection with canto 13, "Auerbachs Keller" became the portal for linking *Faust* with the library of epics.

The project's genesis is reflected in what might seem to be an eccentric emphasis on "Auerbachs Keller" in the book. The two main sections correspond to the two stages of the investigation, albeit in reverse order. Rather than beginning with "Auerbachs Keller," the first four chapters provide a framework for the closer focus on the scene in the final three. Chapter 1 argues that Goethe had solid motives for wanting to write an epic. Like all poets striving to be laureates in their national literatures, Goethe knew that he had to demonstrate mastery of the epic. Superbly educated and bountifully endowed with poetic talent, Goethe was in a unique position to become enshrined as the greatest of German poets. Added to his excellent circumstances was the availability of a suitable subject matter in the Faust legend, which Lessing had brought to public attention. Not everyone would have made the leap to epic. Goethe's discerning eye saw that the material had the required elements: an epic hero (Faust), a villain (Mephistopheles), a quest (to know all things), a sublime conflict (good versus evil), a love story (via Helen of Troy), and elasticity (all arts and sciences, all of history and geography could be accommodated by the plot). These elements could be shaped to the exigencies of epic through emulation and differentiation.

Chapter 2 reviews how the system of European epic functioned and how *Faust* could be linked to it. Connectors include formal features such as openings and quotations; figures in whom the features of antecedents can be recognized; allusions to commonplaces and standard topoi; and variations on set pieces and episodes. The next two chapters are case studies of how *Faust* is tied to the works of Tasso, Ariosto, Dante, and Vergil, all poets Goethe knew well. The primary focus is on the episode that leads to the tapping of the wine from the table in "Auerbachs Keller." Layer by layer, the archeological excavation reveals the care with which Goethe draws upon the sources, down to the level of myth.

The second part concentrates specifically on "Auerbachs Keller," the scene that is a microcosm of the entire universe and of the work as a whole. Much like scenes on the shield of Achilles in the *Aeneid* or Jason's cloak in the *Argonautica*, "Auerbachs Keller" represents, through minute yet sufficient details, human and divine history as well as the order of nature.[6]

---

[6] Entry points to the respective discussions are Stephen Scully, "Reading the Shield of Achilles: Terror, Anger, Delight," *Harvard Studies in Classical Philology* 101 (2003): 29–47; and Anthony Bulloch, "Jason's Cloak," *Hermes* 134.1 (2006): 44–68.

Thus Faust has the opportunity to find "what holds the world together in its essence" and to end his quest happily, but he fails to do so. His melancholic condition confounds his memory so that he cannot recall his future as it was shown in the events made visible to him. Faust forgets the future because he cannot remember the past. Faust's course, unlike that of the Pilgrim of Dante's comedy, who finally does gain insight and understanding, ends tragically. Or rather, it ends where European epic and history began, as Faust replicates the mistake made by the Trojans at the founding of their city, when they presumed to cheat the gods.

Each chapter in the second part demonstrates what "Auerbachs Keller" contributes to the themes of epic in *Faust*. In chapter 5 the crises of the sixteenth and the eighteenth centuries are viewed as continuations of the political crisis that began with the Trojan War and were passed along to the Roman and then the Holy Roman Empires. Chapter 6 shows how subtly Goethe developed the theological (Christian) themes that the Faust material provided and that the epic system since Dante had required. In this light, "Auerbachs Keller" is a theatre in hell where Mephistopheles mocks the faithful, blasphemes against God and Christ, and tortures the damned. The final chapter examines how Goethe responded to the challenge that each epic was supposed to present an up-to-date summary of scientific knowledge. By using Faust as a representative of the premodern scholar who failed to keep pace with the scientific revolution and Mephistopheles as a figure of the cunning scientist, Goethe is able to show science as an evolving body of knowledge, one that no one can outguess.

# 1: Goethe's Epic Ambitions

THE ARCH OF EUROPEAN EPIC rests on Homer as the first and on Milton as the last pillar, encompassing in its sweep major contributors such as Vergil, Dante, Ariosto, Tasso, Chaucer, Spenser, and Milton, as well as lesser ones such as Lucan, Statius, Pulci, Boiardo, Vida, Drayton, Cowley, Camões, and Klopstock. Several of the English Romantics did try to produce an epic. Wordsworth completed *The Prelude*;[1] Keats began an epic with *Hyperion*;[2] and Byron may lay some claim to the tradition with *Don Juan*.[3] On the whole, however, critics have generally been uneasy about the attempts to produce epics since the eighteenth century.[4] David Quint has expressed the consensus near the conclusion of his *Epic and Empire*: "Milton pronounces the demise of epic as a genre, and since he had no great successors, he appears from the perspective of a later literary history to have fulfilled the ambition of every epic poet: to have written the epic to end all epics."[5] Were it not for the fact that German literary historians

---

[1] On Wordsworth's aspirations in the context of eighteenth-century views of epic, see Karl Kroeber, *Romantic Narrative Art* (Madison: U of Wisconsin P, 1960), 78–112; Brian Wilkie, *Romantic Poets and Epic Tradition* (Madison: U of Wisconsin P, 1965), 59–111; Stuart Peterfreund, "*The Prelude*: Wordsworth's Metamorphic Epic," *Genre* 14 (1981): 441–72; and Stuart Curran, *Poetic Form and British Romanticism* (New York: Oxford UP, 1986), 182–90.

[2] Walter Jackson Bate, *John Keats* (Cambridge, MA: The Belknap P of Harvard UP, 1963), 388–417; Wilkie, *Romantic Poets and Epic Tradition*, 145–88; Masaki Mori, *Epic Grandeur: Toward a Comparative Poetics of the Epic* (Albany, NY: SUNY P, 1997), 101–10.

[3] Wilkie, *Romantic Poets and Epic Tradition*, 188–226; Donald H. Reiman, "*Don Juan* in Epic Context," *Studies in Romanticism* 16 (1977): 587–94; and Curran, *Poetic Form and British Romanticism*, 190–98.

[4] On more recent attempts at writing epics, see H. J. Schueler, *The German Verse Epic in the Nineteenth and Twentieth Centuries* (The Hague: Martinus Nijhoff, 1967); L. R. Lind, "The Great American Epic," *Classical and Modern Literature* 17.1 (1996): 7–29; and Joseph Farrell, "Walcott's *Omeros*: The Classical Epic in a Postmodern World," *The South Atlantic Quarterly* 96.2 (1997): 247–73.

[5] David Quint, *Epic and Empire: Politics and Generic Form from Virgil to Milton* (Princeton: Princeton UP, 1993), 340; see also Robert M. Durling, "The Epic Ideal," in *Literature and Western Civilization*, vol. 3: *The Old World: Discovery and Rebirth*, ed. David Daiches and Anthony Thorlby (London: Aldus Books, 1974), 105–46; here, 140.

bear the primary responsibility for the exclusion of Goethe from the precinct of the epic, one might suspect lingering nationalism of the sort that characterized the debates about the ancients and the moderns in the insistence that Milton marks the end of the tradition. Goethe's exclusion is due partly to the difficult genre issues, but a major cause has been the continued emphasis of Goethe scholars upon the notion of Goethe as a solitary genius whose works emerged from the great man's personal experience.[6] Consequently, important domains of research into the intertextualities of *Faust* have been largely overlooked, impoverishing our understanding of the work. Ironically, the more that Germans have clung to an ahistorical model of Goethe's literary production so as to envelop him with glory, the more they have removed him from the awareness of readers who should marvel at his accomplishment in renewing and extending the epic into the modern age.

The motivation behind Goethe's lifelong involvement with the epic *Faust* had its origins in the literary system and the economy of fame. Fame has an implacable logic. Like wealth, with which it has much in common, fame is a relative measure, contingent upon time, circumstance, and the vagaries of fortune.[7] Those who aspire to an enduring fame have to choose their sphere of activity with care, especially if they are to prevent their reputations from being converted into either of fame's antitheses: oblivion or infamy. Although great military conquests such as those of Alexander were once reliable means for becoming famous, that option was made less desirable for Christians because it clashed with the avowed irenic ideals and the hope for an end to wars in Christendom. Nor did monarchs stand securely on the pedestal of fame, as the ruins of empire so starkly reminded everyone, memorably evoked by Shelley:

> "My name is Ozymandias, king of kings:
> Look on my works, ye Mighty, and despair!"
> Nothing beside remains. Round the decay

---

[6] Compare Gerhart von Graevenitz, "Gewendete Allegorie: Das Ende der 'Erlebnislyrik' und die Vorbereitung einer Poetik der modernen Lyrik in Goethes Sonett-Zyklus von 1815/1827," in *Allegorie: Konfigurationen von Text, Bild und Lektüre*, ed. Evan Horn and Manfred Weinberg (Opladen: Westdeutscher Verlag, 1998), 97–117.

[7] On fame in all fields, see Leo Braudy, *The Frenzy of Renown: Fame & Its History* (New York and Oxford: Oxford UP, 1986). Much of the analysis by Richard Helgerson in his book *Self-Crowned Laureates: Spenser Jonson Milton and the Literary System* (Berkeley and Los Angeles: U of California P, 1983) applies to the German literary system, mutatis mutandis.

> Of that colossal wreck, boundless and bare
> The lone and level sands stretch far away.[8]

The field of science had once been a reasonable guarantor of fame, but by the eighteenth century the tremendous growth in the quantity of research and the increasing acceleration of technical progress meant that only a very few would acquire and retain the prominence of a Newton. Nor should it be forgotten that this was an arena in which Goethe also sought to be an active participant.[9]

Confronted by such considerations, a young man such as Goethe was drawn almost inevitably to test himself in the one arena where permanent fame could be constructed, namely in literature. Unlike transitory institutions such as nation states, literary monuments were grounded in language, the most enduring of human accomplishments. When little else remained of the Greeks, Homer's poetry had survived, becoming influential again in the eighteenth century. Even when Latin had yielded supremacy to the vernaculars, Vergil was still studied and respected. Even the fragmentation of the Holy Roman Empire and of the erstwhile universal republic of letters that had been overlaid upon the political system, also increasingly broken into national subsystems, did not undermine the importance of literary fame. Instead, these developments opened up the possibility for the insertion of new supreme poets into the pantheons of their respective national languages. Each language provided space for a national epic. Thus Dante could function in Italian as Vergil did for Latin, as Milton would for English; a poet who wanted to rank with them would have to attempt an epic. As Lawrence Lipking observes, "At one time the prestige of the epic led many poets and critics to believe that nothing but an epic could conclude a career."[10] But their contests for supremacy, for a claim to a place in the canon, were difficult, and they by no means assured an individual success. There were spectacular failures, such as Ronsard's *Franciade*, and often critical acclaim was won at a high personal price, as in the notorious case of Tasso and his *Gerusalemme Liberata*. The respective national literary histories are replete with the names of poets whose obscurity confirms that they did not triumph.[11]

---

[8] Percy Bysshe Shelley, *Poetical Works*, ed. Thomas Hutchinson (London and New York: Oxford UP, 1967), 550.

[9] An good overview is provided by Karl J. Fink, *Goethe's History of Science* (Cambridge and New York: Cambridge UP, 1991), 93–104.

[10] Lawrence Lipking, *The Life of the Poet: Beginning and Ending Poetic Careers* (Chicago and London: U of Chicago P, 1981), 69.

[11] Ample evidence of writers whose works have not led to their being recused from oblivion is found in Paul F. Grendler's article "Chivalric Romances in the Italian

For aspiring German writers in the eighteenth century, there were two major obstacles blocking the production of a great epic. One, frequently lamented by contemporaries, was the absence of a single national capital such as the French had in Paris, where the sovereign might act as a patron and the court would provide a first audience. The other, equally pressing, was the lack of suitable material. All poets faced the same difficulty; one need only recall Wordsworth's discussion of the choices he considered for an epic before he wrote *The Prelude*.[12] German poets had particular difficulty in finding a suitable German hero.[13] To quote Goethe from *Dichtung und Wahrheit*: "Betrachtet man genau, was der deutschen Poesie fehlte, so war es ein Gehalt, und zwar ein nationeller; an Talenten war niemals Mangel."[14] Poor or arbitrary choices could produce only unhappy results, as in the negative example of Johann Ulrich König (1688–1744), pilloried by his contemporaries and damned with faint praise by Goethe. König had been court poet for August the Strong of Saxony and had been commissioned to write an epic on the occasion of an extravagant military pageant staged by the king in June 1730. Such a frivolous occasion could never sustain the weight of an epic, and "August im Lager" did not proceed past the first book. Goethe recorded the caustic reaction of critics:

> Freilich hatte dieser Gegenstand einen inneren Mangel; eben daß es nur Prunk und Schein war, aus dem keine Tat hervortreten konnte. . . . Er mußte den Hof- und Staatskalender zu Rate ziehen, und die Zeichnung der Personen lief daher ziemlich trocken ab; ja schon die Zeitgenossen

---

Renaissance," *Studies in Medieval and Renaissance History* NS 10 (1988): 59–102; Ulrich Langer, "Boring Epic in Early Modern France," in *Epic and Epoch: Essays on the Interpretation and History of a Genre*, ed. Steven M. Oberhelman, Van Kelly, and Richard J. Goslan (Lubbock, TX: Texas Tech UP, 1994), 208–29; Barbara Kiefer Lewalski, *Milton's Brief Epic: The Genre, Meaning and Art of* Paradise Regained (Providence, RI: Brown UP and London: Methuen, 1966), 68–101 and 377–85; Dieter Martin, *Das deutsche Versepos im 18. Jahrhundert: Studien und kommentierte Gattungsbibliographie* (Berlin and New York: de Gruyter, 1993); and David Maskell, *The Historical Epic in France, 1500–1700* (Oxford: Oxford UP, 1973).

   [12] William Wordsworth, *The Five-Book Prelude*, ed. Duncan Wu (Oxford: Blackwell, 1997), 45–47, Version 1: 175–225. The same problems had faced Milton; see Gordon Teskey, "Milton's Choice of Subject in the Context of Renaissance Critical Theory," *ELH* 53 (1986): 53–72.

   [13] See Conrad Wiedemann, "Zwischen Nationalgeist und Kosmopolitismus: Über die Schwierigkeiten der deutschen Klassiker, einen Nationalhelden zu finden," *Aufklärung* 4.2 (1989): 75–101.

   [14] Johann Wolfgang von Goethe, *Dichtung und Wahrheit*, in *Werke: Hamburger Ausgabe in 14 Bänden* ed. Erich Trunz (Munich: C. H. Beck, 1981), 9:264. This "Hamburger Ausgabe" will be cited henceforth in the text as HA.

machten ihm den Vorwurf, er habe die Pferde besser geschildert als die Menschen.[15]

The quest for suitable material led German writers in various directions, as Dieter Martin's thorough study *Das deutsche Versepos im 18. Jahrhundert* recounts.

Compounding the difficulties was the turn that epics had taken towards Christian themes since Dante. Once Milton had staked a claim to the Fall, subsequent poets had turned to other themes, such as the Flood. Klopstock dared to attempt a reworking of the life of Christ in his *Messias* and immediately ran into a conflict between the needs of the genre and the constraints of religion. How far could a poet go in inventing material to fill in the gaps of what was told in the Gospels? The parameters were set by a knowledgeable and committed reading public, as Moses Mendelssohn wrote to Lessing on 2 August 1756:

> Ja vielleicht ist dieser große Dichter auch darin unglücklich, daß alle kleine Umstände seines Subjekts allzu bekannt sind, und daß er nicht den mindesten Umstand darinn ändern könnte, ohne sich in theologische Streitigkeiten einzulassen. Es wäre mehr als ein Wunder, wenn sich eine Begebenheit so in der Natur zugetragen hätte, wie sie der Dichter brauchet.[16]

Because the audience knew Scripture all too well, Klopstock had virtually no room for amplification and elaboration, so that in effect the poem was an extended paraphrase in rhyme, admirable but neither overwhelming nor able to meet the challenges of its epic precursors. With the immediate material associated with Scripture either occupied, exhausted, or unsuitable, the young Goethe at one point contemplated using the story of the "Wandering Jew" as the framework for an epic that could encompass not only Christian but Jewish and world history.[17] The project was not carried out, not least because Goethe came upon much more workable material, which also had the advantage of national interest.

While attempting to emancipate German literature from the predominance of the French, Klopstock had advocated the concept of a "teutonic"

---

[15] Goethe, *Dichtung und Wahrheit*, in HA, 9:265.

[16] Gotthold Ephraim Lessing, *Werke und Briefe*, ed. Wilfried Barner et al., vol. 11.1: *Briefe von und an Lessing, 1743–1770*, ed. Helmuth Kiesel with Georg Braungart and Klaus Fischer (Frankfurt am Main: Deutscher Klassiker Verlag, 1987), 101.

[17] Heinrich Clairmont, "Der ewige Jude," in *Goethe Handbuch in vier Bänden*, ed. Bernd Witte, Theo Buck, Hans-Dietrich Dahnke, Regine Otto, and Peter Schmidt, vol. 1:, *Gedichte*, ed. Regine Otto and Bernd Witte (Stuttgart and Weimar: J. B. Metzler, 1996) 540–46.

tradition that supposedly had run parallel to the Roman and Latin influences. This turn towards a "national" cultural heritage spurred the quest for a "Germanic" hero who could be added to the series continuing from Achilles and Aeneas; Hermann (Arminius) seemed especially suitable.[18] Goethe's participation in the search yielded *Götz von Berlichingen* and drew him to the sixteenth century, where he researched figures such as Hans Sachs and Albrecht Dürer. The difficulty was how to graft such "Germanic" heroes back into a tapestry dominated by eschatological themes, such as those that the story of the "Wandering Jew" could have sustained. The gap would be filled from an unexpected quarter. The story of Faust, first put to higher literary use by Christopher Marlowe, met the key requirements. Set in Germany during a time of transition, the legends about a man who bargained his soul away could represent the crisis of Christian faith as well as the historical crises of the Holy Roman Empire. The legends also came equipped with links to the classics, via Faust's position as a scholar during the Renaissance and via the episode with Helen. Conversely, there were so few concrete historical details known about Faust's life that there were almost no restrictions upon any skilful writer's powers of imagination. To this day, German literary historians have discovered virtually no evidence about the "real historical" Faust against which Goethe's work may be measured and found wanting.[19]

It would be misguided to ask where then Goethe blatantly laid out his intentions to make a national epic on the basis of the *Faust* material. For one thing, any such declaration would have been counterproductive, since the mere declaration of the goal could incline a critical public towards skepticism. The sad example for the destructive interaction of audience and author was present to Goethe's awareness in the example of Torquato Tasso, whose lofty ambitions were so cruelly scorned by his contemporaries. A second and more serious reason is that for a long time Goethe himself

---

[18] See Richard Kuehnemund, *Arminius or the Rise of a National Symbol in Literature* (Chapel Hill: U of North Carolina, 1953); Harro Zimmermann, *Freiheit und Geschichte: F. G. Klopstock als historischer Dichter und Denker* (Heidelberg: Carl Winter, 1987), 234–42; and Hans Peter Hermann, " 'Ich bin fürs Vaterland zu sterben auch bereit': Patriotismus oder Nationalismus im 18. Jahrhundert? Lesenotizen zu den deutschen Arminiusdramen, 1740–1808," in *Machtphantasie Deutschland: Nationalismus, Männlichkeit und Fremdenhaß im Vaterlandsdiskurs deutscher Schriftsteller des 18. Jahrhunderts*, ed. Hans Peter Herrmann, Hans-Martin Blitz, and Susanna Moßmann (Frankfurt am Main: Suhrkamp, 1996), 32–65.

[19] On the search for the historical Faust, see Frank Baron, *Doctor Faustus from History to Legend* (Munich: Fink, 1978); Hans Henning, "Faust als historische Gestalt," *Goethe: Neue Folge des Jahrbuchs der Goethe-Gesellschaft* 21 (1959): 107–39.

had doubts about the viability of the project. After a strong beginning in the early 1770s, various factors undermined his confidence about his abilities and about the project as such. For the former, there was the fate of Werther, whose imitations of epic voices and postures (Homer, Klopstock, Ossian) were indicted as symptoms and causes of social maladjustment.[20] For the latter, Wilhelm Meister's dramatization of a scene from *Gerusalemme Liberata* suggests that Goethe too found himself more persuaded by the possibilities of the theatre than those of the epic poem. Because Goethe destroyed so many of his early papers, the evidence overall is scanty. One of the few recorded traces about his attitude to *Faust* comes in his recollections dated 1 March 1788 in the *Italienische Reise*:

> Das alte Manuscript macht mir manchmal zu denken, wenn ich es vor mir sehe. Es ist noch das erste, ja in den Hauptszenen gleich so ohne Konzept hingeschrieben, nun ist es so gelb von der Zeit, so vergriffen . . . , so mürbe und an den Rändern zerstoßen, daß es wirklich wie das Fragment eines alten Codex aussieht. (HA 11:525)

Interesting here is the comparison of the draft to an "old codex," which suggests at least some residual association of Goethe's manuscript with more ancient texts.[21]

Despite intense scrutiny, the available evidence is so fragmentary that we will probably never know exactly when Goethe conceived or wrote all the scenes of *Faust I*. There is some consensus that by 1772 Goethe had begun to work on the Faust material;[22] the *Urfaust* must have been substantially completed by November 1775. Because of its obvious proximity to the Faust legends, it has been suggested that "Auerbachs Keller in Leipzig" is one of the earliest scenes Goethe wrote, even though there is no hard evidence for this.[23] The exact date of composition seems beyond recovery, not only because of the usual difficulties with the transmission of

---

[20] A subtle and convincing analysis of Werther as a response to Goethe's relationship to Klopstock is provided by Meredith Lee, *Displacing Authority: Goethe's Poetic Reception of Klopstock* (Heidelberg: Universitätsverlag C. Winter, 1999), 161–88.

[21] The importance of the material transmission of epics had been highlighted by the controversy around Macpherson's *Ossian* poems and by the discovery and publication of the *Nibelungenlied*, published 1757 by Johann Jakob Bodmer and 1782 by Christoph Heinrich Myller.

[22] See Hanna Fischer-Lamberg, "Zur Datierung der ältesten Szenen des Urfaust," *Zeitschrift für deutsche Philologie* 76 (1957): 379–406.

[23] The discussion on the origin of the scene is summarized in Valters Nollendorfs, *Der Streit um den Urfaust* (The Hague and Paris: Mouton, 1967), 227–40.

manuscripts, but because Goethe was at that period of his life in a furtive mood, concealing his projects and aspirations even from close friends such as Herder.[24] Looking back in *Dichtung und Wahrheit* on the period from autumn 1770 to spring 1771, Goethe recalled keeping secrets from Herder: "Am sorgfältigsten verbarg ich ihm das Interesse an gewissen Gegenständen, die sich bei mir eingewurzelt hatten und sich nach und nach zu poetischen Gestalten ausbilden wollten. Es waren Götz von Berlichingen und Faust" (HA 9:413). In a famous comparison, Goethe hints at an affinity for both characters:

> Die Lebensbeschreibung des erstern hatte mich im Innersten ergriffen. Die Gestalt eines rohen, wohlmeinenden Selbsthelfers in wilder, anarchischer Zeit erregte meinen tiefsten Anteil. Die bedeutende Puppenspielfabel des andern klang und summte gar vieltönig in mir wider. Auch ich hatte mich in allem Wissen umhergetrieben und war früh genug auf die Eitelkeit desselben hingewiesen worden. Ich hatte es auch auf allerlei Weise versucht und war immer unbefriedigter und gequälter zurückgekommen. (HA 9:413)

Before drawing the conclusion that this is evidence that Goethe and Faust can be equated, we have to recall Goethe's idiosyncratic relationship to his literary inventions. It was not that he identified with them so as to project himself in and through them, but rather that he projected certain negative aspects on to them, almost therapeutically, in order to overcome the personal troubles vicariously. The blatant case was Werther, in whom Goethe overcame his personal fascination with the possibility of suicide and transformed the hapless figure of Jerusalem into a drastic negative example; similar projections can be found in Egmont or Tasso. What Goethe is telling in this passage then is not how he might have resembled Faust at some time, but that he diverged from that character's trajectory. "Early enough" Goethe had been made aware of the "vanity" in "wandering aimlessly through knowledge." And then Goethe adds something in the same paragraph that was obviously connected with these projects in his mind, yet of a different order: "Am meisten aber verbarg ich vor Herdern meine mystisch-kabbalistische Chemie, und was sich darauf bezog, ob ich mich gleich noch sehr gern heimlich beschäftigte, sie konsequenter auszubilden, als man sie mir überliefert hatte" (HA 9:414). The narrative space between

---

[24] On Goethe's almost habitual secretiveness, his unwillingness to put innermost thoughts into words, see Otto Lorenz, "Verschwiegenheit: Zum Geheimnis-Motiv der 'Römischen Elegien,'" *Text + Kritik*, Sonderband: *Johann Wolfgang von Goethe* (Munich: text + kritik, 1982), 130–52; here 134–39; see the literature he cites in note 18.

the mention of Faust's aimless pursuit of knowledge and Goethe's revelation (many years after the event) of his intense, systematic study of the alchemical discourse is significant. Having given up the attitude represented by an earlier self and still represented by the literary character Faust, Goethe had already moved on to serious research.

What is usually referred to as "Goethe's *Faust*" had a complicated publishing history. The so-called *Urfaust* was completed by 1775 and an unauthorized copy was made by Luise von Göchhausen between 1776 and 1780, but this version was not rediscovered until 1887, when Erich Schmidt found it in her papers. Schmidt published it the same year as *Goethes Faust in ursprünglicher Gestalt nach der Göchhausenschen Abschrift*. The text had been revised by Goethe and published in 1790 as *Faust: Ein Fragment* in volume 7 of a collected edition of his works. There were extensive and systematic revisions from the *Urfaust* to the *Fragment*. After that, "Auerbachs Keller in Leipzig" would remain substantially unchanged; however, the work as a whole would not. After letting it lie fallow for several years, Goethe took up the work again in 1797, after he and Schiller had overcome an impasse about the possibility of writing a modern heroic epic poem. *Der Tragödie Erster Teil* was published by Cotta in four editions (1808, 1816, 1821, and 1825). The entire *Faust* would not be completed for decades, and a full text of *Der Tragödie Zweiter Teil* appeared only posthumously.[25]

Because it has some bearing upon how we conceptualize Goethe's attitude to the Faust project, it is worth pausing to look at his decision in 1797 to continue working on what might have remained a torso. Certainly the press of other business associated with the move to Weimar will have played some role in Goethe's decision to publish *Faust: Ein Fragment* as the interim conclusion to the project, salvaging as a drama what could be used of the work he had put into background research and individual sections. The plan for a large-scale philosophical epic on "Die Geheimnisse" was considered by Goethe in the mid-1780s, only to be abandoned.[26] But then in the 1790s Goethe's attention was focused repeatedly on the epic and the conditions for its production. In addition to his intense discussions

---

[25] A handy summary is provided by Theodor Friedrich and Lothar J. Scheithauer in their *Kommentar zu Goethes Faust: Mit einem Faust-Wörterbuch und einer Faust-Bibliographie* (Stuttgart: Reclam, 1994), 68–84. For a detailed summary of the research, see Ulrich Gaier, *Kommentar II*, which is vol. 3 of Johann Wolfgang von Goethe, *Faust-Dichtungen*, ed. Ulrich Gaier (Stuttgart: Philipp Reclam, 1999), 46–151.

[26] Hans-Dietrich Dahnke, "Die Geheimnisse," in Otto and Witte, *Gedichte*, 546–52.

with Schiller,[27] there were stimuli such as Stolberg's and Voss's translations of Homer.[28]

Goethe made several stabs at an epic, including "Achilleis,"[29] "Nausikaa,"[30] "Hermann und Dorothea,"[31] and "Reineke Fuchs."[32] The work eventually written 1826 in prose form as *Novelle* was initially construed in 1797 as an epic poem around the theme of hunting; this was in fact the project that prompted some of Schiller's most extensive reflections about the difficulties confronting the modern epic poet.[33] Important also was the publication in 1795 of Friedrich August Wolf's *Prolegomena ad Homerum*, which made Goethe rethink the fundamental assumptions about the composition and form of the epic.[34] What has not been sufficiently

---

[27] See Richard Littlejohns, "The Discussion between Goethe and Schiller on the Epic and Dramatic and its Relevance to *Faust*," *Neophilologus* 71 (1987): 388–401; and E. L. Stahl, "Schiller and the Composition of Goethe's *Faust*," *Germanic Review* 34 (1959): 185–99.

[28] See Günter Häntzschel, "Die Ausbildung der deutschen Literatursprache des 18. Jahrhunderts durch Übersetzungen: Homer-Verdeutschungen als produktive Kraft," in *Mehrsprachigkeit in der deutschen Aufklärung*, ed. Dieter Kimpel (Hamburg: Felix Meiner, 1985), 117–32; and Gerhard Lohse, "Die Homerrezeption im 'Sturm und Drang' und deutscher Nationalismus im 18. Jahrhundert," *International Journal of the Classical Tradition* 4.2 (1997): 195–231.

[29] Elke Dreisbach, *Goethes "Achilleis"* (Heidelberg: Universitätsverlag C. Winter, 1994); Melitta Gerhard, "Götter-Kosmos und Gesetzes-Suche: Zu Goethes Versuch seines Achilleis-Epos," *Monatshefte* 56.4 (1964): 145–59; Wolfgang Schadewaldt, "Fausts Ende und die Achilleis," in *Weltbewohner und Weimaraner: Ernst Beutler zugedacht*, ed. Benno Reifenberg and Emil Staiger (Zurich and Stuttgart: Artemis, 1960), 243–60; Martin, *Das deutsche Versepos im 18. Jahrhundert*, 295–96; Friedrich Sengle, *Neues zu Goethe: Essays und Vorträge* (Stuttgart: J. B. Metzler, 1989), 69–85; and Christian-Friedrich Collatz, "Achilleis," in Otto and Witte, *Gedichte*, 537–40.

[30] Rüdiger Görner, "Goethe's Ulysses: On the Meaning of a Project," *Publications of the English Goethe Society* NS 44/45 (1993–95): 21–37; and David Constantine, "*Achilleis* and *Nausikaa*: Goethe in Homer's World," *Oxford German Studies* 15 (1984): 95–111.

[31] Sengle, *Neues zu Goethe*, 49–68; Yahya A. Elsaghe, "Hermann und Dorothea," in Otto and Witte, *Gedichte*, 519–37.

[32] Lothar Schwab, *Vom Sünder zum Schelmen: Goethes Bearbeitung des Reineke Fuchs* (Frankfurt am Main: Athenäum, 1971), esp. 27–38 and 92–106. See also Hans-Wolf Jäger, "Reineke Fuchs," in Otto and Witte, *Gedichte*, 508–18.

[33] See the summary of the origins of *Novelle* (HA 6:735–42).

[34] Joachim Wohlleben, "Goethe and the Homeric Question," *Germanic Review* 42 (1967): 251–75; Martin, *Das deutsche Versepos im 18. Jahrhundert*, 249–57; Dreisbach, *Goethes "Achilleis,"* 24–31.

recognized, due in part to the compartmentalization of his works, is that out of this nexus Goethe returns to the *Faust* material. Schadewaldt argued persuasively that Goethe's involvement with the "Achilleis" shaped *Faust II* and in particular the conclusion.[35] What I want to stress are three propositions about the return to *Faust* in the context of the lively German interest in epic in the last decade of the eighteenth century.

First, Goethe's return to the larger epic was possible because he had come to understand, and accept, the historicity of epic as a genre. Each epic not only reflected the subject matter and the philosophical concerns of its gestation period but also embodied the respective historical context in the *form* of its production. Thus it was futile to attempt to recreate with absolute loyalty the metrics of a Homer or the rigorous, numerically governed form of Dante's *Commedia* in the present: style had of necessity to bow to contemporary expectations. Although this may seem a minor shift today, it marked a crucial inversion of aesthetic values in the epic system, for one of the given aspirations of epic had always been to transcend the exigencies of the moment, to forge a timeless, universal work of art. Once the epic was historicized, the poets could insist that only through sinking deeply into the local context of production would an epic achieve uniqueness.

This in turn raised the question of what form the epic should take. From the audience's point of view, the direction was indicated by *Wilhelm Meister*, namely, to blur the boundary between drama and epic.[36] Most readers had long sensed that there were "dramatic" episodes in epics that contrasted with less theatrical, less visually compelling transitions and interludes. Pictorial illustrations of epics drew upon the same experience, so that key scenes came to represent the story lines.[37] The same could be done on the stage. From the author's perspective, the melding of epic and drama was a powerful and liberating tactic, not least because it did away with the requirement for an omniscient epic narrator.[38] By the eighteenth

---

[35] Schadewalt, "Fausts Ende und die Achilleis," 248.

[36] A pertinent example of the crossover from epic to drama was Heinrich Wilhelm von Gerstenberg's *Ugolino* (1768). Not to be underestimated is the influence of operas; Aeneas's abandonment of Dido was an extremely popular story. For an overview of its German reception, see Eberhard Semrau, *Dido in der deutschen Dichtung* (Berlin and Leipzig: Walter de Gruyter, 1930).

[37] See for example Nigel Llewellyn, "Virgil and the Visual Arts," in *Virgil and His Influence: Bimillennial Studies*, ed. Charles Martindale (Bristol: Bristol Classical P, 1984), 117–40, on paintings derived from Virgil; and Rensselaer W. Lee, *Names on Trees: Ariosto into Art* (Princeton: Princeton UP, 1977), on Angelica and Medoro from Canto 19 of *Orlando Furioso*.

[38] An incisive analysis of the narrator's crisis of knowledge in the writing of epics is developed by Eberhard Müller-Bochat in his article "Die Einheit des Wissens

century, the role articulated by Tasso for such a narrator had become implausible, even if Johann Christoph Gottsched still clung to the ideal. Readers were not willing to accept narrators who claimed to have virtually unlimited knowledge of the world, and mocked rather than respected narrating characters who violated laws of time and space.[39] Drama evades the difficulty by transposing the authorial voice into the characters, into the staging, and above all into the plot itself, for on the stage no narrator attempts to convince us by telling us that a poodle turns into Mephistopheles — it just happens.

With the genre problems resolved — or at least shunted aside, there was nothing to block Goethe from completing the *Faust* project. The work on the first part could be integrated relatively seamlessly into a newer, larger project, without recasting the dramatic scenes into the confines of verse. More important, once the second part was completed, the underlying epic themes and allusions that had been intricately woven into *Faust I* would finally come to full resonance. I agree with Schadewaldt that *Faust II* bears the impress of Achilles, but I would also maintain that in Goethe's plan the Faust of the first part had also, from the outset, been conceived of as a type of Achilles. In this connection Jane Brown is correct in detecting allusions to Vergil in *Faust II*;[40] but the network of such allusions was woven into *Faust I* from the beginning.

In addition to a frequent mistaken identification of Goethe the author with Faust the character, there is another odd assumption prevalent in Goethe studies. This is the division of his career into a "non-classicizing" and then a "classicizing" phase. The premises are shaky. The assumption is that as a *Stürmer und Dränger* Goethe shared in the exuberant patriotic sentiments associated with the poets of the "Göttinger Hainbund." Proof for this is found in his use of figures from the fifteenth and sixteenth centuries: Götz von Berlichingen, Dürer, Hans Sachs, the Gothic architect Erwin, and Faust. Behind such assumptions is the idea that Goethe was subscribing to a model of history in which the centre of civilization was moving in that era from Italy (Medieval) to the German Holy Roman Empire (Renaissance and Reformation). Aside from the objective historians' reservations about such a model, there is the matter of Goethe's turn

---

und das Epos: Zur Geschichte eines utopischen Gattungsbegriffs," *Romanistisches Jahrbuch* 17 (1966): 58–81. For an extended discussion, see Robert M. Durling, *The Figure of the Poet in Renaissance Epic* (Cambridge, MA: Harvard UP, 1965).

[39] See Mindele Anne Treip, *Allegorical Poetics & the Epic: The Renaissance Tradition to* Paradise Lost (Lexington: U of Kentucky P, 1994), 106–18.

[40] Jane K. Brown, *Goethe's Faust: The German Tragedy* (Ithaca and London: Cornell UP, 1986), 195–96.

to the classical world to consider. The chronological sequence of when works were published is misleading about Goethe's intellectual development. For example, *Torquato Tasso* was written in the early 1780s, but Goethe had known the poet's works from early childhood. His father, a keen lover of Italian literature and culture, had an extensive library, including the canonical Greek, Latin, and Italian writers.[41] Even where the young Goethe's reading is not documented — Tasso, Boccaccio, and Ovid for instance are — there can be no doubt that he read Vergil, Dante, Ariosto, and much more.[42] To the Greeks in the original Goethe seems to have come somewhat later. In the early 1770s, with impetus from Herder, but doubtless also as an extension of his alchemical research, Goethe began an intensive study of Greek and of Greek literature.[43] "Wandrers Sturmlied" dates from early 1772, that is, it coincides with the gestation of *Faust*. Although *Iphigenie auf Tauris* would not be written until a decade later, Goethe was at this time reading the Greek tragedians.[44] In sum, the blanket exclusion of "classical" influences on the basis of an arbitrary and inaccurate division of Goethe's life into two completely separate phases is unwarranted.

The mingling of "classical" and "non-classical" or "German" themes was thorough. Let us take Goethe at his word when he reported that Helena, that quintessence of the "classical" in *Faust*, had always been in his mind together with Faust.[45] He wrote to Sulpiz Boisserée on 22 October

---

[41] Franz Götting, "Die Bibliothek von Goethes Vater," *Nassauische Annalen: Jahrbuch des Vereins für Nassauischen Altertumskunde und Geschichtsforschung* 64 (1953): 23–69; here, 42–44 and 55–56.

[42] On his extensive familiarity with Renaissance poetry, see Stuart Atkins, "Goethe und die Renaissancelyrik," in *Goethe und die Tradition*, ed. Hans Reiss (Frankfurt am Main: Athenäum, 1972), 102–29, available in a translation by Jane K. Brown as: "Goethe and the Poetry of the Renaissance," in Atkins, *Essays on Goethe*, ed. Jane K. Brown and Thomas P. Saine (Columbia, SC: Camden House, 1995), 92–117.

[43] See Ernst-Richard Schwinge, *Goethe und die Poesie der Griechen* (Mainz: Akademie der Wissenschaften und der Literatur, and Stuttgart: Franz Steiner Verlag Wiesbaden, 1986).

[44] In addition to Schwinge, *Goethe und die Poesie der Griechen*, see Uwe Petersen, *Goethe und Euripides: Untersuchungen zur Euripides-Rezeption in der Goethezeit* (Heidelberg: Carl Winter, 1974); and Ernst Grumach, *Goethe und die Antike: Eine Sammlung* (Potsdam: Verlag Eduard Stichnote, 1949), *passim*.

[45] My discussion and the quotations are derived from Thomas Gelzer, "Helena im Faust: Ein Beispiel für Goethes Umgang mit der antiken Mythologie," in *Mythographie der frühen Neuzeit: Ihre Anwendung in den Künsten*, ed. Walter Killy (Wiesbaden: Otto Harrassowitz for the Herzog August Bibliothek Wolfenbüttel, 1984), 223–53.

1826: "Die 'Helena' ist eine meiner ältesten Conceptionen, gleichzeitig mit 'Faust,' immer nach einem Sinne, aber immer um und um gebildet."[46] And on the same day to Humboldt he mentioned the "Puppenspiel-Überlieferung, daß Faust den Mephistopheles genöthigt, ihm die Helena zum Beilager heranzuschaffen."[47] There is no difficulty in seeing that Goethe carried through on this perceived obligation in *Faust II*. But surely, the critics' reading goes, he must be wrong to suggest that Helena was *always* part of the concept, which would entail her presence in *Faust I*. This is one of the puzzles yet to be solved. Just because we have not detected Helena in the first part does not guarantee that Goethe was mistaken about his own plans or had forgotten what he had written. The more likely possibility is that we have not looked hard enough.

The juxtaposition of Faust and Helena was not Goethe's invention.[48] Paralipomenon 123C records his awareness that the Faust story had always required the episode:

> Die alte Legende sagt nämlich, und das Puppenspiel verfehlt nicht, die Scene vorzuführen: daß Faust in seinem herrischen Uebermuth durch Mephistopheles den Besitz der schönen Helena von Griechenland verlangt, und ihm dieser nach einigem Widerstreben willfahrt habe. Ein solches bedeutendes Motiv in unserer Ausführung nicht zu versäumen war uns Pflicht.[49]

The key word here is "duty." One might read in it nothing more than the poet's sense of obligation to the plot. But the passage to Sulpiz Boisserée hints quite openly at another source of authority to which Goethe was obligated: the requirement that the epic encompass "three thousand years of history." By assuming the burden, Goethe figured himself as a successor in the lineage descended from Homer.

In 1827, Goethe received from the publisher E. Fleischer in Leipzig an inscribed copy of an edition of Italian poetry, *Il Parnasso italiano, ovvero: I quattro poeti celeberrimi italiani: La Divina Commedia di Dante Alighieri; Le rime di Francesco Petrarca; L'Orlando Furioso di Lodovico Ariosto; La Gerusalemme Liberata di Torquato Tasso*. Together with the gift of a beaker, Goethe sent his compliments to the editor:

---

[46] Johann Wolfgang von Goethe, *Goethes Briefe*, ed. Karl Robert Mandelkow and Bobo Morawe, 4 vols. (Hamburg: Christian Wegner, 1962), 4:207.

[47] Goethe, *Goethes Briefe*, 4:205.

[48] See Ulrich Gaier, "Goethes *Faust* als Neu- und Fortschreibung der *Ilias*," in *Europäische Mythen von Liebe, Leidenschaft, Untergang und Tod im (Musik-) Theater: Der Trojanische Krieg; Vorträge und Gespräche des Salzburger Symposions 2000*, ed. Peter Csobadi (Salzburg: Verlag Mueller-Speiser, 2002), 307–18.

[49] Johann Wolfgang Goethe, *Faust: Texte*, ed. Albrecht Schöne (Darmstadt: Wissenschaftliche Buchgesellschaft, 1999), 637.

es ist eine vollständige Bibliothek, die wohl hinreichend wäre, ein ganzes Leben zu beschäftigen und den vollständigen Menschen auszubilden, daher ich Ihnen Glück wünsche, daß Ihre Thätigkeit bis in das Einzelne dieser geheimnißvollen Schätze sich zu versenken den Muth hatte.[50]

The sincerity is unmistakeable and the advice weighty, coming from the grand old man. Despite this and all the other evidence, German critics and literary historians have been loath to acknowledge that Goethe himself might have followed his own advice throughout a long life: that he might have immersed himself in the library of the Italian epic poets and their precursors.[51] Fritz Strich quotes the above passage and insists that there is little to be found of Italian influence in Goethe's poetry.[52] The difficulty in tracing Goethe's creative appropriation from poets such as Ariosto and Tasso, not to mention Boiardo and Pulci, is that they have receded from the domain of common knowledge and are now the preserve of specialists. Fortunately, those specialists have been producing exciting new interpretations and detailed commentaries, so that the work of detecting connections is rewarded once it is begun. With support from a wide range of relevant scholarship on the European epics, it is possible to see *Faust* as an evolution in the system of epic.

---

[50] Letter to Gottlob Heinrich Adolph Wagner, 29 October 1827, in Johann Wolfgang von Goethe, *Goethes Werke*, commissioned by the Grand Duchess Sophie of Saxony (Weimar: Böhlau, 1887–1919), pt. 4, vol. 4:43.

[51] For a compilation of basic facts about Goethe's knowledge of Italian literature, see John Hennig, "Goethes Kenntnis der schönen Literatur Italiens," in *Goethes Europakunde: Goethes Kenntnisse des nichtdeutschsprachigen Europas: Ausgewählte Aufsätze* (Amsterdam: Rodopi, 1987), 128–50; originally published in *Literaturwissenschaftliches Jahrbuch* 21 (1980): 361–83.

[52] Fritz Strich, *Goethe und die Weltliteratur* (Bern: A. Francke, 1946), 133.

# 2: The System of European Epic

RATHER THAN ATTEMPTING A precise definition of the category of the set of "epics," a process in which it would be easy to lose one's way, I shall take the more practical path of referring to the tradition of European epics, taken together, as a system.[1] Systems theory accepts the open-ended, dynamic nature of the interrelationships among the elements of a system. As new elements are introduced, the status, function, and value of all the elements are subtly but decisively transformed. For example, even though the *Aeneid* comes as a successor to the *Iliad* and the *Odyssey*, its presence will henceforth shape the interpretation of the those preceding works. And so it continues down the line. Dante's portrayal of Vergil in the *Divine Comedy* interprets that poet, his work, and his place in literary history, sometimes explicitly, more often implicitly. The allegorizing of the *Divine*

---

[1] The literature on the European epic is vast. In addition to specific studies of particular epics, the following provide an overview of the workings of the epic system; the list is not intended to be comprehensive: Barbara J. Bono, *Literary Transvaluation: From Vergilian Epic to Shakespearean Tragicomedy* (Berkeley and Los Angeles: U of California P, 1984); C. M. Bowra, *From Virgil to Milton* (London: MacMillan and New York: St Martin's P, 1967); Patrick J. Cook, "The Epic Chronotype from Ariosto to Spenser," *Annali d'italianistica* 12 (1994): 115–41; James D. Garrison, *Pietas from Vergil to Dryden* (University Park, PA: Pennsylvania State UP, 1992); A. Bartlett Giamatti, *The Earthly Paradise and the Renaissance Epic* (Princeton: Princeton UP, 1966); K. W. Gransden, "The *Aeneid* and *Paradise Lost*," in *Virgil and His Influence: Bimillennial Studies*, ed. Charles Martindale (Bristol: Bristol Classical P, 1984), 95–116; Thomas Greene, *The Descent from Heaven: A Study in Epic Continuity* (New Haven, and London: Yale UP, 1963); Philip Hardie, "After Rome: Renaissance Epic," in *Roman Epic*, ed. A. J. Boyle (London and New York: Routledge, 1993), 294–313; Hardie, *The Epic Successors of Virgil: A Study in the Dynamics of a Tradition* (Cambridge: Cambridge UP, 1993); Michael Murrin, *The Allegorical Epic: Essays in Its Rise and Decline* (Chicago and London: U of Chicago P, 1980); Murrin, *History and Warfare in Renaissance Epic* (Chicago and London: U of Chicago P, 1994); John M. Steadman, *Milton and the Renaissance Hero* (Oxford: Clarendon, 1967); Steadman, "Two Theological Epics: Reconsiderations of the Dante-Milton Parallel," *Cithara* 35.1 (1995): 5–21; Mihoko Suzuki, *Metamorphoses of Helen: Authority, Difference, and the Epic* (Ithaca and London: Cornell UP, 1989); E. M. W. Tillyard, *The English Epic and Its Background* (London: Chatto and Windus, 1954).

*Comedy*, which set in almost immediately, did not affect only that work: it also extended the reach of allegorizing back over Homer and Vergil and forward to Tasso, Milton, and Goethe. The increasing complexity of the system imposed ever greater obligations on succeeding generations of poets — Milton had to reckon with Tasso and Dante and Vergil and Homer, as well as the Bible and the English epic masters, Chaucer and Spenser. But complexity also offers increasing numbers of options, so that later poets have a greater degree of freedom for expressing themselves by choosing which antecedent element to emphasize more forcefully, and when.

The model of a non-teleological system even accepts the contribution of those works that were not ultimately successful, perhaps not even completed; those works that attempted to alter the direction of the system; and those that belong to the epic system primarily via their differences with it. This systemic flexibility was important for the practitioners of epic, who exploited the elasticity of the system to their own advantage. A major instance is the appropriation of the Bible via typology and allegory to the purposes of epic, a melding greatly indebted to Augustine's parallelism of the divine and worldly cities. Once Adam could be linked typologically to Achilles and Aeneas, then Scriptural history could be grafted on to secular chronology demarcated by events such as the fall of Troy and the founding of Rome.[2] The porous boundaries also allowed for absorption by osmosis of other narrative materials, such as the Arthurian legends[3] and the history of European colonial expansion.[4] The epic system was also quite tolerant of formal experiments. One of the requirements for epic poets was that they had to innovate, that they were obliged to find the style, the meter, and the stanza structures that would simultaneously acknowledge

---

[2] One of the most useful studies of these conflations is D. W. Robertson, Jr., *A Preface to Chaucer: Studies in Medieval Perspectives* (Princeton: Princeton UP, 1970).

[3] See Edmund G. Gardner, *The Arthurian Legend in Italian Literature* (London: J. M. Dent and New York: E. P. Dutton, 1930), 273–94.

[4] In addition to David Quint, *Epic and Empire: Politics and Generic Form from Virgil to Milton* (Princeton: Princeton UP, 1993), see Heinz Hofmann, "The Discovery of America and Its Refashioning as Epic," *Allegorica* 15 (1994): 31–40; Hofmann, "*Adveniat tandem Typhis qui detegat orbes*: COLUMBUS in Neo-Latin Epic Poetry (16th–18th Centuries)," in *The Classical Tradition and the Americas*, vol. 1: *European Images of the Americas and the Classical Tradition*, ed. Wolfgang Haase and Meyer Reinhold (New York: Walter de Gruyter, 1994), 421–656; Hofmann, "Aeneas in Amerika: Komplikationen des Weltbildwandels im Humanismus am Beispiel neulateinischer Columbusepen," *Philologus* 129 (1995): 39–61; and Herbert Knust, "Columbiads in Eighteenth Century European and American Literature," *European Contributions to American Studies* 34 (1996): 33–48.

the inherited forms while making the particular contribution of the new poet evident.[5] By way of analogy, one could say that epic poets had to be as inventive formally as are composers, who similarly cannot simply keep playing the same tune over and over again.

In the long run, the same flexibility that had granted the epic system the capacity to survive innovation and thus to retain its stability and its authority would prove its undoing. By the end of the eighteenth century, the authority of epic in verse yielded to the pressure of prose from one side and of drama from the other. Hegel blamed the circumstances of world history for the marginalization of epic:

> Suchen wir nun in neuester Zeit nach wahrhaft epischen Darstellungen, so haben wir uns nach einem anderen Kreise als dem der eigentlichen Epopoee umzusehen. Denn der ganze heutige Weltzustand hat eine Gestalt angenommen, welche in ihrer prosaischen Ordnung sich schnurstracks den Anforderungen entgegenstellt, welche wir für das echte Epos unerläßlich fanden, während die Umwälzungen, denen die wirklichen Verhältnisse der Staaten und Völker unterworfen gewesen sind, noch zu sehr als wirkliche Erlebnisse in der Erinnerung festhaften, um schon die epische Kunstform vertragen zu können.[6]

Hegel continued by suggesting that the "idyllic epic" was the only viable option, and pointed to Johann Heinrich Voss's *Luise* and Goethe's *Hermann und Dorothea* as examples. Determined to maintain the categorical separation of epic — lyric — dramatic, Hegel was unable or unwilling to countenance another possibility, such as the hybridization of Goethe's *Faust*, where the dramatic form is congruent with the exigencies of epic representation at the end of the eighteenth century. Finally, and by no means least, the shift away from an aesthetics based upon learned and witty allusions to one based upon the primacy of the imagination freed both readers and writers of the obligation to operate within what were increasingly felt to be the confining limits of the epic.[7]

---

[5] Tillyard has pointed out how momentous a decision about the verse form could be for a poet such as Milton: "Not all readers perceive how unconventional Milton was in choosing to write *Paradise Lost* in blank verse, how violently he went against his age in so doing" (*The English Epic and Its Background*, 434).

[6] Georg Wilhelm Friedrich Hegel, *Sämtliche Werke: Jubiläumsausgabe in zwanzig Bänden*, ed. Hermann Glockner, vol. 14:3 *Vorlesungen über die Aesthetik*, ed. Heinrich Gustav Hotho (Stuttgart-Bad Cannstatt: Friedrich Frommann Verlag, 1964), 416–17.

[7] For the English discussions see Ernest Lee Tuveson, *The Imagination as a Means of Grace: Locke and the Aesthetics of Romanticism* (Berkeley and Los Angeles: U of California P, 1960).

What held the epic system together? Employing terminology from linguistics, one might speak of the connectors or linkers that poets used in order to maintain systemic coherence under dynamic, changing conditions.[8] Some of these connectors were meta-textual, such as a declaration that one had written an epic poem and thereby contributed to the system or that one was emulating Homer or Vergil. Others were formal features, including the length (epics were long poems) the verse form, and the persona of the epic narrator (overwhelmingly omniscient third person, objective voices). A regular, predictable connecting device was an echo of the invocation to the muses, which referred to Homer's opening for the *Iliad*: "Sing, goddess, the anger of Peleus' son Achilleus / and its devastation, which put pains thousandfold upon the Achaians."[9] The skill with which an epic poet met the challenge of simultaneously announcing an allegiance to and entering into a competition with Homer was taken as an indication of the entire work's quality.[10] No one could fail to recognize the obligatory allusion in Klopstock's *Messias* to both Homer and Milton:

> Sing, unsterbliche Seele, der sündigen Menschen Erlösung,
> Die der Messias auf Erden in seiner Menschheit vollendet,
> Und durch die er Adams Geschlechte die Liebe der Gottheit
> Mit dem Blute des heiligen Bundes von neuem geschenkt hat.[11]

The phrasing alone echoes Homer, as does the statement of intent. But there is also a difference in the subject matter, since the Christian poet has translated everything out of the framework of the Greek gods into a pious history of salvation. This second dimension compelled Klopstock to let us hear a reference to *Paradise Lost* and to the story Milton told.

Not every epic poet would be so forthcoming in the opening. Wordsworth's invocation of the muse was made considerably subtler when inspiration is assumed to come directly from nature:

---

[8] On connectors, see Hanspeter Ortner, "Syntaktisch hervorgehobene Konnektoren im Deutschen," *Deutsche Sprache* 11 (1983): 97–121.

[9] Homer, *The Iliad of Homer*, trans. Richmond Lattimore (Chicago and London: U of Chicago P, 1961), 59, 1:1–2.

[10] For comparative discussions of epic openings, see Michael von Albrecht, *Rom: Spiegel Europas: Texte und Themen* (Heidelberg: Verlag Lambert Schneider, 1988), 361–403; and Kurt Reichenberger, "Das epische Proömium bei Ronsard, Scève, Du Bartas: Stilkritische Betrachtungen zum Problem von 'klassischer' und 'manieristischer' Dichtung in der 2. Hälfte des 16. Jahrhunderts," *Zeitschrift für romanische Philologie* 78 (1962): 1–31.

[11] Friedrich Gottlieb Klopstock, *Werke in einem Band*, ed. Karl August Schleiden (Munich and Vienna: Carl Hanser Verlag), 197, lines 1–4.

> Oh there is blessing in this gentle breeze
> That blows from the green fields, and from the clouds,
> And from the sky: it beats against my cheek,
> And seems half-conscious of the joy it gives.
> Oh welcome messenger, oh welcome friend![12]

A considerable effort in exegesis is required if one is to recognize the "welcome messenger" as the descendant of the inspiring muse, yet the relationship is there. More muffled still are the echoes in Goethe's "Dedication" ("Zueignung") to *Faust*, written on 24 June 1797 as he recommenced working on the project. Ulrich Gaier has observed that the elevated style is characteristic of Ariosto and Tasso and that the reference to the shades makes a connection to book 11 of the *Odyssey*.[13] The poem may be read as an amplification of the traditional epic opening, filled with foreboding about loss, destruction, and the futility of human endeavors. But at the same time it is a severe reduction of the entirety of the epic system and the fate of that system in the modern world. What purpose can epic have in the modern world without a heroic audience?

> Sie hören nicht die folgenden Gesänge,
> Die Seelen, denen ich die ersten sang;
> Zerstoben ist das freundliche Gedränge,
> Verklungen ach! der erste Widerklang.
> Mein Lied ertönt der unbekannten Menge,
> Ihr Beifall selbst macht meinem Herzen bang,
> Und was sich sonst an meinem Lied erfreuet,
> Wenn es noch lebt, irrt in der Welt zerstreuet.[14]

This is no longer the poet at the beginning of the epic system, filled with the confidence of a founding father, who could tell about the struggles and misfortunes of warrior heroes without himself becoming embroiled in their destiny, whose trajectory rose as states and cities declined and fell in his narrative. Rather, this is a poet who is caught up in history, who knows that his fame is contingent upon mortality and the whims of human affairs. Nevertheless, the ancient urge has not entirely abandoned him: there are stirrings of poetic desire. Not quite the classical muse, but perhaps something close to Wordsworth's natural breeze moves him:

> Und mich ergreift ein längst entwöhntes Sehnen
> Nach jenem stillen ernsten Geisterreich,

---

[12] Wordsworth, *The Five-Book Prelude*, version 1: lines 1–5.
[13] Ulrich Gaier, *Faust-Dichtungen*, vol. 2: *Kommentar I*, 17; 20.
[14] Goethe, "Zueignung" to *Faust*, HA 3:25–32.

> Es schwebt nun in unbestimmten Tönen
> Mein lispelnd Lied, der Äolsharfe gleich,
> Ein Schauer faßt mich, Träne folgt den Tränen,
> Das strenge Herz es fühlt sich mild und weich;
> Was ich besitze seh' ich wie im weiten,
> Und was verschwand wird mir zu Wirklichkeiten.[15]

*Faust* will not share the confident optimism of Klopstock's *Messias*, for it owes too much to Vergil, Ariosto, and above all Milton:

> What in me is dark
> Illumine, what is low raise and support;
> That to the highth of this great argument
> I may assert eternal providence
> And justify the ways of God to men.[16]

More poignantly and personally than anywhere else in the epic system, Goethe's dedication confesses the immense burden that lies upon the epic poet, who must confront the tragic course of history and must do so *alone*, accompanied only by the muse, by his inspiration.

Whether one calls them *topoi*, places, episodes, or themes, the repetition of familiar events was important for the coherence of the epic system. Educated readers could be expected to recognize the references; indeed, being able to identify them qualified one as well-read and as witty. Where the allusions were too subtle and for those without the requisite training, commentators decoded, provided cross-references, and worked out intricate allegories for the respective epics. To cite one relevant example, the motif of a tree that bleeds when wounded and also speaks occurs repeatedly in the series of major epics.[17] It has been easy to follow the series from book 3 of the *Aeneid* through canto 13 of the *Divine Comedy* to Tancred's encounter with Clorinda in the Enchanted Wood of *Gerusalemme Liberata*. Until now, no one has pursued the lead to *Faust*, to "Auerbachs Keller," because Goethe has made it quite difficult to recognize the *topos*.

---

[15] Goethe, "Zueignung," to *Faust*, HA 3:25–32.

[16] John Milton, *The Poems of John Milton*, ed. John Carey and Alastair Fowler (London: Longmans, 1968), 1. 22–26.

[17] For overviews, see Charles Speroni, "The Motif of the Bleeding and Speaking Trees of Dante's Suicides," *Italian Quarterly* 9 (1965): 44–55; Elizabeth J. Bellamy, "From Virgil to Tasso: The Epic Topos as an Uncanny Return," in *Desire in the Renaissance: Psychoanalysis and Literature*, ed. Valeria Finucci and Regina Schwartz (Princeton: Princeton UP, 1994), 207–32; and Jane Tylus, "Tasso's Trees: Epic and Local Culture," in *Epic Traditions in the Contemporary World: The Poetics of Community*, ed. Margaret Beissinger, Jane Tylus, and Susanne Wofford (Berkeley and Los Angeles: U of California P, 1999), 108–30.

Certainly no less important for the participation of the epic in the system than specific topics were the constructions of the hero, his companions and adversaries, and his quest. Eventually the three essential characters had been crystallized as the male hero, another male who was part guide for, part adversary against, the hero, and a woman who would have a complex tragic amorous relationship with the hero. In the *Divine Comedy* the roles are played by the Pilgrim, Vergil the Guide, and Beatrice. In *Paradise Lost*, they are assumed by Adam, Eve, and Satan, while in Goethe's work we have Faust, Mephistopheles, and Margarete. Each figure had his or her own epic genealogy, which could be a fairly direct one (Achilles > Aeneas > Adam > Faust) or more intricate (Helena > Medea + Ariadne > Dido + Eve > Margarete). Mapping all of these and kindred relationships in detail will be an assignment for the future of hypertext models.

The intricacy of the network of allusions to the epic system in *Faust* only dawns on us gradually. Consider the figure of Margarete. To borrow Mihoko Suzuki's felicitous phrase, Margarete appears as one of the "metamorphoses of Helen."[18] Indeed, that is how she is first announced: "Du siehst, mit diesem Trank im Leibe, / Bald Helenen in jedem Weibe" (2603–4). In the epic system, there were many metamorphoses of Helen, including Medea, Ariadne, Dido, Beatrice, and Clorinda. The melding of the Bible into the epic system also implicated the figures of Eve, Mary, and the Bride from the Song of Songs. Aspects of all of these female figures were incorporated by Goethe in the construction of Margarete. The allusion to the epic figures by no means excludes the references to historical figures such as those women accused and convicted of infanticide in Goethe's own time. Although some of these aspects are becoming clearer, there is still a lot of research to be done.

Immediately striking is how Faust and Margarete have been demythologized and secularized. Far from being titans, they are ordinary folk, scarcely heroic at all any more. Faust the studious professor bears little direct resemblance to warriors and leaders of men such as Achilles or Aeneas. Margarete seems utterly remote from the queenly presences of Helen and Dido. By transposing the epic figures into the mundane world, Goethe was following the path away from the world populated by active gods to a world where the divine is known only through mediating presences. The exception is Mephistopheles, modeled on Odysseus and on Vergil the Guide from the *Divine Comedy*, who has the power to move

---

[18] Mihoko Suzuki, *Metamorphoses of Helen*. See also Lawrence Lipking, *Abandoned Women and the Poetic Tradition* (Chicago and London: U of Chicago P, 1988), 1–31, on Ariadne as a type.

between ordinary and celestial realms. Basically, Goethe has taken what Tillyard described as Milton's "domestication" of the epic material one step further.[19] We see Faust and Margarete as the descendants of Adam and Eve, living in a world circumscribed by social norms as they have evolved since the expulsion from Paradise. From the outset, Goethe presents in Faust and Margarete two figures who will have great difficulty in seeing themselves as reflections of epic types. Although they will reenact the fates of the earlier epic couples, they will be unable to articulate an awareness of the ways in which their struggles are just as heroic, just as consequential for the history of mankind. Only the audience can make the connections, having been alerted by the Prologue in Heaven to the cosmic dimension of Faust's biography.

The epic hero is inseparable from the epic quest, which defines his life and gives it a universal significance.[20] What the quest should be changes over time. In the *Iliad*, where the Trojan War is the central conflict, Achilles must stand at the centre as a warrior. Through him the values, motives, and outcome of the war are shaped and made visible to the audience. The qualities of the warrior were so deeply inscribed into the epic hero that all subsequent poets had to find some equivalent to the conflict between the Greeks and the Trojans as a setting, whether that war had actually happened or was a fanciful invention.[21] Tasso used the Crusades, while *Paradise Lost* takes place in the context of a "war in heaven."[22] In *Faust I* war remains on the margins, but it is never far away and will dominate much of *Faust II*.

Paralleling the external conflict represented by military campaigns, there is an internal or symbolic quest each epic hero must carry out. For the construction of this aspect of the hero, Odysseus eventually became more interesting and hence useful as a model for the exploration of psychological conflicts than Achilles. The shrewd advisor and cunning, inquisitive explorer provided the model of a hero seeking knowledge and truth. With the inclusion of Christian themes, the search was elevated to the quest for a knowledge of God's purpose and of the way to salvation, most visibly so in the *Divine Comedy*. The emphasis upon knowing the truth about one's self and

---

[19] Tillyard, *The English Epic and its Background*, 435–38.

[20] Definitive is Dean A. Miller, *The Epic Hero* (Baltimore and London: The Johns Hopkins UP, 2000).

[21] See especially Murrin, *History and Warfare in Renaissance Epic*.

[22] See Arnold Stein, "Milton's War in Heaven — An Extended Metaphor," in *Milton: Modern Essays in Criticism*, ed. Arthur E. Barker (Oxford: Oxford UP, 1965), 264–83; Stella Purce Revard, *The War in Heaven*: Paradise Lost *and the Tradition of Satan's Rebellion* (Ithaca and London: Cornell UP, 1980).

one's destiny could not avoid bringing epistemological theories within the purview of the epic. Instead of Aeneas's anxiety about how to read the intentions of the gods out of portents, the Pilgrim in the *Divine Comedy* will be challenged at every turn by the question of how to distinguish between illusion and reality. Similarly, the knights in *Orlando Furioso*, the crusaders in *Gerusalemme Liberata*, and Adam and Eve in *Paradise Lost* all confront a world where everything depends upon obtaining certain knowledge.

Goethe's selection of Faust for the epic hero was a brilliant move, since it enabled him to continue the development of this quest for certain knowledge in a fallen world. Something of an impasse had been reached with the history of *Paradise Lost*: what was there left for mankind to learn once the prohibition against eating from the Tree of Knowledge had been violated? Milton had also encountered difficulties in incorporating contemporary history and scientific investigation into the epic. The narrative device whereby Michael unfolds human history in book 12 was somewhat clumsy and was only partly compensated for by the allusions earlier in the poem to events of the English Civil War. Since Adam and Eve were located at the beginning of modern history, they did not provide much scope for incorporating references to the rapidly growing body of knowledge scientists were gathering about the natural world. Faust, however, was an ideal candidate, not least because in him the spiritual turmoil was so closely connected to an intellectual crisis. The domain of struggle had shifted from the battlefield to the academic's study, from the warrior to the professor. Goethe has portrayed in Faust an average man of unexceptional qualities yet grand ambitions, who is confronted and ultimately overwhelmed by the influx of new ideas and information. Like Achilles and Aeneas, Faust will be torn apart by the contradiction between the values he has inherited and chooses to live by, and the new values he can not, will not, learn.

One surprising aspect of the epic hero is the influence of some mental or psychological weakness. That a hero should have an affliction of the mind was quite a regular feature in the epic tradition.[23] Achilles himself had manifested strong passions, bordering on rage, and had withdrawn in bouts of dark bitterness, qualities that were not easy to reconcile with the ideal of a hero.[24] Similarly, Aeneas had manifested a savage fury at the end of the

---

[23] For a succinct overview, see Peter Toohey, "Some Ancient Histories of Literary Melancholia," *Illinois Classical Studies* 15 (1990): 143–61.

[24] Steadman summarizes the reservations that Renaissance writers had: "For the poets who took the *Iliad* as their model, Achilles in particular proved a stumbling block. Although they might retain the basic outline of his role as essential to the plot, they could hardly transfer his character whole cloth from Homer without incurring blame for celebrating a vicious hero." *Milton and the Paradoxes of Renaissance Heroism* (Baton Rouge and London: Louisiana State UP, 1987), 45.

*Aeneid*, killing Turnus in a way that still arouses intense debate, both about the meaning of the conclusion and about the implications for our understanding of his psychological state.[25] The title *Orlando Furioso* forthrightly announced the hero's mental plight.[26] And in Tasso's case, melancholy also afflicted the epic poet, who thereby became himself a literary topic, one explored by Goethe in *Torquato Tasso*.[27] To these might be added relevant figures from drama such as Hercules, whose depiction in Seneca's *Hercules Furens* was influential as negative example, and, not least, Hamlet, the melancholic par excellence. In sum, Faust without some sort of emotional-intellectual ailment would have been a glaring deviation in the genealogy of epic heroes. Furthermore, as the chance of history would have it, the sixteenth century was indeed marked by a tremendous outbreak of melancholy, at least according to contemporary witnesses. The reasons for this epidemic of melancholy are even today of considerable interest to cultural historians, as they were to those living at the time, and as they were for Goethe.[28]

Faust's situation is so difficult because he is afflicted at the same time with two ailments of the mind that work to reinforce each other, melancholy

---

[25] On the controversy: Karl Galinsky, "The Anger of Aeneas," *American Journal of Philology* 109 (1988): 321–48; Erich Potz, "Pius furor und der Tod des Turnus," *Gymnasium* 99 (1991): 248–62; Michael Erler, "Der Zorn des Helden: Philodems 'De Ira' und Vergils Konzept des Zorns in der 'Aeneis,'" *Grazer Beiträge: Zeitschrift für die klassische Altertumswissenschaft* 18 (1992): 103–26; and Christopher Gill, "Passion as Madness in Roman Poetry," in *The Passions in Roman Thought and Literature*, ed. Susanna Morton Braund and Christopher Gill (Cambridge: Cambridge UP, 1997), 213–41. When Faust kills Valentin, he unknowingly imitates Aeneas.

[26] On Orlando's condition, see Paolo Valesio, "The Language of Madness in the Renaissance," *Yearbook of Italian Studies* 1 (1971): 199–234, here 204–6; and Philip McNair, "The Madness of Orlando," in *Renaissance and Other Studies: Essays presented to Peter M. Brown*, ed. Eileen A. Millar (Glasgow: University of Glasgow, Department of Italian, 1988), 144–59.

[27] On Tasso's psychology in relation to the intellectual currents of his time, see Walter Stephens, "Tasso and the Witches," *Annali d'italianistica* 12 (1994): 181–202. On his reputation as a melancholic poet, see Maria Moog-Grünewald, "Tassos Leid: Zum Ursprung moderner Dichtung," *arcadia* 21 (1986): 113–32; and Albert Meier, "'Und so war sein Leben selbst Roman und Poesie': Tasso-Biographien in Deutschland," in *Torquato Tasso in Deutschland: Seine Wirkung in Literatur, Kunst und Musik seit der Mitte des 18. Jahrhunderts*, ed. Achim Aurnhammer (Berlin and New York: Walter de Gruyter, 1995), 11–32.

[28] On melancholy as a Renaissance condition, in addition to the monumental study by Raymond Klibansky, Erwin Panofsky, and Fritz Saxl, *Saturn and Melancholy: Studies in the History of Natural Philosophy, Religion and Art* (London: Nelson, 1964), see Hans-Günter Schmitz, "Das Melancholieproblem in Wissenschaft und Kunst der frühen Neuzeit," *Sudhoffs Archiv für die Geschichte der*

and curiosity. Melancholy was something to which men of learning and genius had long been considered prone. There is extensive literature on the topic.[29] The diagnosis that Faust displays the classical symptoms of melancholy has slowly gained acceptance since the suggestion was made by Leonard Forster.[30] Melancholy was caused by excesses that led to an imbalance among the humors. Men of learning were notorious for their one-sided concentration on the life of the mind, which dried the blood and heated the mind. The illness was particularly harmful to the mnemonic capacity, since obsessive attention upon a singular fixed idea or image made it difficult to move to other places in the memory, producing a serious disorientation.[31] Hence the therapy usually prescribed distractions, such as

---

*Medizin und Naturwissenschaft* 60.2 (1976): 135–62; Schmitz, *Physiologie des Scherzes: Bedeutung und Rechtfertigung der Ars Iocandi im 16. Jahrhundert* (Hildesheim and New York: Georg Olms, 1972), esp. 91–183; Bridget Gellert Lyons, *Voices of Melancholy: Studies in Literary Treatments of Melancholy in Renaissance England* (New York: Norton, 1975); Winfried Schleiner, *Melancholy, Genius and Utopia in the Renaissance* (Wiesbaden: Otto Harrassowitz, 1991); and Johann Anselm Steiger, *Melancholie, Diätetik und Trost: Konzepte der Melancholie-Therapie im 16. und 17. Jahrhundert* (Heidelberg: Manutius Verlag, 1996).

[29] The extent of the literature is indicated by John F. Sena, *A Bibliography of Melancholy, 1660–1800* (London: The Nether P, 1970).

[30] Leonard Forster, "Faust and the Sin of Sloth, Mephistopheles and the Sin of Pride," in *The Discontinuous Tradition: Studies in German Literature in Honour of Ernest Ludwig Stahl*, ed. P. F. Ganz (Oxford: Clarendon, 1971), 54–66; and "Faust und die *acedia*: Mephisto und die *superbia*," in *Dichtung, Sprache, Gesellschaft: Akten des IV. Internationalen Germanisten-Kongresses 1970 in Princeton*, ed. Victor Lange and Hans-Gert Roloff (Frankfurt am Main: Athenäum, 1971), 307–19. The diagnosis has been confirmed by Ferdinand van Ingen, "Faust — *homo melancholicus*," in *Wissen aus Erfahrungen: Werkbegriff und Interpretation heute; Festschrift für Herman Meyer zum 65. Geburtstag*, ed. Alexander von Bormann (Tübingen: Niemeyer, 1976), 256–81; Jochen Schmidt, "Faust als Melancholiker und Melancholie als strukturbildendes Element bis zum Teufelspakt," *Jahrbuch der Deutschen Schillergesellschaft* 41 (1997): 125–39; and Thorsten Valk, *Melancholie im Werk Goethes: Genese, Symptomatik, Therapie* (Tübingen: Niemeyer, 2002).

[31] See Markus Bauer, "Melancholie und Memoria: Zur Theorie von Gedächtnisschwund und fixer Idee im 17. Jahrhundert," in *Ars memorativa: Zur kulturgeschichtlichen Bedeutung der Gedächtniskunst, 1400–1750*, ed. Jörg Jochen Berns and Wolfgang Neuber (Tübingen: Max Niemeyer, 1993), 313–30, who cites the commonplace that melancholics had memory problems. Leaving the etiology of melancholy out of consideration, some critics have suggested that Faust actually strives to be more forgetful; examples are Fred Hagen and Ursula Mahlendorf, "Commitment, Concern and Memory in Goethe's Faust," *Journal of Aesthetics and Art Criticism* 21 (1962–63): 473–84; here, 477.

listening to music, gentle conversation, contemplating nature, and physical activity (absolutely prohibited were love affairs and sex, since those exacerbated the humoral imbalance).

Compounding Faust's difficulties is another fascinating development in the history of epistemology and the modalities of knowing: the legitimation of curiosity in the modern period, a shift that is connected to the crisis of knowledge as both cause and symptom.[32] It is hard for us to recall that curiosity was not always a positive quality. Today, when we want people to act in accordance with a psychological model based upon the predations of possessive individualism, curiosity cannot be considered excessive. Parents and schoolteachers are supposed to encourage children to be endlessly curious. But it was not always thus, for the institutions of wisdom set limits upon what and how much any individual should attempt to know. Ancient and medieval philosophy perceived in unchecked curiosity a grave threat to knowledge and insight, to the cosmic order, and even to faith. Those who wanted to know divine secrets and attempted to get them from the gods were punished — Prometheus is an example. For Thomas Aquinas, *curiositas* was grouped with spiritual sins such as *acedia*. The work of Hans Blumenberg has underscored the transformation in the

---

[32] For surveys of the topic see Barbara M. Benedict, *Curiosity: A Cultural History of Early Modern Inquiry* (Chicago and London: U of Chicago P, 2001); Hans Blumenberg, "Neugierde und Wissenstrieb: Supplemente zu *Curiositas*," *Archiv für Begriffsgeschichte* 14.1 (1970): 7–40; the articles in *La curiosité à la Renaissance*, ed. Jean Céard (Paris: Société d'Édition d'Enseignement Supérieur, 1986); Neil Kenny, " 'Curiosité' and Philosophical Poetry in the French Renaissance," *Renaissance Studies* 5.1 (1991): 263–76; Gilbert G. Meilaender, *The Theory and Practice of Virtue* (Notre Dame, IN: U of Notre Dame P, 1984), 127–51; André Labhardt, "Curiositas: Notes sur l'histoire d'un mot et d'une notion," *Museum Helveticum* 17 (1960): 206–24; Hans Joachim Mette, "Curiositas," in *Festschrift for Bruno Snell zum 60. Geburtstag am 18. Juni 1956, von Freunden und Schülern überreicht* (Munich: Beck, 1961), 227–35; Jan-Dirk Müller, "*Curiositas* und *erfarung* der Welt im frühen deutschen Prosaroman," in *Literatur und Laienbildung im Spätmittelalter und in der Reformationszeit: Symposion Wolfenbüttel 1981*, ed. Ludger Grenzmann and Karl Stackmann (Stuttgart: J. B. Metzler, 1984), 252–71; Richard Newhauser, "Towards a History of Human Curiosity: A Prolegomenon to its Medieval Phase," *Deutsche Vierteljahrsschrift* 56 (1982): 559–73; Friedrich Strack, *Im Schatten der Neugier: Christliche Tradition und kritische Philosophie im Werk Friedrichs von Hardenberg* (Tübingen: Niemeyer, 1982), 1–21; and Christian K. Zacher, *Curiosity and Pilgrimage: The Literature of Discovery in Fourteenth-Century England* (Baltimore, MD and London: The Johns Hopkins UP, 1976), 18–41 and 162–43. On attempts to cure melancholy while satisfying curiosity, see Ulrich Breuer, *Melancholie und Reise: Studien zur Archäologie des Individuellen im deutschen Roman des 16.–18. Jahrhunderts* (Hamburg: Lit Verlag Münster-Hamburg, 1994); 130–48 on Faustus.

value of curiosity for the history of modern science.[33] And in a survey immediately relevant here, Horst Rüdiger has succinctly traced the connections of the tradition from Apuleius's *The Golden Ass* through magic science to the figure of Faust.[34]

The crux of the problem for Faust can best be seen via the German word for curiosity: *Neugierde*, literally being greedy for that which is new. Curiosity is connected to melancholy because both are caused by a loss of the mean, the Aristotelian ideal of moderation in all things. They reinforce each other, especially when the melancholic becomes captivated by the desire to know everything, to accumulate all the facts of the world, even at the price of inner harmony. Today we cannot see anything wrong with wanting novelty, not least because we have difficulty in detecting a flaw in unlimited wanting of any kind. But consider Faust's predicament. On the one side, his melancholy comes from his awareness that his hope of becoming a polyhistor is in vain, that he cannot know everything, and that even if he did it might not be the ultimate key to the universe. The more he wants to know, the more his melancholy will intensify. From the other direction, it is also an attribute of melancholics that they are greedy, for they are under the influence of Saturn.[35] The more that influence increases, the more they want gold and treasure and the more tightly they want to cling to their hoard. Thus Faust is caught in a vicious circle, for his curiosity, his greed for novelty, will pull in ever more knowledge of the world and only increase the despair at never being able to master all

---

[33] Blumenberg, "Neugierde und Wissenstrieb: Supplement zu *Curiositas.*"

[34] Horst Rüdiger, "*Curiositas* und Magie: Apuleius und Lucius als literarische Archetypen der Faust-Gestalt," in *Goethe und Europa: Essays und Aufsätze, 1944–1983,* ed. Willy R. Berger and Erwin Koppen (Berlin and New York: de Gruyter, 1990), 66–88. Curiosity as an essential dimension to the Faust figure has also been detected by Hans Joachim Kreutzer, " 'Der edelste der Triebe': Über die Wißbegierde in der Literatur am Beginn der Neuzeit," in *Das neuzeitliche Ich in der Literatur des 18. und 19. Jahrhunderts: Zur Dialektik der Moderne; Ein internationales Symposion,* ed. Ulrich Fülleborn and Manfred Engel (Munich: Wilhelm Fink, 1988), 59–70; here, 66; and Maria E. Müller, "Der andere Faust: Melancholie und Individualität in der Historia von D. Johann Fausten," *Deutsche Vierteljahrsschrift* 60 (1986): 572–608. In a similar vein, Hugh Powell, "A Neglected Faustian Drama and Its Cultural Roots in Seventeenth-Century Germany," in *Faust through Four Centuries: Retrospect and Analysis / Vierhundert Jahre Faust: Rückblick und Analyse,* ed. Peter Boerner and Sidney Johnson (Tübingen: Niemeyer, 1989), 65–77, has drawn attention to the parallels between Johann Valentin Andreae's Latin drama *Turbo* (1616), his condemnation of curiosity in *De curiositatis pernice,* and the Faust story.

[35] John W. Draper, *The Humours & Shakespeare's Characters* (New York: AMS Press, 1970), 73.

knowledge. His turn to magic accelerates his exposure to ever greater quantities of information. With the assistance of Mephistopheles, he is able to undertake experiments, to have experiences, far beyond the confines of a laboratory. By offering Faust the opportunity for unlimited desire, Mephistopheles is cleverly giving him just what he should avoid.[36]

Margarete as the voice of wisdom could have helped Faust to recover from his melancholy and to curb his curiosity. Wisdom, gendered as feminine and initially personified as "Sophia" is mirrored in the Beatrice of Dante's *Divine Comedy* and the Eve of *Paradise Lost* and will finally appear as the "eternal feminine" whose attraction is proclaimed at the end of Goethe's drama. But Faust is stubbornly deaf to wise hints that he change his ways. Blinded by his sexual passions and by his habitual contempt for common people, Faust cannot hear or trust Margarete's deep insights. Instead of hearing her sage advice in the garden, particularly her intuitive aversion to Mephistopheles, Faust chides her for being so simple: "Liebe Puppe, fürcht' ihn nicht!" (3476).[37] Fortunately, Margarete will reappear in *Faust II* as an intensified version of the woman whose pure truth can redeem the hero.

However, wisdom can also be dangerous, since it is a form of knowledge so powerful that it disrupts human institutions designed to contain and channel its energy. As unmediated truth about the universe, past and future, wisdom declares truth in the utterances of oracles, mystics, seers, and prophets. Without careful control, those truths can destroy human beings, as in the ambivalent pronouncements of the witches in *Macbeth*. This duality of wisdom is encapsulated by the two visages of Medea, whose magic powers could help Jason win the Golden Fleece but who could also wreak terrible havoc.[38] In a similar fashion, Dido was the wise queen who founded Carthage, but she was also an adept in sorcery.[39] Traces of these

---

[36] I have found Leonard Forster's *The Man Who Wanted to Know Everything*, The 1980 Bithell Memorial Lecture (London: Institute of Germanic Studies, U of London, 1981), to be the most profound discussion of Faust's epistemological economy. My main reservation concerns Forster's assumption that Goethe wants to depict Faust as "an earnestly striving, though necessarily erring, human being" (22) and demonstrate "the steady development of a character from an initial traumatic experience to final redemption" (23). Without healing from melancholy, Faust cannot and does not develop.

[37] See my "Naming Goethe's Faust: A Matter of Significance," forthcoming in the *Deutsche Vierteljahrsschrift*.

[38] See Alain Moreau, *Le Mythe de Jason et Médée: Le va-nu-pied et la sorcière* (Paris: Les Belles Lettres, 1994).

[39] A.-M. Tupet, "Didon magicienne," *Revue des études latines* 48 (1970): 229–58. On the parallels between Dido and Medea, see Christopher Collard, "Medea and Dido," *Prometheus* 1 (1975): 131–51; here, 149.

disturbing forms of wisdom can also be found in Margarete, as in the scene at the spinning wheel where she foretells her own dire fate and in the prison scene where she echoes Medea's accusations against Jason, directing them against Faust.[40]

The most complicated figure in terms of knowledge modalities is Mephistopheles, who combines cunning and wit with the attitude of the modern scientist. As Albert Fuchs has aptly observed, "Mephisto's intelligence is penetrating and vast."[41] This positive view of Mephistopheles is shared by Harald Weinrich, who describes him as a man of the world, polite, a good conversationalist, enlightened, and the moralist in the drama.[42] Dieter Breuer has evaluated Mephistopheles' competence as a theologian, showing that he is quite well versed in Scripture and able to operate with subtle theological distinctions. But Breuer reminds us that the Devil quotes Scripture for his own purposes, that his theology is a diabolical one.[43] The qualities that make up Mephistopheles are summed up by Werner Keller: "Wer ist Mephisto? Er ist die persongewordene reine Intelligenz — im ersten Teil des *Faust* ein Rationalist ohne Phantasie und ein Realist ohne Empfindung . . . Mephisto ist ein intellektueller Virtuose, der zu verdrehen, zu verwirren versteht, ein Zyniker, der das Leben sieht, wie es ohne Sinngebung wäre, und ein Nihilist, der mit Treue und Glauben skrupellos spielt."[44] The antecedents of Mephistopheles in the epic system are Odysseus and Satan. Odysseus was not only clever; he also became an integral figure in the legitimation of curiosity.[45] In the Christian

---

[40] I have dealt with these scenes in detail in "Gretchen am Spinnrad" (unpublished paper presented at the Goethe Museum Düsseldorf, 13 June 2001) and in "Margarete's Innocence and the Guilt of Faust," *Deutsche Vierteljahrsschrift* 75.2 (2001): 216–50.

[41] Albert Fuchs, Le Faust *de Goethe: Mystère — document humain — confession personnelle* (Paris: Éditions Klincksieck, 1973), 118.

[42] Harald Weinrich, "Der zivilisierte Teufel," in *Interpreting Goethe's* Faust Today, ed. Jane K. Brown, Meredith Lee, and Thomas P. Saine (Columbia, SC: Camden House, 1994), 62–67; here, 62–63.

[43] Dieter Breuer, "Mephisto als Theologe," *Goethe Jahrbuch* 109 (1992): 91–100; here, 100.

[44] Werner Keller, "*Faust: Eine Tragödie* (1808)," in *Goethes Dramen: Neue Interpretationen*, ed. Walter Hinderer (Stuttgart: Reclam, 1980), 244–80; here, 268. Jane K. Brown, in her article "Mephistopheles the Nature Spirit," *Studies in Romanticism* 24 (1985): 475–90, makes good observations on how Mephistopheles stages scenes, as "the actor and producer" (485).

[45] See the chapter on "'Curiositas' o 'Fol Hardement'?" in Fiorenzo Forti, *Magnanimitade: Studi su un tema dantesco* (Bologna: Pàtron Editore, 1977), 161–206; Karlheinz Stierle, "Odysseus und Aeneas: Eine typologische Konfiguration

context, limitless curiosity is a form of rebellion against God, whether in the Garden of Eden or as a driving force in Satan's mission.[46] Precisely this congruence of transgression with the unlimited desire to know is highlighted by the quotation Mephistopheles writes for the student: "Eritus sicut Deus, scientes bonum et malum" (2048).[47] To be sure, the tactics of cunning are very persuasive, as everyone recognized once Machiavelli had codified them. However, as Mephistopheles will need to relearn, cunning cannot in the long run overwhelm wisdom. Even the folk-wisdom of Margarete's mother is enough to frustrate his designs with the casket of jewels.

What then is the extent of Mephistopheles' knowledge? He is much better informed than most academics, primarily because he has advantages in information retrieval. He has lived a long time and is able to range widely through space and time. Over and over again in the drama, he demonstrates prior knowledge of topics that Faust is encountering for the first time. But Mephistopheles is not omniscient; God is the only vessel of omniscience. Mephistopheles cannot know in advance just how he will be thwarted in the wager, although he should be able to anticipate that he will lose. The reason he does not realize this is his excessive pride, which is reinforced by the structures of *Klugheit*. Nor, despite popular misconceptions to the contrary, will Mephistopheles be able to alter the fundamental laws of the universe or to discover a secret truth such that it would give him the ultimate key to mastery of the universe. Far from it: because he has deviated from the quest for wisdom Mephistopheles will, like Dante's Ulysses, achieve only the limited knowledge possible to *Klugheit*, namely know-how, technique. The fateful consequence is that the more Faust emulates his mentor Mephistopheles in imitating technique, the further he will swerve from the ultimate true knowledge available to philosophical investigation.

---

in Dantes *Divina Commedia*," in *Das fremde Wort: Studien zur Interdependenz von Texten; Festschrift für Karl Maurer zum 60. Geburtstag*, ed. Ilse Nolting-Hauff and Joachim Schulze (Amsterdam: Verlag B. R. Grüner, 1988), 111–54; and Piero Boitani, *The Shadow of Ulysses: Figures of a Myth*, trans. Anita Weston (Oxford: Clarendon, 1994).

[46] On the conflation of Odysseus with Satan in *Paradise Lost*, see John M. Steadman, *Milton's Epic Characters: Image and Idol* (Chapel Hill: U of North Carolina P, 1968), 194–208.

[47] Genesis 3:5. In the King James version, "ye shall be as gods, knowing good and evil."

# 3: *Faust* and Epic History

EPIC AND HISTORY HAVE BEEN closely interwoven from the start.[1] History provided the chronological framework in which the events of the hero's life could unfold; epic gave to history the tools and patterns for organizing and assembling a coherent narrative. This bonding presented serious challenges to later epic poets. As history continued to unfold, each successive poet had more, and more complicated, historical events to incorporate. Simply stitching on a summary of what had happened since the last precursor's work was impossible, not only because of the constraints of length and form but because historical change remorselessly altered the readers' world view. The understanding of what history was and what the forces driving change were continued to evolve. Milton, for example, could hardly have expected his readers to believe in the gods who ruled in the *Aeneid*.

As David Quint has shown so lucidly, the fate of epic came to depend on the fate of empire. The eighteenth century did not bode well for either. The evident decline and likely collapse of the Holy Roman Empire was an overriding concern for Goethe throughout his life, both as poet and as subject. In *Faust* he depicted the contemporary crisis — notably in "Auerbachs Keller" — and analyzed its causes. The diachronic analysis developed in the engagement with the system of epic, beginning with Torquato Tasso and then moving back through Ariosto and Dante to Vergil and Homer.

## Tasso and *Gerusalemme Liberata*

By the middle of the eighteenth century, the campaign against the "fantastic" ("das Wunderbare") in literature had taken its toll.[2] Talking animals, birds,

---

[1] See for example the discussions by Mario A. Di Cesare, *The Altar and the City: A Reading of Vergil's* Aeneid (New York and London: Columbia UP, 1974); Jeffrey T. Schnapp, *The Transfiguration of History at the Center of Dante's* Paradise (Princeton: Princeton UP, 1986); Michael Murrin, *History and Warfare in Renaissance Epic* (Chicago and London: U of Chicago P, 1994); and David Quint, *Epic and Empire: Politics and Generic Form from Virgil to Milton* (Princeton: Princeton UP, 1993).

[2] On Tasso as a touchstone of the controversies, see Maria Moog-Grünewald, "Torquato Tasso in den poetologischen Kontroversen des 18. Jahrhunderts," in *Torquato Tasso in Deutschland: Seine Wirkung in Literatur, Kunst und Musik seit der Mitte des 18. Jahrhunderts*, ed. Achim Aurnhammer (Berlin and New York:

stones, or plants were no longer permitted aesthetically, at least not until the Romantics rehabilitated them via "fairy tales." Nevertheless, even during the rise of the Age of Reason, the memory of the topoi from the epic heritage was still vivid and indeed attractive, as William Collins related circa 1749 in "An Ode on the Popular Superstitions of the Highlands of Scotland, Considered as the Subject of Poetry":

> In scenes like these, which, daring to depart
> From sober truth, are still to nature true,
> And call forth fresh delight to fancy's view,
> The heroic muse employ'd her TASSO's art!
> How have I trembled, when at TANCRED's stroke,
> Its gushing blood the gaping cypress pour'd;
> When each live plant with mortal accents spoke,
> And the wild blast up-heav'd the vanish'd sword![3]

Concomitant with the silencing of natural elements in poetry, Collins's reaction notwithstanding, was the progress of scientific investigation of "nature," which no longer was expected to speak directly. The table in "Auerbachs Keller" is silent, but its antecedents in the epic chain going back to Vergil had groaned, sighed, and complained when they were wounded. The episode was one of the set pieces readers had come to expect; in each case the poet's manipulation of the elements of the scene had to be varied yet recognizable. I am not going to examine all the versions. As far as I can tell, Spenser was not a writer Goethe was familiar with, and Boiardo's examples and those of other lesser-known epics are less important for Goethe.[4]

---

Walter de Gruyter, 1995), 382–97; and Klaus Ley, " 'sii grand'uomo e sii infelice': Zur Umwertung des Tasso-Bildes am Beginn des Ottocento; Voraussetzungen und Hintergründe im europäischen Rahmen (La Harpe/Gilbert — Goethe — Foscolo)," *Germanisch-Romanische Monatsschrift* NS 46.2 (1996): 131–73.

[3] Gray, Thomas, and William Collins, *Gray and Collins: Poetical Works*, ed. Austin Lane Poole (London: Oxford UP, 1974), 299.

[4] Charles Speroni gives a basic overview in his article "The Motif of the Bleeding and Speaking Trees of Dante's Suicide," *Italian Quarterly* 9 (1965): 44–55, listing relevant passages from Dante, Vergil, Ovid, Tasso, Ariosto, Boccacio's *Filocolo*, Federico Frezzi's *Quadriregio*, Boiardo's *Orlando Innamorato*, and Spenser. On this motif as an element in the chain linking texts to precursors, see Daniel Javitch, "The Imitation of Imitations in *Orlando Furioso*," *Renaissance Quarterly* 38 (1985): 215–39; here, 235–39. More recently, see Shirley Clay Scott, "From Polydorus to Fradubio: The History of a *Topos*," *Spenser Studies: A Renaissance Poetry Annual* 7 (1987): 27–57; and Elizabeth J. Bellamy, "From Virgil to Tasso," in *Desire in the Renaissance: Psychoanalysis and Literature*, ed. Valeria Finucci and Regina Schwartz (Princeton: Princeton UP, 1994), 207–32. Speroni also cites *Wilhelm Tell*, act 3, scene 3, where Walter asks Tell whether it is

Much as I am persuaded by the analysis of R. A. Shoaf that *Paradise Lost* also makes use of this topos, and much as that would support my argument, I cannot at present detect any evidence that Goethe was consciously alluding to Milton in this instance.[5] Even so, there is considerable material to discuss, and I will take up the scenes from Tasso, Ariosto, Dante, and Vergil in turn. The sequence proceeds against the chronological flow of the dates of composition of the original texts, in order to emphasize that from Faust's vantage point the recognition of the antecedents involves a process of historical investigation, rather than a declension from the origins.

For Goethe the figure of Torquato Tasso was of considerable concern.[6] There is also evidence that the problems surrounding *Torquato Tasso*

---

true that trees wounded by a hatchet can bleed. On Wordsworth's reception of the topos, see my "An Allusion to Tasso in 'The Thorn,'" *The Wordsworth Circle* 33.2 (2002): 77–79.

[5] R. A. Shoaf, *Milton, Poet of Duality* (New Haven and London: Yale UP, 1985), 20–21: "In book I of *Paradise Lost* (lines 612–16), as the fallen angels gather around Satan to hear his first speech to them after the Fall, Milton likens them to blasted trees:

> As when heaven's fire
> Hath scathed the forest oaks, or mountain pines,
> With singed top their stately growth though bare
> Stands on the blasted heath.

The punctuation, which leaves the simile a freestanding syntactic unit, also therefore leaves open the possibility of its reference *forward* as well as backward; in other words, Satan can also resemble a blasted tree as he prepares to speak. I feel sure that this dual reference is intentional, for it enables Milton to go on to suggest a likeness between Piero delle Vigne and Satan. He writes, just before Satan begins to address the fallen angels, that

> Thrice he essayed, and thrice in spite of scorn,
> Tears such as angels weep, burst forth: at last
> *Words interwove with sighs found out their way.*
> (*Paradise Lost*, lines 619–21; emphasis added.)

Sighs, of course, are not blood, and the allusion must be reckoned a distant one. But if distant, it is nonetheless audible, especially between the Italian *insieme* and the English *interwove*, and it invites us to understand that Satan was, albeit in a very special sense, a suicide, now hardening, as it were, with the hardness of a tree trunk."

[6] On the origins of the play, see Johann Wolfgang von Goethe, *Werke: Hamburger Ausgabe in 14 Bänden*, ed. Erich Trunz (Munich: C. H. Beck, 1981), 5:505–6. This "Hamburger Ausgabe" will be cited henceforth as HA. From the secondary literature on the context and meaning of *Torquato Tasso*, see Ernst M. Oppenheimer, *Goethe's Poetry for Occasions* (Toronto: U of Toronto P, 1974), 188–214; William H. McClain, "The Arcadian Fiction in Goethe's Torquato Tasso," in *Vistas and Vectors: Essays Honoring the Memory of Helmut Rehder*, ed. Lee B. Jennings and George Schulz-Berend (Austin: Department of Germanic

are not far from those around *Faust*, if only because Goethe was working on both dramas, on and off, at the same time. As he wrote to Carl August in a passage that is often quoted: "Nun steht mir fast nichts als der Hügel Tasso und der Berg Faustus vor der Nase."[7] Faust the character is a larger, more daunting example of the problems which afflicted the poet Tasso, who had become almost a byword for severe melancholy contributing to mental instability as a touchstone of genius.[8] But, as Goethe's play about him argues, Tasso was also someone who transformed his melancholic anxieties into art. Few commentators have considered the possible direct connections between Tasso's masterpiece, *Gerusalemme Liberata*, and Goethe's other writings.[9]

The process of translating of one's immediate crises into aesthetic representations so as to reassert control of the self over threatening chaos was understood to be the logic of Tasso's allegorical appropriation of history in his theory and practice of epic. The political direction of this appropriation was necessarily conservative, aiming at the restoration of order at all levels, and coincided both with his psychological make-up and the Counter-Reformation.[10] The "key to the allegory" appended by Tasso to *Gerusalemme Liberata* indicates the direction of his politics:

> And such is it in the mind, as the chieftain in an assembly of soldiers: for as of these the office is to obey their princes, which do give directions and commandments to fight against their enemies: so is it the duty of the ireful, warlike, and sovereign part of the mind, to be armed with reason against concupiscence, and with that vehemency and fierceness which is proper unto it, to resist and drive away whatsoever impediment to felicity.[11]

---

Languages, The University of Texas at Austin, 1979), 104–13; and Walter Hinderer, "Torquato Tasso," in *Goethes Dramen: Neue Interpretationen*, ed. Walter Hinderer (Stuttgart: Reclam, 1980), 169–96.

[7] Letter of 16 February 1788, in Johann Wolfgang von Goethe, *Goethes Werke*, commissioned by the Grand Duchess Sophie of Saxony (Weimar: Böhlau, 1887–1919), pt. 4, vol. 8: 347.

[8] See Moog-Grünewald, "Tassos Leid: Zum Ursprung moderner Dichtung," *arcadia* 21 (1986): 113–32.

[9] One exception was Harold Jantz, who mused that there seemed to be some parallel between Faust's journey to The Mothers in *Faust II* and *Gerusalemme Liberata*. See *The Mothers in* Faust: *The Myth of Time and Creativity* (Baltimore: The Johns Hopkins UP, 1969), 52.

[10] See especially Margaret W. Ferguson, *Trials of Desire: Renaissance Defenses of Poetry* (New Haven and London: Yale UP, 1983), 54–136; Andrew Fichter, *Poets Historical: Dynastic Epic in the Renaissance* (New Haven and London: Yale UP, 1982), 112–55; and Quint, *Epic and Empire*, 213–47.

[11] Quoted by Mindele Anne Treip, *Allegorical Poetics & the Epic: The Renaissance Tradition to* Paradise Lost (Lexington: U of Kentucky P, 1994), 61.

All of this could be applied to the condition of Faust, who resembles both Tasso and the allegorized mind in being caught in a struggle between reason and dark emotions. The military language in which Tasso couched the allegory was a convenient device for imagining the conflicts between reason and irrationality; it was a commonplace in Scripture and in the teachings of the Stoics and meshed well with the martial context of the heroic epic. But this was also a political language, one that continually verged on self-deconstruction by reminding everyone that the corollary to obedience was the possibility of disobedience, that commanders were confronted by mutinies and rebellions, as when Argillano revolts against Goffredo.[12] And finally, these discourses were joined to the language of medicine via the topos of the "body politic" through Peter the Hermit's pronouncement near the beginning of the poem:[13]

> Where one man alone does not have the rule, from whom may then depend the judgments about rewards and punishments, by whom responsibilities and offices may be apportioned, there the government is bound to be erratic. Oh, make but one body of your cooperating limbs; make but one head that may direct and restrain the others. Give to one man alone the scepter and the power, and let him hold the place and the semblance of a king.[14]

The mingling of these discourses is important because it opens up the possibility of a political history of melancholy. Not least troubling for those who dealt with melancholy was the question of why it had broken out with epidemic proportions in the fifteenth and sixteenth centuries. There were and continue to be philosophic explanations that note the shock of the age

---

[12] See the analysis by Quint, *Epic and Empire*, 214–22. The article by T. M. Holmes, "Homage and Revolt in Goethe's 'Torquato Tasso,'" *Modern Language Review* 65 (1970): 813–19, does not come to grips with the ways in which Goethe's play reflects the thematization of those two gestures on the basis of Tasso's poem. Quite useful for its many insights is Ulrich Stadler, "Der Augenblick am Hofe: Allgemeines und Besonderes in Goethes Schauspiel *Torquato Tasso*," in *Wahrheit und Wort: Festschrift für Rolf Tarot zum 65. Geburtstag*, ed. Gabriela Scherer and Beatrice Wehrli (Bern: Lang, 1996), 463–81.

[13] See the suggestive remarks by Francesca Savoia, "Notes on the Metaphor of the Body in the *Gerusalemme liberata*," in *Western Gerusalem: University of California Studies on Tasso*, ed. Luisa Del Giudice (New York: Out of London P, 1984), 57–70; and Michael Murrin, *The Allegorical Epic: Essays in Its Rise and Decline* (Chicago and London: U of Chicago P, 1980), 103–7.

[14] Torquato Tasso, *Jerusalem Delivered: An English Prose Version*, trans. and ed. Ralph Nash (Detroit: Wayne State UP, 1987), 1.31. All passages cited are from this translation.

of discovery. But an equally powerful explanation was the discrepancy between the hopes for a universal Christian peace and the apparently unending, indeed intensifying, state of war. The point is not that observers were simply saddened by what they witnessed, but that they were made physically ill because the body, as a microcosm, could not achieve a proper balance of the humors when the *body politic*, a macrocosm, was in disarray.

In this framework, Tasso's key to the allegory was also the prescription for a cure of the individual in tandem with the restoration of order in the Holy Roman Empire. Tasso's choice of subject matter — the supposed unity of Christianity during the Crusades — was to be a corrective to the religious and national conflicts of the sixteenth century. The vision of a unified, multi-national, Christian army that could succeed in capturing the Holy City should have ushered in an era of lasting Christian peace, in the actual world, centered on the liberated Jerusalem. As Quint puts it:

> The *Liberata* thus celebrates the triumph of the imperial, Counter-Reformation papacy: this is the significance for the larger poem of the specific topical allusions that gather around Rinaldo and Argillano. The peculiar trick of these allusions is to portray the two rebels against Goffredo's authority literally as *political subjects* of the Church, inhabitants of papal domains.[15]

The flies in Tasso's ointment were that unity under the sole authority of the Pope was not an agenda appealing to Protestants, and that the plan obviously did not succeed. By the eighteenth century, things would be even worse than two hundred years before, as Protestant Prussia and Catholic Austria vied for supremacy in the Empire. There was also an inherent contradiction in Tasso's argument that peace could be brought about through the conquest of Islam and the "liberation" of Jerusalem. As European expansion continued the impulses of the Crusades, it was the military action in the colonial spaces, on the periphery, that inevitably brought war back to the metropolis, notably in the Seven Years' War (1756–63) which began in the Americas and India. The displacement of inner struggles on to the history of the world had not brought harmony to Europe and had not brought the epidemic of melancholy under control.

With Faust, Goethe returned to the sixteenth century for a reexamination of the political and historical causes of melancholy. Faust was historically a contemporary to Tasso and therefore shares many of the poet's problems, but lacks poetic insight. Whereas Tasso was able to make his predicament a subject *for* history, Faust will never succeed in transcending his status as a subject *of* history. They participated in the course of history

---

[15] Quint, *Epic and Empire*, 230.

at about the same time, but they will remain differentiated by historical fact: Faust could not have read *Gerusalemme Liberata*, which was only published in 1581, by the time he arrives in "Auerbachs Keller." Faust cannot learn from Tasso's example; all he can do is share Tasso's experiences of the age and, should he be capable of doing so, perceive in those experiences the analogy to what had already been described in historical epics. Both the fictional Faust and the historical Tasso are given the opportunity to transcend the limitations of their here and now through casting their lives as coherent stories, but only the latter will succeed.[16]

The ironic juxtaposition becomes starkly apparent for the audience that remembers the key episode from cantos 12 and 13 of *Gerusalemme Liberata* while watching "Auerbachs Keller." The Crusaders are besieging Jerusalem and need wood to build scaling ladders. When Godfrey's men go to cut down some trees, they are frightened by strange apparitions, for the evil sorcerer Ismeno has enchanted the forest, and they flee. Tancred then resolves to penetrate the mysterious forest. After braving enchanted fire and storms, he comes upon a clearing where he reads a warning inscription:

> At length he discovers a broad clearing in the shape of an amphitheater; and in it there is not a single tree, except that in its center a cypress towers high, like a lofty pyramid. Thither he makes his way; and upon examining it, becomes aware that the trunk was carved with various symbols, resembling those that ancient mystic Egypt once used in place of script.
>
> Among the unknown symbols he makes out some phrases in the Syrian language, of which he has a good command: "O you that have dared set foot, bold warrior, within the cloisters of the dead — ah! (if you be not cruel as you are brave) ah! disturb not this secret seat. Have pity on souls that are now deprived of light; the living ought not wage war with the dead." (13.38–39)

The theatrical audience watching Faust and recalling Tasso's poem is startled by the resemblance in function between the strange hieroglyphs, which only the initiated can read, and the stage direction in the text, which Faust never sees and therefore cannot decode, at the entrance to the scene: "Auerbachs Keller. In Leipzig." Tancred is warned that something extraordinary is about to happen, a confrontation of the living with the dead. Faust receives no such warning, but we in the audience grasp how the admonition to Tancred could be applied in the theatre.

The caution is wasted on Tancred, who cannot plumb its hidden meaning even with his proficiency in translating the literal sense. Now

---

[16] Compare Benjamin Bennett, *Goethe's Theory of Poetry:* Faust *and the Regeneration of Language* (Ithaca and London: Cornell UP, 1986), 215.

comes a reenactment of a scene immediately familiar to all readers of Dante's *Inferno*:

> Thus spoke that inscription. He stood intent on the hidden meanings of the cryptic words: meanwhile he heard the wind continually moaning among the leaves and undergrowth of the wood, and drawing from them a sound that seems a plaintive harmony of human sobs and sighs, and instills in his heart I know not what mingled sense of pity, fear and sorrow.
>
> Yet in the end he draws his sword and with his mighty strength he smites the towering tree. Oh marvellous! the split bark issues blood and stains the earth about it crimson. He is completely horrified, and yet redoubles the blow and tells himself to see it through to the end. Then he hears issue forth, as from the tomb, a muffled sorrowing groan that becoming distinguished into words then said: "Alas too much have you wronged me, Tancred; now let this much suffice. From the body that was along with me and because of me my happy abode, you have already cast me forth; why do you yet lay waste the wretched trunk to which my harsh lot bound me? Do you wish, cruel man, after death to assault your enemies in their graves?
>
> Clorinda I was once; and lodge not here the only human soul in this hard and shaggy tree; but every other too, pagan or Frank, that left his limbs at the base of the lofty walls is here constrained by strange and new enchantment, I know not whether to say into this body or this grave. Branches and trunks are animate with sense, and you a murderer, if you cut their wood." (13.40–43)

The similarities and differences between this passage from Tasso and that from Dante have been closely studied.[17] Of interests here are clues linking it textually to "Auerbachs Keller." One such connection is the way in which the wine spills on the ground as the blood from the trees flows over the earth. A second detail picks up on Tancred's remorseless repetition of blows with the sword. Instead of halting at the horrid sight of the blood gushing from the wounded tree, instead of showing mercy as the inscription had enjoined upon him, he continues because of his determination, as the narrator tells us. Is Tancred's doggedness good or bad? That will remain a

---

[17] For analyses of the episode, see William J. Kennedy, "The Problem of Allegory in Tasso's *Gerusalemme Liberata*," *Italian Quarterly* 15 (1972): 27–51; here, 35–38; Colin Burrow, *Epic Romance: Homer to Milton* (Oxford: Clarendon, 1993), 78–79; and Jane Tylus, "Tasso's Trees: Epic and Local Culture," in *Epic Traditions in the Contemporary World: The Poetics of Community*, ed. Margaret Beissinger, Jane Tylus, and Susanne Wofford (Berkeley and Los Angeles: U of California P, 1999), 108–30.

dilemma: it is good for a heroic knight to persevere, but it is bad for a warrior to violate the cosmic order by failing to show mercy. The tree poses no immediate threat to Tancred, and his repeated assaults upon it serve no good purpose. In *Faust*, the wounds into the table are made by Mephistopheles, who of course has no qualms of conscience. Tancred's perseverance shifts into mere butchery, mocking further his killing of Clorinda, reminding us of Turnus's killing of Pallas in the *Aeneid*. The mechanical inflicting of the wounds betrays an indifference to the wonders of the natural world. Clorinda's accusation carries over from Tasso's text to Goethe's: "Branches and trunks are animate with sense, and you are a murderer, if you cut their wood." In the world where allegory was still possible, even trees could lament, whereas the wooden table must remain mute. However, the literary heritage is still alive in the imagination of readers.

One such reader was the young Wilhelm Meister, who reported a special affinity for the story of Clorinda:

> "Das befreite Jerusalem," davon mir Koppens Übersetzung in die Hände fiel, gab meinen herumschweifenden Gedanken endlich eine bestimmte Richtung. Ganz konnte ich zwar das Gedicht nicht lesen; es waren aber Stellen, die ich auswendig wußte, deren Bilder mich umschwebten. Besonders fesselte mich Chlorinde mit ihrem ganzen Tun und Lassen. Die Mannweiblichkeit, die ruhige Fülle ihres Daseins taten mehr Wirkung auf den Geist, der sich zu entwickeln anfing, als die gemachten Reize Armidens, ob ich gleich ihren Garten nicht verachtete.[18]

The young Wilhelm is captivated by the sad story of how Tancred, not recognizing who she was, killed Clorinda in battle. Powerful emotions overcome him when he recalls the episode we have just been analyzing:

> Aber wie ging mir das Herz über, wenn in dem bezauberten Walde Tankredens Schwert den Baum trifft, Blut nach dem Hiebe fließt, und eine Stimme ihm in die Ohren tönt, daß er auch hier Chlorinden verwunde, daß er vom Schicksal bestimmt sei, das, was er liebt, überall unwissend zu verletzen. (HA 7:27)

Ah, but that is not quite what Clorinda said to Tancred; she did not make a general prophecy about his fate or about how he would harm everything he would love. That is an interpretation by Wilhelm of Tasso's text, and, dare I say, an interpretation that could apply rather aptly to *Faust*'s destiny.

---

[18] HA 7:26–27. I am indebted here to Günter Saße, "Wilhelm Meister als Leser Tassos," in *Torquato Tasso in Deutschland: Seine Wirkung in Literatur, Kunst und Musik seit der Mitte des 18. Jahrhunderts*, ed. Achim Aurnhammer (Berlin and New York: Walter de Gruyter, 1995), 370–81.

Moved deeply by the tragic episode, Wilhelm decides to do something that helps us to understand the relationship, not only of this episode, but of epic poetry in general to Goethe's drama. Ignoring abstract rules about genre, Wilhelm is able to grasp the dramatic potential of the epic:

> Es bemächtigte sich die Geschichte meiner Einbildungskraft so, daß sich mir, was ich von dem Gedichte gelesen hatte, dunkel zu einem Ganzen in der Seele bildete, von dem ich dergestalt eingenommen war, daß ich es auf irgendeine Weise vorzustellen gedachte. Ich wollte Tankreden und Reinalden spielen und fand dazu zwei Rüstungen ganz bereit, die ich schon gefertigt hatte. Die eine, von dunkelgrauem Papier mit Schuppen, sollten den ernsten Tankred, die andere, von Silber- und Goldpapier, den glänzenden Reinald zieren. In der Lebhaftigkeit meiner Vorstellung erzählte ich alles meinen Gespannen, die davon ganz entzückt wurden und nur nicht wohl begreifen konnten, daß das alles aufgeführt, und zwar von ihnen aufgeführt werden sollte. (HA 7:27–28)

However, there are numerous obstacles between the imagined transformation and its realization. Where to get trees, for example?

> Für den Wald fanden wir eine gute Auskunft: wir gaben einem alten Bedienten aus einem der Häuser, der nun Förster geworden war, gute Worte, daß er uns junge Birken und Fichten schaffen möchte, die auch wirklich geschwinder, als wir hoffen konnte, herbeigebracht wurden. Nun aber fand man sich in großer Verlegenheit, wie man das Stück, eh' die Bäume verdorrten, zustande bringen könne. Da war guter Rat teuer, es fehlte an Platz, am Theater, und Vorhängen. (HA 7:28)

(Parenthetically, one might observe that the young Wilhelm has done the same kind of harm to the living trees in order to satisfy his imagination that Clorinda had pleaded with Tancred to avoid doing.) The performance is a failure because Wilhelm has forgotten to rehearse the other actors in their roles and no one knows their parts. The lesson Wilhelm draws from the collapse of his plan is that henceforth he would undertake performances only with the most careful consideration beforehand.

One lesson I would like to draw for my purposes from this lengthy summary is that Goethe was very well aware of the dramatic potential residing in epic forms and at the same time knew that generic constraints were not easily transcended. If one were contemplating staging the episode of the wounded and talking tree, the limitations of realism would turn any literal rendering on the stage into farce. Required was careful reworking of the material, with due attention to the requirements of the theatre medium. Otherwise, the effect would be comical and ludicrous, something like the production within *Midsummer Night's Dream*, and would vitiate any sense of the tragic in the plot.

In the transposition of the episode of Tancred and Clorinda to the stage of *Faust I*, the tree falls silent, but so does Faust. Instead of a dialogue with a voice that could tell its story, that could testify about the past, Faust is now in the situation of the historian who must recreate the past out of mute objects and a pantomime. There is no longer a marvelous privileged access to the past: the modern historian has to rely upon memory, insight, empathy, logic, and imagination in order to be able to make sense of what is happening out of the fragments available to him. Certainly there is material in the archive that could fill in background details. Had Faust remembered Dante and Vergil, as Tasso obviously did, he should have been able to recognize himself through the reenactment of the epic scene upon the theatre stage. An advantage of historical memory is that it also provides access, however limited, to the understanding of the present and the future. The poet Tasso could give shape to the chaos of the sixteenth century by recasting the conflicts in terms of the age of the Crusades. He was also able then to discern the transformations imposed by change over time upon the role of the individual subject, as myth gave way to romance and then to Christian allegory. Having forgotten those texts, Faust cannot grasp that now he is the central figure of the history, the successor in the line of epic figures coming down from Achilles to Aeneas.

Faust's forgetfulness should not be blamed upon him personally — he has not willed himself to forget, but rather is suffering one side effect of extreme melancholy. The links between psychological states and forgetfulness are adumbrated in *Gerusalemme Liberata* by what we learn of Tancred's emotions and their effect upon his reason. First, his zeal in combat prevents him from discovering that Clorinda is his opponent. Then when he comes to the inscription in the grove, he is still so caught up in grief that he disregards the warning and perpetrates further harms. An interpolation by the narrator explains that the "enchantment" as a whole might be the result of Tancred's fevered imagination:

> As sometimes the sick man who encounters in a dream [some] dragon or tall chimaera girt with flame, although he suspects or partly knows that the simulacrum is no true shape, yet wants to flee, such terror the horrid and dreadful appearance implants in him; even so the intimidated lover not wholly believes the false deceits, and yet concedes and fears. (13.44)

Had Faust only read these lines! As a trained physician he might have grasped how the demonic images in his world are conjured up as part of his illness; as a trained theologian he might have remembered how susceptible the melancholics were to the temptations of Satan. But Faust does not overcome the distortions of his own imagination and will; instead he follows Tancred's example, succumbs to phantasms and fails to penetrate to the truth. The foil to Tancred is Rinaldo, who does accomplish the task. As C. M. Bowra observed, Rinaldo is steadfast:

> The skies thunder and the earth roars, but Rinaldo does not care, and the devils leave the wood. Rinaldo's triumph over the devilish enchantment is

that of a man who is completely master of himself and no longer a prey to his former weaknesses. So the episode of the wood closes, with its implicit lesson that evil magic of this kind can be encountered successfully only by those who know what evil is and are not moved by its allurements.[19]

Surely this could be taken as an indictment of Faust, who does not truly know what evil is and therefore can be lured by it.

One of the most important morals to be learned from history is that knowledge is limited and therefore mistakes will be made out of sheer ignorance. Tancred's killing of Clorinda highlights this from two sides. Tancred does not know what he is doing, and in his flush of triumph he cannot anticipate how meanings will change as the events unfold. The narrator's apostrophe speaks to us all about the limitations of knowledge that contribute to human suffering:

> Tancred sees his enemy's blood in greater quantity, and himself not hurt so much. He joys and takes pride in it. Alas our foolish minds, that every breath of Fortune can puff up!
>
> Wretched man, for what are you rejoicing? oh how tearful will be your triumphs and luckless your vaunt! Your eyes will pay [if you remain alive] for every drop of that blood an ocean of tears. So, silent and watchful, these bloody warriors ceased a while. (12.58.5–59.6)

The form and content of this intervention are further intensified because they echo the fateful remarks by the narrator in the *Aeneid* after Turnus is boasting about having killed Pallas:

> Ah, mind of man, so ignorant of fate, of what shall befall him,
> So weak to preserve moderation when riding the crest of good fortune!
> For Turnus a time is coming when he'd give everything
> To have Pallas unharmed, and will loathe this day and the spoils
> It brought him.[20]

These warnings, could he only remember them, might have given Faust pause, for they anticipate all the harm that he will still bring into the world, all the suffering he will undergo after Valentin and Margarete are destroyed because of him. Nor will it be possible to exonerate Faust on the grounds that he "did not know": the sequence of events in the epics teaches that the judgment of history is stern. Tancred and Turnus would give anything if they could turn back the clock, and in this they are prefigurations of

---

[19] Bowra, *From Virgil to Milton* (London: MacMillan, and New York: St Martin's P, 1967), 167.

[20] Virgil, *The Aeneid*, trans. C. Day Lewis (Oxford: Oxford UP, 1998), 10.501–5.

Faust. Clorinda accuses Tancred of being a "murderer" when he cuts into the tree — and those words will recur in the "Kerker" when Margarete exclaims: "Laß mich! Nein, ich leide keine Gewalt! / Fasse mich nicht so mörderisch an!" (4576–77). By then it will be too late.

## Ariosto and *Orlando Furioso*

Goethe's visit in the autumn of 1789 to Ferrara was something of a disappointment. During the evening of 16 October, he recorded his negative impressions:

> Zum erstenmal überfällt mich eine Art von Unlust in dieser großen und schönen, flachgelegenen, entvölkerten Stadt. Dieselben Straßen belebte sonst ein glänzender Hof, hier wohnte Ariost unzufrieden, Tasso unglücklich, und wir glauben uns zu erbauen, wenn wir diese Stätte besuchen. Ariosts Grabmal enthält viel Marmor, schlecht ausgeteilt. Statt Tassos Gefängnis zeigen sie einen Holzstall oder Kohlengewölbe, wo er gewiß nicht aufbewahrt worden ist. Auch weiß im Hause kaum jemand mehr, was man will. Endlich besinnen sie sich um des Trinkgeldes willen. (HA 11:100)

Those who make pilgrimages to sites associated with famous persons are particularly upset when they find that the locals either have forgotten to how to honor the person or never knew and have rebuilt the monuments, badly, into a tourist attraction. Having come such a distance to pay homage, Goethe was contemptuous of those citizens of Ferrara who could not remember the two names that had lent glory to their city.[21] Whereas the presence of the drama *Torquato Tasso* has kept some awareness of that poet alive, even if only through the veil of Goethe's text, the same cannot be said for Ludovico Ariosto and his *Orlando Furioso*. As far as I can tell,

---

[21] Basic information about the reception of Ariosto by the Sturm und Drang generation is provided by Gabriele Kroes, "Zur Geschichte der deutschen Übersetzungen von Ariosts *Orlando furioso*," in *Italienische Literatur in deutscher Sprache: Bilanz und Perspektiven*, ed. Reinhard Klescewzki and Bernhard König (Tübingen: Gunter Narr, 1990), 11–26, esp. 12–15. Without placing too much weight upon its implications, it is interesting to note a moment of ironic identification on Goethe's part with Ariosto. On 4 January 1831 he wrote to Zelter to report that the first two acts of *Faust II* were completed: "Die Exclamation des Cardinals von Este, womit er den Ariost zu ehren glaubte, möchte wohl hier am Orte seyn" Johann Wolfgang von Goethe, *Goethes Werke*, commissioned by the Grand Duchess Sophie of Saxony (Weimar: Böhlau, 1887–1919), pt. 4, vol. 48:72. It is notorious that the Cardinal asked the poet something like "Wherever do you get all that stuff?"

no one has pursued any of the evidence in *Faust I* that points in the direction of Ariosto's pervasive influence, although here again Harold Jantz was perceptive.[22] Of course, Ariosto does come into the awareness of Goethe's readers because he is referred to repeatedly in *Torquato Tasso,* where he receives remarkable if indirect praise out of Antonio's mouth in the final scene of the first act. The courtier praises Ariosto in order to humiliate Tasso:

> Wie die Natur die innig reiche Brust
> Mit einem grünen, bunten Kleide deckt,
> So hüllt er alles was den Menschen nur
> Ehrwürdig, liebenswürdig machen kann,
> Ins blühende Gewand der Fabel ein.
> Zufriedenheit, Erfahrung und Verstand
> Und Geisteskraft, Geschmack und reiner Sinn
> Fürs wahre Gute, geistig scheinen sie
> In seinen Liedern und persönlich doch
> Wie unter Blütenbäumen auszuruhn,
> Bedeckt vom Schnee der leicht getragnen Blüten
> Umkränzt von Rosen, wunderlich umgaukelt
> Vom losen Zauberspiel der Amoretten.
> Der Quell des Überflusses rauscht darneben,
> Und läßt uns bunte Wunderfische sehn.
> Von seltenem Geflügel ist die Luft,
> Von fremden Herden Wies und Busch erfüllt.
> Die Schalkheit lauscht im Grünen halb versteckt,
> Die Weisheit läßt von einer goldnen Wolke
> Von Zeit zu Zeit erhabne Sprüche tönen,
> Indes auf wohlgestimmer Laute wild
> Der Wahnsinn hin und her zu wühlen scheint
> Und doch im schönsten Takt sich mäßig hält.
>                               (lines 711–33; HA 5:92–93)

But Antonio's fulsome rhetoric is duplicitous, for Ariosto was anything but a dreamy poet unfamiliar with the turmoils of his age, and *Orlando Furioso* is far more than an unproblematic romance. The gush of clichés could only come from someone who in fact has not read Ariosto and is only repeating vague second-hand impressions, stressing the pastoral and romance dimensions while ignoring or suppressing Ariosto's political criticism. The whole of Antonio's praise of Ariosto is intended by Goethe as ironic barb

---

[22] Jantz, *The Mothers in Faust,* 53 and 81.

against the economy of patronage. Antonio lauds Ariosto because in doing so he is praising the Este family and their patronage in Ferrara: "see how successful we have been in fostering such talents, in encouraging such masterpieces." This praise is merely the payback for the effusive compliments supposedly offered by Ariosto to the Estes in *Orlando Furioso*. There was no need to actually read, appreciate, and understand what Ariosto had written. The Dukes of Ferrara used up the symbolic capital of poets such as Ariosto and Tasso without actually investing in them,[23] as Goethe's notes pithily summarized on that depressing evening in Ferrara: "ein glänzender Hof, hier wohnte Ariost unzufrieden, Tasso unglücklich." But the poets have their revenge, and had Antonio actually paid attention to *Orlando Furioso*, he would surely have been less pleased, for he would have noticed what a careful reader such as Albert R. Ascoli has detected:

> The invocation of the myth of Hippolytus may thus have two opposite and yet equally deleterious effects on the genealogical encomium: it may suggest that the Este lack the Machiavellian *virtù* or personal force to avoid becoming victims of treachery and to rule successfully in a violent world; or it may suggest that they do possess such force, but only at the cost of sacrificing virtue in the more conventional moral sense to the violence of their own desires. Whichever the case, the problems with the family had already been forecast by the title (with its allusion to mad Hercules destroying his family), bolstered by the subsequent reference to Ippolito as "generosa Erculea prole." (1.3.1)[24]

In short, Antonio's trust in the reports he has had of Ariosto's work and of his loyalty are short-sighted. One reason why he would never expect such a subversive politics from a supposedly faithful subject is that he cannot imagine, has conveniently forgotten, that Ariosto was a man of the

---

[23] A concise discussion is that of C. P. Brand, "Ludovico Ariosto — Poet and Poem in the Italian Renaissance," *Forum for Modern Language Studies* 4 (1968): 87–101.

[24] Albert Russell Ascoli, *Ariosto's Bitter Harmony: Crisis and Evasion in the Italian Renaissance* (Princeton: Princeton UP, 1987), 387. See also Herbert Frenzel, "Der Stammbaum der Este: Ein Beitrag zur genealogischen Trojalegende," in *Wort und Text: Festschrift für Fritz Schalk*, ed. Harri Meier and Hans Sckommodau (Frankfurt am Main: Vittorio Klostermann, 1963), 187–99; Robert M. Durling, *The Figure of the Poet in Renaissance Epic* (Cambridge, MA: Harvard UP, 1965), 135–46; Fichter, *Poets Historical*, 70–111; and R. Baillet, "L'Arioste et les princes d'Este: Poésie et politique," in *Le pouvoir et la plume: incitation, contrôle et répression; Actes du colloque internationale organisé par le Centre Interuniversitaire de Recherche sur la Renaissance Italienne et l'Institut Culturel Italien de Marseille, Aix-en-Provence, Marseille, 14–16 Mai 1981* (Paris: Université de La Sorbonne Nouvelle, 1982), 85–95.

world as well as a poet. Long years of service as a diplomat and adminis-
trator for the Este family had placed Ariosto close to the centre of the
political struggles at the end of the fifteenth and beginning of the sixteenth
centuries. He had seen and endured much of the treachery and naked
ambition that characterized his age, matters that Antonio is only too happy
papering over with a pastoral tranquillity. But Goethe *has* read Ariosto dif-
ferently than a duke might, especially because he was still grappling with
the contradictions of his own relationship to Carl August. In that context,
the achievement of Ariosto's "bitter harmony," to use A. R. Ascoli's elegant collocation, as well as the fact that Orlando yet again represents a
moment in the history of melancholy,[25] made *Orlando Furioso* a work with
lasting significance for Goethe.

The full extent of the allusive network weaving *Faust* to *Orlando
Furioso* can not be presented here,[26] but two knots may indicate how firmly
they are tied together. One is the much-discussed translation by Faust of
the New Testament in "Studierzimmer." Surely it is time for readers to
notice Ariosto's satire upon St. John the Evangelist and to ponder some of
its ramifications for *Faust*.[27] Faust, flushed with pride, decides to challenge
Scriptural authority and to reverse cosmic history by putting the deed
before the word: "Auf einmal seh ich Rat / Und schreibe getrost: Im
Anfang war die Tat!" (1235–37). This reversal means that before the
divine Word there would be matter that acted without inspiration, thereby
establishing events, with a secular history, predating the onset of revelation. The serious issues, going to the core of the understanding of
Christian hermeneutics, are presented by Ariosto through the elaborate
ironies of John's meta-historical criticism of all written texts. Inciting the
discussion is the question of how true epic poetry could be:

> Aeneas was not as devoted, nor Achilles as strong, nor Hector as ferocious
> as their reputations suggest. There have existed men in their thousands

---

[25] See Paolo Valesio, "The Language of Madness in the Renaissance," *Yearbook
of Italian Studies* 1 (1971): 199–234, here 204–6; Philip McNair, "The Madness
of Orlando," in *Renaissance and Other Studies: Essays Presented to Peter M. Brown*,
ed. Eileen A. Millar (Glasgow: University of Glasgow, Department of Italian,
1988), 144–59; and Andrea Di Tommaso, "*Insania* and *Furor*: A Diagnostic Note
on Orlando's Malady," *Romance Notes* 14.3 (1973): 583–88. Orlando is of course
an excellent example of someone stricken with "love-sickness"; see Alfredo
Bonadeo, "Note sulla pazzia di Orlando," *Forum Italicum* 4 (1970): 39–57.

[26] I have dealt with one allusion in "The Tell-Tale Chalice: 'Es war ein König
in Thule' and *Orlando Furioso*," *Monatshefte* 92.1 (2000): 20–34.

[27] I am indebted in the following discussion to James Thomas Chiampi,
"Between Voice and Writing: Ariosto's Irony According to Saint John," *Italica* 60
(1983): 340–50; and to Ascoli, *Ariosto's Bitter Harmony*, 264–304.

who could claim preference over them. What has brought them their sublime renown have been the writers honoured with gifts of palaces and great estates donated by these heroes' descendants. / Augustus was not as august and beneficent as Vergil makes him out in clarion tones — but his good taste in poetry compensates for the evil of his proscriptions. And no one would know whether Nero had been wicked — he might even, for all his enemies on earth and in heaven, have left a better name — had he known how to keep friendly with writers. / Homer made Agamemnon appear the victor and the Trojans mere poltroons; he made Penelope faithful to her husband, and victim of a thousand slights from her suitors. But if you want to know what really happened, invert the story: Greece was vanquished, Troy triumphant, and Penelope a whore. / Listen on the other hand to what reputation Dido left behind, whose heart was so chaste: she was reputed a strumpet purely because Vergil was no friend of hers.[28]

In other words, the events that came before the words are betrayed by them: the written accounts are false because of the cupidity of the authors, who have distorted the truth for the sake of material gain. This sounds rather like the deist attacks in the early eighteenth century upon Scripture as being little more than historical fabrications designed to present the Church in a favorable light. Indeed, Ariosto is more than subtle in turning the readers toward such a conclusion, for John readily admits that he, also, was only a "writer":

> Don't be surprised if this embitters me and if I talk about it at some length — I like writers and am doing my duty by them, for in your world I was a writer too. / And I, above all others, acquired something which neither Time nor Death can take from me: I praised Christ and merited from Him the reward of so great a good fortune. (35.27.5–29.4)

Well, if the Evangelist is only a writer, then Faust's vanity in correcting the text could well be justified, especially since he is using the same critical move just demonstrated by John, namely giving priority to the deeds themselves over the written history. What happens when the Bible is set into the series of epic histories if all those histories are lies and distortions commissioned for a price? The truth, then, would not be in the Scriptures but would have to be calculated by negating what the Bible states, and the authors would no longer have divine legitimation and would be subject to a translation that would be other than literal, as it would correct and

---

[28] Ludovico Ariosto, *Orlando Furioso*, trans. Guido Waldman (Oxford: Oxford UP, 1983). Quotations in the text are from this edition, cited by canto/verse/line; here 25.25–28.4. The allusion to the reputation of Dido sheds light on Valentin's cruel denigration of Margarete in the scene "Nacht."

improve.[29] This would take us down the road that Mephistopheles prefers and wants Faust to follow, denying the Gospel and doubting everything written about Christian history. In particular, Mephistopheles could certainly benefit if the plus and minus signs were reversed in front of his and Christ's values — after all, that has been his goal from the beginning.

A second allusion involves the difficult situation of Ariosto's epic in the history of his own time, which was contemporary with the era that is the background to "Auerbachs Keller." One small puzzle in *Faust* has been why Marthe's husband should have died at Padua, as Mephistopheles reports:

> Er liegt in Padua begraben
> Beim heiligen Antonius,
> An einer wohlgeweihten Stätte
> Zum ewig kühlen Ruhebette. (2925–28)

Aside from the unlikely possibility that this should be general knowledge, one wonders why Mephistopheles should have just this information ready. What was so special about Padua that might have roused his diabolical interest? From *Orlando Furioso* we learn that Padua was the site of a siege, made infamous because the army of Maximilian I had fired huge cannons at the town and its inhabitants. The narrator refers to the event in the course of a diatribe against the horrors of modern warfare, one that implicates the Church in the remorseless destructiveness:

> Among the warriors of old, examples of chivalrous and noble conduct were frequently to be seen, but seldom in our own day: aye, wicked practices a-plenty were to be seen or marked, Hippolytus, during the war in which you adorned the churches with captured standards and towed the enemy ships, laden with booty, to your father's shores! / Every cruel, inhuman deed ever practised by Tartar, Turk, or Moor was perpetrated, if not indeed by will of the Venetians (for they have always been of

---

[29] It would take a long digression to expose the political economy of translation being presented here as a critique of unearned production. Such a digression could begin with the analyses by David Raybin, "Translation, Theft, and *Li Jeus de Saint Nicolai*," *Romanic Review* 85.1 (1994): 27–48, and move through Marc Shell's *Money, Language, and Thought: Literary and Philosophical Economies from the Medieval to the Modern Era* (Berkeley and Los Angeles: U of California P, 1982), especially his analysis of *Faust*, 84–130; and would have to extend into the eighteenth century and the history of "copyright," as reviewed by Martha Woodmansee, *The Author, Art, and the Market: Rereading the History of Aesthetics* (New York: Columbia UP, 1994), 35–55.

exemplary justice), by the criminal hand of their mercenaries. I say nothing of all the fires they started, which burned down our farms and country retreats — / though this was indeed an ugly vengeance, especially
against yourself: when you were in the emperor's camp at the siege of
Padua, it was well known that you on more than one occasion forbade the
firing of churches and villages, and had the fires put out once started, for
thus it pleased your innate chivalry. (36.2.1–36.4.8)

The mere mention of "Padua," then, invokes and represents both the civil
conflicts fracturing the Holy Roman Empire and the tremendous increase
in the destructive capacity of armies now armed with cannon. Such battles
erased any difference between "Christians" and "pagans." The fact that
Marthe's husband fell at Padua is of more than peripheral interest to
Mephistopheles; it was another milestone in the degeneration of the policies of Christian states towards each other, with ever more efficient slaughter. The contradiction is underscored when we are told how he died: "Ich
stand an seinem Sterbebette, / Es war was besser als von Mist, / Von hal-
bgefaultem Stroh; allein er starb als Christ" (2952–54). Cruelly,
Mephistopheles enjoys detailing the end of a "Christian" whose life has
been taken by other "Christians" and who perishes under pathetic circumstances, his bed little better than a dung-heap. The allusion to the bed
of straw on which Christ was born gives the usual Mephistophelean
piquancy to the story, as does the oblique blasphemy of the rhyme.[30]

Mephistopheles has reason to be pleased with Padua and with the
spreading effectiveness of weapons of mass destruction, not least because
guns were one of his bequests to human beings. *Orlando Furioso* reminds
us of the legends about how firearms came into the world:

> the Evil One, enemy of human kind, who invented the fire-arm, copying the
> action of the thunderbolt which splits the clouds and falls to earth — the
> Evil One, serving us almost as fatally as when he deceived Eve with
> the apple, saw to it that a sorcerer should recover the weapon in our grand-
> fathers' time, or a little earlier. / The infernal contraption lay hidden for
> many a year under more than a hundred fathoms of water, until it was
> brought to the surface by magic and passed into the possession of the
> Germans; these tried one experiment after another, and the devil sharpened
> their wits until, to our detriment, they eventually rediscovered how to use
> it. (21.22.1–23.8)

---

[30] These little details keep reminding us how cunning Mephistopheles is, since
he could always defend himself by pleading that "Christ" means "Christian," i.e.
Marthe's husband, and not Jesus. Nevertheless, the very act of associating the
highest name with a word for filth has a degrading effect.

The invention of guns and gunpowder has drastically altered the nature of warfare:

> Unhappy soldier, turn in your weapons to be melted down, even to your very sword: carry a musket on your shoulder or an arquebus — else you will go without wages! / Wicked, ugly invention, how did you find a place in human hearts? You have destroyed military glory, and dishonoured the profession of arms; valour and martial skill are now discredited, so that often the miscreant will appear a better man than the valiant. (21.25.4–26.6)

Goethe's comments upon the sixteenth century in the *Geschichte der Farbenlehre* could almost be a paraphrase of the sentiment:

> Im Sittlichen gehen ähnliche große Wirkungen und Gegenwirkungen vor. Das Schießpulver ist kaum erfunden, so verliert sich die persönliche Tapferkeit aus der Welt oder nimmt wenigstens eine andre Richtung. Das tüchtige Vertrauen auf seine Faust und Gott löst sich auf in die blindeste Ergebenheit unter ein unausweichlich bestimmendes, unwiderruflich gebietendes Schicksal. (HA 14:80)

Far from underpinning any paean of praise to the Germans, *Faust* harbors the judgment of history upon them as those whose technological prowess multiplied and intensified human suffering. That the Germans were responsible for the introduction of gunpowder as a dreadful new weapon was a Renaissance commonplace, as was the conviction that Satan must have had a hand in the invention.[31]

One artistic achievement of Ariosto, unpleasant though it was to contemplate, was his modernization of warfare for the purposes of the epic. He could hardly avoid doing so, since technological progress had altered the nature of combat. Henceforth warfare had little use for chivalry and the other trappings of hand-to-hand combat that had been the image and reality since Homer. The remnants of the chivalric world were in Ariosto's time being replaced by a new ethos and by armies made up of mercenaries ("else you will go without wages") such as the *Landsknechte* who sacked Rome. Marthe's husband seems to have been one of the sixteenth-century soldiers whose life could still be told as though it had been filled with adventure but that had in fact been dominated by money and material

---

[31] Murrin, *History and Warfare in Renaissance Epic*, 127. On the reception of guns and cannon in the sixteenth century, see J. R. Hale, "Gunpowder and the Renaissance: An Essay in the History of Ideas," in *From the Renaissance to the Counter-Reformation: Essays in Honor of Garrett Mattingly*, ed. Charles H. Carter (New York: Random House, 1965), 113–44.

pursuits.[32] Although Marthe's summation of his life suppresses most of the dark side to the endless wars of the age, she does point to the aimlessness of his fortune-seeking, where Fortuna is no more than a roll of the dice:

> Es konnte kaum ein herziger Närrchen sein.
> Er liebte nur das allzuviele Wandern,
> Und fremde Weiber, und fremden Wein,
> Und das verfluchte Würfelspiel. (2994–97)

The anonymous husband is the modern everyman, and his picture owes its lineaments to the figures moving through *Orlando Furioso*, driven by insatiable, random desire.[33] With *Orlando Furioso* in mind, we can see that Faust's second utterance in "Auerbachs Keller" could have been written by Ariosto: "Ich hätte Lust nun abzufahren" (2296). The structure of the sentence balances the modern self ("Ich") against the urge to continue somewhere, anywhere ("abzufahren"), and does so on the pivot of desire ("Lust"). This is no longer the sentiment of a heroic knight compelled by the vision of a noble quest heading out for *aventiure*, but the beginning of the tireless peregrination that continues to the present as the longing for "adventure."[34]

Much more could be said in general about the relationships between *Orlando Furioso* and *Faust*, for example on the correspondences between Ruggiero's conversion and what transpires in "Marthens Garten," but for the nonce I will concentrate upon "Auerbachs Keller." Not a specific detail that Goethe has taken from Ariosto but more the matter-of-factness with which the marvelous is recounted concerns us. Ruggiero has tethered his hippogryph to a myrtle bush, which begins to speak in a direct imitation of its precursors in Dante and Vergil:

> While Ruggiero was here, his steed, which he had left in the cool shade
> of a dense thicket, shied away, frightened by I know not what he had
> descried in the tangled wood. He so tore apart the myrtle to which he

---

[32] For the background, see Lothar Knapp, "Ariosts 'Orlando Furioso': Die Kritik der Waffen und der Triumph der Liebe," in *Das Epos in der Romania: Festschrift für Dieter Kremers zum 65. Geburtstag*, ed. Susanne Knaller and Edith Mara (Tübingen: Gunter Narr, 1986), 177–92. It would be worthwhile to reread the character of Marthe — her determination, her interest in a new mate — in light of Knapp's discussion of canto 20, with its argument that long absences of warring men produced strong women back at home.

[33] Behind this sentence are the discussions by Eugenio Donato, "'*Per selve e boscherecci labirinti*': Desire and Narrative Structure in Ariosto's *Orlando Furioso*," *Barroco* 4 (1972): 17–34; and D. S. Carne-Ross, "The One and the Many: A Reading of *Orlando Furioso*, Cantos 1 and 8," *Arion* 5 (1966): 195–234.

[34] Compare also Ulrich Breuer, *Melancholie und Reise*.

was tethered that he became ensnared in the branches strewn underfoot; he tugged at the myrtle, bringing down a shower of leaves, but was unable to pull free. / If a log with but a soft core of pith is placed in the fire, it starts to whine, because the intense heat consumes the vaporous air inside it, and it sizzles noisily so long as the vapour forces a way out. Just so, the damaged myrtle moaned and hissed in vexation, and finally a sad, tearful voice / issued from an open pore, and framed words pronounced with utmost clarity: "If you are good and kind, as your fair looks suggest, loose this animal from my branches. Let my own ill-fortune be sufficient torment without the addition of more evil, more pain inflicted upon me from without." (6.26.1–28.55)

The closer we draw to Vergil the clearer the episode from book 3 of the *Aeneid* becomes. Here the voice is heard from a *bush*, rather than a tree, and the plaintive self-accusation echoes Vergil's Polydorus. Of course Ariosto was not merely imitating his predecessors; the scientific explanation has been updated to fit with the Neoplatonic revival in the wake of Ficino's impact. Nevertheless, Ariosto has taken pains to make sure that his epic is understood as a deepening of the Christian allegory that dominates the *Divine Comedy*, so that the tethered hippogryph alludes to the griffin in *Purgatorio* 32 and the marvelous tree.[35] The "shower of leaves" reminds us of the fact that the tree, a type of the tree of knowledge, is bare of leaves and fruits: "I heard 'Adam' murmured by all, then they encircled a tree stripped of its flowers and of its foliage in every bough" (32.2.37–39). The immense complexity of Dante's text cannot be recapitulated here,[36] but there should be no doubt that Ariosto had more in mind than a charming diversion with this episode. To give one suggestion of where pursuing the allusion to canto 33 might lead: Ariosto has the hippogryph shaking down *some* leaves, but the myrtle bush is not yet entirely bare, because the historical events to be described by Dante are still in progress during the time when *Orlando Furioso* is taking place, that is, the reign of Charlemagne.

---

[35] See Erika Kanduth, "Bemerkungen zu Dante-Reminiszenzen im 'Orlando furioso,'" in *Studien zu Dante und zu anderen Themen der romanischen Literaturen: Festschrift für Rudolf Palgen zu seinem 75. Geburtstag*, ed. Klaus Lichem and Hans Joachim Simon (Graz: Universitäts-Buchdruckerei Styria for the Hugo Schuchardtsche Malwinenstiftung Graz, 1971), 59–70; here, 62.

[36] In addition to Charles Singleton's commentary on the passage (see *The Divine Comedy*), see R. E. Kaske, "Dante's *Purgatorio* XXXII and XXXIII: A Survey of Christian History," *University of Toronto Quarterly* 43.3 (Spring 1974): 193–214; Margherita Frankel, "Biblical Figuration in Dante's Reading of the *Aeneid*," *Dante Studies* 100 (1982): 11–23; and above all the magisterial study by Peter Armour, *Dante's Griffin and the History of the World: A Study of the Earthly Paradise* (Purgatorio, *cantos xxix–xxxiii*) (Oxford: Clarendon, 1989).

The withering of the celestial tree, the tree of knowledge and of justice, is yet to be fulfilled, as is its regeneration. In this context, there is more to Ruggiero's blush in the scene than meets the eye. A. Bartlett Giamatti observes that "The blush reinforces the portrait of the chivalrous young man who realizes he has broken the code by hitching his horse to a man."[37] Yes, but the blush also imitates the sense of shame that Adam and Eve felt after they transgressed against God's law by violating the tree in Paradise. The implications for "Auerbachs Keller" are significant. There the tree is no longer present as living wood at all, but has been cut down and made into a table,[38] and Faust is so removed from Adam that he registers no emotion whatsoever, no shame, no shock, no astonishment.

There is nothing simplistic in Ariosto's text, even though it reads so entertainingly. Surfaces are not the same as essences; seeing is not believing. Astolfo, who became a victim of Alcina along with so many other men because he let himself be caught by desire, forgot "about France and all else," forgot his mission, his destiny, and discovered too late that Alcina was an inconstant lover and an enchantress:

> I was late in discovering the fickleness of her nature, prone to falling in and out of love all at once. I had reigned in her affection for but two months when a new lover was assumed in my place. She drove me out disdainfully, and withdrew her favour from me. Later I learnt that she had meted similar treatment to a thousand lovers before me, and always without cause. / And, to prevent their spreading about the world the story of her wanton ways, she transforms them, every one, planting them here and there in the fertile soil, changing one into a fir-tree, another into an olive, another into a palm or cedar, or into the guise in which you see me on this verdant bank; yet others the proud enchantress changes into liquid springs, or into beasts, just as it suits her. (6.50.1–51.8)

The story of metamorphosis into a myrtle bush, with the shift from a cruel blow that wounds a tree to merely a horse's entanglement with the shrubbery, could easily deceive the unwary reader who is bewitched by the teller's artfulness into taking this all very lightly. Where indeed are the agony and remorse, the crimson gash of blood?

Yet things are darker and more complicated for *Faust* than the surfaces indicate, for with the move back in time from Tasso to Ariosto we are

---

[37] A. Bartlett Giamatti, *The Earthly Paradise and the Renaissance Epic* (Princeton: Princeton UP, 1966), 143.

[38] Marc Harris reminded me of the relevance of Matthew 21:19–21. The replacement of the cross by a table involves very intricate symbolic histories dealing not only with the Cross but also with the Ark and the fact that a table is the sort of furniture that a carpenter would make.

becoming increasingly burdened by the past. The work of memory is becoming harder as we have to keep in mind both earlier and later versions of texts and events. The audience has to remember what happens in "Auerbachs Keller" and how that compares with the episode in *Gerusalemme Liberata* but now has to begin juggling with the awareness that the successive epics give different versions. These have to be reconciled typologically with each other and at the same time each of them has to be seen as a reflex of the author's specific historical situation. The history of production and the history of transmission, the whole of the process summed up by "tradition," must be brought to mind. We know that Ariosto was "continuing" Boiardo and that Tasso was "modernizing" Ariosto — how shall we describe and understand Goethe's renewal of the epic? All the while, more information is being brought to light about the past through these sources, and questions arise about how to construct an orderly history out of the whole. The scene "Auerbachs Keller" is a cosmological microcosm, but it is also one of a series of vignettes about history as chronicle *and* as prophecy, a treatment of history that had become a set piece in epic, where the hero confronts his own past that is also a future. Aeneas sees the recapitulation of the fall of Troy in the temple frieze in book 1 of the *Aeneid* (30) and is compelled to encounter himself as a subject of history.[39] In *Orlando Furioso*, Astolfo is told about the history yet to come: that is, the events leading up to Ariosto's era are told as prophecy:

> I see Charles acceding to the crown of Italy under the faithful escort of this captain of whom I speak, for he shall open the gates to the emperor. And I see that the captain does not keep for himself the reward he wins for his assistance, but has it made over to his own city, Genoa: at his instance, he obtains the liberation of his city, when others would perhaps have obtained its subjection to themselves. . . . Let them blush, and whoever else presumes to enslave his homeland; let them not dare to raise their eyes when they hear Andrea Doria's name pronounced. I see Charles increasing his reward, for in addition to the freedom he shall enjoy in common with his fellow-citizens, the emperor shall give him the rich territory where the Normans are to establish the foundations of their greatness in Apulia. (15.32.1–8; 34.1–8)

---

[39] I am indebted at this point and in the section to follow on the *Aeneid* to the analysis by Reinhart Herzog, "Aeneas' epische Vergessen: Zur Poetik der memoria," in *Memoria: Vergessen und Erinnern*, ed. Anselm Haverkamp and Renate Lachmann, with Reinhard Herzog (Munich: Wilhelm Fink, 1993), 81–116; here, 96. On the use of *ekphrasis* in conjunction with the epic poet's confrontation with history and historiography, see Page Dubois, *History, Rhetorical Description and the Epic: From Homer to Spenser* (Cambridge: D. S. Brewer, and Totowa, NJ: Biblio Distribution Services, 1982).

These vignettes serve to historicize the hero, for he must learn that his actions too shape the future, in ways that can be predicted from a knowledge of the past.[40] Neither Aeneas nor Astolfo learns enough to be able to avoid contributing further to the cycles of violence and destruction that would gradually engulf the whole known world. Similarly, Faust, although he is shown the reality of political history in "Auerbachs Keller," will go on to participate in imperial warfare in *Faust II*. Although the historical Faust could not have read *Gerusalemme Liberata*, the potential existed for him to have read *Orlando Furioso* and to have learned from it, since it was published during his lifetime. Like his contemporaries who were still familiar with the classical canon, he would have noticed the connections to tradition, would have noticed, as everyone has, that Ariosto referred to Dante and to Vergil. Astolfo, as we will see shortly, corresponds to Dante's Pier della Vigna, and through him to Polydorus; Ruggiero and Astolfo correspond to aspects of Dante the pilgrim and thence to Aeneas. It is increasingly difficult in this archaeology to decode the system of correspondences and hence to garner clues about their meaning and their implications for *Faust* without opening the gates to the antecedent texts.

The typological links are intricate, as each of the authors shifts attributes and deeds from one figure to another; it is not simply a matter of identifying X as a copy of Y. The actions and responses of Ruggiero in the episode with the myrtle bush are largely consistent with what has been said about Faust's indifference in "Auerbachs Keller." To quote William J. Kennedy:

> Much of the torment in Vergil and Dante derived from the fact that the encounter wounded Aeneas and Dante's pilgrim no less than the bushes themselves. In each instance the heroes seem stunned and then aroused by fear to a heightened awareness of the unusual situation. Ruggiero, however, is hardly moved to the core of his being. His initial reaction amounts only to flustered incomprehension; he is *stupefatto* (6.29), but he soon regains his innate sense of *cortesia* (6.32), which prompts him to alleviate the myrtle's irritation. . . . Ruggiero, for his part, accepts the myrtle's plea without reflection, without suspicion, without skepticism, and in so doing he exposes himself to the danger of being deceived for the second time in his brief career.[41]

---

[40] On the congruence of past and contemporary history with allegory in *Orlando Furioso*, see Lothar Knapp, "Ariosts 'Orlando Furioso': Die Kritik der Waffen und der Triumph der Liebe," in *Das Epos in der Romania: Festschrift für Dieter Kremers zum 65. Geburtstag*, ed. Susanne Knaller and Edith Mara (Tübingen: Gunter Narr, 1986), 177–92.

[41] William J. Kennedy, "Ariosto's Ironic Allegory," *Modern Language Notes* 88.1 (1973): 44–67; here, 48–49.

This is important for Faust's genealogy as a figure, since all his other equiv-
alents in the version of the episode — Aeneas, Dante the pilgrim, Tancred
(and indeed Adam) — react strongly to their wounding of the trees.
Mephistopheles is of course the exception, because Goethe has transposed
the actual deed on to him and away from Faust. Such reworking of the figures is standard operating procedure in the tradition of the epic, as some
qualities are retained in a figure while others are relocated or redefined.
Ruggiero is not exactly congruent with Tancred, since the latter actually
cuts into the enchanted tree whereas the former is only a bystander while
the hippogryph disturbs the bush. In this respect, Faust's inactivity resembles the passivity of Ruggiero. But they are connected at a more fundamental level as types of the epic hero through the theme of *pietas.*[42]

A telling phrase is uttered by Astolfo when he politely addresses
Ruggiero: "If you are good and kind, as your fair looks suggest"
(6.28.3–4). The restrained request begins a series of polite exchanges:
Ruggiero inquires about how the voice came to be in the bush, and Astolfo
opens his tale with a formulaic politeness marker: "Your courtesy so pre-
vails upon me" (6.32.5). It is unlikely that Ariosto was trying to teach the
audience the importance of manners under extreme circumstances. Rather,
the politeness of Ruggiero and of Astolfo is consistent here with the death
of chivalry in the modern world.[43] Ruggiero's polite inquiry is an empty
ritual: he is acting out the abstract rules of courtly society, without anchoring his expressions in genuine feelings. The contrast of this superficial
politeness to the anguish of Dante the pilgrim in canto 13 is remarkable,
as Erika Kanduth observes.[44] Something has gone awry with courtesy by
the time of the world of *Orlando Furioso.* Politeness now represents a fundamental indifference to others, no matter how much they might be
undergoing pain and suffering. This indifference has come into the world
together with the terrible new forms of warfare, since only those who can
alienate themselves totally from their feelings can participate in the whole-
sale slaughter of anonymous human beings. A key word for tracing the
history of this dissociation of self from feelings is *pietas.* Once a word

---

[42] Cf. James D. Garrison, *Pietas from Vergil to Dryden* (University Park:
Pennsylvania State UP, 1992).

[43] See A. Bartlett Giamatti, "Introduction," in Ludovico Ariosto, *Orlando
Furioso*, trans. William Stewart Rose, ed. Stewart A. Baker and A. Bartlett Giamatti
(Indianapolis and New York: Bobbs-Merrill, 1968), xxxvi–xxxvii.

[44] Kanduth, "Bemerkungen zu Dante-Reminiszenzen im 'Orlando furioso,'"
62–63.

betokening the most serious commitments to paternity, to the divine order, to the past and to others, in *Orlando Furioso* it is no longer binding morally and has been reduced to the fixed phrase "cortese e pio" ("courteous and pious").[45]

The decline from *pietas* as a lived principle to the polished husk of courtesy as manifested in the transformations of the epic hero helps to explain Faust's behavior. In "Auerbachs Keller," Faust reenacts the empty politeness with his greeting to the four companions: "Seid uns gegrüßt, ihr Herrn!" (2183). The greeting is stiff and is awkwardly inappropriate, since the four drunken companions do not warrant the honorific. The effect of the shift to the passive voice is to emphasize the wooden lack of empathy in Faust's greeting, his demurral at interacting directly with the others. Far from being praiseworthy, Faust's courtesy, taken over from Ruggiero and the world of the late fifteenth century, betrays a subversion of civil society by the politics and manners of an era that gave us the concept "machiavellian." The self is now hidden behind social masks and routine ploys of interaction. What has gone missing are the emotions upon which authentic social selves could be grounded. Unless rooted in lived emotions, concepts such as *pietas* cannot have any transformative influence in the social world, but become themselves false tokens, inverting their original value. *Pietas* that is only a formula is a self-contradiction and is tantamount to the *impiety* that characterizes Faust. His politeness in "Auerbachs Keller" is on a par with his formulaic invocation of Christian teachings: he does not really believe in either. Impiety disguises itself in the rote repetition of empty social forms that will rarely be challenged openly; it perdures in the awareness of others and the past but refuses to acknowledge any obligation to them. Within the chivalric code, the fact that piety has become inauthentic makes a mockery of the knight's pretense of loyalty and of love, for those are predicated on a genuine, serving subordination of the self. A. Bartlett Giamatti saw in *Orlando Furioso* a "failure of the chivalric code to dictate meaningful patterns for behaviour" and noted the deviation of chivalric love away from the ideal.[46] Looking forward in the drama, we can anticipate through Faust's false courtesy the tragic consequences of his equally specious "love" for Margarete. That love will be false because it will be artificially induced by the love potion, one that will not induce constancy but that will make him see "Helen in *every* woman." While each woman might wish to be treated with courtesy as if she were Helen, none would be flattered to be loved no better than every and any other one.

---

[45] Kennedy, "Ariosto's Ironic Allegory" points out that " 'Cortese e pio' is a conventional formula that recurs throughout the poem" (48, n. 10).

[46] A. Bartlett Giamatti, "Introduction," xxxvi–xxxvii.

The crisis of courtesy is also a crisis of modern epistemology, because those who lack genuine piety will be unable to learn the laws of nature. Grossly put, Faust's religious impiety is inseparable from his failings as a scientist. A recognition of the lessons of *Orlando Furioso* might have helped Faust avoid joining the wrong side in the development of modern science. We know that he has opted for the illusions of "black magic," and thereby rejected the other option available in the Renaissance, namely the Neoplatonic philosophical attitude to nature. As Goethe would stress in his history of the theory of color, a contribution of the sixteenth century was the swing to the critical, rational examination of traditions and appearances (HA 14:69). The ability to differentiate the genuine from the phony is, as Goethe goes on to observe, very much the same for the history of scientific progress and for the progress in the critique of written authorities such as the works of Plato and Aristotle. Through a careful process of studying the authoritative texts and comparing them with other evidence, a finer understanding gradually emerges. Goethe saw in the sixteenth century a decisive period in the development of modern science. In this he basically agrees with what many historians of science would say, but he has also grasped that Ariosto's *Orlando Furioso* is a demonstration of the questioning, critical mind at work.[47] There is an important distinction to be made between the characters in the poem and the author's critical ideology. Faust approximates figures such as Ruggiero but does not correspond to the skeptical mind of Ariosto, who was both aware of and in sympathy with a critical scientific attitude. The narrator of *Orlando Furioso* must be ironic because of the author's realization that progress is a mixed blessing — the invention of gunpowder brings previously unimagined horror into warfare — that truth dissolves cherished traditions even as it introduces new possibilities.

The case that is of direct relevance to "Auerbachs Keller" is the metamorphosis of Alfonso into the myrtle bush. Of course, no one is expected to believe that such shape-shifting is possible in the modern era. So why tell it? One might simply take the episode at face value as a transmitted fragment of antiquity, in the way that works on natural history had been accepted for centuries, and be amused by it as a bizarre shard of anachronistic romance. However, the close reader will be alerted to the differences with the theoretical issues raised by the metamorphosis in "Auerbachs Keller" and in *Gerusalemme Liberata*. Goethe has gone to great lengths to make the scientific infrastructure appropriate to Faust's time. Tasso had relied upon a psychological explanation: the enchantment is explicable as a figment of troubled minds. What moves into the foreground in *Orlando Furioso* is precisely, for the first time, the need for the epic poet to take the

---

[47] Here I follow Ascoli's *Ariosto's Bitter Harmony*.

epistemological questions seriously. The gods are long since departed and Christian faith is in dispute, so that skepticism now intrudes upon the epic narrative, forcing readers to question their own assumptions about the logic of the natural world as they observe the characters learning to be experimenters. There is considerable humor in this for us because the characters are not very skeptical yet. Alfonso has been enchanted because he was deceived by the surface appearance of Alcina and her island. Only after undergoing the embarrassing change into a myrtle bush does he realize that the alluring island was entirely the product of earlier enchantments:

> Later I learnt that she had meted similar treatment to a thousand lovers before me, and always without cause. / And, to prevent their spreading about the world the story of her wanton ways, she transforms them, every one, planting them here and there in the fertile soil, changing one into a fir-tree, another into an olive, another into a palm or cedar, or into the guise in which you see me on this verdant bank; yet others the proud enchantress changes into liquid springs, or into beasts, just as it suits her. (6.50.5–51)

The demonstration and the analysis could not be more explicit: do not trust the world you see; it may be radically different than it seems; the phenomena are virtual enchantments. (Parenthetically, but appositely: this warning has been offered just before Faust will head to the Witches' Kitchen). Ruggiero, unable and unwilling to place trust in Astolfo's report, almost immediately undergoes the same experience (experiment):

> Little did it profit him to have been warned by the myrtle of her evil, treacherous nature — it did not seem to him possible for deceit and perfidy to keep company with so charming a smile. / On the contrary, he preferred to believe that if she had changed Astolfo into a myrtle by the sandy shore, it was because he had treated her with stark ingratitude, and so deserved his fate and worse. (7.16.4–17.4)

The pretense of courtesy towards Astolfo was in fact only that, for Ruggiero is quite ready to discredit the latter's report, impugning dishonor to him. The breakdown of the chivalric code retards the progress of science, because individuals must trust the reports of others if they are to avoid replicating mistakes over and over again.[48] Ruggiero's blatant disregard for

---

[48] The connection between civility and modern science has increasingly drawn the interest of historians of science, notably in Steven Shapin's *A Social History of Truth: Civility and Science in Seventeenth-Century England* (Chicago and London: U of Chicago P, 1994). On the eighteenth century, see Alice N. Walters, "Conversation Pieces: Science and Politeness in Eighteenth-Century England," *History of Science* 30 (1997): 121–54. See also the subtle analysis by Gordon Teskey, "'And therefore as a stranger give it welcome': Courtesy and Thinking," *Spenser Studies* 18 (2003): 343–59.

Astolfo's report is something that we have already identified in Faust, namely, the refusal to learn from other scholars and scientists. The difficulty is how one can be alert and skeptical about appearances without succumbing to an extreme skepticism that cannot learn from experience and tradition. The ironic reversal is that by rejecting everything completely — the great refusal of Faust's opening monologue! — Ruggiero ends up enchanted in turn.

Once the correspondences between Ruggiero and Faust are visible, one glimpses how the figure of Mephistopheles shares traits with Alcina. The whole of "Auerbachs Keller" is analogous to her enchanted island, which is as enticing as the lands glimpsed by the four companions in the "grape trick" illusion. What the four see is a replication of the beautiful landscape used by Alcina to lure her victims. The disappearance of the illusions is consistent with the unreality and hence impossibility of romance in the material world. Mephistopheles is no more committed to the illusion than Alcina is to true forms. Faust, as a contemporary of Ariosto's who could have been delighted and enlightened by *Orlando Furioso*, takes no warning from Ruggiero's fate. Nor does he reflect upon how Alcina beguiles the hapless knights, much as Mephistopheles has managed to charm Faust.[49] The urbane and elegant Mephistopheles quickly makes Faust forget his original quest and blinds him to the dangers of unexplained metamorphoses. Faust is ready to continue to the Witches' Kitchen, where enchantments will prevail, and where he will begin his descent into a life of illusionary infatuation that parallels Ruggiero's sojourn with Alcina: "how he was passing his time now in amusements, in dancing and feasting, in soft, pampered indolence, forgetful of his Liege, of his beloved, of his own renown" (7.39.3).

Lacking piety, Faust is not sufficiently loyal to the past to investigate seriously the history revealed in "Auerbachs Keller." Had he done so, he would have been brought face to face with disturbing truths about himself as a child of his own era. Ariosto does not paint a pretty picture of the times. Violence, war, delusion, and folly are the pervasive themes, but ultimately they all pale by comparison to the greatest scourge of the modern era, the beast of avarice:

> This cruel beast issued forth from the depths of hell at the time when lands were assigned boundaries, when weights and measures were established, and agreements written. At first he did not roam all over the world — many

---

[49] The switch from Alcina (feminine) to Mephistopheles (masculine) as the enchanting agent has implications for the history of the latter, for the problems around his gender identity, and for the nature of his relationship to males such as Faust.

countries he left inviolate. In our own time he brings distress to many parts of the world, but it is the commoners, the lowly rabble whom he attacks. From his advent to our own day he has kept growing, and he shall continue to grow until he shall eventually be the greatest monster that ever lived, and the most dreadful. (26.40.1–41.4)

As we are moving back in time, the motor force of modern history becomes easier to discern.[50] Faust would doubtless prefer not to have his own motive named so bluntly, choosing to forget why he has entered into the wager with Mephistopheles, refusing to see the history lesson through "Auerbachs Keller." It is telling that Ariosto has identified the written contract with the advance of avarice, for the importance of such writing for the success of Satan is what the versions of the Faust legend also stressed. What the audience in the theatre will not be spared but must be compelled to learn is the history of greed as it manifests itself in every historical period, growing, as Ariosto put it, more and more powerful, voracious, threatening. Greed as the most devastating force in history was also at the centre of Dante's analysis in canto 13.

## Dante and the *Divina Commedia*

Goethe scholars have been in a state of denial about his relationship to Dante, resisting particularly any attempts to connect *Faust* to the *Divine Comedy*. Fritz Strich spoke for the majority when he declared that "Goethe never acquired a really inward relationship to Dante."[51] Willi Hirdt has

---

[50] Reciprocally, the prophecy within *Orlando furioso*, which looks forward to Ariosto and his time, will become even more visible by the time of *Faust II*, where Avaritia will appear on stage in the Mummenschanz as "Der Abgemagerte." On the Biblical allusions in that passage, see Frank Möbus, "Des Plutus zwiefache Rede: Eine kryptische Bibelanspielung in der Mummenschanz des *Faust II*," *Zeitschrift für deutsche Philologie* 107: *Sonderheft* (1988): 71–84.

[51] Fritz Strich, *Goethe und die Weltliteratur* (Bern: A. Francke, 1946), 130–31; Horst Rüdiger, "Dante als Erwecker geistiger Kräfte in der deutschen Literatur," in *Festschrift für Richard Alewyn*, ed. Herbert Singer and Benno von Wiese (Cologne and Graz: Böhlau, 1967), 17–45; here, 26–29; Kurt Wais, "Die *Divina Commedia* als dichterisches Vorbild im XIX. und XX. Jahrhundert," *arcadia* 3 (1968): 27–47; here, 30–31. Goethe owned various editions and translations of Dante; see John Hennig, "Goethes Kenntnis der schönen Literatur Italiens," in his *Goethes Europakunde: Goethes Kenntnisses des nichtdeutschsprachigen Europas* (Amsterdam: Rodopi, 1987), 128–50; here, 133. No one heaped scorn on those who sought a "key" to *Faust* in the *Divine Comedy* more forcefully than Erich Schmidt, "Danteskes in Faust," *Archiv für das Studium der neueren Sprachen und Litteraturen* 107 (1901): 241–52; here, 241.

recently reevaluated the question in an informative article.[52] He sums up the force of the negative conclusions drawn by Emil Sulger-Gebing's rigorously positivistic study *Goethe und Dante: Studien zur vergleichenden Literaturgeschichte* (1907), which is still the standard study of the problem. Sulger-Gebing's work is meticulous, yet paradoxically its one serious defect is its extreme rigor, whereby no influence can be acknowledged that is not blatant, explicit, or direct. But Goethe had his own reasons for being evasive about revealing sources and intertexts. Even without that personal trait one should expect that all poets engaged in the great game of epic will make demands on readers. Yet there is no way around Sulger-Gebing's study and its presentation of the facts. It was he who firmly enshrined the notion that Goethe's first reference to Dante comes in 1796 with the translation of Cellini's autobiography. How reliable is this claim? Hirdt reminds us that Goethe's early education makes his familiarity with Dante more than probable. Goethe's father was keenly interested in Italian culture and had given his son extraordinary opportunities to learn the language and study the literature and become familiar with Dante.[53] Holding to caution, Hirdt nevertheless sought explicit textual confirmation for an earlier dating, which he finds in passages in *Götz von Berlichingen* that bear a strong resemblance to the Ugolino episode in the *Divine Comedy*. On the basis of this evidence, Hirdt asserted with confidence that we can at least go back to November 1771 in dating Goethe's familiarity with Dante. But even without the background information about Goethe's study of Italian — what else would a language teacher who was an Italian have used for textbook material besides the best from the canon? — we can push back the date to 24 November 1768, according to this passage from a letter by Goethe to Oeser:

> Meine Gedancken über den Idris, und den Brief an Riedeln, über den Ugolino, über Weissens Grosmuth für Grosmuth, über die Abhandlung von Kupferstichen, aus dem Englischen, sind zwar zum erzälen ganz erträglich, zum Schreiben noch lange nicht ordentlich, nicht richtig genug.[54]

---

[52] Willi Hirdt, "Goethe und Dante," *Deutsches Dante-Jahrbuch* 68–69 (1993–94): 31–80. This is an expanded version of his "Goethe e Dante," *Studi Danteschi* 62 (1990): 97–115. Two other recent surveys are by Arnold Münster, *Über Goethes Verhältnis zu Dante* (Frankfurt am Main: R. G. Fischer, 1990); and V. A. Avetisyan, *Gete i Dante* (Izhevsk: Isdatel'stvo Udmurtskovo Universiteta, 1998). Ulrich Gaier's commentary to his edition of *Faust-Dichtungen*, 3 vols. (Stuttgart: Philipp Reclam jun., 1999), pays systematic attention to the Dante allusions in *Faust II*.

[53] Hirdt, "Goethe und Dante," 55.

[54] Goethe, *Goethes Briefe*, ed. Karl Robert Mandelkow and Bodo Morawe, 4 vols. (Hamburg: Christian Wegner, 1962), 1:80.

Hirdt does cite one other important piece of evidence, although he draws back from its implications. A diary entry by Goethe on 7 August 1779 suggests a more profound identification of Goethe with the narrator of the *Divina Commedia*:

> Zu Hause aufgeräumt, meine Papiere durchgesehen und alle alten Schaalen verbrannt. Andre Zeiten andre Sorgen. Stiller Rückblick aufs Leben, auf die Verworrenheit, Betriebsamkeit Wissbegierde der Jugend, wie sie überall herumschweift um etwas befriedigendes zu finden. Wie ich besonders in Geheimnissen, duncklen Imaginativen Verhältnissen eine Wollust gefunden habe. Wie ich alles Wissenschafftliche nur halb angegriffen und bald wieder habe fahren lassen, wie eine Art von demütiger Selbstgefälligkeit durch alles geht was ich damals schrieb. Wie kurzsinnig in Menschlichen und göttlichen Dingen ich mich umgedreht habe. Wie des Thuns, auch des Zweckmäßigen Denckens und Dichtens so wenig, wie in zeitverderbender Empfindung und Schatten Leidenschafft gar viel Tage verthan, wie wenig mir davon zu Nuz kommen und da die Hälfte des Lebens vorüber ist, wie nun kein Weg zurückgelegt sondern vielmehr ich nur dastehe wie einer der sich aus dem Wasser rettet und den die Sonne anfängt wohlthätig abzutrocknen.[55]

It is a powerful emotional outburst and there can be no doubt that Goethe meant to invoke the opening lines of the *Inferno*.[56] Like the real Dante and his poetic namesake in *The Divine Comedy*, Goethe had turned fifty and come to that awareness now called "mid-life crisis." Unmistakable are the familiar themes of melancholy and the desultory casting about for a purpose in life that beset Goethe and that made him find kinship in great melancholic forebears, to which group Dante's name can be added. The image of regeneration in the sunlight of one who is "rescuing himself," who is overcoming sloth and despair, reminds us of canto 7 of the *Inferno*:

> and I would also have you know for certain that down under the water are people who sigh and make it bubble at the surface, as your eye tells you wherever it turns. Fixed in the slime they say, "We were sullen in the sweet air that is gladdened by the sun, bearing within us the sluggish fumes; now we are sullen in the black mire." (7.121–26)[57]

---

[55] Johann Wolfgang von Goethe, *Goethes Werke*, commissioned by the Grand Duchess Sophie of Saxony (Weimar: Böhlau, 1887–1919), pt. 3, vol. 1:93–94.

[56] Hirdt, "Goethe und Dante," 56.

[57] Dante Alighieri, *The Divine Comedy: Inferno 1: Italian Text and Translation*, trans. Charles S. Singleton (Princeton: Princeton UP, 1970). Quotations are from this edition.

Those who surrender to *acedia*, to sloth, are sinners and therefore must be punished accordingly.[58] But Goethe is rousing himself out of the state, is standing erect and is preparing for the ascent through the second half of life, a trajectory described by the *Divina Commedia*.

Goethe was by no means alone in rediscovering Dante in the second half of the eighteenth century. If the Enlightenment was antithetical to Dante,[59] then it is not surprising to find the *Sturm und Drang* generation drawn to him, especially those who tended towards the aesthetics promulgated by Bodmer,[60] responding to Johann Nikolaus Meinhard's *Versuche über den Charakter und die Werke der besten italienischen Dichter* (1763–1764).[61] German translations of the *Divina Commedia* in 1769 (prose) and then in 1780 (blank verse) also kept interest alive.[62] Wieland was open to the Italians, and *Agathon* bears traces of Dante.[63] The same principles that made Shakespeare suddenly acceptable and exemplary also created a space for a positive reception of Dante.

One of the strangest obstacles in the path to studying the relationship between Dante and Goethe has been a dull-witted understanding of an anecdote from Goethe's second trip to Rome (1787–88). Everything Goethe published about his travels to Italy should be taken with more than

---

[58]  See Wolf-Günther Klostermann, "Acedia und Schwarze Galle: Bemerkungen zu Dante, Inferno VI, 115 ff.," *Romanische Forschungen* 74 (1964): 183–93; and Giuseppe Mazzotta, *Dante, Poet of the Desert: History and Allegory in the Divine Comedy* (Princeton: Princeton UP, 1979), 179.

[59]  Alfred Noyer-Weidner, *Umgang mit Texten*, vol. 2: *Von der Aufklärung bis zur Moderne*, ed. Gerhard Regn (Stuttgart: Franz Steiner, 1986), 403–25.

[60]  On Bodmer's defense of Dante, see Max Wehrli, *Johann Jakob Bodmer und die Geschichte der Literatur* (Frauenfeld and Leipzig: Huber, 1936), 108–12.

[61]  The close connections between the discourse on melancholy and the reception of Dante was underscored by the publication in 1768 of Riedel's *Denkmal des Herrn Johann Nikolaus Reinhard*, which Mattenklott describes as one of the "Lebensbilder von Melancholikern" being read in the *Sturm und Drang*; see Gert Mattenklott, *Melancholie in der Dramatik des Sturm und Drang* (Stuttgart: J. B. Metzler, 1968), 17.

[62]  Noyer-Weidner, *Umgang mit Texten*, 131–32. Whether Goethe had read Lebrecht Bachenschwanz's *Dante Alighieri von der Hölle: Aus dem Italiänischen übersetzt und mit Anmerkungen begleitet* (Leipzig, 1767) is an open question.

[63]  Giorgio Padoan, "Un'eco della 'Divina Commedia' nell' 'Agathon' di Wieland," in *Miscellanea di studi offerta a Armando Balduino e Bianca Bianchi per le Loro Nozze, Vicenza — giugno 1962* (Padova: Presso Il Seminario di Filologia Moderna dell'Universita, 1962), 67–69.

a grain of salt,[64] and this episode is no exception. Goethe begins by signaling his disagreement with and distance from the conversation:

> Beim Grafen Fries fanden sich außer den Kunsthändlern auch wohl derart Literatoren, wie sie hier in Abbétracht herumwandern. Mit diesen war kein angenehmes Gespräch. Kaum hatte man von nationaler Dichtung zu sprechen angefangen und sich über einen andern Punkt zu belehren gesucht, so mußte man unmittelbar und ohne weiteres die Frage vernehmen, ob man Ariost oder Tasso, welchen von beiden man für den größten Dichter halte. Antwortete man: Gott und der Natur sei zu danken, daß sie zwei solche vorzügliche Männer einer Nation gegönnt, deren jeder uns nach Zeit und Umständen, nach Lagen und Empfindungen die herrlichsten Augenblicke verliehen, uns beruhigt und entzückt — dies vernünftige Wort ließ niemand gelten. Nun wurde derjenige, für den man sich entschieden hatte, hoch und höher gehoben, der andere tief und tiefer dagegen herabgesetzt. (HA 11:380)

Goethe's irritation verges on contempt for the dilettantes, who show no genuine appreciation of the literary and aesthetic problems at stake and are unwilling to respect informed discussion. The quarrel is especially tiresome since it is a shabby replication of the intense debates around the question of Tasso versus Ariosto as they had been fought in the sixteenth century. In the words of a literary historian from a later century, "The controversy whether Ariosto or Tasso's poem is the greater epic, as it was one of the most obstinately interminable ever raised by academic pedantry, is also one of the idlest."[65] These eighteenth-century literary priests are merely going through empty rituals of criticism, reducing it to a social diversion. One

---

[64] Some of the complexities are explored by Robert Gould, "Problems of Reception and Autobiographical Method in the 'Zweiter römischer Aufenthalt' of Goethe's *Italienische Reise*," *Carleton Germanic Papers* 22 (1994): 71–85. On Goethe's discussions of poets and writers, see János Riesz, "Goethe's 'Canon' of Contemporary Italian Literature in his *Italienische Reise*," in *Goethe in Italy, 1786–1986: A Bi-Centennial Symposium November 14–16, 1986, University of California, Santa Barbara: Proceedings Volume*, ed. Gerhart Hoffmeister (Amsterdam: Rodopi, 1988), 133–46.

[65] Richard Garnett, *A History of Italian Literature* (New York: D. Appleton & Co., 1898), 146. The highlights of the controversy are summarized by Bernhard Weinberg, *A History of Literary Criticism in the Italian Renaissance* (Chicago: U of Chicago P, 1961), 1:646–56; and examined in detail by Daniel Javitch, *Proclaiming a Classic: The Canonization of* Orlando Furioso (Princeton: Princeton UP, 1991). Since the comparison was a commonplace of Italian literary history, the suggestion that a foreigner such as Goethe might not be familiar with the positions had to be somewhat insulting.

can hardly imagine how Goethe, who had immersed himself in the background for the writing of *Torquato Tasso*, remained polite. But the situation was even worse when the acme of Italian literary achievements was mentioned. Hoping for serious engagement with people who after all defined their nationality through Dante's literary achievement, Goethe grew increasingly exasperated and finally resorted to a drastic riposte:

> Viel schlimmer aber war es, wenn Dante zur Sprache kam. Ein junger Mann von Stande und Geist und wirklichem Anteil an jenem außerordentlichen Manne nahm meinen Beifall und Billigung nicht zum besten auf, indem er ganz unbewunden versicherte, jeder Ausländer müsse Verzicht tun auf das Verständnis eines so außerordentlichen Geistes, dem ja selbst die Italiener nicht in allem folgen könnten. Nach einigen Hin- und Widerreden verdroß es mich denn doch zuletzt, und ich sagte, ich müsse bekennen, daß ich geneigt sei, seinen Äußerungen Beifall zu geben; denn ich habe nie begreifen können, wie man sich mit diesen Gedichten beschäftigen möge. Mir komme die "Hölle" ganz abscheulich vor, das "Fegefeuer" zweideutig und das "Paradies" langweilig; womit er sehr zufrieden war, indem er daraus ein Argument für seine Behauptung zog: dies eben beweise, daß ich nicht die Tiefe und Höhe dieser Gedichte zum Verständnis bringen könne. Wir schieden als die besten Freunde; er versprach mir sogar einige schwere Stellen, über die er lange nachgedacht und über deren Sinn er endlich mit sich einig geworden sei, mitzuteilen und zu erklären. (HA 11:380–81)

It is quite hilarious to imagine Goethe, who probably knew Italian literature better than any German of his time and whose respect for Dante was based on long, careful study, feigning complete ignorance and offering a preposterous judgment. Anyone with a modicum of perception would have recognized this as the ploy it was, but the young and chauvinistic Italian was only too happy to be confirmed in his prejudices. What is amazing about this is the reception that the anecdote has been given by many a German critic who quotes Goethe's riposte as though it should be taken at face value.[66] People with no sense for irony should stay away from certain writers.

The deep respect Goethe felt towards Dante and his accomplishments is attested on various occasions. Taken together, they make claims that Goethe did not know Dante or disparaged the *Divina Commedia* altogether implausible:

---

[66] One is almost dumbfounded to find even Ernst Robert Curtius, *European Literature and the Latin Middle Ages*, trans. Willard R. Trask (Princeton: Princeton UP for the Bollingen Foundation, 1973) taking the episode at face value as evidence that "Goethe's relation to Dante was ambivalent" (348)!

1805: "Die wenigen Terzinen, in welche Dante den Hungertod Ugolinos und seiner Kinder einschließt, gehören mit zu dem Höchsten, was die Dichtkunst hervorgebracht hat: denn eben diese Enge, dieser Lakonismus, dieses Verstummen bringt uns den Turm, den Hunger und die starre Verzweiflung vor die Seele. Hiermit war alles getan, und hätte dabei wohl bewenden können.[67]

1821: [Summing up his response to Tommaso Grossi's *Ildegonda*]: Die Stanzen sind ganz fürtrefflich, der Gegenstand modern unerfreulich, die Ausführung höchst gebildet nach dem Charakter großer Vorgänger: Tassos Anmut, Ariosts Gewandtheit, Dantes widerwärtige, oft abscheuliche Großheit, eins nach dem andern wickelt sich ab.[68]

1824: [In conversation with Eckermann about a new bust]: "Es ist Dante," sagte Goethe. "Er ist gut gemacht, es ist ein schöner Kopf, aber er ist doch nicht ganz erfreulich. Er ist schon alt, gebeugt, verdrießlich, die Züge schlaff und herabgezogen, als wenn er eben aus der Hölle käme. Ich besitze eine Medaille, die bei seinen Lebzeiten gemacht worden, da ist alles bei weitem schöner." Goethe stand auf und holte die Medaille. . . .

Und so kam das Gespräch wieder auf die vor uns stehende Büste des Dante und dessen Leben und Werke. Besonders ward der Dunkelheit jener Dichtungen gedacht, wie seine eigenen Landsleute ihn nie verstanden, und daß es einem Ausländer um so mehr unmöglich sei, solche Finsternisse zu durchdringen. "Ihnen," wendete sich Goethe freundlich zu mir, "soll das Studium dieses Dichters von Ihrem Beichtvater hiermit durchaus verboten sein."

Goethe bemerkte ferner, daß der schwere Reim an jener Unverständlichkeit vorzüglich mit schuld sei. Übrigens sprach Goethe von Dante mit aller Ehrfurcht, wobei es mir merkwürdig war, daß ihm das Wort Talent nicht genügte, sondern daß er ihn eine Natur nannte, als womit er ein Umfassenderes, Ahnungsvolleres, tiefer und weiter um sich blickendes ausdrücken zu wollen schien."[69]

1826: "Bekennen wir nur im ähnlichen Falle, daß wir ein Gedicht wie *Dantes Hölle* weder denken noch begreifen können, wenn wir nicht stets im Auge behalten, daß ein großer Geist, ein entschiedenes Talent, ein würdiger Bürger aus einer der bedeutendsten Städte jener Zeit, zusamt

---

[67] From a review in *Jenaer Allgemeine Literaturzeitung*, 14 February 1805, quoted in Emil Sulger-Gebing, *Goethe und Dante: Studien zur vergleichenden Literaturgeschichte* (Berlin: Verlag von Alexander Duncker, 1907), 8.

[68] Quoted in Sulger-Gebing, *Goethe und Dante*, 17.

[69] Conversation of 3 December 1824, quoted in Sulger-Gebing, *Goethe und Dante*, 22–23.

mit seinen Gleichgesinnten von der Gegenpartei in den verworrensten Tagen aller Vorzüge und Rechte beraubt, ins Elend getrieben worden."[70]

In light of such testimony, it is implausible to maintain that Goethe neither knew nor respected Dante. Quite the contrary. As the chiding instruction to Eckermann signals, Goethe was convinced that Dante's masterpiece was a work that could only benefit those readers with the requisite poetic and philosophic insight.

If we have any doubt that Goethe included himself among that select company, one need only examine his translation from canto 12 of the *Inferno*, which he provided as a corrective to the translation undertaken by Karl Streckfuß. Goethe's justification of his versions demonstrates how well he read the complexity of Dante's poem, its language, and its allegory:

> Die Wanderer nähern sich nunmehr dem Blutgraben, der, bogenartig, von einem gleich runden ebenen Strande umfangen ist, wo Tausende von Kentaurn umhersprengen und ihr wildes Wächterwesen treiben. Vergil ist auf der Fläche schon nah genug dem Chiron getreten, aber Dante schwankt noch mit unsicherem Schritt zwischen den Felsen; wir müssen noch einmal dahin sehen; denn der Kentaur spricht zu seinen Gesellen:
>
> > "bemerkt: der hinten kommt, bewegt,
> > Was er berührt, wie ich es wohl gewahrte,
> > Und wie's kein Totenfuß zu machen pflegt."
>
> Man frage nun seine Einbildungskraft, ob dieser ungeheure Berg- und Felsensturz im Geiste nicht vollkommen gegenwärtig geworden sei?
>
> In den übrigen Gesängen lassen sich bei veränderter Szene eben ein solches Festhalten und Ausmalen durch Wiederkehr derselben Bedingungen finden und vorweisen. Solche Parallelstellen machen uns mit dem eigentlichsten Dichtergeist Dantes auf den höchsten Grad bekannt und vertraut.[71]

With the weight of all this evidence and more, some Goethe scholars have conceded that there are more than approximate parallels between the *Divina Commedia* and *Faust*. However, these have been primarily been localized to the "Prologue in Heaven" and to *Faust II*.[72] The presence of

---

[70] From *Über Kunst und Altertum*, quoted in Sulger-Gebing, *Goethe und Dante*, 26.

[71] Letter of 9 September 1826, quoted in Sulger-Gebing, *Goethe und Dante*, 34–35.

[72] Sulger-Gebing, *Goethe und Dante*, 78–111; Hirdt, "Goethe und Dante," 68–80; Wais, "Die *Divina Commedia* als dichterisches Vorbild im XIX. und XX. Jahrhundert," 30–33; The. Absil, "La Divina Commedia en Faust: Uitreksel uit een overweging," in *Verzamelde Opstellen: Geschreven door oud-Lerlingen von*

Dante's influence throughout has hardly been mentioned, although Jane Brown has suggested that the "Walpurgis Nacht" has Dantean reflections.[73]

It is more than a little ironic that a comparison of "Auerbachs Keller" with the *Inferno* should pit against each other two passages whose reception has been so very different. "Auerbachs Keller" has been largely overlooked, on the presumption that nothing or very little of consequence happens there. Canto 13 is one of the best-known and most closely analyzed parts of Dante's poem.[74] To quote Patrick Boyde:

---

*Professor Dr. J. H. Scholte*, ed. The. C. Van Stockum, H. W. J. Kroes, and D. J. C. Zeeman (Amsterdam: J. M. Meulenhoff, 1947), 110–40; Luciano Zagari, "Natur und Geschichte: Metamorphisches und Archetypisches in der *Klassischen Walpurgisnacht*," in *Bausteine zu einem neuen Goethe*, ed. Paolo Chiarini (Frankfurt am Main: Athenäum, 1987), 148–85; Cyrus Hamlin, "Tracking the Eternal-Feminine in Goethe's *Faust II*," in *Interpreting Goethes* Faust *Today*, ed. Jane K. Brown, Meredith Lee, and Thomas P. Saine, in collaboration with Paul Hernadi and Cyrus Hamlin (Columbia, SC: Camden House, 1994), 142–55.

[73] Jane Brown, *Goethe's Faust: The German Tragedy* (Ithaca and London: Cornell UP, 1986), 124.

[74] In addition to the extensive commentary by Charles Singleton to his translation, I have benefited from or consulted the following: J. C. Barnes, "Inferno XIII," in *Dante Soundings: Eight Literary and Historical Essays*, ed. David Nolan (Dublin: Irish Academic P, and Totowa, NJ: Rowman and Littlefield, for The Foundation for Italian Studies, University College, Dublin, 1981), 28–58; Douglas Biow, "From Ignorance to Knowledge: The Marvelous in *Inferno* 13," in *The Poetry of Allusion: Virgil and Ovid in Dante's* Commedia, ed. Rachel Jacoff and Jeffrey T. Schnapp (Stanford, CA: Stanford UP, 1991), 45–61 and 261–64; Patrick Boyde, "*Inferno* XIII," in *Cambridge Readings in Dante's* Comedy, ed. Kenelm Foster and Patrick Boyde (Cambridge and London: Cambridge UP, 1981), 1–22; Anthony K. Cassell, *Dante's Fearful Art of Justice* (Toronto and Buffalo: U of Toronto P, 1984), 32–56 and 126–40; and Cassell's "Pier della Vigna's Metamorphosis: Iconography and History," in *Dante, Petrarch, Boccaccio: Studies in the Italian Trecento in Honor of Charles S. Singleton*, ed. Aldo S. Bernardo and Anthony L. Pellegrini (Binghamton, NY: Center for Medieval and Renaissance Texts and Studies, SUNY Binghamton, 1983), 31–76; Joan M. Ferrante, *The Political Vision of the* Divine Comedy (Princeton: Princeton UP, 1984); David H. Higgins, "Cicero, Aquinas, and St. Matthew in *Inferno* XIII," *Dante Studies* 93 (1975): 61–94; Robin Kirkpatrick, *Dante's* Inferno: *Difficulty and Dead Poetry* (Cambridge: Cambridge UP, 1987), 173–95; Jon D. Levenson, "The Grundworte of Pier Delle Vigne," *Forum Italicum* 5 (1971): 499–513; Richard Neuse, *Chaucer's Dante: Allegory and Epic Theater in* The Canterbury Tales (Berkeley and Los Angeles: U of California P, 1991), 181–91; Leonard Olschki, "Dante and Peter de Vinea," *Romanic Review* 31 (1940): 105–11; Aldo Scaglione, "XIII," *Lectura Dantis. Nr. 6 Supplement*, ed. Tibor Wlassics (Spring 1990): 163–72; R. A. Shoaf, " 'Dante in ynglyssh': The *Prologue* to the *Legend of Good Women* and *Inf.* 13 (Chaucer and Pier della Vigna)," *Annali d'Italianistica* 8

It has been said that any great narrative must contain passages of great drama, and there could hardly be a more striking instance of this truism than the thirteenth canto of the *Inferno*. A scene is set where acts of violence succeed each other in an atmosphere of mystery and suspense. Six actors reveal themselves in the sharply characterised words they are given to speak (almost two thirds of the canto being cast in the form of direct speech). The plot advances through the interaction of these six characters as they misunderstand and hurt each other, interrupt, taunt, plead for sympathy, or suffer pain and remorse.[75]

Mutatis mutandis this could also be a summation of "Auerbachs Keller." I do not consider it to be just a coincidence that Goethe has exactly the same number of actors in "Auerbachs Keller," divided into similar groups, consisting of the two "visitors" versus the four "regular inhabitants." Tasso, Ariosto, and Vergil do not have this constellation for their episodes of wounded and talking trees.

Canto 13 is replete with the imagery of trees, vines, and vineyards, with all the expected Biblical overtones, complicated by the puns on Pier della Vigna's name. The amplitude of the symbolic languages of the trees cannot even begin to be reviewed here, given the extensive secondary literature, but one example is worth citing. In order to establish his veracity, Pier takes an unusual oath: "By the new roots of this tree I swear to you that I never broke faith with my lord, who was so worthy of honor" (13.73–75)." Pier makes his oath "by the new roots of this tree," refusing to accept that his wood is dead, is no longer a *lignum vitae*, and therefore cannot be given new life through verbal grafts. The vineyards of "Auerbachs Keller" and of canto 13 cannot be made to yield anything except matter. J. C. Barnes points out the emptiness of the gesture and its mockery of the judicial system.[76] We see here parallels to the wager, which also made no reference to God and whose authenticity was also guaranteed by reference to Faust's own blood/sap — by no means the only point of similarity between him and Pier.

The contrast between Dante's vividly charged, dramatic account and what is presented in a relatively understated way in "Auerbachs Keller" was

---

(1990): 384–94; Leo Spitzer, "Speech and Language in 'Inferno' XIII," in Leo Spitzer, *Representative Essays*, ed. Alban K. Forcione, Herbert Lindenberger, and Madeline Sutherland (Stanford, CA: Stanford UP, 1998), 143–71 and 461–63 [originally in *Italica* 19 (1942): 81–104]; and William A. Stephany, "Pier della Vigna's Self-Fulfilling Prophecies: The 'Eulogy' of Frederick II and 'Inferno' 13," *Traditio* 38 (1982): 193–212.

[75] Boyde, "*Inferno* XIII," 1.

[76] John C. Barnes, "Inferno XIII," 44–45.

part of Goethe's overall intention. The overriding themes of canto 13 are those of ignorance, greed, ambition, and suicide on one side and justice on the other. With its focus on suicide, the scene bonds *Faust* and the *Divina Commedia* tightly together. Suicide was an explicit theme from the opening scenes of Faust, where his melancholy is taking a turn for the worse, until he is prevented from carrying out the sinful deed by the intervention of Easter music. Like *Faust*, the *Divina Commedia* begins *in media res*, with the narrator speaking in the first person and regretting, much like Faust, that his life until this juncture has been empty and meaningless. Both characters begin their respective journeys in dark despair and will eventually be saved through divine grace. Faust's arrival in "Auerbachs Keller" is his first entry into a version of Hell, whereas Dante the Pilgrim has already had some drastic experiences before coming to the woods of canto 13. Even so, both characters display naivety, not wanting to accept how horrible damnation can be. The narrator's arrival in canto 13 brings an intensification of the terrors of the underworld, introduced by Vergil's warning: "And the good master began to say to me, 'Before you enter farther, know that you are in the second ring, and shall be, until you come to the horrible sand. Look well, therefore, and you shall see things that would make my words incredible'" (12.6–21). This explicit warning set before the episode corresponds to the Syrian inscription that Tancred reads in *Gerusalemme Liberata*. Similarly, it might be compared with the preparation of Faust by Mephistopheles:

> FAUST
> Wohin soll es nun gehn?
> MEPHISTOPHELES
>     Wohin es dir gefällt.
> Wir sehn die kleine, dann die große Welt.
> Mit welcher Freude, welchem Nutzen
> Wirst du den Cursum durchschmarutzen! (2051–54)

Both guides are forecasting the shifting scene and both obviously have foreknowledge of what will be presented and of how it might affect the viewer. And in both instances, there are definite hints that the respective guides already know those residing at the destination. Vergil speaks directly to Pier della Vigna: "But tell him who you were" (13.51) and Mephistopheles addresses the four companions as though they were on familiar terms with him: "Viel Grüße hat er uns an jeden aufgetragen" (2194) and "Still, altes Weinfaß!" (2308). However, Vergil's compassion for Dante the Pilgrim is contrasted with the glee that Mephistopheles feels at the sufferings Faust is to witness and also to undergo.

    A major difference in the scenes is that the wounded trees are permitted to tell their stories in the *Inferno*. The lengthiest of these is that of Pier della Vigna, who is never mentioned by name and must be recognized by readers who can fill in the historical background from subtle clues. One unmistakable sign points to the story of Pier della Vigna. Mephistopheles incorporates the plot of Pier della Vigna's career in the "Song of the Flea" and alludes to it by introducing the reference to the "Weinstock," a telling epithet. The name "della Vigna" had been particularly suitable for Dante's purposes, since all contemporaries were aware of the Biblical overtones it evoked.[77] The context in which the imagery of the vineyard and of the *lignum vitae* emerges through canto 13 is one entirely consistent with the interests of Mephistopheles.

Pier della Vigna turns out to be an example, a *type*, for anchoring eschatology in secular history. His actual rebellion against Frederick II, culminating in suicide, imitates on the historical level the original rebellion of Satan. Once we know Pier della Vigna's story, the relevance of Mephistopheles' song about corruption and court intrigue is clear. The "Song of the Flea" may be taken as a sort of historical ballad. The first stanza recalls the special favor Pier della Vigna had won at the court of Frederick II:

> Es war einmal ein König,
> Der hatt' einen großen Floh,
> Den liebt' er gar nicht wenig,
> Als wie seinen eignen Sohn. (2211–14)

The second stanza describes him at the height of his influence:

> In Sammet und in Seide
> War er nun angetan,
> Hatte Bänder auf dem Kleide,
> Hatt' auch ein Kreuz daran,
> Und war sogleich Minister,
> Und hatt' einen großen Stern.
> Da wurden seine Geschwister
> Bei Hof' auch große Herrn. (2222–30)

The reference to "even having a Cross" touches on Pier della Vigna's usurpation of Church authority, at least in his rhetoric. The final stanza deals with his sudden fall from favor and into disgrace because of court intrigue:

> Und Herrn und Frau'n am Hofe,
> Die waren sehr geplagt,
> Die Königin und die Zofe
> Gestochen und genagt,

---

[77] Cassell, *Dante's Fearful Art of Justice*, 34; Stephany, "Pier della Vigna's Self-Fulfilling Prophecies," 202–4.

> Und durften sie nicht knicken
> Und weg sie jucken nicht.
> Wir knicken und ersticken
> Doch gleich, wenn einer sticht. (2231–38)

Essentially, the same history is related by Pier della Vigna in canto 13:

> I am he who held both the keys of Frederick's heart, and turned them, locking and unlocking, so softly that from his secrets I kept almost every one. So faithful was I to the glorious office that for it I lost both sleep and life. The harlot that never turned her whorish eyes from Caesar's household — the common death and vice of courts — inflamed all minds against me; and they, inflamed, did so inflame Augustus that my glad honors were changed to dismal woes. (13.58–63)

Having risen to be the most important and influential person at the court of the Emperor, Pier had, if we believe his interpretation of events, aroused the envy of others, who conspired against him. The "inflammation" of rumors and innuendo would be a nice comparison to the reddening caused by flea bites. When his fortunes reversed, Pier committed suicide in despair, a tragic conclusion that picks up once more on the theme of melancholy and its excesses.

Aware of Mephistopheles' duplicity as a narrator we are alerted to the congruence between the "Song of the Flea" and Pier della Vigna's confession. Mephistopheles is unreliable — could this cast doubt on Pier's credibility? Indeed there is more to the history than he has admitted. Since he is an actual historical figure, it becomes possible to check the facts and to assess whether he was truly an innocent victim or whether he bore some culpability for his fate. The plot thickens considerably once we consult a historian such as Thomas Curtis van Cleve:

> Rightly or wrongly, Frederick was convinced of the guilt of his most trusted friend and official. But there remains always the possibility that at a moment when he was most sensitive to his own financial difficulties, Frederick lent his ear too readily to calumniators who affected to see in Piero della Vigna the fortunate embezzler that they themselves might have been. That he was guilty of peculation there can be no reasonable doubt; his trial and the sentence imposed appear to have confirmed his guilt. Peculation, however, was a crime not uncommon among the much-tempted officials of Frederick's court.[78]

---

[78] Thomas Curtis Van Cleve, *The Emperor Frederick II of Hohenstaufen: Immutator Mundi* (Oxford: Clarendon, 1972), 521. See also Ernst Kantorowicz, *Frederick the Second, 1194–1250*, trans. E. O. Lorimer (New York: Frederick Ungar, 1957), 663–69; Cassell, "Pier della Vigna's Metamorphosis," 37–44; and Ferrante, *The Political Vision of the* Divine Comedy, 107–8; 156–58.

Beyond the facts, there were also many rumors that grew around Pier, to the point where history and legend blended in a fateful way. The heady brew was especially potent because of the involvement of and proximity to Frederick II, one of the most controversial of the Holy Roman Emperors. He becomes important for the interlocking series of epics in two directions, into the past and into the future. Because he claimed to be a successor to the *Roman* emperors, his reign was analogous to the era that had framed the *Aeneid* for Vergil, namely a time of transition from one empire to another. Vergil had concentrated upon the shift from the Trojans to those who would become the Romans, in order to show how positive traits that would make Rome great as well as flaws that would corrupt the republic were translated together. In the figure of Frederick II, Dante could see the ambition to preserve Rome's grandeur and the unity of the Empire but also the seeds of decline.[79] For Goethe, the series would be continued with Maximilian I, another Holy Roman Emperor who would emulate Augustus and Frederick II and also try to legitimate his authority by casting himself as their rightful heir.[80] The problem was that Rome was not only the symbolic centre of a political domain; it was also the seat of Papal authority, so that all claims for supremacy by the Holy Roman Emperor were bound to clash with those of the Pope.[81] The conflicts between State

---

[79] On the continuities, see Craig Kallendorf, "Virgil, Dante, and Empire in Italian Thought, 1300–1500," *Vergilius* 34 (1988): 44–69.

[80] Maximilian was by no means the only Emperor to attempt to legitimate himself in this way, but he did achieve considerable heights of historical propaganda. See Marie Tanner, *The Last Descendant of Aeneas: The Hapsburgs and the Mythic Image of the Emperor* (New Haven and London: Yale UP, 1993), 100–107. Of course the effort at emulation included projects of epic poetry: Paul Gwynne, " 'Tu alter Caesar eris': Maximilian I, Vladislav II, Johannes Michael Nagonius and the *renovatio Imperii*," *Renaissance Studies* 10.1 (1996): 56–71; Elisabeth Klecker, "Kaiser Maximilians Homer," *Wiener Studien: Zeitschrift für klassische Philologie und Patristik* 107/108 (1994–95): 613–37.

[81] Quentin Skinner provides a good overview in *The Foundations of Modern Political Thought*, vol. 1: *The Renaissance* (Cambridge: Cambridge UP, 1978), 3–22. For the constitutional issues and on the language of rebellion, see the analysis by Gunther Wolf, "Universales Kaisertum und nationales Königtum im Zeitalter Kaiser Friedrichs II. (Ansprüche und Wirklichkeit)," in *Universalismus und Partikularismus im Mittelalter*, ed. Paul Wilpert (Berlin: de Gruyter, 1968), 243–69. The symbolic value of "Rome" is reviewed by Charles T. Davis, "Rome and Babylon in Dante," in *Rome in the Renaissance: The City and the Myth, Papers of the Thirteenth Annual Conference of the Center for Medieval and Early Renaissance Studies*, ed. Paul A. Ramsey (Binghamton, NY: Center for Medieval and Early Renaissance Studies, 1982), 19–40.

and Church were encapsulated in the story of Pier della Vigna, who had been willing to be ruthless in advancing the cause of Frederick II. The facts and the legends converge on the inevitable conflict that arose for Pier della Vigna when he became caught between his loyalty as a political subject and his obligations as a Christian to the Pope. The dilemma had its fascinations for contemporaries and led to wild speculations. Matthew Paris chronicled the story, for which there seems to be no evidence, that Pier della Vigna had changed sides and conspired with the Pope to poison Frederick.[82] The same point is made by Dante in the *Divina Commedia*, when Pier, whose first name identified him with St. Peter, the first Pope and also the foundation of the Church, says that he held the keys to Frederick's heart, thereby inviting a comparison with the papal insignia.[83] He has let ambition move him into rebellion against the Church and hence against Christian faith. Worse still, the fawning loyalty continues even after his death, for Pier della Vigna is still comparing Frederick II to Augustus, still hoping that his loyalty to the secular ruler might compensate for disobeying spiritual authority. What Dante the Pilgrim and the readers have already discovered, having encountered him in canto 10 of the *Inferno*, is that Frederick has also been consigned to Hell, ostensibly because of his epicureanism.[84] All of this should instruct Faust and give him pause. By siding with Mephistopheles, Faust is imitating the erroneous choice of Pier della Vigna in setting personal ambition ahead his loyalty to the Church.

Frederick II did not become the founder of a stable, peaceful Empire. Despite his attempts to portray himself as a new Augustus, his reign was filled with turmoil, intrigue, and schism, and it would be followed by the total collapse of order, leading to the Interregnum (1254–73). Historians have not been much kinder to Frederick in their judgments of him than Dante was. His policies contributed directly to the weakening of the Holy Roman Empire:

> Frederick's aggressions in Italy evoked the opposition of a revived Lombard League and the implacable hostility of the papacy. He gave up lands and royal rights in Germany with an almost careless abandon in order to keep the peace with the German princes and win their support for his persistent but inconclusive Italian campaigns. . . . In 1245 the

---

[82]  Van Cleve, *The Emperor Frederick II of Hohenstaufen*, 522.

[83]  Robin Kirkpatrick, *Dante's* Inferno: *Difficulty and Dead Poetry*, 183.

[84]  For the details of Frederick's offense, in addition to Singleton's commentary, see Clotilde Soave-Bowe, "Dante and the Hohenstaufen: From Chronicle to Poetry," in *Dante and the Middle Ages: Literary and Historical Essays*, ed. John C. Barnes and Cormac Ó Culleanáin (Dublin: Irish Academic P for The Foundation for Italian Studies, University College, Dublin, 1995), 181–210; here, 186.

pope presided over a universal council of the Church at Lyons which condemned and excommunicated Frederick II. The emperor was deposed, a rival emperor was elected in his place, and a Crusade was called to rid the empire of its ungodly tyrant.[85]

This gives some sense of the political implications of canto 13.[86] Dante knew only too well what harm the dissension in the realm meant for individuals, since his own exile from Florence derived from dynastic strife. The struggle for supremacy between the Emperor and the Pope would still not be settled at the beginning of the sixteenth century, when it would reemerge with brutal urgency during the reign of Maximilian I. History, both real and imagined, could have seemed to be repeating the events from Dante's time. On the real plane, for example, Dante's political treatise *De Monarchia*, a key document in the history of the discussion of relations between Pope and Emperor, was invoked directly.[87] On the level of fantasy, there were subversive rumors about the return of "the German Emperor, Frederick, the Last Emperor," with nervous undertones about the end of history.[88] The question posed by Brander — "Das liebe, heil'ge

---

[85] C. Warren Hollister, *Medieval Europe: A Short History* (New York: John Wiley & Sons, 1964), 184.

[86] Although Dante was not interested in "progress" as it is understood today, he was concerned for the renewal of empire, its *renovatio*. As James T. Chiampi observes in his "*Consequentia Rerum*: Dante's Pier della Vigna and the Vine of Israel," *Romanic Review* 75 (1984): 162–75, the immobility of Pier has important political implications (167).

[87] See John M. Headley, "The Habsburg World Empire and the Revival of Ghibellinism," *Medieval and Renaissance Studies* 7 (1978): 93–127, here 98–105. On the *Monarchia*, see also Karl Brandi, "Dantes Monarchia und die Italienpolitik Mercurino Gattinaras," *Deutsches Dante-Jahrbuch* 24 (1942): 1–19; and Walter Ullmann, "Dante's 'Monarchia' as an Illustration of a Politico-Religious 'Renovatio,'" in *Traditio — Krisis — Renovatio aus theologischer Sicht: Festschrift Winfried Zeller zum 65. Geburtstag*, ed. Bernd Jaspert and Rudolf Mohr (Marburg: N. G. Elwert, 1976), 101–13. Goethe would have read *De Monarchia* as part of the background preparation for his dissertation on State-Church relations; cf. Alfons Pausch and Jutta Pausch, *Goethes Juristenlaufbahn: Rechtsstudent Advokat Staatsdiener; Eine Fachbiographie* (Cologne: Verlag Dr. Otto Schmidt, 1996), 87–95.

[88] On the background to the myths, see Frank L. Borchardt, *German Antiquity in Renaissance Myth* (Baltimore, MD and London: The Johns Hopkins UP, 1971), *passim*. On the growing importance of the myth around 1500, see Norman Cohn, *The Pursuit of the Millennium: Revolutionary Millenarians and Mystical Anarchists of the Middle Ages* (1957; repr. London: Paladin, 1970), 108–26; and Marjorie Reeves, *The Influence of Prophecy in the Later Middle Ages: A Study in Joachimism* (Oxford: Clarendon, 1969).

Römische Reich, / Wie hält's nur noch zusammen?" (2090–91) — was not one that had arisen in the eighteenth century. It was the perennial problem of the Empire, and the failure to achieve stable harmony was a severe indictment of imperial politics.

The discord on the macrocosmic plane of the Empire was a reflection of what was transpiring in the political microcosm. The jealousies and spiteful intrigues alluded to by Pier della Vigna were both a cause and an anticipation of the collapse of political order after Frederick II's death in 1250. A close reading of canto 13 reveals that Dante has carefully replicated a rude discourse of incivility, with the interruptions, accusations, and recriminations that make harmony impossible. Thus the whole of canto 13 is a demonstration of life in a domain torn by civil unrest, just as "Auerbachs Keller" is. The actions and allusions of "Auerbachs Keller" play against the background of the wars, invasions, and sieges experienced by Ariosto and woven into *Orlando Furioso*. It will not be long before Faust enters the service of a ruler who resembles the greedy, ambitious Frederick II. Faust's first task will be an imitation of Pier della Vigna's main duty, namely, getting money to fill the insatiable demands of the Emperor. But we also know that Goethe modeled the Kaiser of *Faust II* on Maximilian I and that the contours were not edifying:

> Ich habe in dem Kaiser. . . , einen Fürsten darzustellen gesucht, der alle möglichen Eigenschaften hat, sein Land zu verlieren, welches ihm denn auch später wirklich gelingt. Das Wohl des Reiches und seiner Untertanen macht ihm keine Sorge; er denkt nur an sich und wie er sich von Tag zu Tag mit etwas neuem amüsiere. Das Land ist ohne Recht und Gerechtigkeit, der Richter selber mitschuldig und auf der Seite der Verbrecher; die unerhörtesten Frevel geschehen ungehindert und ungestraft. Das Heer ist ohne Sold, ohne Disziplin und streift raubend umher, um sich seinen Sold selber zu verschaffen und sich selber zu helfen, wie es kann. Die Staatskasse ist ohne Geld und ohne Hoffnung weiterer Zuflüsse. Im eigenen Haushalt des Kaisers sieht es nicht besser aus: es fehlt in Küche und Keller, der Marschall, der von Tag zu Tag nicht mehr Rat zu schaffen weiß, ist bereits in den Händen wuchernder Juden, denen alles verpfändet ist, sodaß auf den Kaiserlichen Tisch vorweggegessenes Brot kommt. Der Staatsrat will seiner Majestät über all diese Gebrechen Vorstellung tun und ihre Abhilfe beraten, aber der gnädigste Herr ist sehr ungeneigt, solchen unangenehmen Dingen sein hohes Ohr zu leihen; er möchte sich lieber amüsieren. Hier ist nun das wahre Element für Mephisto der den bisherigen Narren schnell beseitigt und als neuer Narr und Ratgeber sogleich an der Seite des Kaisers ist.[89]

---

[89] Johann Peter Eckermann, *Gespräche mit Goethe in den letzten Jahren seines Lebens*, ed. Ernst Beutler, vol. 24 of the *Gedenkausgabe* (Zurich: Artemis, 1949), conversation of 1 October 1827. The passage is quoted by Hermann Wiesflecker,

Goethe always kept some information in reserve, some clues occluded. Here it is useful to combine two facts from epic and history. First, Ariosto and the Este family wanted to be descended from heroes, and the poet reminded everyone that Orlando's distant ancestor was Hercules, who was known not only to be strong and virtuous but also as someone who sporadically went berserk. Second, as part of his propaganda of self-legitimation, Emperor Maximilian I had also styled himself as a Hercules Germanicus.[90] Thus by inscribing the Emperor who would have been contemporaneous with Faust into the text, Goethe has imitated on the imperial level the subversion through genealogy performed by Ariosto for the Dukes of Ferrara. However, all of this is lost on Faust, who ignores the lessons of history and subordinates himself to a ruler who will continue the tradition of warfare in the Empire and whose reign will be followed by the devastations of the wars between Protestants and Catholics. What Faust could not know, but Goethe's audience will recognize, is that the paradigm continued into the eighteenth century, when another Frederick II appeared.[91] He was not an emperor, only a king, but one termed "the Great" and one whose territorial ambitions destroyed the last vestiges of the Holy Roman Empire. For those in the audience reckoning in

---

the author of a magisterial biography of Maximilian I, in a careful article arguing for him as the prototype of the "Kaiser." The historian points to *Faust*: "Immerhin ergibt sich aus diesem Gespräch, wie stark Goethe seinen *Kaiser* auch für die besonderen Bedürfnisse des Dramas zurechtgemacht hat. Wenn auch zahlreiche Einzelzüge und das Zeitkolorit auf eine überraschende Weise stimmen, so ist doch vieles für die besondere Rolle, die der *Kaiser* im Drama zu spielen hat, frei erfunden" (275–76). ("Der Kaiser in Goethes Faust: Beobachtung über Goethes Verhältnis zur Geschichte," in *Tradition und Entwicklung: Festschrift Eugen Thurnher zum 60. Geburtstag*, ed. Werner M. Bauer, Achim Masser, and Guntram P. Plangg [Innsbruck: Institut für Germanistik der Universität Innsbruck, 1982], 271–82).

[90] Georg Braungart, "Mythos und Herrschaft: Maximilian I. als Hercules Germanicus," in *Traditionswandel und Traditionsverhalten*, ed. Walter Haug und Burghart Wachinger (Tübingen: Niemeyer, 1991), 77–95. On efforts at legitimation through heroic and epic genealogy see Marie Tanner's *The Last Descendant of Aeneas: The Hapsburgs and the Mythic Image of the Emperor*, 1993).

[91] The resistance to any critique of Prussian absolutism leads to remarkable contortions, as when Theodor Schieder reports that Frederick II was called a "Gegenkaiser" but immediately defuses the explosive potential. See his " 'Der junge Goethe im alten Reich': Historische Fragmente aus 'Dichtunge und Wahrheit,' " in *Staat und Gesellschaft im Zeitalter Goethes: Festschrift für Hans Tümmler zu seinem 70. Geburtstag*, ed. Peter Berglar (Cologne and Vienna: Böhlau, 1977), 131–45; here, n. 14.

thousands of years, the association Goethe was making between the Prussian king and his precursors should be easy to follow, if not to accept.

Another set of associations extends from Goethe to Dante — those around melancholy as a political problem. The suicide of Pier della Vigna implicitly resurrected the predicament embodied by the life and writings of Boethius. How can one be good in an evil time? Despair overwhelmed Pier della Vigna and might well have overwhelmed Dante, who nevertheless resisted. What the literature on melancholy seemed to indicate was that there was a persistent conflict between public service and being a good person. Dante, Ariosto, and Tasso all dealt with the corruption of the world by turning away from materialism and ambition and by devoting themselves to their writings. The tension represented in *Torquato Tasso* was more than a psychological aberration: it was a fundamental crisis of the political order.

However, the political crisis could not be resolved unless the true causes of the discord were known, so that human actions could be brought into alignment with divine order. The contribution of canto 13 to such a resolution is Dante's argument that the suicide committed by Pier della Vigna was simultaneously an act of despair and a political act. Today we might be surprised to find suicide subsumed as a vice under the categories of avarice or greed, because we no longer see individual actions as integral components of a general economy. Within the divine economy, suicide represents an attempt to take something from God that belongs rightfully to Him: our lives are part of His plan, our bodies are under His care. By taking one's own life, one is rebelling against the authority of God. Thus, Pier della Vigna's final actions are not a repudiation of his life but rather an extension of the principles of insurrection against the established order upon which he and Frederick II had based their politics.

As Anthony K. Cassell has shown in *Dante's Fearful Art of Justice*, understanding canto 13 requires us to recognize the final figure, who is mentioned almost in passing. The anonymous Florentine says in the final line: "I made me a gibbet of my own house" (13.151). In the Old Testament, it is Achitophel who hanged himself in his own house because Absalom ignored his counsel (Samuel 2:17–23). Typologically, he was matched with Judas in the New Testament, who also betrayed the one he served.[92] Cassell proposes that the figure of Judas is used by Dante to draw

---

[92] Cassell, *Dante's Fearful Art of Justice*, 50–51. For an overview of the philosophical and theological condemnation of suicide, especially of suicide as a rebellion, see Jeffrey R. Watt, "Calvin on Suicide," *Church History* 66.3 (1997): 468–76.

attention to the symbolic meaning of Pier della Vigna's life: "Just as the discarded minister Achithophel clearly parallels the discarded minister della Vigna, so Judas' selling the Innocent Blood for money parallels the love of money which led Piero to embezzle from the state and persecute the innocent for gain."[93] Through Judas, the themes of suicide, betrayal, and avarice are knotted together. The implications are even more far-reaching, since the betrayal of Christ by Judas follows the rebellion by Lucifer.[94] Judas threw away the gift of grace and chose immediate material gain instead, a choice that was replicated in suicide. By contemplating suicide, Faust was letting himself be swayed by material concerns — his relative poverty, his melancholic brooding — and thereby risking becoming another Judas. "Auerbachs Keller" offers a number of opportunities for him to reflect upon his own situation and therefore to change course. In addition to the allusions to Pier della Vigna, there are the four companions who are condemned for their gluttony, a sin close to avarice. And finally there is Dante the Pilgrim. His actions at the beginning of canto 13 are also open to criticism as a variation on greed, since he insists upon reaching out and breaking the branch from the bush, so that he might have more knowledge. The cry of the bush, even though it comes from a condemned sinner, calls out for mercy according to immutable laws of justice: " 'Why do you tear me? Have you no spirit of pity? We were men, and now are turned to stocks. Truly your hand ought to be more merciful had we been souls of serpents' " (13.35–39). The violence was not necessary. Had Dante the Pilgrim remembered what he had read in Vergil's text, he would have been able to understand: " 'If he, O wounded spirit, had been able to believe before,' replied my sage, 'what he had never seen save in my verses, he would not have stretched forth his hand against you' " (13.46–50). Because he refused to take on faith what he had read in the *Aeneid*, Dante the Pilgrim has contributed needlessly to the suffering of the bush, wounding it in order to gain tangible, material confirmation. The text was not sufficient for his mind; he had to grasp the world with his hands, in an effort to seize the totality of meaning. Such a seizure is an epistemological avarice and a betrayal of the spirit for the sake of matter. Dante commentaries have equated Dante the Pilgrim's act and attitude with the skepticism of doubting Thomas, who would not believe until he had laid his hands in Christ's wounds,[95] but there are also parallels to Judas, who clung

---

[93] Cassell, *Dante's Fearful Art of Justice*, 52.

[94] The traces of avarice are visible when Mephistopheles finds it so hard to part with the gold for Faust's courtship.

[95] Boyde, "*Inferno* XIII," 8.

to the immediate reward of silver and refused to accept Christ's promise of the intangible. What this implies for Faust is that his immoderate grasping for all knowledge resembles Judas closely and that his spiritual greed has already made him, like Judas, an adherent of Mephistopheles. Before the curtain falls, Faust will have ample opportunity to destroy innocent lives in relentless pursuit of a knowledge that he wants to be his alone, the embodiment of unlimited epistemological avarice, of modern curiosity. But the victims of greed are not silenced. In the *Divina Commedia*, it is Pier della Vigna who cries out for mercy; in *Gerusalemme Liberata* it was Clorinda; in *Faust* it will be Margarete.

# 4: The Roots of Evil

GOETHE AND VERGIL SEEMS AN UNPROMISING conjunction, given the received opinions that the former was totally captivated by Homer[1] and that the latter was generally neglected by Germans in the eighteenth century.[2] There can be no doubt that Goethe was able to and did read the *Aeneid* from an early age.[3] Goethe's father knew that fluency in Latin would be essential for the all-important career as a lawyer he intended for his son. In book 6 of *Dichtung und Wahrheit*, Goethe recalled his early facility in the language.[4] Goethe also reports that at one point he had hoped to become a professor of Classical Philology; surely he would have prepared himself with a thorough study of the secondary as well as the primary texts. Not least, he would have followed closely the publication of Christian Gottlob Heyne's Vergil edition in four volumes (Leipzig 1767–75). Of particular interest is his report, with some mischievous undertones, of how his uncle had satisfied a young boy's desire:

> Hier lernte ich zuerst den Homer kennen, und zwar in einer prosaischen Übersetzung, wie sie im siebenten Teil der durch Herrn von Loen besorgten "Neuen Sammlung der merkwürdigsten Reisegeschichten," unter dem Titel "Homers Beschreibung der Eroberung des Trojanischen Reichs," zu finden ist, mit Kupfern im französischen Theatersinne

---

[1] Still informative are E. M. Butler, *The Tyranny of Greece over Germany* (1935; repr., Boston: Beacon P, 1958), 83–154; and Humphry Trevelyan, *Goethe and the Greeks* (Cambridge: Cambridge UP, 1941; repr., New York: Octagon Books, 1972). For a thorough discussion, see Joachim Wohlleben's "Goethe and the Homeric Question," *Germanic Review* 42 (1967): 251–75. On Goethe's plans for an *Achilles* epic, see Elke Dreisbach, *Goethes "Achilleis"* (Heidelberg: Universitätsverlag C. Winter, 1994).

[2] According to Theodore Ziolkowski, *Virgil and the Moderns* (Princeton: Princeton UP, 1993), 77, Homer displaced Vergil in Germany in the second half of the century.

[3] Examples of the seven-year-old's translations *into* Latin are quoted and evaluated by Eckard Lefèvre, "Goethe als Schüler der alten Sprachen, oder vom Sinn der Tradition," *Gymnasium* 92 (1985): 288–98; here, 290–91.

[4] Johann Wolfgang von Goethe, *Werke: Hamburger Ausgabe in 14 Bänden*, ed. Erich Trunz (Munich: C. H. Beck, 1981), 9:239. This "Hamburger Ausgabe" will henceforth be cited as HA.

geziert. Diese Bilder verdarben mir dermaßen die Einbildungskraft, daß ich lange Zeit die Homerischen Helden mir nur unter diesen Gestalten vergegenwärtigen konnte. Die Begebenheiten selbst gefielen mir unsäglich; nur hatte ich an dem Werke sehr auszusetzen, daß es uns von der Eroberung Trojas keine Nachricht gebe, und so stumpf mit dem Tode Hektors endige. Mein Oheim, gegen den ich diesen Tadel äußerte, verwies mich auf den Virgil, welcher denn meiner Forderung vollkommen Genüge tat. (HA 9:42)

Even as a child, then, Goethe knew that the epic continuation of Homer led to Vergil. We also have good reason to believe that Goethe knew at least the first half of the *Aeneid* extremely well, for he mentions it explicitly in *Dichtung und Wahrheit* as an example of his mnemonic prowess: "Ich hatte von Kindheit auf die wunderliche Gewohnheit, immer die Anfänge der Bücher und Abtheilungen eines Werks auswendig zu lernen, zuerst der fünf Bücher Mosis, sodann der Äneide und der Metamorphosen" (HA 9:158). It would be truly surprising if there were *no* echoes of Vergil in Goethe's texts, but only recently has any attempt been made to identify Goethe's experiments with the imitation of Vergil.[5] Jürgen Paul Schwindt has cautiously but convincingly pointed to the parallels between the meeting of Werther and Lotte and that of Aeneas and Dido.[6] Closer to the drama, Jane Brown has reemphasized the links between the *Aeneid* and the "Klassische Walpurgisnacht."[7] Even more important here is her keen observation that Vergilian traces are also already felt in *Faust I*.[8] She comments on parallels between the opening of *Faust I* and the beginning of the *Aeneid*:

> *Faust*, ll. 464–72; *Aeneid*, III, 192–99. In *Aeneid* III the advent of the storm that drives the Trojan fleet onto the coast of the Harpies (note the

---

[5] On Goethe's specific mentions of Vergil, see Ernst Grumach, *Goethe und die Antike: Eine Sammlung* (Potsdam: Verlag Eduard Stichnote, 1949), 1:353–60; and the brief entry under "Goethe, Johann Wolfgang," by Fritz Bornkamm in the *Enciclopedia Virgiliana,* directed by Francesco della Corte, with Ferdinando Castagnoli, Massimiliano Pavan, Giorgio Petrocchi, and Umberto Cozzoli (Rome: Instituto della Enciclopedia Italiana, 1985–1991) 2:776–78. Bornkamm notes that no study of Vergil in Goethe exists and refers primarily to Grumach.

[6] Jürgen Paul Schwindt, "Dido, Klopstock und Charlotte Buff: Vergilreminiszenz(en) in Goethes 'Werther'?" *Antike und Abendland* 42 (1996): 103–18; Geoffrey Atherton, Disiciendi membra poetae: *Vergil and the Germans in the Eighteenth Century* (PhD diss., Yale U, 1996), 386–421.

[7] Jane K. Brown, *Goethe's Faust: The German Tragedy* (Ithaca and London: Cornell UP, 1986), 195.

[8] Brown, *Goethe's Faust*, 196.

unexpected shipwreck motif in Goethe) is described in terms of the arrival of a dark cloud overhead, increasing darkness, then lightning — the same sequence of events as in Faust's speech.[9]

The thesis that Vergil had an extensive influence on *Faust I* is supported by Ulrich Gaier's commentary to lines 149–56 of the *Urfaust*. Gaier sees strong parallels to *Aeneid* 6.724–51.[10] These observations push rather firmly in the direction of the conclusion that Vergil played a role in Goethe's conception of *Faust*, as did Dante, Ariosto, and Tasso. The full extent of that role cannot be measured here, in what are necessarily exploratory pages, but it was neither incidental nor trivial.

Moving back from Dante's world to Vergil's, everything seems radically simple. This simplicity is an illusion; the longer we dwell in the *Aeneid*, the more complicated that world becomes, and the more events are interwoven synchronically and diachronically. Consider the complexities of the episode of Polydorus in book 3. The Trojans have come to Thrace and hope to found a new city, but the space is not empty. When Aeneas needs material for a pyre to commemorate both the beginning of the city and the memory of his mother, when he is acting according to *pietas* with utmost circumspection, the proceedings are shattered:

> There was a dune nearby, as it chanced, topped by brushwood
> Of cornel and of myrtle sprouted with thick-set shafts.
> I approached it, wanting some foliage to festoon over the altar,
> And tried to root up its dense greenery: as I did so
> I saw an uncanny thing, which horrifies me to speak of.
> From the first sapling that I tore up, its roots dissevered,
> There oozed out, drop by drop, a flow of black blood
> Fouling the earth its stains. My whole frame shook in a palsy
> Of chilly fear, and my veins were ice-bound. Well, I proceeded
> To pluck out the whippy shaft of another sapling; I wanted
> To investigate the mystery and get at the reason for it.
> From the bark of this one too there issued the black blood.
> Pondering much, I prayed to the deities of the woodland
> And Gradivus who looks after the Thracian fields, that they should
> Take the sting out of the omen and turn it to our advantage.
> But when, with my knees deep in the sand to get a purchase,
> I was putting forth a still greater effort upon a third shaft —
> Shall I say it aloud or be silent? — then, a pathetic moan

---

[9] Brown, *Goethe's Faust*, 196, n. 28.

[10] Ulrich Gaier, *Faust-Dichtungen: Kommentar I*, in Goethe, *Faust-Dichtungen*, ed. Ulrich Gaier, 3 vols. (Stuttgart: Philipp Reclam jun., 1999), 147.

Came from the depth of the dune, a voice was saying to me: —
   Aeneas, you're tearing me! I am buried here. Don't hurt me!
Don't dishonour your guiltless hands. I am a Trojan,
No foreigner. That blood is drawn not from the wood.
Get away from this cruel land, from these hard-fisted shores!
I am Polydorus. The spears that nailed me down here have sprouted
An iron crop above me, a thicket of javelin wood.
   Then an acute conflict appalled my mind. I stood there
Dazed: my hair was on end and my voice stuck in my throat.
This Polydorus had been unluckily sent by Priam
With store of gold, in secret, to lodge with the Thracian king,
At a time when Priam began to have doubts about the resistance
Of Troy, perceiving how the blockade of the city was tightening.
That king, when the Trojan fortunes ebbed and our power was crushed,
Went over to Agamemnon, tagged on to the winning side,
Breaking all laws of good faith. He murdered Polydorus
And seized the gold. What lengths is the heart of man driven to
By this cursed craving for gold![11]

The analogies to the versions of the episode found in Dante, Ariosto, and
Tasso are evident: in all of them we find the myrtle bush, the blood that
gushes from the wood and "stains the soil," the groans from whoever is
trapped within, and the pleas for relief.

   Precise details over and above the general constellation indicate how
subtly Goethe has assimilated this source. Vergil's account enumerates the
repeated attempts by Aeneas explicitly: there are *three*. A check confirms
that, yes, the stage directions state that Mephistopheles drills ("bohrt")
exactly three times into the table, whereas the *Urfaust* uses the term only
twice and then says "wie oben" ("as above") for the last time. The explicit
repetition has been noticed by Michael C. J. Putnam, who blames Aeneas
for the act:

> But what strikes the reader is the persistence of his violence, even after the
> appearance of blood. Greed, already associated with Polydorus, now cen-
> ters not on money but on knowledge. "To make trial of causes hidden
> deep within" drives Aeneas three times to rend the foliage at its roots, as
> if the preliminary sight of blood aroused in the perpetrator a desperate
> need for understanding, even at the cost of further hurt.[12]

---

[11] Vergil, *The Aeneid*, trans. C. Day Lewis (Oxford: Oxford UP, 1998),
3.22–57. All quotations are from this translation.

[12] Michael C. J. Putnam, *Virgil's Aeneid: Interpretation and Influence* (Chapel
Hill and London: U of North Carolina P, 1995), 52.

Not everyone would judge Aeneas so harshly. Kenneth J. Reckford took a more sympathetic view, seeing Aeneas as a "good leader of men" who "keeps a stiff upper lip, encourages his men, and does quickly without apparent reluctance what has to be done."[13] Dividing these two views are judgments about the value of Aeneas as a hero, which depend in turn on political positions. If Aeneas should have hesitated, should have listened to the cries of the wounded being, then all his actions would be open to the same sort of criticism. But if his determination to carry on in spite of dire portents is laudable, then the project of colonization should be accepted, no matter how much blood is shed along the way. I incline to Putnam's view. Aeneas has transgressed against the dead, but not innocently, for in his confident mood as he prepares to build a new city, one to be named for *him*, he forgets the reach of the gods, forgets humility, and forgets the laws of divine economy. A small pyre and one ox are not going to be enough sacrificial offerings to guarantee the prosperity of an entire new city, much less a new empire. Trojans did not have a good record in the matter of propitiating the gods when it came to founding cities, and Aeneas is close to forsaking his *pietas*. The sudden eruption of dark blood serves as a stark reminder that much blood, human blood, will have to soak the ground before Rome is founded. Because he did not remember the recent past well enough, Aeneas has been given an opportunity to hear directly from someone who was there. The boundary of death has been momentarily suspended so that Aeneas might come to a profounder understanding of the meaning of his history, which is also a glimpse of his future. Polydorus was a Trojan who represented a last desperate attempt to escape from history, to evade the judgment of the gods by fleeing to another country, but although he could elude the specific conflict between the Greeks and the Trojans, he fell victim to the universal causes of war: treachery, mistrust, and greed. Aeneas does not comprehend this and will have to go to the Underworld himself to receive even harsher history lessons. There the plucking of the Golden Bough will repeat the gesture of breaking a reluctant plant already seen in book 3:

> And in a gentle breeze the gold-foil foliage rustled.
> Aeneas at once took hold of the bough, and eagerly breaking
> It off with one pull, he bore it into the shrine of the Sibyl.
> (6.208–11)[14]

---

[13] Kenneth J. Reckford, "Some Trees in Virgil and Tolkien," in *Perspectives of Roman Poetry: A Classics Symposium*, ed. G. Karl Galinsky (Austin and London: U of Texas P for the College of Humanities and the College of Fine Arts of The University of Texas at Austin, 1974), 57–91; here, 68.

[14] Putnam observes: "The personified golden bough in book 6 hesitates before Aeneas' tugging, an event strange in itself — and much discussed by scholars — because

A significant difference between Aeneas and Faust is the latter's reticence in "Auerbachs Keller." We are struck by how loquacious Aeneas is and by what he says. As the first-person narrator, his exclamation of horror has an immediacy that is moving: "Cold horror shook *my* limbs; fear froze *my* blood." Faust will speak only two lines and tell us nothing about the scene or the action, even though the genre of the drama would make it possible for him to speak to us directly. Something has gone wrong with history. Can it be possible that the pagan Aeneas, who did not have the benefit of Christian teachings, should be more compassionate than Faust? It would help to redeem Faust in this comparison if we could suspect that he is so moved by compassion that words fail him, but there too Aeneas has the advantage, explaining: "Then an acute conflict appalled my mind. I stood there / Dazed: my hair was on end and my voice stuck in my throat." Faust's silence is the zenith of a trend that can be followed from Vergil through the other epic poets. The modern man no longer believes in gods, miracles, romance, the marvelous; unable to wonder, he is unmoved by wonders.

The story of Polydorus concludes with a frank mention of gold, the source of the ills that befell Polydorus: "What lengths is the heart of man driven to / By this cursed craving for gold!" By the time Dante reworks the story, the gold will be hidden in the text, visible only indirectly through the greed of Pier della Vigna and, behind that, in the insatiable demand for revenue by Emperor Frederick II. Ariosto depicts the menace as the Beast of Avarice, and one might have expected a continually more abstract language the farther one is removed from the origins. Counteracting this trend, however, was the history of the impact of alchemy, for the alchemists blatantly made gold-seeking their primary goal. For some, gold was purely symbolic, but for many the intent literally was to have unlimited access to wealth.[15] In *Faust I* it is Mephistopheles who provides real gold jewelry in order to tempt Margarete. She finds herself lured by the treasures, knowing the force they have in the social world:

---

the Sibyl had earlier maintained that the bough would follow easily the touch of those fated to pluck it (6.211). Perhaps it is a last, thoughtful resistance to Roman might or even a premonition that the implementation of the Roman mission would have its less than idealistic moments" (Vergil, *Aeneid*, 156).

[15] Compare Hans Christoph Binswanger, *Money and Magic: A Critique of the Modern Economy in the Light of Goethe's* Faust, trans. J. E. Harrison (Chicago and London: U of Chicago P, 1994), originally published in German as *Geld und Magie: Deutung und Kritik der modern Wirtschaft anhand von Goethes* Faust (Stuttgart: Weitbrecht Verlag in K. Thienemanns Verlag, 1985).

Ein Schmuck! Mit dem könnt' eine Edelfrau
Am höchsten Feiertage gehn.
Wie sollte mir die Kette stehn?
Wem mag die Herrlichkeit gehören?
*Sie putzt sich damit auf und tritt vor den Spiegel.*
Wenn nur die Ohrring' meine wären!
Man sieht doch gleich ganz anders drein.
Was hilft euch Schönheit, junges Blut?
Das ist wohl alles schön und gut,
Allein man läßt's auch alles sein;
Man lobt euch halb mit Erbarmen. (2792–801)

She concludes with a sentence that closely echoes Aeneas's lament: "Nach Golde drängt, / Am Gold hängt / Doch alles. Ach wir Armen!" (2802–4). In both instances, the overriding sentiment is one of sad resignation, a heartsick sigh about the power that gold exerts over human hearts. The pronouncement about the power of gold is uttered in such a way that it could stand alone, outside and above all the remaining action.[16] Readers and characters who could remember the dark saying would have a key not only for the actions in these works but for life. The power of gold was something that Goethe knew from personal experience; even as a youngster he could have read his uncle Johann Michael Loen's semi-satirical piece "Beweis, daß das Geld den ersten Rang habe," a tongue-in-cheek encomium upon "Geld."[17] The satire undercuts itself because it was all too accurate in describing how

---

[16] The line is highlighted because of the controversy around its invocation by Statius in Dante's *Divine Comedy: Purgatorio 1: Italian Text and Translation*, trans. and with a commentary by Charles S. Singleton. (Princeton: Princeton UP, 1989), 22, 40–41: "Per che non reggi tu, o sacra fame / de l'oro, l'appetito de mortali?" ("To what do you not drive the appetite of mortals, O accursèd hunger of gold?") See, in addition to the commentary by Singleton to his translation, Giuseppe Mazzotta, *Dante, Poet of the Desert: History and Allegory in the Divine Comedy* (Princeton: Princeton UP, 1979), 222. Gaier, in his *Faust-Dichtungen: Kommentar I*, 353, cites Vergil and Dante, as well as Molière's *Dom Juan* 2.2.

[17] Johann Michael Loen, *Gesammelte kleine Schriften (1749–1752)*, ed. J. C. Schneider (Frankfurt am Main: Athenäum, 1972), 3: 333–34. The pun on "Geld" / "gelten" returns in *Faust II*, when the Kaiser is amazed that paper money works: "Und meinen Leuten gilt's für gutes Gold? / Dem Heer, dem Hofe gnügt's zu vollem Sold? / So sehr mich's wundert, muß ich's gelten lassen" (6083–85). See Werner Hamacher's scintillating analysis, "Faust, Geld," *Athenäum: Jahrbuch für Romantik* 4 (1994): 131–87; here, 174.

the bourgeois understood money to be a universal social solvent, one that neither customs nor traditions could withstand.[18]

The usual interpretation is that in the *Aeneid* the lament about gold is nothing more than an explanation of the crime committed by the King of Thrace against Polydorus: "the supernatural occurrence reflects an *unnatural* (in the sense of *inhuman*) deed, the impious murder of Polydorus."[19] But the syntactic detemporalization of the sentence is more consistent with a sort of "moral of the story" summation that the audience should take away from the immediate context and apply more generally.[20] Turned against Aeneas even in the narrow compass of the opening of book 3, one could put his actions into a different light. His declared purpose has been to offer sacrifices to the gods — but whose bull and whose wood will he use? Has he asked permission of the Thracians? Since he has not, then his visible *pietas* is grounded upon unremarked trespass and theft in broad daylight.[21] He is so sure that this land somehow already belongs to him that he does not take the gush of blood as a warning against stealing, but instead redoubles his efforts. Aeneas is greedy for knowledge, but that comes after the initial appropriation of material things; knowledge and grasping cannot be kept separate. This analysis fits with Putnam's interpretation of the repetition of such theft when the Trojans arrive on the Strophades.[22] The reign of gold gives rise to a wide variety in the forms of

---

[18] On the real and symbolic importance of gold in the sixteenth and seventeenth centuries, see M. G. Flaherty, "Money, Gold, and the Golden Age in Germany," in *Literature and Western Civilization,* vol. 3: *The Old World: Discovery and Rebirth*, ed. David Daiches and Anthony Thorlby (London: Aldus Books, 1974), 363–411.

[19] Brooks Otis, *Virgil: A Study in Civilized Poetry* (Oxford: Clarendon, 1963), 256.

[20] Cf. the commentary by R. D. Williams in Vergil [P. Vergili Maronis], *Aeneidos liber Tertius* (Oxford: Clarendon, 1962), to lines 49–57.

[21] E. L. Harrison, "Foundation Prodigies in the *Aeneid*," *Papers of the Liverpool Latin Seminar* 5 (1985): 131–64; here, 150, also senses that something is amiss. He suggests that the offense arises because the corpse of Polydorus belongs to others, namely, the gods.

This is a fitting point at which to acknowledge a debt to Franz Vonessen, "Das Opfer der Götter," in *Dialektik und Dynamik der Person: Festschrift für Robert Heiss zum 60. Geburtstag am 22. Januar 1963*, ed. Hildegard Hiltmann and Franz Vonessen (Cologne and Berlin: Kiepenheuer & Witsch, 1963), 265–85, not only here but throughout. See also the trenchant remarks by Walter Burkert, "Offerings in Perspective: Surrender, Distribution, Exchange," in *Gifts to the Gods: Proceedings of the Uppsala Symposium, 1985*, ed. Tullia Lunders and Gullög Nordquist (Uppsala: Acta Universitatis Upsaliensis, 1987), 43–50.

[22] Putnam, *Virgil's Aeneid*, 51–52.

greed: avarice, lust, desire, miserliness. Having come back this far, we see in its original contours the crime that will shape all the subsequent versions of the episode. Not the object of greed or avarice is condemned — gold is a polyvalent sign — but the specific logic of investment calculation. The Trojans and Polydorus try to hoard against the future, to speculate against history. The refusal to spend generously and to give gifts when it is right to do so upsets the entire economy as it deprives others of their share of life. Like Polydorus's fellow citizens, the miser's neighbors must carry on bravely managing with less and less while he prospers. Divine justice makes the punishment fitting, as Polydorus loses not only this life but the life to come. The one who tried to keep himself safe and to invest himself shrewdly is now squandered literally as his blood gushes out, not in honorable sacrifice of his life for the city, but through the clumsy accident of a wound inflicted by a countryman. Aeneas had wanted to conduct a proper ritual, something underscored by the elaborate preparations,[23] yet what happens is a sad travesty of sacrifice. Polydorus has wasted his life and his death and his fame. Or, to be more precise, he will live on in infamy, a marginal figure representing the worst of human qualities.

Not least, the *Aeneid* also teaches that unchecked desire for wealth is the root of imperial conquest, and that gold is the fuel of destruction.[24] The discovery of greed as the origin of empire necessarily raises the question of whether it also governs epic. Can the poet can imagine an alternative, an epic without empire?

---

[23] Cf. A. W. Allen, "The Dullest Book of the *Aeneid*," *The Classical Journal* 47 (1951–52): 119–23; here, 121.

[24] Cf. A. J. Boyle, "The Meaning of the Aeneid: A Critical Inquiry, Part II: *Homo Immemor*: Book VI and its Thematic Ramifications," *Ramus: Critical Studies in Greek and Roman Literature* 1.2 (1972): 113–52: "It is not without purpose that Virgil points to the golden nature of the temple at Cumae (*aurea*, 15) and then subtly associates this 'goldenness' with failure, death and non-fulfilment (*in auro*, 32); for the golden bough (VI, 136ff. and 201ff.), so the golden promises of history (*aurea saecula*, 'golden ages,' VI, 793ff., VIII, 324ff.), and the golden shield made by Vulcan (VIII, 625ff.) lead not to ideological triumph and glory but to frustration and tragic death, when the studs on the golden belt of Pallas (*auro*, X, 499) blind Aeneas to all thoughts of *humanitas* and of pity (XII, 941ff.). The dire connection of gold with suffering, death and failure, of which Aeneas has often been the witness (e.g. I, 348fff., III, 56ff.), will simply repeat itself in the actuality of his own experience" (119).

# Investment and Sacrifice

The logic of the symbolic economy is diametrically opposed to the laws of the material economy. Those who are rich in worldly things will be poor in divine reckonings; those who give their worldly possessions away will gain wealth beyond all dreaming. Goethe was steeped in such ideals from the Pietist circles in which he moved and from the philosophical interpretation of the alchemical-hermetic literature.[25] At the same time, he was intensely aware of the real political economy of the eighteenth century and its contradictions. The tensions present in his mind are recorded in a famous passage written to Charlotte von Stein on 6 March 1779, while he was working on *Iphigenie auf Tauris*: "Hier will das Drama gar nicht fort, es ist verflucht, der König von Tauris soll reden, als wenn kein Strumpfwürker in Apolde hungerte."[26]

In "Auerbachs Keller," we can see how greed appears in the modern world as the cunning of calculation and investment. When Mephistopheles and Faust arrive, the companions immediately try to discover if the strangers are rich, if they have business news or secrets, if they are aristocrats or influential persons:

> SIEBEL
> Für was siehst du die Fremden an?
> FROSCH
> Laß mich nur gehn! Bei einem vollen Glase
> Zieh' ich, wie einen Kinderzahn,
> Den Burschen leicht die Würmer aus der Nase.
> Sie scheinen mir aus einem edlen Haus,
> Sie sehen stolz und unzufrieden aus.
> BRANDER
> Marktschreier sind's gewiß, ich wette!
> ALTMAYER
> Vielleicht.
> FROSCH
>       Gib Acht, ich schraube sie! (2173–180)

These companions know nothing of the laws of hospitality and in their cunning, repressed violence they resemble the murderous Thracians. As

---

[25] On gold as a "life symbol," see especially Wilhelm Emrich, *Die Symbolik von Faust II: Sinn und Vorformen* (Frankfurt am Main and Bonn: Athenäum, 1964), 199–200.

[26] Goethe, *Goethes Briefe*, ed. Karl Robert Mandelkow and Bodo Morawe, 4 vols. (Hamburg: Christian Wegner, 1962), 1:264.

gluttons, the four companions in "Auerbachs Keller" are even more demanding than the miserly kings of Troy and Thrace. Whereas the miser invests for the future by hoarding, the glutton, having concluded that there will be no tomorrow, spends everything in the present. At least that way, should the future never arrive or arrive and take everything away, the glutton does not lose anything to others, such as heirs. The companions have risked their lives, have lost the gamble, and are consigned to Hell, where their punishment is never to be satiated. No less than Polydorus or Pier della Vigna, they cling to the logic that directed their lives. Although Mephistopheles warns them that the wine in the cellar belongs to someone else, Siebel flippantly accepts the debt and the consequences: "Nur immer her! ich nehm's auf mich" (2251). It is an easy agreement to make — pleasure will be here and now; the bill might never be delivered. As Mephistopheles acerbically remarked earlier, "So lang' der Wirt nur weiter borgt, / Sind sie vergnügt und unbesorgt" (2166–67). The four companions do not worry about how they are to pay, and certainly give no thought to the global economy.

Faust should recognize himself in the various figures of greed and gluttony that populate "Auerbachs Keller" and its antecedents, for he too is caught by the logic of money and investments. After years of study, he laments at length that he has gained nothing:

> Auch hab' ich weder Gut noch Geld,
> Noch Ehr' und Herrlichkeit der Welt;
> Es möchte kein Hund so länger leben! (374–76)

Faust overlooks all that his life is worth because the sum of it cannot be converted to money; all his efforts seem to be a failed investment. Now he resolves to rededicate himself to investment thinking by staking everything he still has in order to get the windfall, the secret to the universe, the fabulous wealth he is convinced he deserves. When Mephistopheles makes him the offer he cannot refuse, Faust is eager to accept. And what a bargain! Misers and gluttons would be filled with envy at the chance to have everything they want at a price of something they have already discarded as worthless, namely, their lives.

The figure of Faust is singularly apt as the representation of the sixteenth century's contribution to the history of greed. Disagree as one may with the details of timing and so forth, Max Weber's thesis pointing to a fundamental transformation in the constellation of economic ideas and attitudes around the sixteenth century appears valid.[27] Ariosto's fearful

---

[27] Max Weber, *The Protestant Ethic and the Spirit of Capitalism*, trans. Talcott Parsons (New York: Charles Scribner's Sons, 1958). For sympathetic critiques of

vision of the triumph of Avarice was a vision of that era's present. Economic history would tend to confirm his argument that somewhere between 1400 and 1600 there was a decisive shift in European thinking about the theological implications of wealth. Where before usury and self-interest had been condemned, that era saw the legitimation of investment and calculation as good for everyone. And what was good in the business world was also good for the life of the mind. The Faust legend is the embodiment of the imaginative effort to understand the avaricious quest for knowledge, a quest that was unlimited in itself and also held the promise of making individuals enormously wealthy. "Secret magic" that had been suppressed for centuries suddenly emerged in the figure of the Magus as a positive hero who would first conquer, then dominate the world. An alliance was forged between the figure of the omnipotent ruler and the omniscient magician, in fantasy and in reality. Emperor Maximilian I was seriously interested in the possibility that alchemy might provide the revenue he needed for his imperial ambitions, and he sponsored a wide range of alchemists and astrologers.[28] Such things had to evoke the memory of

---

Weber, see Benjamin Nelson, "The Medieval Canon Law of Contracts, Renaissance 'Spirit of Capitalism,' and the Reformation 'Conscience': A Vote *for* Max Weber," in *Philomathes: Studies and Essays in the Humanities in Memory of Philip Merlan*, ed. Robert B. Palmer and Robert Hamerton-Kelly (The Hague: Martinus Nijhoff, 1971), 525–48; Joyce Oldham Appleby, *Economic Thought and Ideology in Seventeenth-Century England* (Princeton: Princeton UP, 1978), 12–14. Complementing Weber are the classical studies by R. H. Tawney, *Religion and the Rise of Capitalism: A Historical Study* (1926; repr., Harmondsworth, UK: Penguin, 1990); and C. B. Macpherson, *The Political Theory of Possessive Individualism: Hobbes to Locke* (1962; repr., Oxford: Oxford UP, 1977). The shift in values is traced by Albert O. Hirschman, *The Passions and the Interests: Political Arguments for Capitalism before Its Triumph* (Princeton: Princeton UP, 1977).

For examples of the permeation of religious imagery by the language of commerce, see Marc Shell, *Money, Language and Thought: Literary and Philosophical Economies from the Medieval to the Modern Era* (Berkeley and Los Angeles and London: U of California P, 1982), 24–46; Bernard Knieger's study, "The Purchase-Sale: Patterns of Business Imagery in the Poetry of George Herbert," *Studies in English Literature* 6 (1966): 111–24; and Winfried Schleiner, *The Imagery of John Donne's Sermons* (Providence, RI: Brown UP, 1970), 122–37.

[28] The seriousness with which rulers desperate for revenue took the promises of alchemists should not be underestimated. For case studies, see R. J. W. Evans, *Rudolf II and His World: A Study in Intellectual History, 1576–1612* (Oxford: Clarendon, 1973); Pamela H. Smith, *The Business of Alchemy: Science and Culture in the Holy Roman Empire* (Princeton: Princeton UP, 1997); and Smith, "Alchemy as a Language of Mediation at the Habsburg Court," *Isis* 85 (1994): 1–25.

Frederick II and his mysterious advisor, Pier della Vigna. Vivid evidence of the association was the circulation in the early sixteenth century of legends about the return of Frederick II; Goethe understood that the pendant to that companion to that ghost of history could be figured as Faust. Looking back from the eighteenth century, Goethe was appalled by the triumph of investment thinking. Everywhere he looked, he could see the poverty and misery, the wars and rebellions, the greed and mistrust that dominated society. The small German states such as Baden or Weimar, city-states such as Frankfurt am Main, and even the whole Holy Roman Empire were perennially short of revenue. Every opportunity to increase wealth had to be exploited, including the impoverished mines at Ilmenau.

The impact of investment thinking is felt throughout *Faust*. He wagers against Mephistopheles because he reckons that he cannot lose. What he does with Margarete takes place under the aegis of calculation. The "gifts" he brings her are intended to buy her love, and that love is an instrument to his pleasure. The high priest of investment banking is Mephistopheles, who gives nothing away for free. At times, he seems to be generous, but everything is staged with the long-term return in mind. Hence his supreme irritation when he is "cheated" of Faust at the end, leading him to bemoan the injustice of it all, using the language of business law:

> Bei wem soll ich mich nun beklagen?
> Wer schafft mir mein erworbenes Recht?
> Du bist getäuscht in deinen alten Tagen,
> Du hast's verdient, es geht dir grimmig schlecht.
> Ich habe schimpflich mißgehandelt,
> Ein großer Aufwand, schmählich! ist vertan (11,832–37)

Mephistopheles is bitter because he feels betrayed according to the logic of investments: after so much effort has been expended, he should have received what he *earned*: Faust's soul should be his as payment. Alas for him, it was not to be, since the divine economy is based on gifts, not profits, and Faust will be saved by grace, not deeds. The end of the drama is preordained and in "Auerbachs Keller" the hope of the divine economy was already evident.

## The World at War

Goethe was not a sentimental apologist for Christianity; *Faust* is not *Gerusalemme Liberata* or *Paradise Regained*; Goethe did not have the kind of faith held by Dante, Tasso, or Milton. The challenge posed by history to Christianity was obvious in the eighteenth century. If one took a long view, the so-called Christians were falling further and further away from any ideal community and were more and more estranged from the

Bible and from Christ's teachings. The heritage of violence and destruction had been passed on from Troy to Rome, had spread throughout the Holy Roman Empire, and was conquering the rest of the world in colonial expansion. The analyses in epic poems had somehow not yet penetrated to the root causes of the deflection of history from the goals of peace and harmony. With Milton, a culmination had been reached in the deconstruction of the epic hero as a prototype for Satan,[29] but Milton could not avoid figuring Christ also as a type of hero and "imperialist."[30] The conundrum of an "unheroic hero" had to be solved if there was to be an "epic without empire."[31] One of the strongest indications that Faust is one who will continue the martial, imperial heritage is introduced in act 3 of *Faust II* with the stage-direction "Signale, Explosionen von den Türmen, Trompeten und Zinken, kriegerische Musik, Durchmarsch gewaltiger Heereskraft." A vast army is being assembled under Faust's command. The marshalling of the troops is another set piece of the epic, going back to similar lists in Herodotus and to Homer's catalogue of the captains and ships in the *Iliad*.[32] It was imitated by Boiardo in his *Orlando*

---

[29] On Satan as a refiguring of Caesar, see William Blissett, "Caesar and Satan," *Journal of the History of Ideas* 18 (1957): 221–32; on him as a general, see James A. Freeman, *Milton and the Martial Muse*: Paradise Lost *and European Traditions of War* (Princeton: Princeton UP, 1980); on him as an imperialist, see Linda Gregerson, *The Reformation of the Subject: Spenser, Milton, and the English Protestant Epic* (Cambridge: Cambridge UP, 1995), 217–30. In a sense, Milton was trapped by the imitation of the epic language into the adaptation of martial imagery; see the discussion on the ensuing difficulties by Arnold Stein, "Milton's War in Heaven — An Extended Metaphor," in *Milton: Modern Essays in Criticism*, ed. Arthur E. Barker (Oxford: Oxford UP, 1965), 264–83; and Michael Murrin, *The Allegorical Epic: Essays in Its Rise and Decline* (Chicago and London: U of Chicago P, 1980), 162–71.

[30] See John M. Steadman, *Milton and the Renaissance Hero* (Oxford: Clarendon, 1967); Merritt Y. Hughes, "The Christ of *Paradise Regained* and the Renaissance Heroic Tradition," *Studies in Philology* 35 (1938): 254–77; and for an incisive critique using the categories of Foucault, see David Weisberg, "Rule, Self, Subject: The Problem of Power in *Paradise Lost*," *Milton Studies* 30 (1993): 85–107. On the contradictions of Milton and empire, see Paul Stevens, "*Paradise Lost* and the Colonial Empire," *Milton Studies* 34 (1996): 3–21, and the literature he cites in note 2.

[31] See my "Narratives for a Post-Heroic Age: Peter Bichsel's Short Prose," *The University of Dayton Review* 19.2 (Summer 1988–89): 55–68, and the literature cited there.

[32] Edward Courtney, "Vergil's Military Catalogues and their Antecedents," *Vergilius* 34 (1988): 3–8.

*Innamorato*,[33] by Tasso in the *Gerusalemme Liberata* (1.35–46), by Milton in *Paradise Lost* (book 1.375–521), and by Wieland in his "Cyrus" (4.1–13).[34] In *Faust II*, the parallels to Godfrey's crusaders are evident as various representatives of the European nations are being given their assignments. However, they are not liberating Jerusalem; they are occupying classical Greece and will make Sparta its capital:

> Germane du! Corinthus Buchten
> Verteidige mit Wall und Schutz,
> Achaia dann mit hundert Schluchten
> Empfehl ich Gote deinem Trutz.
> Nach Elis ziehn der Franken Heere,
> Messene sei der Sachsen Los,
> Normanne reinige die Meere
> Und Argolis erschaff er groß.
> Dann wird ein jeder häuslich wohnen,
> Nach außen richten Kraft und Blitz;
> Doch Sparta soll euch überthronen,
> Der Königin verjährter Sitz. (9466–76)

The military seizure of the topography of the classical world turns the tradition of conquest back upon the source of epic. Having disseminated a history of empire into the world, the original domain of epic itself is now to fall victim to the generals and armies of Europe, who have been inspired by the examples of the Greeks, the Romans, and the Crusaders. The lure Faust holds out is the instauration of the hitherto elusive realm of peace, a return to arcadia at the end of history. But the hope founders on the contradiction between the means and the end, and the new empire will be a dictatorship built on universal mistrust and possessive individualism, as the Chorus intones:

> Seinen Befehl vollziehn sie treu,
> Jeder sich selbst zu eignem Nutz
> Wie dem Herrscher zu lohnendem Dank,
> Beiden zu höchlichem Ruhmes-Gewinn. (9496–99)

If there is to be a way out of the vicious circle of commanding and obeying versus rebelling and disobeying, Faust has not found it and indeed will

---

[33] Michael Murrin, *History and Warfare in Renaissance Epic* (Chicago and London: U of Chicago P, 1994), 63–64.

[34] Christoph Martin Wieland, *Wielands gesammelte Schriften: Erste Abteilung: Werke*, ed. Deutsche Kommission der Königlich Preußischen Akademie der Wissenschaften (Berlin: Weidmannsche Buchhandlung, 1909–), 3:128–29.

not find it, for he is bound to repeat the attitudes and actions of his heroic, martial precursors.

## St. Lycurgus

In a popular paperback on cures for hangovers one finds a reference to the drastic remedy of one Lycurgus, who had torn up the vineyards in Thrace.[35] This story turns out to be of considerable consequence for getting us back to one of the earliest stages of Goethe's thinking about epic, myth, and history in "Auerbachs Keller."

One detail that has puzzled commentators about the Polydorus in the *Aeneid* is the description of how he was killed and where he is buried. According to R. D. Williams:

> The grim and weird story of Polydorus and the drops of blood trickling from the myrtle shoots is not found in Classical literature before Virgil. In the very varied tradition about Polydorus we do not anywhere find a trace of this sequel to his death; nor is there any certain indication that the Polydorus story figured in any form in the Aeneas legend before Virgil.[36]

He also noticed the verb "beheading" ("obtruncat") in line 5, which points to a discrepancy with lines 45–46, where Polydorus was pierced by spears. Williams senses that "Virgil is combining two different sources for the story" and this turns out to be a useful hypothesis.

A different account is found in Euripides' *Hecuba*. There the ghost places special emphasis on his watery grave:

> And having killed me, he abandoned me to the swelling sea, so he might keep the gold himself at home.
>
> I lie (at times) upon the shore, at other times in the tossing sea, carried on the waves' constant ebb and flow, unwept, unburied; and now I glide above my dear mother.[37]

---

[35] I would like to thank Keith Neilson for drawing my attention to the ultimate hangover cure at just the right moment.

[36] R. D. Williams, commentary in Vergil, *Aeneidos liber Tertius*, 57–58; Franco Caviglia, "Polidoro," in *Enciclopedia Virgiliana* (Roma: Istituto della Enciclopedia Italiana, 1998), 4:162–64, here 163. Richard Heinze had ventured the same opinion that some other source must have been at work (*Virgils epische Technik* [1915, repr., Leipzig and Berlin: B. G. Teubner, 1928], 105).

[37] Euripides, *Hecuba*, trans. and ed. Christoph Collard (Warminster: Aris + Phillips, 1991), 55 and 57.

Basically the same story is told by Ovid's *Metamorphoses*:

> When Troy's fair fortune fell, that wicked king
> Took his sharp sword and slit his charge's throat,
> And then, as though removal of the corpse
> Removed the crime, he threw it from a cliff
> Down to the waves below. (13.435–39)

Those conversant with Greek mythology prick up their ears at all this talk of burial at sea, one that does not seem to mark a final demise, since there is one figure routinely associated with death and rebirth in the water: Dionysos.[38] Somehow the stories of Polydorus seem have become mixed up with stories of Dionysos.

The crossover point that made the conflation possible is the figure of Lycurgus. He was mentioned more or less in passing by Aeneas: "acri quondam regnata Lycurgo" (3.14; "ruled once by hot-tempered Lycurgus"). In order to find out more about this Thracian ruler, we turn to book 6 of the *Iliad*, where Hector has been taunting the Trojans, and Diomedes replies, using an anecdote to reinforce the rhetoric of his response:

> know that I will not fight against any god of the heaven,
> since even the son of Dryas, Lykourgos the powerful, did not
> live long; he who tried to fight with the gods of the bright sky,
> who once drove the fosterers of rapturous Dionysos
> headlong down the sacred Nyseian hill, and all of them
> shed and scattered their wands on the ground, stricken with an ox-goad
> by murderous Lykourgos, while Dionysos in terror
> dived into the salt surf, and Thetis took him to her bosom,
> frightened, with the strong shivers upon him at the man's blustering.
> But the gods who live at their ease were angered with Lykourgos,
> and the son of Kronos struck him to blindness, nor did he live long
> afterwards, since he was hated by all the immortals.[39]

Aeneas obviously did not communicate anything like this in the simple phrase with which he mentioned Lycurgus. At least one might have heard

---

[38] For a survey of the topic, see Maria Daraki, "ΟΙΝΟΨΠΟΝΤΟΣ: La mer dionysiaque," *Revue de l'Histoire des Religions* 199.1 (1982): 3–22.

[39] Homer, *The Iliad of Homer*, trans. Richmond Lattimore (1951; repr., Chicago and London: U of Chicago P, 1961), 156–57. Cf. Albert Henrichs, "Der rasende Gott: Zur Psychologie des Dionysos und des Dionysischen in Mythos und Literatur," *Antike und Abendland* 40 (1994): 31–58; here, 41–47. We know that Goethe knew Homer in the original text, since we have his detailed paraphrase of the entire *Iliad* (Grumach, *Goethe und die Antike*, 1:138–202).

some hint, some overtone or undertone, of a fate that should inspire awe. Aeneas could hardly claim not to know the story, given his proximity to the events at Troy, where Diomedes had the story immediately to hand, even under the pressure of the battlefield. The story reverberates with mighty crimes and dreadful punishments and should serve as a warning to all mortals. Aeneas is silent on all of this and even elides the epithet "murderous." Either he wants to forget the background or, having come now to Thrace, his thoughts are full and he has remembered more than he will tell to Dido and the audience.

If in fact he had already been thinking about Lycurgus and all the dire connotations around that name, then the extremity of his reaction to the first sight of blood from the plant is more than just a psychological response to something extraordinary. Not just the immediate experience[40] but a sudden flash of insight into the possible meaning of what was happening made him shiver with fright. The intensity of the moment had fused what he knew from the present — they were in Thrace, on the shore, near the sea, a plant was bleeding, something supernatural was at work — with old and dark stories about Lycurgus.[41] Just for an instant, Aeneas fears that, for reasons and ways still unknown to him,[42] he has been cast by the gods into the role of Lycurgus, the foe of Dionysos. That he has turned his mind to the possibility is confirmed by his prayer to the dryads, the woodland nymphs. They were routinely associated with Dionysos but had been explicitly mentioned in the story conveyed through the *Iliad*: the nymphs of Nyssa had been the nurses of the child Dionysos and had been driven away by Lycurgus. Aeneas does not dare pronounce the name of the god directly, but prays for intercession from beings close to him, ones who might have some influence with him. The reference to "Gradivus, Lord of

---

[40] Gordon Williams, *Technique and Idea in the* Aeneid (New Haven and London: Yale UP, 1983) suggests that the episode was one of two that "seem likely to have been introduced by him [Vergil] at a late stage precisely to provide authentic emotional eye-witness experiences for Aeneas" (273–74).

[41] William J. Kennedy, "Irony, Allegoresis and Allegory in Virgil, Ovid and Dante," *arcadia* 7 (1972): 115–34, suggests that Aeneas should have suspected a betrayal (124).

[42] As James J. O'Hara points out, there are correspondences between the deceptiveness and unreliability of divine messages and the political climate of general mistrust; see his *Death and the Optimistic Prophecy in Vergil's* Aeneid (Princeton: Princeton UP, 1990), 119–20. Wolfgang Hübner, "Poesie der Antipoesie: Überlegungen zum dritten Buch der *Aeneis*," *Grazer Beiträge: Zeitschrift für die klassische Altertumswissenschaft* 21 (1995): 95–120, connects the "unsureness and uncertainty" of the Trojans with their errant exile (109–12).

Getic fields" is another evasive substitution, for Dionysos had come from northern Thrace, the home of the Getae.

Aeneas leaps to the possibility that he has been singled out to relive the fate of Lycurgus because he knows more about Dionysos than was told by Homer. There were many fragments of the myth in circulation, and they could not always be reconciled according to a linear chronology, especially not for Dionysos, whose biography was already complicated because he had been born twice. A number of the stories dealt with the transgressions of Lycurgus against the god. The exact nature of the crime varied, although it usually involved violating laws of hospitality, a transgression that brought terrible punishments. There were different versions of the story.[43] One is that told by Homer, quoted above. Particularly detailed is the version by Apollodorus. Dionysos was returning to Thrace from his triumphs in India, only to be expelled by Lycurgus, who also captured the Bacchae and the Satyrs. These were released, but in order to punish him Dionysos made Lycurgus demented. In his delusion, Lycurgus thought that his own son was a grapevine that he wanted to cut down, and so he killed the boy with an axe. Only after he had hacked off the limbs did he come to his senses. Since the land had become barren, Dionysos promised to restore its fertility if Lycurgus were dead, so the people had him killed by horses.[44] In another version, Lycurgus refused to accept the divinity of Dionysos. While drunk, he violated his own mother and had the vineyards torn up because they produced wine. He was deluded again and actually killed his wife and son, and Dionysos threw him to the panthers. Finally, one version told that in his befuddlement, whether drunk or under a mania produced by Dionysos, he thought that he himself was a grapevine and cut into his own flesh.

We can see how this material could enter into the *Aeneid* and how intricate the relationships between myth and history become in Vergil's reworking of the material. The stories of Lycurgus and his crimes had been myth in the *Iliad*, a myth that was reenacted in historical time by Polymestor's murder of Polydorus. The similarity between Lycurgus and Polymestor had already been apparent in *Hecuba*, where Polydorus suffers both blindness and exile.[45] Before Aeneas wounds the plant, he does not

---

[43] W. H. Roscher, *Ausführliches Lexikon der griechischen und römischen Mythologie* (Hildesheim: Georg Olms, 1965), 2.2, "Lykurgos," cols. 2191–204; here, cols. 2193–94.

[44] Apollodorus, *The Library*, trans. James George Frazer, Loeb Classical Library (London: William Heinemann and Cambridge, MA: Harvard UP, 1967), 3.5.1 (324–31).

[45] Charles Segal, *Euripides and the Poetics of Sorrow: Art, Gender and Commemoration in* Alcestis, Hippolytus *and* Hecuba (Durham: Duke UP, 1993), xxx.

know about the *new* crime committed by Polymestor against Polydorus; he only knows about elements of the myth. Unforgettable are the horrible images of Lycurgus confusing grapevines with people and cutting into, killing, or wounding either his son, his wife, or himself as a result. The punishment is consistent with the ancient identification between Dionysos and wine.[46] Lycurgus in his blasphemy attacks Dionysos as though he were in the grapevines, only to discover that the grapevines he imagines in his delusion are human beings. The metamorphoses of wine and blood erupt for Aeneas with the force of the myth behind them.

There are actually three different stories that overlap. In the myth, Lycurgus transgresses against hospitality by expelling Dionysos and is punished in being made to harm innocent people. On the historical plane, it is Polymestor who violates the laws of hospitality and Polydorus is actually turned into a person-plant. Finally, Aeneas, who has arrived in Thrace to be a new ruler, ends up wounding the plant-person. The blindness of Lycurgus is reenacted when Aeneas is unable to see past the surfaces and makes the plant bleed and suffer. Unfortunately, when Aeneas hears the history of Polydorus there is little reassurance for him, because the fact that Polydorus is a fellow Trojan and not a random stranger tightens the parallel back to Lycurgus, who violated a familiar (Thracian) god and was punished by making him assault his own kin. Thus the final verb "obtruncat" (3:55) signals that the myth hangs heavy on Aeneas's mind, since it refers to the way in which Lycurgus killed his son — beheading — and not to the reports of how Polymestor murdered Polydorus.

The parallels in the stories about Lycurgus and Dionysos to certain events in "Auerbachs Keller" are noteworthy. In particular, the "grape trick" evokes the wounding of Lycurgus by himself while deluded:

FROSCH
Weinberge! Seh' ich recht?
SIEBEL
   Und Trauben gleich zur Hand!
BRANDER
Hier, unter diesem grünen Laube,
Seht, welch ein Stock! seht, welche Traube!
   *Er faßt Siebeln bei der Nase, die andern tun es wechselseitig und heben die Messer.* (2317–319)

---

[46] Walter Burkert, *Griechische Religion der archaischen und klassischen Epoche* (Stuttgart: W. Kohlhammer, 1997), comments: "Vatertod und Mädchenopfer werfen ihren Schatten auf den Genuß des Weins . . . . Vielleicht hat man insgeheim viel direkter vom Tod des Gottes selbst gesprochen: die Assoziation von Wein und Blut, die Rede vom Wein als 'Blut der Reben' ist alt und verbreitet" (255).

Mephistopheles envelops the four companions with delusion and they almost cut into their bodies, imagining them to be grapes on vines.

But the skeptical reader will want to know if this is not entirely far-fetched. What evidence is there that Goethe knew the story of Lycurgus, or indeed was thinking about it in connection with *Faust*? One could of course respond with a reference to the mythological compendium of Hederich, upon which Goethe relied.[47] But one can do better than that. In *Dichtung und Wahrheit* Goethe provides ample evidence that he was familiar with these stories and their implications. It was May 1775 when Christian and Friedrich Leopold Stolberg and Graf Haugwitz arrived in Frankfurt am Main, where they were frequent dinner guests at the home of Goethe's parents. Goethe gives a vivid and detailed account of the evening; the passage is long, but must be quoted in its entirety, so that the dramatic impact may be felt and because it is the final piece to the intricate puzzles of "Auerbachs Keller":

> Zu meiner Mutter machte sich ein eigenes Verhältnis; sie wußte in ihrer tüchtigen graden Art sich gleich ins Mittelalter zurückzusetzen, um als Aja bei irgend einer lombardischen oder byzantinischen Prinzessin angestellt zu sein. Nicht anders als Frau Aja ward sie genannt, und sie gefiel sich in dem Scherze und ging so eher in die Phantastereien der Jugend mit ein, als sie schon in Götz von Berlichingens Hausfrau ihr Ebenbild zu erblicken glaubte.
>
> Doch hiebei sollte es nicht lange bleiben, denn man hatte nur einige Male zusammen getafelt, als schon nach ein und der andern genossenen Flasche Wein der poetische Tyrannenhaß zum Vorschein kam, und man nach dem blute solcher Wütriche lechzend sich erwies. Mein Vater schüttelte lächelnd den Kopf; meine Mutter hatte in ihrem Leben kaum von Tyrannen gehört, doch erinnerte sie sich in Gottfrieds "Chronik" dergleichen Unmenschen in Kupfer abgebildet gesehen zu haben: den König Kambyses, der in Gegenwart des Vaters das Herz des Söhnchens mit dem Pfeil getroffen zu haben triumphiert, wie ihr solche noch im Gedächtnis geblieben war. Diese und ähnliche aber immer heftiger werdenden Äußerungen ins Heitere zu wenden, verfügte sie sich in ihren Keller, wo ihr von den ältesten Weinen wohlunterhaltene große Fässer verwahrt lagen. Nicht geringere befanden sich daselbst als die Jahrgänge 1706, 19, 26, 48, von ihr selbst gewartet und gepflegt, selten und nur bei feierlichen bedeutenden Gelegenheiten angesprochen.

---

[47] Benjamin Hederich, "Lycurgus," in *Gründliches mythologisches Lexikon*, ed. Johann Joachim Schwabe (1770; repr., Darmstadt: Wissenschaftliche Buchgesellschaft, 1967), cols. 1494–97. Goethe could also have read about the Bacchic connection in Servius's commentary to the *Aeneid*.

Indem sie nun in geschliffener Flasche den hochfarbigen Wein hin-
setzte, rief sie aus: "Hier ist das wahre Tyrannenblut! Daran ergötzt euch,
aber alle Mordgedanken laßt mir aus dem Hause!" "Ja wohl
Tyrannenblut!" rief ich aus; "keinen größeren Tyrannen gibt es, als den,
dessen Herzblut man euch vorsetzt. Labt euch daran, aber mäßig! denn
ihr müßt befürchten, daß er euch durch Wohlgeschamck und Geist unter-
joche. Der Weinstock ist der Universaltyrann, der ausgerottet werden
sollte; zum Patron sollten wir deshalb den heiligen Lycurgus, den
Thrazier, wählen und verehren; er griff das fromme Werk kräftig an, aber
vom betörenden Dämon Bacchus verblendet und verderbt, verdient er in
der Zahl der Märtyrer obenan zu stehen.

Dieser Weinstock ist der allerschlimmste Tyrann, zugelich Heuchler,
Schmeichler und Gewaltsamer. Die ersten Züge seines Blutes munden
euch, aber ein Tropfen lockt den andern unaufhaltsam nach; sie folgen
sich wie eine Perlenschnur, die man zu zerreißen fürchtet."

Wenn ich hier, wie die besten Historiker getan, eine fingierte Rede
statt jener Unterhaltung einzuschieben in Verdacht geraten könnte, so
darf ich den Wunsch aussprechen, es möchte gleich ein Geschwindschreiber
diese Peroration aufgefaßt und uns überliefert haben. Man würde die
Motive genau dieselbigen und den Fluß der Rede vielleicht anmutiger
und einladender finden. Überhaupt fehlt dieser gegenwärtigen
Darstellung im ganzen die weitläufige Redseligkeit und Fülle einer
Jugend, die sich fühlt und nicht weiß, wo sie mit Kraft und Vermögen
hinaus soll. (HA 10:126–27)

It must have been quite an evening! The whirl of allusions, barbs, and
reversals makes this a remarkable vignette, one whose ramifications only
strike readers who are as familiar with "Auerbachs Keller" as we now are.[48]
Four young male companions, drinking and carousing together in the
presence of the two parents, makes up a grouping of six (four plus two)
that matches the one in the play. The references to the famous family wine
cellar (exactly four vintages are chosen) further evoke the scene from the
drama, as do Goethe's invitation to the others to drink, tempered with a
caution, and his use of the word "Patron." However, the situations are so
opposed to each other, Hell there and a bourgeois idyll here, that the relationship can only be intended to be satirical. The spirit of satire dominates
the playing upon the metaphor of wine as "tyrants' blood," although the
insistent repetition of blood, blood, blood and the talk of drinking
"Tyrannenblut" starts to sound weird enough to bring to mind the "cannibalism" of the four in "Auerbachs Keller."

---

[48] I was led to this passage by Leonard Willoughby's " 'Wine that maketh
glad . . . ': The Interplay of Reality and Symbol in Goethe's Life and Work,"
*Publications of the English Goethe Society* 47 (1976–77): 68–133.

Any doubts about whether Goethe knew of Lycurgus are dispelled completely with the direct allusion to him and to details of his campaign against the vineyards, of his blinding, and of his miserable end. But an earlier allusion also hints at Lycurgus. Goethe's mother remembers the story of Cambyses because it is so horrible. The critical notes in the *Hamburger Ausgabe* are helpful:

> In Gottfrieds "*Chronik*" . . . wird geschildert, wie der Tyrann Cambyses, nachdem er viel Wein getrunken, dem Prexaspes beweist, daß er seiner Sinne mächtig sei; er schießt mit Pfeil und Bogen auf dessen Sohn, trifft ihn, läßt die Leiche öffnen und zeigt, daß der Pfeil genau ins Herz ging. (HA 10:632)

It is not a pleasant tale and bears strong resemblances yet again to the hints of infanticide while intoxicated that were attached to Lycurgus. It also sets up a contradiction between what we remember about the arbitrary violence of tyrants and the mock praise of Lycurgus as a "patron," a "saint," and a "martyr." For everyone familiar with the context, these epithets can only be satirical. One trick of satire is to invert praise and condemnation. If the polarities are reversed, then the real meaning would become apparent: it is the victim Dionysos who should be sanctified and ranked among the martyrs. Wine would be the universal liberator, not an implacable tyrant. But where is one to stop this play of signifiers? Does blood then become wine and vice versa? Is Goethe playing at being Mephistopheles, telling us "the vine bears grapes" but meaning something else? Does Goethe become the advocate of inebriation in the presence of his parents and thereby intimate a rebellion against the pater familias? Will temperance no longer be the mark of Christian virtue, something that frees good people from the "tyranny of drink," and become instead the force that imprisons wildness and ecstasy and therefore should be repudiated? Would the satirical attack on Dionysos be elevated, in the mouth of a satyr-izing young Goethe, into a dithyramb of praise for the "Genius of the Age"?

The inverted world is turned right side up with the interruption of the calm voice of the historian, who tells us that what has just transpired is only an invented report. It is not an actual document; no one was there taking the conversation down. Reason sways us again, as we are invited to imagine how other historians have made up speeches in similar circumstances. The distance between experience and narration, between "Dichtung" (fiction) and "Wahrheit" (truth), gapes once again as a chasm that cannot be bridged. Yet all is not forgotten, for the memory of the illusion lingers that we were present, drinking, joking, laughing with Goethe and his friends. So does a feeling of skepticism about "the best historians" and the reliability of their accounts. If Lycurgus can be so quickly elevated here to saint and martyr, then the whole history of constructing heroes, from the Greek gods down the present, seems to hang by a thread. As John the

Evangelist had said in *Orlando Furioso*: "If you want to know what really happened, invert the story: Greece was vanquished, Troy triumphant, and Penelope a whore."[49] Bacchus, so long banished as the source of tyranny, might in fact be the liberator who should be sanctified and celebrated.

Remembering that 1775, the time of the Stolbergs' visit, was near the beginning of Goethe's project sheds light on Faust's figurative genealogy. His ancestor is Lycurgus, representing the principle opposed to Dionysos. From the perspective of Lycurgus, the symbol of oppression is wine: "tyrants' blood." What he does not *see* — therefore his blindness is one just punishment — is that all his actions, driving out the nymphs or tearing up vineyards, are the true operations of tyranny. Failing to overcome his own lack of self-control, Lycurgus projects into the wine a bane that was not there naturally. His legacy will be passed on to all subsequent heroes. The fears of Aeneas *were* realized and he *has* been cast to replay the role of Lycurgus, as his complaint against gold reveals. Gold is no more to blame for the violence that men do than wine; there is nothing in the essence of the metal that inclines to good or to evil; it is greed that makes gold an object of desire. The *Aeneid* will continue to tell how heroic greed shapes government and builds empires. Goethe knew how the epics continued. It will not be a coincidence that Erichtho, transported from Lucan's post-Vergilian *Pharsalia*, the epic of bloody civil war, will lament in the "Klassische Walpurgisnacht":

> Wie oft schon wiederholt sich's! wird sich immerfort
> In's Ewige wiederholen . . . Keiner gönnt das Reich
> Dem Andern; dem gönnt's keiner der's mit Kraft erwarb
> Und kräftig herrscht. Denn jeder, der sein innres Selbst
> Nicht zu regieren weiß, regierte gar zu gern
> Des Nachbars Willen, eignem stolzem Sinn gemäß . . . .
>
> (7012–17)

---

[49] Ludovico Ariosto, *Orlando Furioso*, trans. Guido Waldman (Oxford: Oxford UP, 1983), 425.

# 5: "Auerbachs Keller" and Epic History

THREE MILLENNIA MAKE A LONG PERIOD and perhaps it is too much to demand or expect that Faust or the audience be able to grasp the totality and discern patterns in such a vast history. Yet, in a short poem in the "Westöstlicher Divan," Goethe expected us to operate with such a span of time:

> Wer nicht von dreitausend Jahren
> Sich weiß Rechenschaft zu geben,
> Bleib im Dunkeln unerfahren,
> Mag von Tag zu Tage leben.[1]

He indicated that the same vast expanse of time governs *Faust*:

> Ich habe von Zeit zu Zeit daran fortgearbeitet, aber abgeschlossen konnte das Stück nicht werden als in der Fülle der Zeiten, da es denn jetzt seine volle 3000 Jahre spielt, von Trojas Untergang bis zur Einnahme von Missolonghi. Dies kann man also auch für eine Zeiteinheit rechnen, im höheren Sinne; die Einheit des Orts und der Handlung sind aber auch im gewöhnlichen Sinn aufs genauste beobachtet.[2]

Confronted by the overwhelming presence of the totality of human history, Faust cannot cope and lives "from day to day." In "Auerbachs Keller" the actions of the four companions towards each other and towards Mephistopheles enact on the stage the causes and the consequences of the fall of empire: this is the *theatrum mundi* of world history.[3]

---

[1] Johann Wolfgang von Goethe, *Werke: Hamburger Ausgabe in 14 Bänden*, ed. Erich Trunz (Munich: C. H. Beck, 1981), 2:49. This "Hamburger Ausgabe" will henceforth be cited as HA.

[2] Goethe, *Goethes Briefe*, ed. Karl Robert Mandelkow and Bodo Morawe, 4 vols. (Hamburg: Christian Wegner, 1962), 4:205, letter of 22 October 1826 to Wilhelm von Humboldt. Missolonghi, a town in Greece, had been taken from the Turks on 1 November 1821, only to be retaken by them after a long siege on 22 April 1826. The name is also associated with Byron and his efforts on behalf of Greek independence, since he died there on 19 April 1824.

[3] On this topic, see Jean Jacquot, "Le Théâtre du Monde," *Revue de Littérature Comparée* 31 (1957): 341–72; Frank J. Warnke, "The World as Theatre: Baroque Variations on a Traditional Topos," in *Festschrift für Edgar Mertner*, ed. Bernhard Fabian and Ulrich Suerbaum (Munich: Wilhelm Fink,

## The Crisis of the Empire

The most obvious historical allusions in "Auerbachs Keller" are to the political affairs of the sixteenth century but they can also apply to the eighteenth. The political crisis was, in short, perpetual. From his training in law, Goethe knew first-hand the legal and constitutional problems that beset the "Holy Roman Empire," problems that would occupy him throughout his public career. Even in his early play, *Götz von Berlichingen*, the divergence between the ideal polity of the City of God and the messy reality of the City of Man is a theme throughout the play and is caught in the exchange between Olearius, a doctor of law, and the Abbot of Fulda. The focal point is the Justinian Code:

> OLEARIUS. Man möcht's wohl ein Buch aller Bücher nennen; eine Sammlung aller Gesetze; bei jedem Fall der Urteilsspruch bereit; und was ja noch abgängig oder dunkel wäre, ersetzen die Glossen, womit die gelehrtesten Männer das vortrefflichste Werk geschmückt haben.
> ABT. Eine Sammlung aller Gesetze! Potz! da müssen auch wohl die zehn Gebote drin sein.
> OLEARIUS. Implicite wohl, nicht explicite.
> ABT. Das mein ich auch, an und vor sich, ohne weitere Explikation.
> BISCHOF. Und was das Schönste ist, so könnte, wie Ihr sagt, ein Reich in sicherster Ruhe und Frieden leben, wo es völlig eingeführt und recht gehandhabt würde. (HA 4:94)

Of course, the Bishop's claim rings hollow in the world of continual strife and justice endlessly delayed shown in the play. Nor was there much hope for reconciling Scripture with the legal codes, for the two sets of legislation had over the course of centuries developed their respective and powerful institutions, each of which claimed supremacy over the other and thereby contributed in no small measure to the discord of the realm.[4]

---

1969), 185–200; Frances F. Yates, *Theatre of the World.* (Chicago: U of Chicago P, 1969); Carl Joseph Hering, "Das Welttheater als religions- und rechtsdidaktisches Gleichnis," in *Aequitas und Toleranz: Gesammelte Schriften von Carl Joseph Hering,* ed. Erich Fechner, Ernst von Hippel, and Herbert Frost (Bonn: Bouvier Verlag Herbert Grundmann, 1971), 199–221; Peter N. Skrine, *The Baroque: Literature and Culture in Seventeenth-Century Europe* (London: Methuen, 1978), 1–24; Howard D. Pearce, "A Phenomenological Approach to the *Theatrum Mundi* Metaphor," *PMLA* 95.1 (1980): 42–57; and William N. West, "The Idea of a Theater: Humanist Ideology and the Imaginary Stage in Early Modern Europe," *Renaissance Drama* NS 28 (1999): 245–87.

[4] For brief overview, see Constantin Fasolt, "Visions of Order in the Canonists and Civilians," in *Handbook of European History, 1400–1600: Latin Middle Ages,*

Political history is introduced considerably more subtly in *Faust* than in *Götz von Berlichingen* — so much so that the former is hardly ever discussed as historical drama. Nevertheless, indications of the political conditions of Faust's time are present. Best known as a political allusion are Frosch's famous lines: "Das liebe heil'ge Röm'sche Reich, / Wie hält's nur noch zusammen?" (2090–91). Commentators are usually content to note that this was a direct reference by Goethe to the precarious situation of the Empire in the late eighteenth century, when the rise of Prussia had exposed the inability of Imperial institutions to cope with serious challenges. Pointedly, the song is broken off at the question, without giving any solution to the threat of imminent collapse or disintegration. It is ironic is that people had been asking what held the Empire together for centuries. The lines must simultaneously be read in context as applying to the turbulent sixteenth century, when religion, princely ambition, and popular discontent fuelled some of the most vicious civil wars imaginable. Erasmus lamented about the state of affairs in 1526:

> Charles is preparing to extend the boundaries of his realm. Ferdinand has his hands full in Germany. Bankruptcy threatens every court. The peasants raise dangerous riots and are not swayed from their purpose, despite so many massacres. The commons are bent on anarchy; the Church is shaken to its very foundations by menacing factions; on every side the seamless coat of Jesus is torn to shreds. The vineyard of the Lord is now laid waste not by a single boar but at one and the same time the authority of priests (together with their tithes), the dignity of theologians, the splendour of monks is imperiled; confession totters; vows reel; pontifical ordinances crumble away; the Eucharist is called in question; Antichrist is awaited; the whole earth is pregnant with I know not what calamity.[5]

This is the historical backdrop against which we should see the events of *Faust* and of "Auerbachs Keller." References to the conflicts of those times are heard in the crass rhetoric of the four drinkers. The ad hominem attack upon Luther as a "plump rat" suggests the vituperation that the participants in the public debates during the Reformation heaped upon each other.

---

*Renaissance and Reformation*, vol. 2: *Visions, Programs and Outcomes*, ed. Thomas A. Brady, Jr., Heiko A. Oberman, and James D. Tracey (Leiden and New York: E. J. Brill, 1995), 31–59.

[5] Quoted by Timothy J. Reiss, "The Idea of Meaning and the Practice of Order in Peter Ramus, Henri Estienne, and Others," in *Humanism in Crisis: The Decline of the French Renaissance*, ed. Philippe Desan (Ann Arbor: U of Michigan P, 1991), 125–52; here, 15, from Desiderius Erasmus, *Colloquies* [1518–33], trans. Craig R. Thompson (Chicago: U of Chicago P, 1965), 269–70.

Further evidence is revealed by the references in the scene to the topography of Christian Europe, for they are replete with sectarian overtones. The organization of both space and time according to symbolic cities was nothing new: Babylon, Jerusalem, and Rome were standard reference points,[6] as were Homer's Troy, Vergil's Carthage, Dante's Florence, or the Ferrara of Ariosto and Tasso. In order to recover something of the symbolic value of the named cities, it is necessary to recall the events of the sixteenth century. "Leipzig" serves as a reminder of the famous Leipzig Disputation of 1519 — where Luther was welcomed by Dr. Auerbach — and of the role of Frederick the Wise, Elector of Saxony, as Luther's protector.[7] Thus the city functioned as something of a capital for the Protestants, and was satirized by Catholics as a new Babylon:

> And this Protestant doctrine was born and nourished in Germany; and principally in Saxony, whence as I have said issued the book of this furious spirit, and thence, catching like a plague, goes travelling through the world. This is therefore that proud and bold woman, this fat whore, that goes fornicating with the Princes of the Earth, removing them from the true worship of God; this is she who is stained with the blood of the saints and prophets, who have been oppressed by the Princes and by the people who have endeavoured to destroy the Catholic faith. She has made herself the habitation of devils and the haven of all unclean spirits; and this is the great Babylon that is fallen; Babylon signifies confusion: and where was there ever greater confusion and where are Catholics more travailed and persecuted than in those regions? Where did so many heresies ever exist at one time?[8]

---

[6] "Jerusalem is usually golden, Babylon is almost always brazen, and the glitter of Rome is often ambiguous" (Davis, "Rome and Babylon in Dante," in *Rome in the Renaissance: The City and the Myth*, Papers of the Thirteenth Annual Conference of the Center for Medieval and Early Renaissance Studies, ed. Paul A. Ramsey [Binghamton, NY: Center for Medieval and Early Renaissance Studies, 1982], 19–40; here, 19).

[7] On Luther's reception by Auerbach, see Gustav Wustmann, *Der Wirt von Auerbachs Keller: Dr. Heinrich Stromer von Auerbach, 1482–1542* (Leipzig: Hermann Seemann Nachfolger, 1902), 31–35. For a brief background on the politics of the Reformation, see Winfried Schulze, *Deutsche Geschichte im 16. Jahrhundert, 1500–1618* (1987; repr., Darmstadt: Wissenschaftliche Buchgesellschaft, 1997), 78–88.

[8] Girolamo Muzio, *L'Heretico infuriato* (1562) translated and quoted by Quint, *Epic and Empire: Politics and Generic Form from Virgil to Milton* (Princeton: Princeton UP, 1993), 218–19. Complicating the imagining of events at the time was the assertion by some Protestants, including Luther, that Frederick of Saxony was the fulfilment of the prophecy about the return of Emperor Frederick, a topic discussed by Reeves, *The Influence of Prophecy in the Later Middle Ages: A Study in Joachimism* (Oxford: Clarendon, 1969), 372–74.

Conversely, Protestants saw in Paris a centre of Catholic resistance to the Reformation, culminating in the St. Bartholomew's Day massacre in 1572.[9] The juxtaposition "Mein Leipzig lob ich mir! Es ist ein klein Paris" mocks the conflict between the factional oppositions: surely someone who can favor both a Protestant and a Catholic capital at the same time might be able to show tolerance to others.[10] Mephistopheles' statement "Wir kommen erst aus Spanien zurück, / Dem schönen Land des Weins und der Gesänge" (2205–6) is one of his cruel little jokes in this context, for Spain was and would remain notorious well into the eighteenth century as the home of the Inquisition.[11] Earlier, Mephistopheles had indicated some familiarity with the role of Spain in the Counter-Reformation when he mentioned the "Spanish boots," a cruel instrument of torture, in connection with controlling the mind: "Da wird der Geist Euch wohl dressiert, / In spanische Stiefeln eingeschnürt" (1912–13).[12] Perhaps, then, there is a

---

[9] On the centrality of the Sorbonne in the religious controversies, see David Nicholls, "Heresy and Protestantism, 1520–1542: Questions of Perception and Communication," *French History* 10.2 (1996): 182–205, esp. 184–87. Goethe may also have had in mind Ariosto's vivid descriptions of the siege of Paris (*Orlando Furioso*, cantos 14–15) as well as the devastations of the Seven Years' War, in which Saxony was a main theatre of operations.

[10] The mention of cities in an underworld is always fraught with ambiguities. Referring to the towns listed by Anchises in book 6 of the *Aeneid* (773–76) as part of the prophecy of future greatness, D. C. Feeney points out in his "History and Revelation in Vergil's Underworld," *Proceedings of the Cambridge Philological Society* NS no. 31 (1985): 1–24, the irony that for Vergil's audience the names would have been quite ordinary.

[11] Compare Jochen Schmidt, "Gesellschaftliche Unvernunft und Französische Revolution in Goethes '*Faust*': Zu den Szenen 'Auerbachs Keller' und 'Hexenküche,' " in *Gesellige Vernunft: Zur Kultur der literarischen Aufklärung: Festschrift für Wolfram Mauser zum 65. Geburtstag*, ed. Ortrud Gutjahr, Wilhelm Kühlmann, and Wolf Wucherpfennig (Würzburg: Königshausen & Neumann, 1993), 297–310; here, 300. The association of Spain with the Inquisition, with the conquest of the Americas, and with the suppression of the Netherlands together formed the basis for the so-called "Black Legend." See William S. Maltby, *The Black Legend in England: The Development of Anti-Spanish Sentiment, 1558–1660* (Durham: Duke UP, 1971); Baerbel Becker-Cantarino, "Die 'Schwarze Legende': Zum Spanienbild in der deutschen Literatur des 18. Jahrhunderts," *Zeitschrift für deutsche Philologie* 94.2 (1975): 183–203.

[12] On the methods of torture in the Inquisition, especially on the "binding" with increasingly tight ropes, see Henry Kamen, *The Spanish Inquisition* (1965; repr., London and Toronto: White Lion Publishers, 1976), 173–78. Note that Mephistopheles is putting himself in the position of the Inquisitors, when in fact one of the main targets of the Inquisition was any association, however slight, with the Devil.

dark pun in "des Weins und der Gesänge" (wine and songs) on "des Weinens und der Gesänge" (weeping and songs), evoking the tears and the screams of the victims of religious fanaticism.[13] Alert readers must be genuinely puzzled about the reference to a trip to Spain, since there is nothing in the preceding action to indicate that Mephistopheles and Faust had gone to or had planned to go to Spain. One commentator has tried to find a logical motive for the deception, suggesting that Goethe was avoiding censorship.[14] I would propose that in this case Mephistopheles is blatantly telling a lie, but that the intertextual function of that speech act is not so simple, for it recalls an infamous episode from the *Odyssey*, the story Odysseus tells to the Phaiakians about his adventures. The ambivalent status of what seem to be "tall tales" and their beguiling effects are characteristic of the wily Odysseus and of Mephistopheles.[15]

Before examining the political philosophy and tactics of Mephistopheles more closely, I would like to suggest the immediate historical background to Brander's allusions to choosing a Pope. He exclaims:

> Ein garstig Lied! Pfui! ein politisch Lied
> Ein leidig Lied! Dankt Gott mit jedem Morgen
> Daß ihr nicht braucht fürs Röm'sche Reich zu sorgen!
> Ich halt' es wenigstens für reichlichen Gewinn,
> Daß ich nicht Kaiser oder Kanzler bin.
> Doch muß auch uns ein Oberhaupt nicht fehlen;
> Wir wollen einen Papst erwählen. (2092–98)

These lines refer directly to affairs contemporary with Faust's life. After Maximilian I died in 1519, the struggles between Francis I, king of France, and Charles of Spain, crowned Emperor Charles V in 1520, presented a sorry spectacle of Christian rulers at war, with Italy as the main battleground.[16] The climax of horror came on 6 May 1527 when German mercenary troops, the *Landsknechte*, sacked Rome. Historian Robert Ergang

---

[13] Johann Wolfgang Goethe, *Faust: Eine Tragödie*, ed. Franz Carl Endres (Basel: Benno Schwabe, 1949), 1:129.

[14] Goethe, *Faust: Eine Tragödie*, 1:129.

[15] For overviews of the issues, see Hugh Parry, "The *Apologos* of Odysseus: Lies, All Lies?" *Phoenix* 48 (1994): 1–20; and Werner Suerbaum, "Die Ich-Erzählungen des Odysseus: Überlegungen zur epischen Technik der Odysee," *Poetica* 2 (1968): 150–77; here, 165–71.

[16] Robert W. Scheller, "Imperial Themes in Art and Literature of the Early French Renaissance: The Period of Charles VIII," trans. Michael Hoyle, *Simiolus* 12.1 (1981–82): 5–69. The article offers much material, textual and iconographic, that is directly relevant to the thread of Goethe's argument in *Faust*.

sums up the horror: "Once the city was taken, the army, augmented by hordes of Italians equally thirsty for booty, pillaged and looted Rome without hindrance. For eight days, during which thousands lost their lives, the sack continued unabated."[17] For anyone who read historical events symbolically, this sacking was a counterpoint to the fall of the Roman Empire to the barbarians, but in this case the city fell to ostensible Christians. Those with apocalyptic anxieties had concrete evidence that the end was near.[18] What force could hold the Holy Roman Empire together under such circumstances? Certainly not the influence of the Church. During the sack of Rome, Pope Clement VII (1523–34) had been imprisoned and the citizens of Florence seized the opportunity to exile the Medici and establish a republican government. However, the Republic was short-lived. The Pope turned to Charles V and promised to legitimate his rule by crowning him officially as Holy Roman Emperor; in return, the Imperial army was sent in the summer of 1530 to besiege and dislodge the Republican government of Florence. Alessandro de' Medici became the "Duke of the Florentine Republic," virtually a monarch.[19]

One might now ask, how does this all connect with *Faust*? An initial response could refer to Benvenuto Cellini, a figure in whom Goethe was intensely interested. Cellini, who even claimed to have been the one who shot the Duke of Bourbon, had been in Rome in 1527. His autobiography gave eye-witness access not only to the sack of Rome but to the beginnings of Medici rule. Even before he translated Cellini's autobiography, Goethe was intrigued by him, not least because of similarities between his life and that of Dürer. I will discuss the significance of Cellini in more detail below.

On a more general level, "Auerbachs Keller" replicates microcosmically the chaos, fragmentation, and strife at the beginning of the sixteenth century. What Brander's words highlight are the problems associated with the translation of the popular will into elections and policies. The period was marked by the contradictions of representative government. From one direction, the Protestants were asserting the primacy of individual conscience over traditional hierarchies. From another, there was the example

---

[17] Robert Ergang, *Europe from the Renaissance to Waterloo* (Boston: D. C. Heath, 1954), 1:154.

[18] On the apocalyptic, prophetic implications, see Marjorie Reeves, "A Note on Prophecy and the Sack of Rome (1527)," in *Prophetic Rome in the High Renaissance Period: Essays*, ed. Marjorie Reeves (Oxford: Clarendon P, 1992), 271–78.

[19] Eric Cochrane, *Florence in the Forgotten Centuries, 1527–1800: A History of Florence and the Florentines in the Age of the Grand Dukes* (Chicago and London: U of Chicago P, 1973), 3–10.

of the ill-fated attempt at the reestablishment of republican government in Florence. Opposing these moments were the brutal facts of military force, vividly represented by the German *Landsknechte* taking matters into their own hands and wreaking only devastation. Not least, there were scheming, ruthless rulers, including the princes of the Church, who were willing to sacrifice honor and their subjects in the quest for power. The challenge of how to translate the unruly will of the common subjects into a mechanism for election ("einen Papst erwählen" [2098]) came to the fore after 1500. The tensions between representative government and Machiavellian manipulation of the masses had hardly been resolved for the German-speaking Holy Roman Empire by 1800 and are depicted through the interactions in "Auerbachs Keller."

One of the sources of divisiveness for the Holy Roman Empire was a nascent patriotic sentiment, evident for example in the identification of the "German" *Landsknechte* versus the "Italian" defenders of Rome and Florence.[20] This sentiment contributes in the four drinkers to a coarse intolerance of foreigners, which manifests itself in their sloganeering when they choose their wines.[21] Frosch is bluntly patriotic: "Gut! wenn ich wählen soll, so will ich Rheinwein haben. / Das Vaterland verleiht die allerbesten Gaben" (2264–65). Brander is willing to put specific desires above his own patriotic sentiments:

> Man kann nicht stets das Fremde meiden,
> Das Gute liegt uns oft so fern.
> Ein echter deutscher Mann mag keinen Franzen leiden,
> Doch ihre Weine trinkt er gern. (2270–74)

The lines mock the very notion of what "a proper German" could or should be. No doubt Goethe was taking aim at his own contemporaries who continually railed against "French" influences but were nevertheless willing to consume French commodities.

The expressions of antipathy to otherness are reinforced by the inhospitable attitude of the companions to their guests. Rather than greeting Mephistopheles and Faust warmly, they regard them with suspicion as

---

[20] This was of course not yet the full-blown nationalism that emerged in the late eighteenth century. As Cochrane notes in *Florence in the Forgotten Centuries*, even during the siege of Florence, many disaffected Florentines fought against their compatriots (7–8).

[21] Cf. the laconic observation by Stuart Atkins, *Goethe's Faust: A Literary Analysis* (Cambridge, MA: Harvard UP, 1958), 61: "Here none will object to Brander's Francophobia, for this world is a place of beasts devouring one another. . . ."

"strangers." Siebel asks, "Für was siehst du die Fremden an?" (2173). A universal mistrust against outsiders has already divided what should be a community, since they presumably are all Christians and speak the same language. Frosch's language is filled with aggression as he moves to confront the newcomers:

> Laßt mich nur gehn! Bei einem vollen Glase
> Zieh' ich, wie einen Kinderzahn,
> Den Burschen leicht die Würmer aus der Nase.
> Sie scheinen mir aus einem edlen Haus,
> Sie sehen stolz und unzufrieden aus. (2174–278)

And then, after interruptions by Brander and Altmayer, he declares: "Gib Acht, ich schraube sie!" (2180). This a far cry from the "Gastfreundlichkeit," the hospitality, on which Germans prided themselves. The verb "schrauben" comes from the language of torture, where various methods of screwing fingers and limbs — such as the "Spanish boots" — were used to extract information.[22] Until this point, the four have made no effort to greet the new arrivals, but have spent their time in speculating about the strangers and projecting various possible interpretations onto them. Before any sort of dialogue, the others have already been stereotyped and reduced to passive objects. I am insisting here on Goethe's depiction of the micro-politics of the encounter typical of the age of European expansion. What we see is how the dislike of the various European "nations" towards each other was the training ground for the hermeneutics of suspicion and politics of exclusion when the Europeans came upon those who were "exotic" and from "far away":

> Die kommen eben von der Reise,
> Man sieht's an ihrer wunderlichen Weise;
> Sie sind nicht eine Stunde hier. (2168–2170)

---

[22] Another historical dimension behind these conversational tactics is the gradual legitimation of interrogation, including torture, as a procedure necessary for the modern state. One crossover point was the eagerness of someone such as Christian Thomasius to teach rulers the art of conversational *Klugheit*, his "discovery of a well-founded science, absolutely necessary for the common body" with which they would learn "to recognize against their will in daily conversation that which was hidden in the heart of other people." Cited from his *Erfindung der Wissenschaft anderer Menschen Gemüt zu erkennen* (1692) by Claudia Henn-Schmölders, "Ars conversationis: Zur Geschichte des sprachlichen Umgangs," *arcadia* 10 (1975): 16–33.

That which is "wonderful" might become the source of admiration ("Bewunderung") but instead it is debased into contempt.[23] Frosch's imagery reduces the others to "children" with "worms in the nose" and simultaneously accuses them of being "proud and malcontented." Altmayer's first words to Faust are an open insult: "Ihr scheint ein sehr verwöhnter Mann" (2188). Subtly but surely the allusions to "pride" and "being spoiled" remind us of the other dimension of mistrust in the society of the sixteenth century, namely the increasingly vocal resentment of the lower classes against the aristocratic and the wealthy, a resentment that exposes itself as rudeness in ordinary interactions. The politics of suspicion recall the tense situation when the Trojans land secretly outside Carthage. Because they were potentially invaders and because they did not know how much the Carthaginians might be informed about the outcome of the war, they cannot trust their hosts, nor can they be trusted.

The veiled threats that take the place of a congenial welcome are matched by the naked attempt at violence against the guests a while later, as the four draw their weapons and make moves against Mephistopheles. The four unite in their violence against outsiders; at all other times they are divided against each other. They interrupt, argue, insult, and assault each other, violating all the norms of *civil* conversation. Indeed, they are rehearsing on the microcosmic stage the patterns of civil war. The political implications of their uncivil behavior are far-reaching. From Plato via Ficino and Stefano Guazzo, the ideal interaction of a small group of friends had been proposed as the model for governance in the republic.[24] The main activities set on the agenda of such symposia were polished conversation, elegant dining, moderate drinking, and harmonious music. The aim

---

[23] Cf. the history of "first contact" episodes from the history of European exploration and colonial expansion.

[24] Out of the extensive literature, see John L. Lievsay, *Stefano Guazzo and the English Renaissance, 1575–1675* (Chapel Hill: U of North Carolina P, 1961); Manfred Hinz, *Rhetorische Strategien des Hofmannes: Studien zu den italienischen Hofmannstraktaten des 16. und 17. Jahrhunderts* (Stuttgart: J. B. Metzler, 1992), 327–66); Emilio Bonfatti, *La "Civil Conversazione" in Germania: Letteratura del Compartamento de Stefano Guazzo a Adolph Knigge, 1574–1788* (Verona: Del Bianco Editore, 1979); Elizabeth C. Goldsmith, *"Exclusive Conversations": The Art of Interaction in Seventeenth-Century France* (Philadelphia, PA: U of Pennsylvania P, 1988); Dena Goodman, *The Republic of Letters: A Cultural History of the French Enlightenment* (Ithaca and London: Cornell UP, 1994), 111–19; David S. Shields, *Civil Tongues & Polite Letters in British America* (Chapel Hill and London: U of North Carolina P, for the Institute of Early American History and Culture, 1997); Shapin, *A Social History of Truth: Civility and Science in Seventeenth-Century England* (Chicago and London: U of Chicago P, 1994), 114–25.

was first to harmonize each participant's body and soul and then the bodies and souls of all together. On the same logic that sought a correspondence between the microcosm and the macrocosm generally, there was a conviction that such miniature societies would provide the moderate tone and set the example for all political activity. Beginning from the micropolitical realm, the concordia would resonate throughout the realm, bringing peace and order to all by means of love and friendship.[25] These were ideas that concerned Goethe deeply throughout his life, as he attempted to realize them, if only in the small community of Weimar.[26]

Of those present in "Auerbachs Keller," only Mephistopheles has the wit necessary to enliven a conversation. Faust, in keeping with the stereotype of the pedant, contributes absolutely nothing to civility and the common well-being. His single utterance is entirely selfish — he is not the sort of guest one would invite a second time. Nor do the four companions seem to be faring much better, despite the subtitle to the scene announcing that this is a "lively drinking party," at least judging by Frosch's complaint:

> Will keiner trinken? keiner lachen?
> Ich will euch lehren Gesichter machen!
> Ihr seid jah heut wie nasses Stroh,
> Und brennt sonst immer lichterloh. (2073–76)

The drastic violations of decorum, including the brusque direct questions, the insults, and then the threats, will hardly improve matters. There is no hope that the four companions will emancipate themselves from their degraded political state; rather, they will transgress against every precept of the ideal republic.

A raucous indicator of this is the disharmony in their "singing," which consists largely of shouting and making loud noises. In the political therapeutic of Neoplatonism, music would cut through the politics of discord by teaching people to be harmonious via song: they would become good

---

[25] On the theological aspects of conversation, see Dennis Costa, "Domesticating the Divine Economy: Humanist Theology in Erasmus's *Convivia*," in *Creative Imitation: New Essays on Renaissance Literature in Honor of Thomas M. Greene*, ed. David Quint, Margaret W. Ferguson, G. W. Pigman III, and Wayne A. Rebhorn (Binghamton, NY: Medieval and Renaissance Texts and Studies, 1992), 11–29.

[26] E. Heyse Dummer, "Goethe's Literary Clubs," *The German Quarterly* 22.4 (1949): 195–201. Goethe explored these issues in *Torquato Tasso*. Lieselotte Blumenthal draws out the connections in her "Arkadien in Goethes 'Tasso,'" in *Goethe: Jahrbuch der Goethe-Gesellschaft* NS 21 (1959): 1–24.

singer-citizens by singing and performing in harmony.[27] We cannot decide whether the four sing badly because they mistrust each other and therefore cannot cooperate or whether they have not learned to act in concert and thus cannot produce beautiful music. The performance begins miserably, even though Siebel begins by invoking a prohibition against disunity, albeit in language not likely to soothe the disharmonious soul:

> SIEBEL
> Zur Tür hinaus wer sich entzweit!
> Mit offner Brust singt Runda, sauft und schreit!
> Auf! Holla! Ho!
> ALTMAYER
>       Weh mir, ich bin verloren!
> Baumwolle her! der Kerl sprengt mir die Ohren!
> SIEBEL
> Wenn das Gewölbe widerschallt,
> Fühlt man erst des Basses Grundgewalt.
> FROSCH
> So recht, hinaus mit dem, der etwas übel nimmt!
> A! tara lara da!
> ALTMAYER
> A! tara lara da!
> FROSCH
> Die Kehlen sind gestimmt. (2081–89)

Despite Frosch's declaration, they are not achieving harmony with the music. The lyrics also contradict the possibility of harmonious interaction, with the threats by Siebel and Frosch that anyone who is not "in tune" should be banned from the group. That is emphatically not how the influence of music should spread through the whole community: the point is to charm those "out of tune" by melodious example, not to exile them. The violent political language is reinforced by interruptions and by

---

[27] Music as a paradigm and instrument for political harmony has a long history going back to the *Timaeus*, to Pythagoras, and to Boethius. Fundamental is the study by Leo Spitzer, *Classical and Christian Ideas of World Harmony: Prolegomena to an Interpretation of the Word "Stimmung,"* ed. Ann Granville Hatcher (Baltimore: The Johns Hopkins UP, 1963). See also John Hollander, *The Untuning of the Sky: Ideas of Music in English Poetry, 1500–1700* (New York: W. W. Norton, 1970); S. K. Heninger, Jr., *Touches of Sweet Harmony: Pythagorean Cosmology and Renaissance Poetics* (San Marino, CA: The Huntington Library, 1974); and David Chamberlain, "The Music of the Spheres and *The Parlement of Foules*," *The Chaucer Review* 5 (1970–71): 32–56.

Altmayer's harsh critique of Siebel. At the end, the best that has been achieved is a base harmonization of the bodies, without any corresponding tuning of the spirit or soul.[28]

Showing complete disregard for the effect of the music, which should after all elevate the spirits, Frosch chooses two songs that arouse negative passions. Brander interrupts the first song with extreme, negative emotions: "Ein garstig Lied! Pfui! Ein politisch Lied!" (2091). Siebel is made unhappy by Frosch's other attempt, a sort of love song, and wants to hear no more. Frosch disregards the other's feelings and imposes his will, compelling the listeners when he cannot persuade them, only to be interrupted in turn. They also mar Mephistopheles' performances with disruptions; if these four ever knew decorum, they have forgotten it. The best they can do together is to chime in loudly with Brander's and Mephistopheles' refrains. The latter is particularly unsuitable for polite society, with its grating sounds and ghastly imagery: "Wir knicken und ersticken / Doch gleich wenn einer sticht" (2238–39). For both songs, the stage direction is "jauchzend," *con gusto*, underscoring the distance from any harmony in the singing. The stage performances of the songs today, which make them rather boisterous and convivial, distort the message of the text by giving audiences too much tuneful harmony, whereas raucous, incompetent noise-making is called for. Frosch exclaims "Bravo! Bravo! Das war schön!" (2241) but he is not a reliable critic. Beautiful and ugly are empty terms when the judgment has been so badly skewed, and the aesthetics of the four companions are anything but admirable. The depth of their coarseness is reached when they sing in unison a song that transgresses against the underlying humanistic ideal of elevating human being and the human spirit: "Uns ist ganz kannibalisch wohl, / Als wie fünfhundert Säuen!" (2293–94).

Mephistopheles' sarcastic remark right after this is steeped in political language and in controversy: "Das Volk ist frei, seht an, wie wohl's ihm geht!" (2295). Since they have just described themselves as, and acted like, "swine," the description of them as the "Volk" resurrects the harsh rhetoric of Luther's broadside against the peasants in his *Wider die räuberischen und mörderischen Rotten der Bauern* (1525).[29] Here,

---

[28] Worth noting is that there was a discordant music of Hell, in opposition to the harmony of Heaven: Reinhold Hammerstein, *Diabolus in Musica: Studien zur Ikonographie der Musik im Mittelalter* (Bern and Munich: Francke, 1974), 16–19 and *passim*.

[29] Martin Luther, "Auch wider die räuberischen und mörderischen Rotten der anderen Bauern," in *Studienausgabe*, ed. Hans-Ulrich Delius, with Helmar Junghans, Joachim Rogge, and Günther Wartenberg (Berlin: Evangelische Verlagsanstalt, 1979–92), 3:140–47.

Mephistopheles is quick to echo Luther's unchristian and anti-democratic sentiments, for the negative view of the common people serves the larger diabolic plan. Karl-Heinz Hucke has drawn attention to some of the ironies involved,[30] but has understated a key point. Mephistopheles is speaking. He repeatedly refers to "Volk" and to "freedom." If we collate these passages, an interesting pattern emerges:

> Dem Volke hier wird jeder Tag ein Fest. (2161)

> Den Teufel spürt das Völkchen nie,
> Und wenn er sie bei'm Kragen hätte. (2181–82)

> Ich tränke gern ein Glas, die Freiheit hoch zu ehren,
> Wenn eure Weine nur ein bißchen besser wären. (2245–46)

> Ich stell' es einem jeden frei. (2262)

> Das Volk ist frei, seht an, wie wohl's ihm geht! (2295)

These contradictory utterances trace the outlines of a political philosophy that is cynical in the extreme; it is Machiavellian. On the one hand, Mephistopheles knows, and openly admits to the audience, that these people are not free, since he has them collared. The four characters are de facto imprisoned in this setting: they are there when the scene begins and remain there when it ends.[31] They have some illusions that they can act freely, they know the slogan "Es lebe die Freiheit!" and Mephistopheles is willing to goad them on by granting them "freedom of choice" in picking wine. That is an extremely limited version of freedom, comparable to the supposed freedom offered to consumers today when they are permitted to choose between different brands of identical products or different yet interchangeable candidates for political office, when actually the exercise of those choices does not alter the status quo. Mephistopheles also knows, as we shall see, that the four are shackled by their humoral natures to their material desires, so that the freedom of choice with the wines is a further mystification. The four are just as bound to their mortal bodies as are the hungry rat and the thirsty flea. And not least, Mephistopheles' denigration of the "Volk" is another veiled attack on God's authority, via a mockery of the proverb "Vox populi vox Dei."[32]

---

[30] Karl-Heinz Hucke, *Figuren der Unruhe: Faustdichtungen* (Tübingen: Niemeyer, 1992), 171.

[31] Unlike in the *Urfaust*, where they are permitted to leave the stage.

[32] "The voice of the people is the voice of God." See George Boas, *Vox Populi: Essays in the History of an Idea* (Baltimore: The Johns Hopkins UP, 1969), esp. 3–38.

The "voice of the people" is utterly powerless in this scene, not least because the four companions have no concept of their role in the drama as a whole. They do not know why Mephistopheles and Faust have arrived, and they do not have an overview of how they are participating in the history being unfolded through the plot. Furthermore, democratic election is impossible. Brander's reference to "electing" a Pope ("einen Papst erwählen") serves as a reminder that neither the Pope nor the Emperor was elected by popular ballot, since they both claimed to derive their authority from God. Similarly, the four companions do not choose Mephistopheles as a leader but merely acknowledge him as "Ein pfiffiger Patron!" (2195). Mephistopheles is totally in charge, functioning as the director who knows in advance what the actors are to play, and they are all too willing to follow his lead. Even the slightest hint of rebellion is suppressed with overwhelming force. The insurrection begins with a denunciation of Mephistopheles and quickly escalates into an attempt to outlaw the governor: "Stoßt zu! der Kerl ist vogelfrei!" (2312). The attempt to invert the hierarchy of power must fail, because the four have no capacity to dethrone Mephistopheles by force of arms. Mephistopheles is inviolable because he is able to deflect their aggression, first by offering them utopian visions and then by turning their violence back upon the community.[33] They emerge from the entranced interlude ready to commit atrocities of the sort found in any civil war, indicated by the stage direction: "Er faßt Siebeln bei der Nase. Die andern tun es wechlseitig und heben die Messer." The last words of Mephistopheles in the scene reassert his total domination: "Und merkt euch, wie der Teufel spaße" (2321).

Cunningly invoking freedom at key moments, Mephistopheles is able to blind the four to their actual condition of servitude. Rather mindlessly, they shout "Es lebe die Freiheit!" and forget to analyze their situation. Caught up in the immediacy of action, they have no coherent narrative of what has happened in the scene or what has happened to them. They have no history and no philosophy of history, for they are unable to connect the micro-politics of their lives with the macro-political structures of the Holy Roman Empire and the course of world history, whether divine or secular. Without access to a masterful historical narrative, concepts such as "freedom" are only hollow slogans. Even when they might regain access to the meta-narrative, as in the "Song of the Rat" or the "Song of the Flea," which provide entry to an understanding of the Christian historical framework, they hear the words without grasping the meaning. The "Rattenlied" tells that after the Fall the human condition is to be unfree; work and

---

[33] The tactics closely resemble those of Satan's declaration of war in the first book of *Paradise Lost*.

suffering are the conditions of human imprisonment in this material world, even though free will remains. Only in the circumscribed world of "Auerbachs Keller" could the illusions be temporarily sustained that life can be easy, that wine and pleasure flow without labor, and that there is no end to secular history, that time has been brought to a standstill.[34]

The height of Mephistopheles' cynicism (or the depth of his cruelty) resides in the fact that he himself represents the spirit of rebellion, the cause of his fall from God's favor. He proudly retells that history in the allegory of the fleas:

> MEPHISTOPHELES *singt*
>     Es war einmal ein König,
>     Der hatt' einen großen Floh —
> FROSCH
>     Horcht! Einen Floh! Habt ihr das wohl gefaßt?
>     Ein Floh ist mir ein saub'rer Gast.
> MEPHISTOPHELES *singt*
>     Es war einmal ein König,
>     Der hatt' einen großen Floh,
>     Den liebt' er gar nicht wenig,
>     Als wie seinen eignen Sohn.
>     Da rief er seinen Schneider,
>     Der Schneider kam heran:
>     Da, miß dem Junker Kleider
>     Und miß ihn Hosen an!
> BRANDER
>     Vergeßt nur nicht, dem Schneider einzuschärfen,
>     Daß er mir aufs genauste mißt,
>     Und daß, so lieb sein Kopf ihm ist,
>     Die Hosen keine Falten werfen!
> MEPHISTOPHELES
>     In Sammet und in Seide
>     War er nun angetan,
>     Hatte Bänder auf dem Kleide,
>     Hatt' auch ein Kreuz daran,
>     Und war sogleich Minister,
>     Und hatt' einen großen Stern.
>     Da wurden seine Geschwister
>     Bei Hof' auch große Herrn.

---

[34] For this insight into the frozen time in this scene, I am indebted to Ernst M. Oppenheimer.

> Und Herrn und Fraun am Hofe,
> Die waren sehr geplagt,
> Die Königin und die Zofe
> Gestochen und genagt,
> Und durften sie nicht knicken,
> Und weg sie jucken nicht,
> Wir knicken und ersticken
> Doch gleich, wenn einer sticht.
> CHORUS *jauchzend*
> Wir knicken und ersticken
> Doch gleich wenn einer sticht.

The one consensus among critics is that the song must be a political satire.[35] The immediate support for this interpretation is sought in book 15 of *Dichtung und Wahrheit*, where Goethe offers a lengthy critique of life at court and includes the lines "Willst du die Not des Hofes schauen: / Da wo dich's juckt, darfst du nicht krauen!" (HA 10:54). Following Witkowski, reference is now also made to the political poem "Der Hahn und der Adler" ("The Rooster and the Eagle") published by Christian Friedrich Daniel Schubart in his *Deutsche Chronik*.[36] More distantly, some have pointed to the older tradition of political satires via flea-themes. Ulrich Gaier refers to "La polece" in the *Pentamerone* of Giambattista Basile.[37] The editors of the Munich edition mention the possible Schubart allusion and go on to cite other possible influences, such as Fischart's *Flohhatz*.[38] In addition to Fischart, one should certainly add the Jupiter episode from Grimmelshausen's *Simplicissimus*.[39] But flea-poems dealing with erotic themes were part of an

---

[35] Hans Arens, *Kommentar zu Goethes Faust I* (Heidelberg: Winter, 1982), 218.

[36] Georg Witkowski, *Kommentar und Erläuterungen*, vol. 2 of *Goethes Faust* (1910; Leiden: E. J. Brill, 1950), 233; Arens, *Kommentar zu Goethes Faust I*, 218; Theodor Friedrich and Lothar J. Scheithauer, *Kommentar zu Goethes Faust: Mit einem Faust-Wörterbuch und einer Faust-Bibliographie* (Stuttgart: Reclam, 1994), 189.

[37] Ulrich Gaier, ed. *Faust-Dichtungen: Kommentar I*. 3 vols. (Stuttgart: Philipp Reclam jun., 1999), 285.

[38] Johann Wolfgang von Goethe, *Sämtliche Werke nach Epochen seines Schaffens: Münchner Ausgabe*, ed. Karl Richter, with Herbert G. Göpfert, Norbert Miller, Gerhard Sauder, and Edith Zehm (Munich: Carl Hanser, 1985–1998), 6.1:1012.

[39] On Fischart's *Flöh Hatz Weiber Tratz* (1573) see Hugo Sommerhalder, *Johann Fischarts Werk: Eine Einführung* (Berlin: de Gruyter, 1960), 40–51. The fleas return in: Hans Jacob Christoffel von Grimmelshausen's *Simplicissimus Teutsch*, in his *Werke*, ed. Dieter Breuer (Frankfurt am Main: Deutscher Klassiker Verlag, 1989), 1.1, book 3, chap. 4, 263–66. There was also a tradition of the

interesting corner of the European literary heritage.[40] Much to the modern reader's amazement, the tradition goes back to the pseudo-Ovidian "Elegia de Pulice" and had many witty repercussions, culminating in the famous anthology *La Puce de Madame Des-Roches* (1582).[41] For whatever reason, the Renaissance seems to have enjoyed witty references to fleas, so that Marlowe could refer to the topic twice in *Dr. Faustus*:

> *Clown.* No, no sir. If you turn me into anything, let it be in the likeness of a little pretty frisking flea, that I may be here and there and everywhere: O, I'll tickle the pretty wenches' plackets, I'll be amongst them i'faith! (1.iv)

And with explicit reference to the classical antecedents:

> *Pride.* I am Pride, I disdain to have any parents, I am like to Ovid's flea, I can creep into every corner of a wench: sometimes like a periwig I sit upon her brow; next like a necklace I hang about her neck; then like a fan of feathers, I kiss her lips; and then, turning myself to a wrought smock, do what I list. But fie, what a smell is here? I'll not speak a word more, unless the ground be perfumed and covered with cloth of arras. (2.iii)[42]

---

mock-heroic epyllion on the deeds of a flea, *Culex*, attributed to Vergil. For the much-disputed reception, see Glenn Most, "The 'Virgilian' *Culex*," *Homo Viator: Classical Essays for John Bramble*, ed. Michael Whitby, Philip Hardie, and Mary Whitby (Bristol: Bristol Classical P, and Oak Park, IL: Bochazy-Carducci Publishers, 1987), 199–209. If Goethe knew this text, as is likely, then it may have lent to the "Flohlied" some of its mock-heroic overtones.

[40] See the bibliography compiled by Hugo Hayn and Alfred N. Gotendorf, *Floh-Litteratur (de pulicibus) des In- und Auslandes vom XVI. Jahrhundert bis zur Neuzeit* (Berlin: n.p, 1913); see 26–27 for pamphlets claiming Goethe as the author of scurrilous flea-texts.

[41] The outlines of the tradition were admirably sketched by Marcel Françon, "Un motif de la poésie amoureuse au XVIᵉ siècle," *PMLA* 56.2 (1941): 307–36. Further examples, mainly from Spanish poets, were discovered independently of Françon (whose title could have been more explicit) by R. O. Jones, "Renaissance Butterfly, Mannerist Flea: Tradition and Change in Renaissance Poetry," *Modern Language Notes* 80 (1965): 166–84. H. David Brumble, "John Donne's 'The Flea': Some Implications of the Encyclopedic and Poetic Flea Traditions," *Critical Quarterly* 15.2 (1973): 147–54, includes his translation of the "Elegia de Pulice" (148–49). On Madame Des Roches, see Cathy Yandell, "Of Lice and Women: Rhetoric and Gender in *La Puce de Madame des Roches*," *Journal of Medieval and Renaissance Studies* 20 (1990): 123–35; and Ann Rosalind Jones, "Contentious Readings: Urban Humanism and Gender Difference in *La Puce de Madame Des-Roches* (1582)," *Renaissance Quarterly* 48 (1995): 109–28.

[42] Christopher Marlowe, *Doctor Faustus: A 1604-Version Edition*, ed. Michael Keefer (Peterborough, ON and Lewiston, NY: Broadview P, 1991), 25 and 47.

Because of an old argument, based primarily on narrow patriotism, German critics have always been unwilling to consider Marlowe's influence on Goethe,[43] thereby foregoing important opportunities for further insight. Notice that Marlowe has brought together two different aspects of the flea tradition, taking the erotic elements from the theme of the flea exploring a woman's body intimately and linking them with the emblematic tradition depicting the sin of pride as a flea. Before pursuing the theology of the flea more closely, we need to digress briefly to general insect theology in *Faust*.

That Mephistopheles is singing should give us pause. We might recollect that several scenes earlier, in the "Prologue in Heaven," the archangels Raphael, Gabriel, and Michael had been celebrating the glories of creation, individually and then in chorus. Naturally, Mephistopheles does not join the hymn of praise. All he brings are sour words, because, he claims, "ich kann nicht hohe Worte machen" (275). Mephistopheles is not courteous — he refuses to imitate what, from his viewpoint, is the empty flattery typical of the hypocrisy at any court. Unlike the fawning archangels, Mephistopheles presents himself as an independent being, and as the one with a genuine social conscience. Others may spend their heavenly eternity praising God, but Mephistopheles expresses his concern (feigned, to be sure) for suffering humanity: "Von Sonn' und Welten weiß ich nichts zu sagen, / Ich sehe nur, wie sich die Menschen plagen" (279–80). The scene depicts the sort of social criticism an honest subject of a realm might bring to the court of a tyrant, bearding tyranny at its centre for the sake of the common people. Never to be forgotten, however, is that his view of things, as well as his attitude towards them, is perverse, for God is neither tyrant nor collector of sycophants. Hence the Lord's calming response:

> Hast du mir weiter nichts zu sagen?
> Kommst du nur immer anzuklagen?
> Ist auf der Erde ewig dir nichts recht? (293–95)

Mild and gracious words fail to turn away wrath and only provoke Mephistopheles to further insolence: "Nein, Herr! Ich find' es dort, wie immer, herzlich schlecht" (296).[44]

Behind the dialogue, we catch glimpses of an ancient history that forms the background to the give and take. Despite his posturing, Mephistopheles knows that his exclusion from the harmony of the angelic

---

[43] See Otto Heller, *Faust and Faustus: A Study of Goethe's Relation to Marlowe* (repr., New York: Cooper Square, 1972).

[44] This pattern of heightened insolence on the part of subordinates may be seen elsewhere in Goethe's writings, e.g., in Werther's and Tasso's refusals to be calmed.

chorus is of his own doing, since he rebelled against the divine order. An important source of background information for the history of this rebellion will have been Milton's *Paradise Lost*.[45] Book 5 retells the story:

> but not so waked
> Satan, so call him now, his former name
> Is heard no more in heaven; he of the first,
> If not the first archangel, great in power,
> In favour and pre-eminence, yet fraught
> With envy against the Son of God, that day
> Honoured by his great Father, and proclaimed
> Messiah king anointed, could not bear
> Through pride that sight, and thought himself impaired.
> Deep malice thence conceiving and disdain,
> Soon as midnight brought on the dusky hour
> Friendliest to sleep and silence, he resolved
> With all his legions to dislodge, and leave
> Unworshipped, unobeyed the throne supreme
> Contemptuous, and his next subordinate
> Awakening, thus to him in secret spake. (5.656–73)

The blame is cast squarely on Satan's pride, which caused him to rebel and which will keep him unrepentant. In Satan's version of history, he is the shining hero and it is God who is the oppressor:

> What though the field be lost?
> All is not lost; the unconquerable will,
> And study of revenge, immortal hate,
> And courage never to submit or yield:
> And what is else not to be overcome?
> That glory never shall his wrath or might
> Extort from me. To bow and sue for grace

---

[45] For a brief survey of Milton's possible influence on *Faust*, see James Boyd, *Goethe's Knowledge of English Literature* (Oxford: Clarendon, 1932), 85–88. For some specific traces, see Momme Mommsen, "Zur Entstehung und Datierung einiger Faust-Szenen um 1800," *Euphorion* 47 (1953): 323–26. Inka Mülder-Bach, " 'Schlangenwandelnd': Geschichten vom Fall bei Milton und Goethe," in *Von der Natur zur Kunst zurück: Neue Beiträge zur Goethe-Forschung; Gotthart Wunberg zum 65. Geburtstag*, ed. Moritz Baßler, Christoph Brecht, and Dirk Niefanger (Tübingen: Max Niemeyer, 1997), 79–94, raises important questions about Miltonic influence upon "Mahomets Gesang" (1773), i.e., during the period when *Faust* was taking shape.

With suppliant knee, and deify his power,
Who from the terror of his arm so late
Doubted his empire, that were low indeed,
That were an ignominy and shame beneath
This downfall . . . (1.105–16)

This posture is the one we see Mephistopheles adopting in the "Prolog im Himmel," refusing to lend "glory" to God by yielding to His will. Just how we judge the resistance hinges upon our own ideology. Torn out of context, Satan's words could be applauded as grand determination to fight for one's cause, even when the cause is known to be lost from the very beginning. However, the contextual question must be: "Is the cause just?" The mistake that both Satan and Mephistopheles make is in confusing the claims of autonomy derived from possessive individualism with the goals of achieving power.

Unable to make his case in Heaven because he is unwilling to try, Mephistopheles takes the opportunity in an environment more hospitable to him, to rewrite the history of his fall from grace for the admiring audience in Hell. Like Milton's Satan, Mephistopheles uses language borrowed from the realm of political affairs in order to narrate the events. The "Flohlied" is his impudent rejoinder to the pro-God chroniclers.[46] As one might expect, all the negative aspects, such as envy and rebellion, are conveniently omitted. The allegory of the song attempts rather to inscribe Mephistopheles as the Lord's favorite courtier. The Son is only mentioned in passing and only in secondary position: in the text the flea is literally only four words and one line from the King in the text while the Son is fifteen words and three lines away. From the perspective of Mephistopheles, the important events are those pertaining to him. Cast in the language of the court, echoing the imagery of Milton's Satan, Mephistopheles tells of a heaven where he was not the outcast but instead the Lord's favorite. This is the ultimate power-fantasy of Mephistopheles, to be recognized as the Prime Minister in Heaven, to be outfitted in splendid garments and insignia of authority! The offhand reference to the Cross, which would in this version of history be merely a bauble, an ornament on the frock of Mephistopheles, mocks the Crucifixion and the displaced Son.

---

[46] Compare Jean Marjorie Burns and Laureen K. Nussbaum, "'Das Flohlied' in Goethe's *Faust*: Mephistopheles' Parable of the Politics of Heaven," *Papers on Language and Literature* 16.1 (1980): 81–89, who anticipate some of my analysis.

# The Body Politic

Each of the major epic poets had sought to reckon with his own age and its troubles by going back to a decisive founding moment in an earlier period and exploring its logic through the fate of the epic hero. Dante exposed the tragedy of Florentine history, which he experienced directly, as the enduring of flaws inherited from a pagan Rome.[47] In doing so, he was imitating and also transcending Vergil, who had previously traced the crises of the Roman Republic back to unresolved contradictions transmitted by the Trojans to Italy. For Goethe, living in the days of the Holy Roman Empire's ossification and demise, the early sixteenth century was crucial because that was when the schismatic national or dynastic differences that were destroying the political realm had also overtaken the Church through the Reformation and the Counter-Reformation. Instead of moving to greater unity, what had been one Roman Empire and then one, if loosely held together, Holy Roman Empire, was beginning to break up into modern nation states. The eighteenth century was dominated by fierce wars between Christians now organized along national lines, most notably in the conflict between Prussia and Austria.[48] As Goethe noted in *Dichtung und Wahrheit*, looking back from the vantage point of the eighteenth century, the death of Maximilian I represented an end to a unified Holy Roman Empire:

> Maximilianen hörten wir als einen Menschen- und Bürgerfreund loben, und daß von ihm prophezeit worden, er werde der letzte Kaiser aus einem deutschen Hause sein; welches denn auch leider eingetroffen, indem nach seinem Tode die Wahl nur zwischen dem König von Spanien, Karl dem Fünften, und dem König von Frankreich, Franz dem Ersten, geschwankt habe. Bedenklich fügte man hinzu, daß nun abermals eine solche Weissagung oder vielmehr Vorbedeutung umgehe: denn es sei augenfällig, daß nur noch Platz für das Bild eines Kaisers übrig bleibe; ein Umstand, der, obgleich zufällig scheinend, die Patriotischgesinnten mit Besorgnis erfülle. (HA 9:20–21)

What we see in "Auerbachs Keller" is a foreshadowing of how, over the next two centuries after Faust's era, the internal and external politics of

---

[47] Particularly suggestive is the discussion by Jeffrey T. Schnapp, *The Transfiguration of History at the Center of Dante's Paradise* (Princeton: Princeton UP, 1986).

[48] The issues and recent historical analyses of them are reviewed by Edgar Wolfrum, "Die Kultur des (Un-)Friedens vom 17. bis zum 19. Jahrhundert: Dimensionen einer Gesamtsicht," *Zeitschrift für Geschichtswissenschaft* 48 (2000): 894–908.

ostensibly Christian states would degenerate into endless warfare.[49] Two questions demand answers. What is Faust's role in this history? And what is the underlying cause of the tragedy of European history?

To begin with the obvious: everything shown in "Auerbachs Keller" has been produced for Faust. The history and politics in the scene should teach him something about the patterns that underlie the events of his age and of world history, but as before he seems entirely oblivious to what he is being shown. Faust is a silent witness, yet he cannot be an innocent bystander, for he is visibly inside the scene, present during the events. The pretense that he could somehow be perched outside of history as a disinterested observer is a delusion. Time and again, his mere presence will alter events, while he will remain unaware of or indifferent to his influence. More important, Faust has already made a choice that has grave consequences: he has allied himself with Mephistopheles.

According to Jochen Schmidt, "Auerbachs Keller" reflects primarily Goethe's reactionary response to the events of the French Revolution.[50] For him the scene betrays Goethe's negative assessment of the potential that democracy could function successfully.[51] Aside from the awkward matter that the depiction of the four companions was completed long before the French Revolution, Schmidt has left unconsidered the intentions of Mephistopheles and the influence of his leadership, indeed his very presence, upon the assembled group.

If we are to understand the logic of Goethe's political critique, we cannot operate with our contemporary models of government where representation is an arbitrary relationship such as the one proposed for linguistic signs by Saussure. Rather, we must keep in mind the model of politics and government that was consonant with the doctrine of correspondences as preserved in the image of the "body politic." Associated with the microcosm-macrocosm correspondence, this was an ancient analogy going back to Plato and Aristotle, but strongly reinforced for Christian thinkers by its deployment in the exposition in Paul's First Epistle to the Corinthians (Corinthians 12:14–26).[52] With the setting of the equivalence of

---

[49] Goethe summarized and indicted the emergence of national sentiments in the vague yet persistent rumors about the last emperor. For the historians' perspective, see Dietrich Kurze, "Nationale Regungen in der spätmittelalterlichen Prophetie," *Historische Zeitschrift* 202 (1966): 1–23; and Reeves, *The Influence of Prophecy in the Later Middle Ages*, 359–73.

[50] Jochen Schmidt, "Gesellschaftliche Unvernunft," 300.

[51] Schmidt, "Gesellschaftliche Unvernunft," 301.

[52] In addition to Leonard Barkan, *Nature's Work of Art: The Human Body as Image of the World* (New Haven and London: Yale UP, 1975), 61–115, see David

body = political realm, it was to be expected that the respective discourses on medicine and politics would fructify each other. Thus a troubled country could be spoken of as having an imbalance of the humors, as we can read in Robert Burton's *The Anatomy of Melancholy*:

> But whereas you shall see many discontents, common grievances, complaints, poverty, barbarism, beggary, plagues, wars, rebellions, seditions, mutinies, contentions, idleness, riot, epicurism, the land lie untilled, waste, full of bogs, fens, deserts, &c., cities decayed, base and poor towns, villages depopulated, the people squalid, ugly, uncivil; that kingdom, that country, must needs be discontent, melancholy, had a sick body, and had need to be reformed.[53]

Consequently, a good ruler could be compared to a careful physician, who kept the whole commonwealth regulated, healthy, and in good order. By contrast, we have observed Mephistopheles doing the opposite in the realm of "Auerbachs Keller." Rather than restoring the humoral balance in the four companions and in Faust, Mephistopheles uses wine to worsen their condition. As they drink, their internal harmony becomes less and less balanced, producing increasingly aggressive language and behavior. They were perhaps crude citizens at the outset, but Mephistopheles worsens their condition until they openly disrupt the political order and attempt to rebel. Normally within the framework of the discourse on the body politic, this would be reason to criticize him as an incompetent ruler, as a weak governor, but this judgment is sullied by the fact that political turmoil is the effect that Mephistopheles wanted to achieve. The legitimation of rebellion subverts the ideal of cosmic harmony and ultimately might exonerate his own first rebellion. The contradiction in rebelling is, as Karl Moor in Schiller's *Die Räuber* would discover, that it renders the position of the leader highly unstable, as his followers begin to imitate his actions.[54] Even — or especially — in Hell, where the Devil might be expected to reign supreme and secure, the subjects can be revolting, as Satan discovers to his undoing in *Paradise Lost*:

---

George Hale, *The Body Politic: A Political Metaphor in Renaissance English Literature* (The Hague and Paris: Mouton, 1971); Anthony J. Parel, *The Machiavellian Cosmos* (New Haven and London: Yale UP, 1992), 100–112, on humors and the body politic; and James Simpson, *Sciences and the Self in Medieval Poetry: Alan of Lille's* Anticlaudianus *and John Gower's* Confessio amantis (Cambridge: Cambridge UP, 1995), 92–133.

[53] Quoted by Hale, *The Body Politic*, 113–14.

[54] On the location of Moor in the pantheon with Satan, see Mario Praz, *The Romantic Agony*, trans. Angus Davidson (Oxford: Oxford UP, 1951), 57–58.

> a while he stood, expecting
> Their universal shout and high applause
> To fill his ear, when contrary he hears
> On all sides, from innumerable tongues
> A dismal universal hiss, the sound
> Of public scorn            (10.504–9)

The hissing monsters are creatures made in the semblance of Satan,[55] just as the violent carousers imitate the leadership and the ingratitude of Mephistopheles.

Mephistopheles' contempt for and treatment of the four companions has complex analogues in the epic system via his identification with Ulysses. Most revealing is the comparison with the speech by Ulysses in *Inferno* 26, in which he encourages the crew by appealing to their higher nature:

> "O brothers," I said, "who through a hundred thousand dangers have reached the west, to this so brief vigil of our senses that remains to us, choose not to deny experience, following the sun, of the world that has no people. Consider your origin: you were not made to live as brutes, but to pursue virtue and knowledge." (26.112–20)

Mephistopheles, on the other hand, plays upon the baser, animal nature of the four drinkers, encouraging their lusts for things of the flesh. They are roused to declaring themselves swine and cannibals and to attacking their "captain," instead of embarking on a quest for uncharted knowledge.

Both Ulysses and Mephistopheles see through people and thus can manipulate them with a blend of flattery and incitement. The turmoil Mephistopheles foments serves his purpose by leading the four into extremities of thought and deed. Their excesses are despicable and will never carry them to new countries; they only glimpse an illusory promised land. As an instigator of revolt, Mephistopheles betrays the ideals of the good governor and wise leader, who must be mindful of the group's well-being. A crew or a country led by Mephistopheles is doomed to shipwreck, just as Dante's Ulysses steers his ship to disaster:

> We rejoiced, but soon our joy was turned to grief, for from the new land a whirlwind rose and struck the forepart of the ship.

---

[55] Cf. C. M. Bowra, *From Virgil to Milton* (London: MacMillan and New York: St Martin's P, 1967). On Satan's shortcomings in this regard, see also Steadman, *Milton and the Renaissance Hero* (Oxford: Clarendon, 1967), 78–107. Behind Satan stands the figure of Lucan's Julius Caesar: William Blissett, "Caesar and Satan," *Journal of the History of Ideas* 18 (1957): 221–32.

> Three times it whirled her round with all the waters, and the fourth
> time it lifted the stern aloft and plunged the prow below us, as pleased
> Another, till the sea closed over us. (26.136–42)

To the keen observer, it should be apparent that Mephistopheles is taking
a course that will bring Faust into peril, not into a safe haven. Those who
recall the fate measured out to Ulysses by Dante will also anticipate that
Mephistopheles too will find his plans dashed to ruin at the end of *Faust
II*.[56]

## The Trojan War: To Be Continued

Although the history of the Trojan War is pervasive elsewhere in the text,
only one small detail explicitly links "Auerbachs Keller" to the war that
began epic history. The tiny detail has enormous consequences. It comes
via Frosch's pronouncement: "Mein Leipzig lob' ich mir! / Es ist ein klein
Paris, und bildet seine Leute" (2171–72). The usual assumption is that the
lines are meant to praise the city:

> In his description of Leipzig in 1768 the city is called "Paris in minia-
> ture," just as Trömer had called Berlin "Small-Paris" [1745]. In 1787 the
> work *Free Observations about Berlin, Leipzig and Prague* it says "Leipzig
> is doubtless one of the loveliest cities in Germany, therefore is always
> called little Paris." Goethe writes Easter 1766 to his sister, "On se croirait
> presque à Paris" and later (to Fritsch, 9 March 1790): "Leipzig is also
> known as little Paris," certainly recalling this passage, which is ironic and
> still missing in *Urfaust*.[57]

But why should a comparison with Paris flatter another city? Were the
staunch Protestants of Saxony completely pleased at being compared to a
citadel of Roman Catholicism?[58] Worth noting is also that in the odd

---

[56] Out of the immense secondary literature on the voyage of Ulysses, see John
A. Scott, "Inferno XXVI: Dante's Ulysses," *Lettere Italiane* 23.2 (1971): 145–86;
Richard Kay, "Two Pairs of Tricks: Ulysses and Guido in Dante's *Inferno*
XXVI–XXVII," *Quaderni d'italianistica* 1.2 (1980): 107–24; Werner Ross, "Der
Held in der Hölle: Ein Versuch über den Odysseus-Gesang des Inferno," *Deutsches
Dante-Jahrbuch* 64 (1989): 61–74; and Edward Peters, "The Voyage of Ulysses
and the Wisdom of Solomon: Dante and the *vitium curiositatis*," *Majestas* 7
(1999): 75–87.

[57] Witkowski, *Kommentar und Erläuterungen*, 233.

[58] On Paris as a focal point of opposition to Lutheranism, see R. J Knecht,
*Renaissance Warrior and Patron: The Reign of Francis I* (Cambridge: Cambridge
UP, 1994), 156–64; and Nicholls, "Heresy and Protestantism, 1520–1542."

amalgamation of myth, legend, epic, and history the genealogy of the two cities alludes directly to an ancient conflict, for it was believed that the "Franks" were descended from the Trojans whereas the "Saxons" were descended from the Greeks.[59] Thus the political and theological rivalry between the two centers could be taken as another manifestation of the deep-seated antagonisms that threatened the integrity of the Holy Roman Empire. Significantly, it is Frosch who quotes the "political song" about how the Empire is not holding together and also raises the specter of competition by comparing Paris and Leipzig. The use of the adjective "garstig" is an aesthetic qualifier used to express opinions about what is ugly and what is not. All such comparisons are in some degree invidious and remind us that ultimately any mention of the name "Paris" when preferences are being expressed must also evoke the famous judgment made by the son of Priam, the choice that sparked the Trojan War.

Making such connections depends, as Goethe emphasized, on the ability to see simultaneously the beginning and end of three thousand years. However, identifying traces of the Trojan War through the ages can be misleading unless the mythological prologue is also recalled. The myths tell how the Trojans were largely responsible for their own downfall because they reneged on their contractual obligation to Poseidon, who had helped erect the city's walls. When the work was done, they refused to pay him. In due course, he avenged himself by having two sea serpents crush Laocoön and his sons, opening the way for bringing the wooden horse filled with Greeks into Troy. All of this comes to mind when, at the end of his life, Faust is attempting to win land from the sea — attempting to cheat Poseidon. There has been no progress and the same human failings that led to the Trojan War continue to shape history. That is why Goethe could, with a straight face, insist that the unities of time and place have been strictly observed in *Faust*.

---

[59] Borchardt, *German Antiquity in Renaissance Myth* (Baltimore and London: The Johns Hopkins UP, 1971), 24, and *passim*; Jörn Garber, "Trojaner — Römer — Franken — Deutsche: 'Nationale' Abstammungstheorien im Vorfeld der Nationalstaatsbildung," in *Nation und Literatur in der Frühen Neuzeit: Akten des 1. Internationalen Osnabrücker Kongresses zur Kulturgeschichte der Frühen Neuzeit*, ed. Klaus Garber (Tübingen: Niemeyer, 1989), 108–63.

# 6: *Faust* as a Christian Epic

WELL-INFORMED CHRISTIANS IN THE eighteenth century augmented their knowledge of Scripture by a library of commentaries whose messages were conveyed in sermons, hymns, festivals and holy days, and religious art and concordances, as well as through conversation. Knowledge of at least the commonplaces was taken for granted. In the case of Goethe, we can presume a detailed knowledge of Scripture, since he has left us with a vivid account of his interest in the Bible. As a young boy, he determined that he would have to learn Hebrew in order to be able to understand the Bible fully:

> Ich eröffnete daher meinem Vater die Notwendigkeit, Hebräisch zu ler-
> nen, und betrieb sehr lebhaft seine Einwilligung: denn ich hatte noch
> einen höhern Zweck. Überall hörte ich sagen, daß zum Verständnis des
> Alten Testaments so wie des Neuen die Grundsprachen nötig wären. Das
> letzte las ich ganz bequem, weil die sogenannten Evangelien und
> Episteln, damit es ja auch Sonntags nicht an Übung fehle, nach der
> Kirche rezitiert, übersetzt und einigermaßen erklärt werden mußten.
> Ebenso dachte ich es nun auch mit dem Alten Testamente zu halten, das
> mir wegen seiner Eigentümlichkeit ganz besonders von jeher zugesagt
> hatte.[1]

A tutor was hired and soon enough the pupil began putting endless questions about the meaning of this or that place. The exasperated Dr. Albrecht recommended a massive German translation of an English annotated Bible, which appeared between 1749 and 1770 in 19 volumes.[2] The English annotations had been augmented by the German translators and editors, so that a great deal of information was conveniently available at

---

[1] Johann Wolfgang von Goethe, *Werke: Hamburger Ausgabe in 14 Bänden*, ed. Erich Trunz (Munich: C. H. Beck, 1981), 9:124. This "Hamburger Ausgabe" will henceforth be cited as HA.

[2] According to the notes in the *Hamburger Ausgabe* (9: 682) the translation appeared in nineteen volumes (1749–70); by 1762 nine volumes had been published. Apparently, each page gives Scripture at the top, then the commentaries by the English theologians, followed by the commentaries of the German theologians, who were careful to distinguish Lutheran positions from the Calvinist-Anglican ones.

one time (HA 9:128–29).[3] The typological reconciliation of the Old and the New Testaments was one of the main reasons why such concordances had to exist, and through the network of annotations Goethe would have acquired the tactics of comparing places so as to be able to harmonize their meaning.[4] Just this technique is referred to by Goethe in the episode when he and Susanne von Klettenberg attempted to make sense of the hermetic-alchemical writings. In order to orient himself in Welling's *Opus mago-cabbalisticum*, Goethe followed the procedure of annotation and cross-referencing:

> Meine vorzüglichste Bemühung an diesem Buche war, die dunklen Hinweisungen, wo der Verfasser von einer Stelle auf die andere deutet und dadurch das, was er verbirgt, zu enthüllen verspricht, aufs genauste zu bemerken und am Rande die Seitenzahlen solcher sich einander aufklären sollenden Stellen zu bezeichnen. (HA 9:342)

Goethe was "bibelfest," solid in the Bible and could both quote and allude freely.[5] Nor did these interests of Goethe's come to an end. He continued to follow the discussions around the interpretation and translation of the Bible closely, and there was much to ponder as theology was being transformed through the critical onslaught of the Enlightenment.[6]

---

[3] The attention that Goethe has lavished upon this episode is noteworthy, particularly the contrast between the schoolmaster reading Lucian and the pupil studying the edifying Scriptures. Surely the passage alludes to Augustine's famous account of how he almost lost his soul through too much reading of the pagan classics, notably the story of Dido's death.

[4] Or fail to harmonize them, as Herbert Schöffler points out in his informative article, "Der junge Goethe und das englische Bibelwerk," in *Deutscher Geist im 18. Jahrhundert: Essays zur Geistes- und Religionsgeschichte* (Göttingen: Vandenhoeck + Ruprecht, 1967), 97–113, and 309. He indicates how systematically the German, *Lutheran* commentators distanced themselves from their English counterparts, and suggests that this might have been an impulse for the young Goethe's own attempt at a syncretic faith.

[5] See Hanna Fischer-Lamberg, "Das Bibelzitat beim jungen Goethe," in *Gedenkschrift für Ferdinand Josef Schneider (1879–1954)*, ed. Karl Bischoff (Weimar: Hermann Böhlaus Nachfolger, 1956). 201–21; Willy Schottroff, "Goethe als Bibelwissenschaftler," *Evangelische Theologie* 44 (1984): 463–85; and the contributions to the volume *Goethe und die Bibel*, ed. Johannes Anderegg and Edith Anna Kunz (Stuttgart: Deutsche Bibelgesellschaft, 2005).

[6] On Goethe's abiding interest in the history of Christianity, see Peter Meinhold, *Goethe zur Geschichte des Christentums* (Freiburg im Breisgau and Munich: Verlag Karl Alber, 1958). A brief overview of the developing historical critique of Scripture is provided by Walter Sparn, "Vernünftiges Christentum: Über die geschichtliche Aufgabe der theologischen Aufklärung im 18. Jahrhundert in

# Faust in Hell

The strategies for assimilating history, both secular and scriptural, to epic were well established by the time Goethe decided the Faust material would sustain an epic. Allegorization and typological interpretation could find in the struggle for Faust's soul a parallel to the epic striving of heroes such as Achilles, Aeneas, and Adam. One detail from the Faust legends was especially fortuitous: Faust's expressed wish to know more about hell. A descent into the underworld was a standard topic in the epic system.[7] In the chapbook version, Faustus is taken to see hell. Or perhaps he only imagines that he has seen it; the text hints that he never actually made the descent.[8] Marlowe cleverly transposed hell to the stage:

> Faustus. Where are you damn'd?
> Meph. In hell.
> Faustus. How comes it then that thou art out of hell?
> Meph. Why this is hell, nor am I out of it (act 1, scene 3, 74–76)

Without even being aware of it, Faustus and the audience have been instantly transported to hell, here and now on the stage.[9]

Generally, the assumption is that Goethe postponed the standard descent into the underworld until the second part of the drama.[10] But Goethe adhered to Faust material more closely than that. The first hint in the text about where hell can be found in *Faust I* comes when the wine spills and Siebel shouts "Helft! Feuer! Helft! Die Hölle brennt!" (2299) His words are given increased weight with the threat by Mephistopheles: "Für diesmal war es nur ein Tropfen Fegefeuer" (2301). Are these references to Hell and to purgatory merely incidental? Or is something hidden

---

Deutschland," in *Wissenschaften im Zeitalter der Aufklärung: Aus Anlaß des 250 jährigen Bestehens des Verlages Vandenhoeck & Ruprecht*, ed. Rudolf Vierhaus (Göttingen: Vandenhoeck & Ruprecht, 1985), 18–57.

[7] Ronald R. Macdonald, *The Burial-Places of Memory: Epic Underworlds in Vergil, Dante, and Milton* (Amherst: U of Massachusetts P, 1987).

[8] August Kühne, ed., *Das älteste Faustbuch: Wortgetreuer Abdruck der editio princeps des Spies'schen Faustbuchs vom Jahr 1587* (repr. Amsterdam: Rodopi, 1970), 54–58.

[9] On this move and its influence on Milton, see Neil Forsyth, *The Satanic Epic* (Princeton: Princeton UP, 2003), 152–55; 217–38. Forsyth's comments on Milton's puns on *dis-* remind us that in German *höll* and *hell* are near rhymes. The space in the theatre that must be brightly lit is the stage.

[10] Erich Franz, "Die verlorene Hades-Szene in Goethes Faust II," *Germanisch-Romanische Monatsschrift 38* (1957): 343–49.

in plain sight here? As far as I know, the only critic to suggest that "Auerbachs Keller in Leipzig" may be a version of Hell has been R. M. Browning in his discussion of the "Urfaust."[11] Without further amplification, Browning's observation has had little influence, but I am going to take it as my provocative working hypothesis that this scene is set in the underworld, in a version of Hell.

The first obstacle to accepting such a view lies in the scene's title. "Auerbachs Keller in Leipzig" seems so definite and so solidly based upon the historical evidence of the Faust legend and the autobiographical support from Goethe's student years in Leipzig that deconstructing this signpost is a challenge. Even today most readers immediately confirm the "reality" of the scene by referring to the restaurant of the same name that tourists still frequent when they visit Leipzig. The facticity of a "Leipzig" and of an "Auerbachs Keller" is incontrovertible, but accepting that does not exhaust their potential for disclosing meanings. For instance, what is implied by the comparison of "Leipzig" to "little Paris"? In an odd corner, Goethe left a clue that opens up a theological dimension of a name that in the eighteenth century was already a byword for licentiousness. Goethe's translation of the autobiography of Benvenuto Cellini conveys a starkly different epithet for Paris:

> Als nun einmal zwei Edelleute bloß als Zuschauer hereindringen wollten, tat ihnen jener Türhüter den stärksten Widerstand. Da sah der Richter hin und rief: Stille, stille! Satan, fort, stille! und zwar klingen diese Worte im Französichen folgendermaßen: paix, paix, Satan, allez paix. Ich, der ich die französische Sprache sehr wohl gelernt hatte, erinnerte mich bei diesem Spruche eines Ausdrucks welchen Dante gebraucht, als er mit Virgil seinem Meister in die Tore der Hölle tritt; und ich verstand nun den dunkeln Vers; denn Dante war mit Giotto dem Maler in Frankreich und am längsten in *Paris* gewesen, und wahrscheinlich hat er auch *diesen Ort, den man wohl eine Hölle nennen kann,* besucht, und hat diesen hier gewöhnlichen Ausdruck, da er gut französisch verstand, auch in seinem Gedichte angebracht. Nun schien es mir sonderbar daß man diese Stelle niemals verstanden hat. Wie ihn denn überhaupt seine Ausleger wohl manches sagen lassen, was er weder gedacht noch geträumt hat.[12]

Granted, Goethe did not translate Cellini's autobiography until the mid 1790s, but he had read it earlier and was obviously fascinated by him (that

---

[11] Robert M. Browning, "On the Structure of the *Urfaust*," *PMLA* 68 (1953): 458–95; here, 471.

[12] Goethe, *Sämtliche Werke nach Epochen seines Schaffens: Münchner Ausgabe,* 7:306–7; my emphasis.

Cellini was another famous melancholic may have been a factor).[13] Frosch's words were already in *Faust: Ein Fragment* from a decade earlier. However, one detail does suggest that Goethe may have left us a clue in how to read the earlier text. The nature and quality of Goethe's translation needs closer scrutiny and comparison with the original:

> On one occasion, when two gentlemen were pushing their way in as spectators, and the porter was opposing them with violence, the judge raised his voice, and spoke the following words precisely as I heard them: "Keep peace, Satan, begone, and hold your tongue." These words in the French tongue sound as follows: *Phe phe, Satan, phe phe, alé, phe!* Now I had learned the French tongue well; and on hearing this sentence, the meaning of that phrase used by Dante came into my memory, when he and his master Virgil entered the doors of Hell. Dante and the painter Giotto were together in France, and particularly in the city of Paris, where owing to the circumstances I have just described, the hall of justice may be truly called a hell. Dante, then, who also understood French well, made use of the phrase in question, and it has struck me as singular that this interpretation has never yet been put upon the passage; indeed, it confirms my opinion that the commentators make him say things which never came into his head.[14]

The words "und ich verstand nun den dunkeln Vers" were evidently added by Goethe in the translation, since there is nothing to correspond to them in the original; he has discreetly melded his voice with that of the narrator.[15] There can be no doubt that Goethe had set the equation of Leipzig = Paris = Hell. Although hidden in an odd corner, the clue tells us where the missing hell is located. When the stage direction says "Auerbachs Keller in Leipzig," it is repeating what Marlowe's Mephastophilis had first said: "This is hell."

---

[13] See the informative article by Dorothy Koenigsberger, "*Leben des Benvenuto Cellini*: Goethe, Cellini and Transformation," *European History Quarterly* 22 (1992): 7–37.

[14] Benvenuto Cellini, *The Life of Benvenuto Cellini, Written by Himself*, trans. John Addington Symonds (London: Phaidon, 1960), 291–92.

[15] Noted by Emil Sulger-Gebing, *Goethe und Dante: Studien zur vergleichenden Literaturgeschichte* (Berlin: Verlag von Alexander Duncker, 1907), 4–5. On Goethe's practice in translating Cellini, see Vito R. Giustiniani, "Goethes Übersetzungen aus dem Italienischen," in *"Italien in Germanien": Deutsche Italien Rezeption von 1750–1850: Akten des Symposiums der Stiftung Weimarer Klassik, Herzogin Anna Amalia Bibliothek, Schiller-Museum, 24.-26. März 1994*, ed. Frank-Rutger Hausmann, with Michael Knoche and Harro Stammerjohann (Tübingen: Gunter Narr, 1996), 275–99; here, 287–90.

# The Divine Cellar

But why would it be important to stress that the tavern is simultaneously a cellar? The implications arise from Goethe's reading of Origen and of Origen's allegorization of the Song of Songs. A series of articles in the last decades have established beyond any doubt that Goethe had been reading Origen while writing *Faust*. The primary emphasis in these studies has been upon implications of the influence for the drama as a whole, particularly upon the question of apocatastasis ("the return of all things," a theory suggesting that all creatures, including the damned and the demons, shall be brought into the divine embrace at the end of time) and the possible salvation of Satan.[16] These weighty matters would have been in Goethe's mind from when he began to work on *Faust* until the very end; they were brought to his attention early through his reading of Gottfried Arnold's *Unparteyische Kirchen- und Ketzer-Historie von Anfang des neuen Testaments biß auff das Jahr Christi 1688* (1699).[17] But there was another, smaller, project that would have drawn Goethe to Origen, one that has gone relatively unremarked. This was the translation of the "Song of

---

[16] Elizabeth M. Wilkinson, "The Theological Basis of Faust's *Credo*," *German Life and Letters* NS 10 (1947): 229–39; Arthur Henkel, "Das Ärgernis Faust," in *Versuche zu Goethe: Festschrift für Erich Heller; Zum 65. Geburtstag am 27.3.1976*, ed. Volker Dürr and Géza von Molnár (Heidelberg: Lothar Stiehm, 1976), 282–304; Renate Knoll, "Zu Goethes erster Erwähnung des Origenes," in *Geist und Zeichen: Festschrift für Arthur Henkel, zu seinem sechzigsten Geburtstag dargebracht von Freunden und Schülern*, ed. Herbert Anton, Bernhard Gajek, and Peter Pfaff (Heidelberg: Carl Winter Universitätsverlag, 1977), 192–207; Dieter Breuer, "Origenes im 18. Jahrhundert in Deutschland," *Seminar: A Journal of Germanic Studies* 21.1 (1985): 1–30. For a stern critique, see Rolf Christian Zimmermann, "Goethes 'Faust' und die 'Wiederbringung aller Dinge': Kritische Bemerkungen zu einem unkritisch aufgenommenen Interpretationsversuch," *Goethe-Jahrbuch* 111 (1994): 171–85. Dieter Breuer offers his final word on the topic in "Bergschluchten: Die Schlußszene von Goethes *Faust*," *Ernst Meister Gesellschaft Jahrbuch* 2002 [2003]: 75–101.

[17] Well-known is Goethe's own testimony in *Dichtung und Wahrheit* (HA 9:350) about Arnold's influence. A good survey of Arnold's influence on Goethe is Meinhold, *Goethe zur Geschichte des Christentums*, 3–10. The standard study on Arnold is Erich Seeberg, *Gottfried Arnold: Die Wissenschaft und die Mystik seiner Zeit: Studien zur Historiographie und zur Mystik* (1923; repr., Darmstadt: Wissenschaftliche Buchgesellschaft, 1964). On Arnold's reception, see Eitel Timm, *Ketzer und Dichter: Lessing, Goethe, Thomas Mann und die Postmoderne in der Tradition des Häresiegedankens* (Heidelberg: Carl Winter, 1989).

Songs," which Goethe undertook between August and the beginning of October 1775.[18] The allegorical reading of the "Song of Songs" by Origen was integral to Goethe's conceptualization of the "Rattenlied" and of "Auerbachs Keller in Leipzig." In Origen's allegory, the "wine cellar" is given spiritual meanings, beginning with the gloss on "Bring ye me into the house of wine":

> It is still the Bride who speaks, but her words are now addressed, I think, to the friends and intimates of the Bridegroom, whom she is asking to bring her into the house of gladness, where wine is drunk and a banquet prepared. For she who had already seen the royal chamber desires now to be admitted also to the royal feast, and to enjoy the wine of gladness. . . .
>
> The Church, therefore, or the individual soul who longs for the things that are perfect, hastens to enter this house of wine and to enjoy the teachings of wisdom and the mysteries of knowledge as the sweetness of a banquet and the gladness of wine.
>
> We must however recognize the fact that besides this wine which is pressed from the dogmas of truth and mingled in Wisdom's bowl, there is another wine of an opposite nature with which sinners and those who accept the harmful dogmas of false learning wickedly get drunk.[19]

From Origen on, the eroticism of the "Song of Songs" had been assimilated hermeneutically by presupposing that it was the story of the union of the Church to Christ or the Soul and the Word.

Such an abstract approach could not entirely repress the erotic elements, and so the bond between spiritual and carnal love continually threatened to slip completely into an emphasis upon the body.[20] The

---

[18] *Der junge Goethe: Neu bearbeitete Ausgabe in fünf Bänden: Band 5: Januar-Oktober 1775*, ed. Hanna Fischer-Lamberg (Berlin and New York: Walter de Gruyter, 1973), 487. Essential is James Simpson, *Goethe and Patriarchy: Faust and the Fates of Desire* (Oxford: European Humanities Research Centre, University of Oxford, 1998). See also Otto Pniower, "Goethes Faust und das Hohe Lied," *Goethe-Jahrbuch* 13 (1892): 181–98; Benno Badt, "Goethe als Übersetzer des Hohenliedes," *Neue Jahrbücher für Philologie und Paedagogik* 51 (1881): 346–57; John Baildam, *Paradisal Love: Johann Gottfried Herder and the Song of Songs* (Sheffield: Sheffield Academic P, 1999); and my "Typology and History in the 'Rattenlied' (*Faust I*)," *Goethe Yearbook* 10 (2001): 65–83. As well as in Scripture, Goethe encountered the Song of Songs in the *Divine Comedy*, see Paul Priest, "Dante and the 'Song of Songs,'" *Studi Danteschi* 49 (1972): 79–115.

[19] Origenes, *The Song of Songs: Commentary and Homilies*, trans. R. P. Lawson (Westminster, MD: Newman P, and London: Longman, Greens, 1957), 186–87.

[20] See Ann W. Astell, *The Song of Songs in the Middle Ages* (Ithaca and London: Cornell UP, 1990).

tension between the two modes of love was the essence of the medieval discussions in *minne* poetry, of which Frosch gives a snippet:

> Schwing' dich auf, Frau Nachtigall,
> Grüß' mir mein Liebchen zehentausendmal. (2101–2)

Siebel interrupts him and brings the tone down to the carnal:

> Ein braver Kerl von echtem Fleisch und Blut
> Ist für die Dirne viel zu gut. (2115–16)

Paralleling Siebel's inversion on Frosch's song, the "Rattenlied" will strip the body of all its spiritual potential and portray it as dross matter. The subjunctive of the refrain "Als hätte sie Lieb im Leibe" challenges the validity of the Christian allegory and its assumption that the eros described so lushly in the "Song of Songs" was a reflex of divine, spiritual love. Look again, argues the "Rattenlied": no love, no mercy, no ascent, no salvation are apparent in the world, only greed, fear, suffering, and agony. For the allegorist, human desires are the spark of love, leading to the spiritual union with God. For the literalist, there is only lust, culminating in death. In the allegorical reading of the "Song of Songs," everything that has been provided in the world is designed with a view to divine wedding, the marriage of the Bride and the Bridegroom. The wine in the cellar is indeed a dowry, since it is the gift of wisdom to the Bride, as well as part of the feast.[21] Without any spiritual or symbolic values, everything served in the "Rattenlied" might as well be poison, since it can do no more than feed the body and thereby contribute, in the long run, to death.[22] For the Bride, all temptations are good if and when they draw her towards happy reunion. For the Rat, temptations bring no translation and release: they are simply the impulses of the body.

The full extent to which the "Song of Songs" permeates *Faust* cannot be mapped here, but a hint is given in "Wald und Höhle" where both Faust and Mephistopheles fall into the language of the allegorical tradition:

---

[21] On the mystical tradition of wine, see Hans Lewy, *Sobria Ebrietas: Untersuchungen zur Geschichte der antiken Mystik* (Gießen: Verlag von Alfred Töpelmann, 1929) with a discussion of Origen, 122–28; and Florence M. Weinberg, *The Wine & the Will: Rabelais's Bacchic Christianity* (Detroit: Wayne State UP, 1972), 89–90. Without Weinberg's analysis, I would never have seen Origen's influence in the "Rattenlied."

[22] On the theology of the Fall as tantamount to the introduction of a poison into Paradise, establishing a congruence between the onset of mortality and the beginning of sexual awareness, see Arthur Groos, *Romancing the Grail: Genre, Science, and Quest in Wolfram's* Parzival (Ithaca and London: Cornell UP, 1995), 165–69, and the sources he cites.

FAUST
Ja, ich beneide schon den Leib des Herrn
Wenn ihre Lippen ihn indes berühren.
MPEHISTOPHELES
Gar wohl, mein Freund! Ich habe Euch oft beneidet
Ums Zwillingspaar, das unter Rosen weidet. (3334–37)[23]

Following this and other tracks would lead us inevitably to a reinterpretation of the scene "Kerker," where Margarete would be seen to be typed as a "Bride of Christ."

# "Choosing a Pope"

Brander's resolution "Wir wollen einen Papst erwählen" (2097) has been read as a colorful detail taken from the seamier side of student life, referring to coarse drinking rituals.[24] Commentators have been torn between exposing the bawdy and bowdlerizing the text. That the line alludes to the testicular inspection has met with resistance or been passed over in silence.[25] Kuno Fischer rejected the hypothesis: "It would be entirely wrong to think here with Goedeke and Loeper of the story of Pope Joan and the masculine quality of the Pope who is to be selected (the 'habet, habet') since in the student's papacy the sole determining quality is none other than the excessive drinking."[26] Indeed, it is difficult to see what

---

[23] Mephistopheles' words allude to the text of the Song of Songs but Faust's allude to the allegorical reading.

[24] Friedrich Kluge, "Wir wollen einen Papst erwählen (Goethes Faust I V. 2098)" first published in the *Beilage* to the *Allgemeine Zeitung* No. 137 (1895): 5–6; repr. in his *Bunte Blätter: Kulturgeschichtliche Vorträge und Aufsätze* (Freiburg im Breisgau: J. Bielefelds Verlag, 1910), 101–8.

[25] Karl Goedeke, "[Review]: *Faust: Eine Tragödie von Goethe*, Mit Einleitung und erläuternden Anmerkungen von G. von Loeper. Berlin. Gustav Hempel. 1870. LXIV und 173, und LXXX und 272 S. 8°," *Göttingsche gelehrte Anzeigen* 10 (6 March 1872): 361–77; here, 375.

[26] Kuno Fischer, *Goethes Faust*, ed. Victor Michels, vol. 3: *Die Erklärung des Goetheschen Faust nach der Reihenfolge seiner Szenen: Erster Teil* (Heidelberg: Carl Winter, 1913), 126. Adolf Trendlenburg, in his book *Goethes Faust erklärt* (Berlin and Leipzig: Vereinigung wissenschaftlicher Verleger Walter de Gruyter, 1922), 293, seems to find it plausible and also points out that Goethe would have been able to read the story in Gottfried Arnold. For the sources and reception of the notorious fable, see J. P. Kirsch, "Joan, Popess," in *The Catholic Encyclopedia*, ed. Charles G. Herbermann, et al. (New York: Robert Appleton, 1910), 8:407–9; Klaus Herbers, "Die Päpstin Johanna: Ein kritischer Forschungsbericht,"

purpose such an allusion might serve.[27] Others have skirted around the issue of just what the drinking ritual entailed. Some commentators cited sources pointing to activities of the sort that one might encounter in rowdy fraternity houses to the present day.[28] Nothing serious seems to happen. Whether the line refers to excessive, competitive beer-drinking or not, the jest is that once again the coarse desire of the gluttons gets no direct satisfaction. More distantly, the allusion to the testicular inspection that supposedly was instituted after the embarrassing incident of a female pope hints ever so indelicately at Origen's biography; more on that later.

The most obvious allusion in "choosing a Pope" remains to be considered, namely to the theological controversies of the sixteenth century about who should have the authority to carry out such an election or if indeed it could *be* an election. This was a fundamental issue in the Reformation, with far-reaching political consequences. Luther took the position that all Christians began as equals in faith and that therefore officers of the Church were not elevated as Christians by virtue of their office:

> Dan was ausz der tauff krochen ist / das mag sich rumen / das es schon priester Bischoff vnd Bapst geweyhet sey / ob wol nit einem yglichen zympt / solch ampt zu vben. Dan weyl wir alle gleich priester sein / muß sich niemant selb erfur thun / vnd sich vnterwinden / an vnszer bewilligen vnd erwelen / das zuthun / des wir alle gleychen gewalt haben.[29]

---

*Historisches Jahrbuch der Görres-Gesellschaft* 108 (1988): 174–94; and the entry "Päpstin Johanna" in Elisabeth Frenzel, *Stoffe der Weltliteratur: Ein Lexikon dichtungsgeschichtlicher Längsschnitte* (Stuttgart: Alfred Kröner, 1988), 584–86. Goethe might have also known either Boccaccio's *De claris mulieribus* (ca. 1370–75) or Hans Sachs's *Die Historia von Johanna Anglica der Päpstin* (1558).

[27] Unless one could develop an argument about the implications of "Pope Joan" for the story of Margarete, especially the detail of the legendary female Pope's unexpected public delivery of a child, which led to her death by stoning, or the theme of a pact with the Devil. A feminist approach that could prove useful for such a perspective is Elisabeth Gössmann, "Die 'Päpstin Johanna': Zur vor- und nachreformatorischen Rezeption ihrer Gestalt," in *Eva — Verführerin oder Gottes Meisterwerk? Philosophie- und theologiegeschichtliche Frauenforschung*, ed. Dieter R. Bauer and Elisabeth Gössmann (Stuttgart: Akademie der Diözese Rottenburg-Stuttgart, 1987), 143–66.

[28] Witkowski, *Kommentar und Erläuterungen*, vol. 2 of *Goethes Faust* (1910; repr., Leiden: E. J. Brill, 1950), 232.

[29] Martin Luther, "An den christlichen Adel deutscher Nation von des christlichen Standes Besserung," in *Studienausgabe*, ed. Hans-Ulrich Delius, with Helmar Junghans, Joachim Rogge, and Günther Wartenberg (Berlin: Evangelische Verlagsanstalt, 1979–92), 2:96–167; here, 100.

Complementing this was the idea that any group of Christians would have the authority to elect officers of the Church from their midst. In a famous passage, Luther imagined what might happen if a group of Christians were set into an ungoverned realm:

> Vnd das ichs noch klerer sag / Wen ein heufflin fromer Christen leye(n) wurden gefangen vnnd in ein wusteney gesetzt / die nit bey sich hetten einen geweyheten priester von eine(m) Bischoff / vnn wurden alda der sachen eynisz / erweleten eynen vnter yhn / er were ehlich odder nit / vnd befihlen ym das ampt zu teuffen / mesz halten / absoluieren / vnd predigenn / der were warhafftig ein priester / als ob yhn alle Bischoffe vnnd Bepste hetten geweyhet.[30]

Goethe, who was familiar with the relevant discourse on Church-State relations from his dissertation, may well have known this passage explicitly, as well as its gist. There does seem to be in the assumption by the four companions of their right to "choose a pope" an extended parody of Luther's analogy. The four are isolated from the rest of society and do propose to elect a pope.

However, they fail to translate their equality and democracy as a community of Christians into a viable order. As their jostling for power over each other indicates, they are not the "priests of equal standing" envisioned by Luther. They wrangle amongst themselves and finally abrogate their authority by submitting to the authority of Mephistopheles. He will become their "high priest," the one whose deceptions replicate the abuses of power Luther had condemned when attacking the corrupt Papacy. Shortly after he arrives, Mephistopheles is declared by Siebel to be a splendid patron, "Ein pfiffiger Patron!" Following his lead, they all join in with the refrain and then celebrate him:

> FROSCH
> Bravo! Bravo! das war schön!
> SIEBEL
> So soll es jedem Floh ergehn!
> BRANDER
> Spitzt die Finger und packt sie fein!
> ALTMAYER
> Es lebe die Freiheit! Es lebe der Wein! (2241–44)

Quite literally, they have "elected" Mephistopheles to be their leader; the Devil is the only version of pope permitted in Hell. Invigorated by his rousing song, they are ready to head off to battle — against fleas.

---

[30] Luther, "An den christlichen Adel deutscher Nation von des christlichen Standes Besserung," 100.

The identification of Mephistopheles as the "pope" is confirmed by an intricate intertextual allusion. Let me quote again from the autobiography of Cellini as translated by Goethe: "Da sah der Richter hin und rief: Stille, stille! Satan, fort, stille! und zwar klingen diese Worte im französischen folgendermaßen: paix, paix, Satan, allez paix."[31] The reference is to one of the most famous cruxes in Dante's *Inferno*, the opening lines of canto 7: "'Pape Satàn, pape Satàn aleppe!' Plutus began with a clucking voice" (7.1–2). As the narrator in Cellini's autobiography observes, the strange language of the first line has proven intractable and the fact that Pluto speaks it is puzzling. Charles Singleton quotes Boccaccio's commentary approvingly: "Pluto marvels, then, for this is something never seen hitherto: that a living man should be walking through Hell. Fearing that this might redound to his harm, he invokes the aid of his superior. And, in order to render him more disposed to help, he laments."[32] Within the structure and sequence of "Auerbachs Keller in Leipzig," this could be pertinent, for if the four companions are in Hell, they are about to encounter, in Faust, someone who is also a living man. Now one message of the passage from the Cellini autobiography is that the words of the mysterious "Pape Satàn, pape Satàn aleppe!" can be mangled in translation — it is a considerable and unlikely leap to "paix, paix, Satan, allez paix." If anything, a punning German ear could make better sense of "Papa Satan" or "Papst Satan," which would have the added advantage of a cross-pun on the etymology of "Papst." Because it is nonsense and because it is so well-known, the Dante line sticks in the mind with tenacity once it has been uttered several times. I cannot help but hear the echoes in "Walpurgisnachtstraum" in the lines spoken by the "Satiric Verses":

> Als Insekten sind wird da,
> Mit kleinen scharfen Scheren,
> *Satan, unsern Herrn Papa,*
> Nach Würden zu verehren. (4303–6; emphasis added)

The equivalence of "Satan" with the honorific "Herr" and the familiar "Papa" mingles the terms in a greeting, just as the line in Dante functions as an opening. The evidence is circumstantial and distant, but plausible, that "let's elect ourselves a pope" needs to be read in this intertextual web, that the four companions accept Mephistopheles' leadership because he is their spiritual father. There is no contradiction between "choosing a pope"

---

[31] Goethe, *Sämtliche Werke*, 7:306–7.

[32] Charles S. Singleton, in Dante Alighieri, *The Divine Comedy: Inferno. 2. Commentary*, trans. and commentary Charles S. Singleton, 6 vols. (Princeton: Princeton UP, 1989), 109.

and carrying out whatever crude, obscene rituals are associated with the traditions of drunken students, for there could be no better way to celebrate the rule of the Devil than with more and more determined sinning.

## Getting to Paradise

The episode that serves, dare I say, as a pendant to "choosing a pope" is the so-called "grape trick" ("Traubenzauber"), where the obscene phallic comedy becomes more explicit and is performed on stage. Just after Faust says he is ready to leave, Mephistopheles announces a fuller revelation of "bestiality": "Gib nur erst Acht, die Bestialität / Wird sich gar herrlich offenbaren" (2297–98). As the four draw their blades and move menacingly towards him, Mephistopheles makes a "serious gesture" and they are overcome by an illusion

> MEPHISTOPHELES *mit ernsthafter Gebärde*
> Falsch Gebild und Wort
> Verändern Sinn und Ort!
> Seid hier und dort!
> > *Sie stehn erstaunt und sehn einander an.*
> ALTMAYER
> Wo bin ich? Welches schöne Land?
> FROSCH
> Weinberge! Seh' ich recht?
> SIEBEL
> > Und Trauben gleich zur Hand!
> BRANDER
> Hier unter diesem grünen Laube,
> Seht, welch ein Stock! Seht, welche Traube!
> > *Er faßt Siebeln bei der Nase. Die andern tun es wechselseitig und heben die Messer.* (2313–19)

After Mephistopheles and Faust depart, the four find themselves in very odd positions:

> > *Er verschwindet mit Faust, die Gesellen fahren auseinander.*
> SIEBEL
> Was gibt's?
> ALTMAYER
> > Wie?
> FROSCH
> > War das deine Nase?
> BRANDER *zu Siebel*
> Und deine hab' ich in der Hand! (2321–24)

The episode has attracted virtually no further comment, since everything seems to be straightforward. The "trick" had already been ascribed to Faust in the sixteenth century.[33] The naïve reader, with fewer sources and yet a somewhat livelier imagination, might have some questions nevertheless. If the trick turns on the jest of duping the fellows into almost cutting off bunches of fake grapes, how do noses get into the act? Another anatomical region on the male seems far better suited structurally for the trick of cutting off a pendant cluster. The suspicion that "nose" has been substituted euphemistically for "penis" is borne out by a much earlier version of the ribald story. It was discovered by Richard G. Salomon in diary notes preserved in a manuscript in the Vatican Library, dating from 1337:

> I have heard that one cardinal, called the White Cardinal, an expert in magic arts, once by order of the Pope, and as a joke, produced the unseasonable appearance of a vine with clusters of ripe grapes. He ordered each one present to put his knife over the grapes, but not to cut. Then he made an end to the fantastic or magic vision; and the audience found themselves holding their knives over their own virilia and saw that they had been duped.[34]

As Salomon points out, it will be impossible to say when and where the anecdote originated and how widely it circulated. The substitution of "nose" for the more logical penis when the anecdote entered written circulation is unremarkable and unproblematic, since euphemizing oral traditions when they were written down was a common phenomenon.[35] Given Goethe's mind, and his extensive research into the carnivalesque while preparing to write about Hans Sachs, there is no doubt that he would have seen the original structure behind the transmitted variants. The grape trick carries through on the theme adumbrated by the phallic allusions — in the testicular inspection and in the drinking games — of "choosing a pope," bringing the lewd interest of the companions in the male genitals into sharper focus. The importance of phallic display for the reign of Mephistopheles will return even more grossly in the "Walpurgisnacht." Observing that the company in "Auerbachs Keller in Leipzig" is all male, some observers might be inclined to read into the scene a hegemony of the phallus as a positive world. Granted, the homosocial bonding toys with crossing the line from the potential to the actual male-male interaction. But even that substitute for the satisfaction of their sexual desires is denied

---

[33] Witkowski, *Kommentar und Erläuterungen*, 235.

[34] Richard G. Salomon, "The Grape Trick," in *Culture in History: Essays in Honor of Paul Radin*, ed. Stanley Diamond (New York: Columbia UP for Brandeis University, 1960), 533–34; his own translation.

[35] Mikhail Bakhtin, *Rabelais and His World*, trans. Hélène Iswolsky (Bloomington: Indiana UP, 1984), 87 and 316–17.

the four companions: although the audience has no doubt which parts are *meant*, illusion and euphemism frustrate everyone.

The deception of the companions by Mephistopheles has definite Biblical undertones. Scripture is filled with figural language relating to grapes, vines, and harvests. Matthew warns that false prophets may be known by the fruits they bring forth:

> Beware of false prophets, which come to you in sheep's clothing, but inwardly they are ravening wolves.

> Ye shall know them by their fruits. Do men gather grapes of thorns, or figs of thistles?

> Even so every good tree bringeth forth good fruit; but a corrupt tree bringeth forth evil fruit. (Matthew 8:15–17)

Eager to accept the authority of Mephistopheles, the companions will be deceived. Greedy to consume unearned delicacies, they fail to recognize the diabolical nature of Mephistopheles' grapes, which are no more edible or satisfying than thorns and thistles. Brander's exclamation should be heard as an admonition: "*Seht*, welch ein Stock! *Seht*, welche Traube!" (2319; emphasis added) But they cannot see. The four believe they are catching a glimpse of a paradise where the grapes will be ripe for the picking; however, their vision is nothing more than a tantalizing illusion, a false prophecy of the promised land. With genuine diabolical humor, Mephistopheles mocks precisely the teaching to be aware of false prophets as he departs: "Und merkt euch, wie der Teufel spaße" (2321).

Once we see that the "noses" signify the phallus, the topic of castration has been broached. The next obvious association is with the use of castration made by J. M. R. Lenz in his play *Der Hofmeister* (1774), where Läuffer, afraid that he cannot control his sexual urges any longer, cuts off the offending parts. When Läuffer confesses to the schoolmaster Wenzeslaus what he has done, the latter puts the deed into a theological framework:

> LÄUFFER. Bleibt — Ich weiß nicht, ob ich recht getan — Ich habe mich kastriert . . .

> WENZESLAUS. Wa — Kastrier — Da mach ich Euch meinen herzlichen Glückwunsch drüber, vortrefflich, junger Mann, zweiter Origenes! Laß Dich umarmen, teures, auserwähltes Rüstzeug! Ich kann's Euch nicht verhehlen, fast — fast kann ich dem Heldenvorsatz nicht widerstehen, Euch nachzuahmen. So recht, werter Freund! Das ist die Bahn, auf der Ihr eine Leuchte der Kirche, ein Stern erster Größe, ein Kirchenvater selber werden könnt.[36]

---

[36] Jakob Michael Reinhold Lenz, *Der Hofmeister*, in *Werke: Dramen Prosa Gedichte*, ed. Karen Lauer (Munich: Deutscher Taschenbuch Verlag, 1992), act 5,

However, when Läuffer confesses that he rues his act, Wenzeslaus remonstrates in the language of enthusiasm:

> Wie, es gereut ihn? Das sei ferne, werter Herr Mitbruder! Er wird eine so edle Tat doch nicht mit törichter Reue verdunkeln und mit sündlichen Tränen besudeln? Ich seh schon welche über Sein Augenlid hervorquellen. Schluck' Er sie wieder hinunter und sing' Er mit Freudigkeit: ich bin der Nichtigkeit entbunden, nun Flügel, Flügel, Flügel her.

The specific function of this persiflage for Lenz's drama cannot concern us here; what is of interest are the dimensions of theology and of the history of the Church that Wenzeslaus knows so well that he can immediately apply them to the situation. The key is "Origen," whose name was a byword for self-castration.[37]

As the confused remarks by Wenzeslaus display, the response to Origen and his act was mixed and filled with turbulent controversy. It was certainly possible to read the castration as the ultimate sacrifice in the battle against temptation and a fulfilment of Scripture:

> For there are some eunuchs, which were so born from *their* mother's womb: and there are some eunuchs, which were made eunuchs of men: and there be eunuchs, which have made themselves eunuchs for the kingdom of heaven's sake. He that is able to receive *it*, let him receive *it*. (Matthew 19:12)

The obvious question is whether these words should be taken literally or figuratively. Lenz caricatures in Läuffer those who would take the injunction at face value. The opponents of Origen doubtless took comfort from the thought that he, one of the most subtle exegetes of Scripture, had also fallen prey to the letter instead of heeding the spirit.

---

scene 3. Lauer notes (498) that Lenz was personally acquainted with August Wilhelm Hupel, author of *Origenes oder von der Verschneidung, über Matt. 19 v. 10–12: Ein Versuch zur Ehrenrettung einiger gering geachteten Verschnittenen* (Riga, 1772).

[37] I have not had an opportunity to see Hupel's *Origenes oder von der Verschneidung, über Matth. 19 v. 10–12: Ein Versuch zur Ehrenrettung einiger gering geachteten Verschnittenen* (Riga, 1772). But I suspect that it is part of the discourse investigated by John Rogers, *The Matter of Revolution: Science, Poetry, and Politics in the Age of Milton* (Ithaca and London: Cornell UP, 1996) in his chapter on "Marvell and the Action of Virginity." The "revolutionary potential of virginity" (97) would certainly fit with Lenz's politics. Also in the precinct is Hamann's identification of abstraction and rationalism with castration, in the context of an erotics of epistemology. See James C. O'Flaherty, *The Quarrel of Reason with Itself: Essays on Hamann, Michaelis, Lessing, Nietzsche* (Columbia, SC: Camden House, 1988), 147–50.

Castration was an extreme measure to enforce abstinence, but there could also be a middle ground, established by the conjunction of theological teaching with medical theory. Again, Lenz's Wenzeslaus is a convenient witness:

> Die Essäer, sag' ich, haben auch nie Weiber genommen; es war eins von ihren Grundgesetzen und dabei sind sie zu hohem Alter kommen, wie solches im Josephus zu lesen. Wie die es nun angefangen, ihr Fleisch so zu bezähmen; ob sie es gemacht, wie ich, nüchtern und mäßig gelebt und brav Toback geraucht, oder ob sie Euren Weg eingeschlagen — So viel ist gewiß, in amore, in amore omnia insunt vitia und ein Jüngling, der diese Klippe vorbeischifft, Heil, heil ihm, ich will ihm Lorbeern zuwerfen . . . (act 5, scene 3)

Virginity could thereby be prescribed both for the soul and the body. Wenzeslaus is parroting in a debased version ideas that had found their clearest expression among radical Protestants in the sixteenth century. Van Helmont in his medical treatise *Ortus Medicinae* (1648) had declared: " . . . the Almighty hath chosen his Gelded Ones, who have Gelded themselves for the Kingdom of God its sake . . . those only shall *rise again changed*, who shall *rise again glorified* in the Virgin-Body of Regeneration."[38] Theology and medicine could coincide in prescribing a personal regime of sexual self-restraint, curing religious despair and the melancholy induced by physical disorders simultaneously. The claim by Wenzeslaus that his orderly life and consumption of tobacco will accomplish the same goals is a dim reflection, but reflection nonetheless, of these ideas.

One implication of all this for "Auerbachs Keller in Leipzig" is that it glosses the illusionary effect of the "grape trick." Although Mephistopheles lets the four companions come very close to achieving the status of eunuchs, the final cuts are not made. Doing so would be a gesture away from gluttony towards abstinence and would raise the possibility that the four companions might be released from Hell. It is just as they are about to castrate each other that they have the vision of Paradise, but Mephistopheles releases the spell and thereby prevents them from carrying out the actions. Unlike Origen they cannot become eunuchs "for the kingdom of heaven's sake," but remain imprisoned in their desires. Faust also fails to learn anything from the episode, although there was much that related to his condition in all the references to male genitals and their removal. First, he might have been reminded of the dangers that letting those parts dominate him could bring, an obvious moral associated with the stories of Origen and of Abelard and one that Faust ignores when he

---

[38] Quoted in Rogers, *The Matter of Revolution*, 97.

encounters Margarete. Then, on the medical plane, the references to castration point to the need for melancholics to preserve semen; amputation would be a drastic but effective cure. Finally, on the mythological level, these references serve as reminders that as a melancholic Faust stands under the influence of Saturn. Relevant here is that Saturn was doubly marked by castration: literally because he castrated his father and symbolically because he devoured his children.[39]

## Among the Swinish Cannibals

Whereas the "Flohlied" and the "Rattenlied" merely *tell* about evil, the tapping of the wines from the table will actually *show* the audience how Mephistopheles blasphemes. The choice of this trick as the climax is no coincidence. The mysteries of wine and its transformation are at the heart of Christian faith and are the key miracles upon which Christ's reputation was founded. It was therefore to be expected that during the Reformation the theological issues would be in the foreground, as indeed were the forms of all Church rituals and institutions.[40] If Mephistopheles is to prevail over his great rival and at the same time to impress Faust, then he has to accomplish something that resembles a miracle.

Although the tapping of the wine from the table is spectacular, most commentators have been complacent about it, on the grounds that it was a set piece dictated by the Faust legends.[41] As far as I know, the only critic who has been alert to some of the serious themes being enacted on the stage is Osman Durrani, whose inclusive approach in *Faust and the Bible* included "Auerbachs Keller in Leipzig" and to whom I am indebted here.[42]

---

[39] Samuel L. Macey, *Patriarchs of Time: Dualism in Saturn-Cronus, Father Time, the Watchmaker God, and Father Christmas* (Athens and London: U of Georgia P, 1987), 24–31.

[40] On the visible, ritual dimensions of religion at the time, see Lee Palmer Wandel, "Setting the Lutheran Eucharist," *Journal of Early Modern History* 2.2 (1998): 124–55; and R. W. Scribner, "Ritual and Popular Religion in Catholic Germany at the Time of the Reformation," *Journal of Ecclesiastical History* 35.1 (1984): 47–77.

[41] Trendlenburg, *Goethes Faust erklärt*, 305; Witkowski, *Kommentar und Erläuterungen*, 234; and Arens, *Kommentar zu Goethes Faust I* (Heidelberg: Winter, 1982), 219.

[42] Osman Durrani, *Faust and the Bible: A Study of Goethe's Use of Scriptural Allusions and Christian Religious Motifs in Faust I and II* (Bern and Frankfurt am Main: Peter Lang, 1977).

Durrani's starting point is the allusion of "Als wie fünfhundert Säuen!": "For one thing, they start singing immediately after drinking Mephisto's wine, which suggests the possibility that their beverages contain some additive that will deprive them of their free will in the latter part of the scene." Theologically, no "additive" is needed; this can be Origen's "wine of an opposite nature with which sinners and those who accept the harmful dogmas of false learning wickedly get drunk."[43] Judged by its effects, it is not a wine of wisdom and gladness, since it makes the four behave rudely and obscenely. The allusion of the companions' description of themselves as swine has reminded more than one critic of Christ's casting of the devils into the swine as told in the Bible:

> And there was a good way off from them an herd of many swine feeding.
> So the devils besought him, saying, If thou cast us out, suffer us to go away into the herd of swine.

> And he said unto them, Go. And when they were come out, they went into the herd of swine: and, behold, the whole herd of swine ran violently down a steep place into the sea, and perished in the waters. (Matthew 8:30–32)

The narrative does not end when Christ has cast the devils into the swine and they have perished. We are told, as so often, that the miracle prompts a response: "And they that kept them fled, and went their ways into the city, and told every thing, and what was befallen to the possessed of the devils" (Matthew 8:33). In other words, witnesses to a miracle should be astounded — but the audience in "Auerbachs Keller in Leipzig," Faust, remains strikingly indifferent, as Durrani reports without further comment.[44]

Durrani also points to the parallels to the transformation of water into wine at the Marriage of Cana (John 2:1–11) and to Mephistopheles' competition with Christ:

> The end product is identical, and in both cases the transformation provides the first example of the supernatural powers of the person who performs it, Christ's representing the beginning of his miracles (Jn. 2.11), and Mephisto's the first public demonstration of his capabilities. He manages to outshine his model at least in as far as he is able to offer four different brands from the same source.[45]

---

[43] Origenes, *The Song of Songs: Commentary and Homilies*, 187.

[44] Durrani, *Faust and the Bible*, 79.

[45] Durrani, *Faust and the Bible*, 79. Cf. Gaier, *Faust-Dichtungen: Kommentar I*, 286–87.

His comments are acute, especially his observation that the sequence in the plot of *Faust* corresponds to the sequence in the narration of the life of Christ. And it is correct that Mephistopheles seems to outdo Christ, at least in terms of consumer choice, by offering four different wines. But what does it mean when he "outshines" Christ? Is he truly superior to Christ, or should we be on our guard and see this as an example of Mephistopheles's grandiose blustering that he could do a better job of running things, that he would offer humans a better deal than God has proposed? And we should not be so dazzled by what Mephistopheles does that we confuse his trick with a miracle. Throughout, the intent of Mephistopheles is to compare himself with Christ and to gull people into switching their allegiances.

Instead of waiting politely for an invitation to join the four companions, it is he who invites himself, with words that emphasize the rudeness of this reversal: "Ich tränke gern ein Glas, die Freiheit hoch zu ehren, / Wenn eure Weine nur ein Bißchen besser wären" (2245–46). Mephistopheles is parodying the words spoken by Mary at the wedding fest in Cana: "They have no wine" (John 2:3).[46] These words, rich with typological possibilities because they were taken as Mary's expression of charity and her anticipation of Christ's ultimate giving, introduce the miraculous transformation of water into wine, itself a foreshadowing of the Last Supper:

> Jesus saith unto them, fill the waterpots with water. And they filled them up to the brim.
>
> And he saith unto them, Draw out now, and bear unto the governor of the feast. And they bare *it*.
>
> When the ruler of the feast had tasted the water that was made wine, and knew not whence it was (but the servants which drew the water knew;) the governor of the feast called the bridegroom.
>
> And saith unto him, Every man at the beginning doth set forth good wine; and when men have well drunk, then that which is worse; *but* thou hast kept the good wine until now.
>
> This beginning of miracles did Jesus in Cana of Galilee, and manifested forth his glory; and his disciples believed on him. (John 2:7–11)

Mephistopheles is well aware of the Scriptural text, as indicated by his elevation of the four companions with the title "werthe Gäste," evoking the wedding guests. But he also knows that he has excluded himself from the

---

[46] My analysis is obligated here to the discussion by Christopher Kleinhenz, "Dante and the Bible: Biblical Citation in the *Divine Comedy*," in *Dante: Contemporary Perspectives*, ed. Amilcare A. Iannucci (Toronto and Buffalo: U of Toronto P, 1997), 74–93, particularly 77–78.

circle of those who will partake of the wine of charity, again echoing Scripture's "the good wine": "Statt eines *guten Trunks*, den man nicht haben kann, / Soll die Gesellschaft uns ergetzen" (2186–87). Mephistopheles refuses to accept the grace that could be his too, claiming that "one cannot have it," even though that is not true. Instead, he will pretend to be able to perform his own miracle for "those who have no wine." He has nothing to lose, for if the four companions and the audience suspect that it is only some sort of trick, a bit of charlatanry, then that will still serve his long-term interests by making people more sceptical about the literal truth of Scripture.

There is another, somewhat complicated, attack by Mephistopheles on the authority of the Bible. This is located in the possibility of four different wines being chosen by four different individuals. The image evoked by this constellation is that of the four rivers of Paradise (Phison, Geon, Tigris, and Euphrates). Each of these was traditionally associated with a different "liquid": milk, oil, honey, and wine. The parallels to the four wines with different qualities that can be factored as indices of those liquids (sweet vs. dry, heavy vs. light, red vs. white), labelled with geographic designations, strengthen the allusion. The four rivers were in turn matched up with the four cardinal virtues.[47] Thus, choosing a liquid from one of four should be a reminder of the topography of Paradise and of the attraction the virtues should hold for spiritually thirsty souls. However, in "Auerbachs Keller," a negative mirror to Paradise, there are no hints of virtue in the choosing.

As a trained theologian, Faust might also have recalled that the four rivers were glossed as corresponding to the four Gospels and the four Evangelists. The notion that the four companions should evoke Matthew, Mark, Luke, and John seems far-fetched, but what is being staged in "Auerbachs Keller" is precisely a satire organized by Mephistopheles. The thrust of the satire goes beyond a straightforward parody and aims at the core of the thorny problem raised by the fact that the four Gospels were

---

[47] On the typology of the four rivers of Paradise, see Ernst Schlee, *Die Ikonographie der Paradiesflüsse* (Leipzig: Dieterich'sche Verlagsbuchhandlung, 1937); J. Poeschke, "Paradiesflüsse," in *Lexikon der christlichen Ikonographie*, ed. Engelbert Kirschbaum, SJ, with Günter Bandmann, Wolfgang Braunfels, Johannes Kollwitz, Wilhelm Mrazek, Alfred A. Schmid, and Hugo Schnell (Freiburg im Breisgau: Herder, 1971), 3: cols. 382–84; Paul Underwood, "The Fountain of Life in Manuscripts of the Gospels," *Dumbarton Oaks Papers* 5 (1950): 43–138; here, 72–73; Francis Lee Utley, "The Prose *Salomon and Saturn* and the Tree Called Chy," *Medieval Studies* 19 (1957): 55–78; here, 65 and n. 75.

not identical. The reconciliation or harmonization of the four was most urgent, and could be nicely imagined as the flowing together of the waters from four different sources.[48] However, in "Auerbachs Keller" the four companions do not harmonize in their interpretations (nor, it should be stressed, in their music). After the "grape trick," they bicker about what they have seen and what it might mean.[49] In other, Mephistophelean words, their lack of agreement mocks the existence of differences in the New Testament. The unsubtle implication is that those differences should prompt doubt about the veracity of the Gospels, should raise questions about the reliability of the Evangelists as witnesses. Instead of having to trust unreliable accounts, we are offered the possibility of accepting the evidence of our eyes, for here Mephistopheles has vividly demonstrated his ability to "perform miracles." Finally, Mephistopheles has drawn our attention to the paradoxical pronouncement of Christ that He has not come to bring peace. Any thinking person should understand that the true meaning of Christ's words can only be grasped if they are not taken literally, but the taunt of Mephistopheles is to insist that they are only literal and nothing more, that the reign of Christ will never bring peace.

If we are on our guard, we know that Mephistopheles does not perform a miracle, since he is not permitted to do so on theological grounds. How then do we understand what happens when he draws the wine from the table? Using the principles of humoral medicine and alchemy, Mephistopheles converts blood into wine and thereby blasphemously parodies the Last Supper and the doctrine of transubstantiation. Whereas Christ transforms His blood into wine, Mephistopheles uses human blood

---

[48] See Underwood, "The Fountain of Life in Manuscripts of the Gospels," appendix A: "Notes on the *Symphonia* of the Evangelists," 118–31, on the tradition of the harmonizing of the Gospels. On the rich symbolism of the source as a fountain or spring, see also David Quint, *Origin and Originality in Renaissance Literature: Versions of the Source* (New Haven and London: Yale UP, 1983). A harmonious fountain, with three wines in one water, is found in Rabelais's *Gargantua and Pantagruel*, discussed below. For an example of the theological discussion, see Herder's "Regel der Zusammenstimmung unsrer Evangelien, aus ihrer Entstehung und Ordnung," published in his *Christliche Schriften: Dritte Sammlung* (1797), reprinted in Johann Gottfried Herder, *Sämtliche Werke*, ed. Bernhard Suphan (1880; repr. Hildesheim: Georg Olms, 1967), 19:380–424. He speaks of "eine Symphonie der Evangelien" "in der jede Dissonanz sich selbst erklärte" (424).

[49] Compare Durrani, *Faust and the Bible*, 79: "Just as the 'miracle' of *Auerbachs Keller* relies on the excessive credulity of four somewhat biased witnesses, the deeds of Christ are reported by four not impartial chroniclers, and it is one of the functions of this episode in *Faust* to illustrate the possibility that the biblical miracles may have been based on similar delusions on the part of the observers."

for the purpose. Let us look closely at the scene for textual evidence, beginning with Mephistopheles' actions:

> MEPHISTOPHELES *mit seltsamen Gebärden*
> Trauben trägt der Weinstock!
> Hörner der Ziegenbock;
> Der Wein ist saftig, Holz die Reben,
> Der hölzerne Tisch kann Wein auch geben.
> Ein tiefer Blick in die Natur!
> Hier ist ein Wunder, glaubet nur! (2284–89)

If the "strange gestures" and the incantation are not sufficient to remind us of the celebration of the Mass, then the last line is a giveaway, echoing the very words. Alert listeners catch the phrase "wine is juicy" and recall an earlier line pronounced by Mephistopheles at a decisive moment: "Blut ist ein ganz besonderer Saft" (1740). The use of "juicy" and "sap" is one of Mephistopheles' intricate jokes, punning upon the immense theological discourse on blood and its symbolic, allegorical values, a discourse that also, for obvious reasons, operated with the language of wine and vineyards. Those who fail to grasp where Mephistopheles is about to get the wines will miss the point. Worse still, they will find themselves in the predicament of the four companions, who sing "Uns ist so *kannibalisch* wohl" (2294; emphasis added) without recognizing the literal truth of the line. Since no miracle of (reverse)-transformation can take place, the wines still bear the essence of the blood from which they have been drawn: the four companions are indeed cannibals. Even if they did know this, there is reason to suspect that they would have accepted Mephistopheles and his blasphemy in any case, for they have forgotten Christian teachings and rituals and do not recoil from what they see. In the Old Testament, cannibalism was a drastic punishment imposed on those who had rejected God's designated prophet.[50] The forgetfulness of the companions is all the more lamentable because precisely the obligation to remember had been emphasized by Christ at the Last Supper. The readiness with which the four companions identify themselves as "cannibals" suggests furthermore that as "moderns" of the sixteenth century, they are familiar with what was then a new term. Imposed upon the indigenous Others of the "New World" in

---

[50] On theological ramifications of cannibalism, see John Casteen, "*Andreas*: Mermedonian Cannibalism and Figural Narration," *Neuphilologische Mitteilungen* 75 (1974): 74–78; Ronald B. Herzman, "Cannibalism and Communion in *Inferno* XXXIII," *Dante Studies* 98 (1980): 53–78; and Rachel Jacoff, "The Hermeneutics of Hunger," in *Speaking Images: Essays in Honor of V. A. Kolve*, ed. Robert F. Yeager and Charlotte C. Morse (Asheville, NC: Pegasus P, 2004), 95–110.

the European conquest, the term quickly was deployed in the polemics of the Reformation, as Protestants hurled the accusation against Catholics.[51] How pleasing to the ears of Mephistopheles to hear the erstwhile Christians describe themselves in such uncharitable language!

The allusions to swine and to cannibals also connect again to epic. Faust's reliance upon Mephistopheles as a reliable guide might be excused more readily because it has been made under the influence of melancholy. Watching Mephistopheles delude the four companions with enchantments, and with their words of self-description "als wie fünfhundert Säuen" still ringing in his ears, Faust could have made the connection to Circe, notorious for turning men into swine.[52] Not so apparent to the reader who is not a philosopher — but had Faust not boasted of having studied "Philosophie durchaus, mit heißem Bemühen"? — was the connection from there to Boethius's *Consolation of Philosophy*. There Faust would have found again an extended philosophical discourse that deals explicitly with the problems of "Auerbachs Keller" and those of the entire drama, a discussion centred on the questions of metamorphosis and on the story of Circe. The figure of Philosophy offers an allegorical interpretation of the transformation of humans into animals:

> This means that anything which turns away from goodness ceases to exist, and thus that the wicked cease to be what they once were. That they used to be human is shown by the human appearance of their body which still remains. So it was by falling into wickedness that they also lost their human nature. . . .
>
> The result is that you cannot think of anyone as human whom you see transformed by wickedness. You could say that someone who robs with violence and burns with greed is like a wolf. A wild and restless man who is for ever exercising his tongue in lawsuits could be compared to a dog yapping. . . . And a man wallowing in foul and impure lusts is occupied by the filthy pleasures of a sow.[53]

Recognizing the intertextual chain back to Boethius entails little more than a recognition of commonplaces that should have been immediately

---

[51] See Frank Lestringant, "Le cannibale et ses paradoxes: Images du cannibalisme au temps des guerres de religion," *Mentalities/Mentalités* 1.2 (1983): 4–19.

[52] Incidentally, there is also a connection between Circe and the discourse on melancholy, pointed out by Gert Mattenklott in his book *Melancholie in der Dramatik des Sturm und Drang* (Stuttgart: J. B. Metzler, 1968): "Als 'Zauberin' erscheint die Einbildungskraft bei Bodmer — barocke Melancholie-Darstellungen versinnbildlichen sie als Circe, die aus Menschen Tiere macht" (36, n. 67).

[53] Boethius, *The Consolation of Philosophy*, trans. V. W. Watts (Harmondsworth, UK: Penguin, 1969), 125.

apparent for someone trained in philosophy during Faust's time.[54] Nevertheless, despite all his vaunted scholarship, Faust is unable to apply the relevant philosophical passages to his situation, his condition, or his intentions. Having just witnessed the four companions "unable to rise to a divine condition" and therefore reduced to animal behavior — it does not seem to be a coincidence that they refer to themselves as "swine," the animals selected by Circe — Faust draws no good conclusions but on the contrary will yield in the very next scene to the lusts of his material nature.

Serious undertones lurk in Mephistopheles' incantation, which has sometimes been dismissed as a "children's rhyme," mere doggerel.[55] "Trauben trägt der Weinstock" must be read in light of the Bible's allegory of Christ as a grapevine. Note the parody, unmistakable if we read the German translation, underscored by the structure and rhythm, of Christ's declaration:

> I am the true vine, and my Father is the husbandman.
>
> Every branch in me that beareth not fruit he taketh away; and every *branch* that beareth fruit, he purgeth it, that it may bring forth more fruit.
>
> Now ye are clean through the word which I have spoken unto you.
>
> Abide in me, and I in you. As the branch cannot bear fruit of itself, except it abide in the vine; no more can ye, except ye abide in me.
>
> I am the vine, ye *are* the branches: He that abideth in me, and I in him, the same bringeth forth much fruit: for without me ye can do nothing.
>
> If a man abide not in me, he is cast forth as a branch, and is withered; and men gather them, and cast *them* into the fire, and they are burned. (John 15: 1–6)

The grapes may be compared to the faithful borne by the body and teachings of Christ. Medieval allegorizers went one step further and depicted Christ in the winepress, with His blood being collected as the juice is gathered at winemaking.[56] Mephistopheles knows Scripture well and turns it to

---

[54] S. K. Heninger, *Touches of Sweet Harmony: Pythagorean Cosmology and Renaissance Poetics* (San Marino: Huntington Library, 1974), reports the positive reception of Boethius early in the Renaissance (53). The importance of Boethius for *Faust*, particularly the analysis of the paradox of divine foreknowledge and free will, has not been explored.

[55] Witkowski, *Kommentar und Erläuterungen*, 234; Arens, *Kommentar zu Goethes Faust I*, 219.

[56] On Christ in the winepress, see Alois Thomas, *Die Darstellung Christi in der Kelter: Eine theologische und kulturhistorische Studie, zugleich ein Beitrag zur Geschichte und Volkskunde des Weinbaus* (1936; repr., Düsseldorf: Pädagogischer

his purposes, for now *he* is the vintner, "harvesting" the wine and pouring it for the companions. A subtle jibe is added by his insistence on the wood-enness of the table, implying that the living wood of Christ-the-vine is now dead, that Christ is not an everlasting *lignum vitae*.[57] Recalling that all of this occurs in the drama just after Easter, the snide hint that Christ has been crucified, that the wood can not bear fruit, lends added force to the blasphemy. Despite all his blustering, Mephistopheles is aware that there are limits upon what he may do. Notably, he does not drink any of the wine, even though he had claimed he would gladly drink a glass. The conditional is not used for politeness alone; in fact Mephistopheles is forbidden to drink any of the wine. The prohibition derives from the fact that this wine, having been transformed from blood, still bears traces of divine essence.[58] Mephistopheles, as we know from the "Prolog im Himmel," can do many things to humans, but he may not himself do violence to them. He cannot prevail ultimately against the truth of Christ's teachings and protection.

The contradictions of Mephistopheles' duplicity are evident whenever one looks closely at his parodies. Durrani has pointed out that the words uttered to quell the flames, "Sei ruhig, freundlich Element" (2300) allude

---

Verlag Schwann, 1981); and Thomas, "Christus in der Kelter," in *Reallexikon zur deutschen Kunstgeschichte*, ed. Ernst Gall and L. H. Heydenreich (Stuttgart: Alfred Druckenmüller, 1954), 3, cols. 673–87. On the blood of Christ as a sacred fountain, see W. v. Reybekiel, "Der 'Fons vitae' in der christlichen Kunst," *Niederdeutsche Zeitschrift für Volkskunde* 12 (1934): 87–136; here, 116–25.

[57] On the wounded Cross, see Leslie Moore, "'Instructive Trees': Swift's *Broom-Stick*, Boyle's *Reflections*, and Satiric Figuration," *Eighteenth-Century Studies* 19.3 (1986): 313–32; A. Joan Bowers, "The Tree of Charity in *Piers Plowman*: Its Allegorical and Structural Significance," in *Literary Monographs*, vol. 6: *Medieval and Renaissance Literature*, ed. Erich Rothstein and Joseph Anthony Wittreich, Jr. (Madison and London: U of Wisconsin P, for the Department of English, U of Wisconsin, 1975), 3–34, 157–60; Eleanor Simmons Greenhill, "The Child in the Tree: A Study of the Cosmological Tree in Christian Tradition," *Traditio* 10 (1954): 323–71; and Karl Josef Höltgen, "Arbor, Scala und Fons vitae: Vorformen devotionaler Embleme in einer mittelenglischen Handschrift (B.M. Add. MS 37049)," in *Chaucer und seine Zeit: Symposion für Walter F. Schirmer*, ed. Arno Esch (Tübingen: Max Niemeyer, 1968), 355–91; here, 361–74, and the sources cited there.

[58] A revealing detail in this regard is that at the moment when Faustus draws his blood to sign the contract in the *Faustbuch* the blood displays a warning: "O Homo fuge"; ("Man, flee." Cf. Ps. 139:7–8: "Whither shall I go from thy spirit? or whither shall I flee from thy presence? If I ascend into heaven, thou art there: if I make my bed in hell, behold thou art there.") See Kühne, *Das älteste Faustbuch*, 21.

to the calming of the storm by Christ.[59] Durrani quotes only Mark 4:39, but the subsequent lines are also relevant:

> And he arose, and rebuked the wind, and said unto the sea, Peace, be still. And the wind ceased, and there was a great calm.
>
> And he said unto them, why are ye so fearful? how is it that ye have no faith?
>
> And they feared exceedingly, and said one to another, What manner of man is this, that even the wind and the sea obey him? (Mark 4:39–41)

The control over the elements and the ability to calm them requires divine powers, and those are what Mephistopheles desires for himself. But we notice a difference in which elements he and Christ address: the latter commands air and water, while Mephistopheles has only fire as a "friendly element." Within the post-Paracelsian framework, Mephistopheles is permitted to claim fire as *his* element because it was superfluous to Creation. Furthermore, it is only destructive. Both reasons, once understood, undermine completely the pretension of Mephistopheles to be an equivalent of Christ in the domain of control over the elements.[60] The four companions do not make the association with Scripture.

Another elaborate attack by Mephistopheles against Christ comes in the first two lines of the incantation. "Hörner trägt der Ziegenbock" stands in counterpoint to "Trauben der Weinstock." Who is being contrasted with Christ? Not Mephistopheles alone, as one might think initially, particularly given the depictions of the witches' sabbath. Here, the reference surely must be to the god Pan, who had the legs, horns, and beard of a he-goat, as well as qualities resembling those of Satyrs, that is, excessive sexual energy, often represented by a prominent phallus (in Asia Minor, Pan was indeed identified with Priapus). On its own, the comparison might be enough to give offence, setting the pagan god on the same pedestal as Christ. However, a deeper insult is at work. Mephistopheles has mentioned Christ *before* Pan, reversing the correct historical order, in which Christianity should supplant paganism.[61]

---

[59] Durrani, *Faust and the Bible*, 79.

[60] There are further complexities to be investigated. Medieval allegorizers noticed parallels between Christ as a helmsman calming the storm and Odysseus. See Ruedi Imbach, "experiens Ulixes: Hinweise zur Figur des Odysseus im Denken der Patristik, des Mittelalters und bei Dante," in *Lange Irrfahrt — Grosse Heimkehr: Odysseus als Archetyp — zur Aktualität des Mythos*, ed. Gotthard Fuchs (Frankfurt am Main: Verlag Josef Knecht, 1994), 59–80. Since Odysseus is also a paradigm for the figure of Mephistopheles, his gesture of imitation has a certain claim to poetic if not theological legitimacy.

[61] Mephistopheles will repeat the introduction of Pan in *Faust II*; important is Frank Möbus's article, "Des Plutus zwiefache Rede: Eine kryptische Bibelanspielung

At stake is the famous passage in which Plutarch tells of the sailor during the reign of Tiberius who hears a mysterious voice telling him, upon reaching his destination, to proclaim "the great god Pan is dead."[62] Since this coincided in time with the Crucifixion, much learned effort was expended in deciding whether the correct interpretation was that the era of paganism had come to an end (with the death of Pan) or, more problematically, whether Pan had somehow been absorbed into Christ so that the two were figurally related (the dying Pan as Christ being crucified).[63] Mephistopheles does not appear interested in making the argument for melding of Christ and Pan, stressing rather their difference and writing the sequence as a succession, with Christ dead and Pan very much alive. Thus he is taking a position diametrically opposed to that of Herder, who argued in his "Vom neuern Gebrauch der Mythologie" for the coincidence of pre-Christian and Christian figures.[64] With his usual penetrating wit, Wieland pointed in his glossary for *Oberon* to the ironies of the Christian discourse on Pan: "Übrigens ist es . . . eben nicht

---

in der Mummenschanz des Faust II," *Zeitschrift für deutsche Philologie* 107: Sonderheft (1988): *71–*84.

[62] On the astral origins of this story (Pan = Sirius), see Giorgio de Santillana and Hertha von Dechend, *Hamlet's Mill: An Essay on Myth and the Frame of Time* (1969; repr., Boston: David R. Godine, 1977), 275–87. Whether Goethe understood that origin by the time he wrote "Auerbachs Keller" is moot. The story floated around on into the eighteenth century and was given prominence by Bernard Le Bovier de Fontenelle's use of it as an example of the unreliability of such stories in his critical *Histoire des oracles*, ed. Louis Maigron (Paris: Librairie Droz, 1934), 16–17. This work was first published in 1686, with editions in 1698, 1701, 1713, 1742, etc.

[63] Compare the entry for "Pan" in Hederich, *Gründliches mythologisches Lexikon*, ed. Johann Joachim Schwabe (1770; repr., Darmstadt: Wissenschaftliche Buchgesellschaft, 1967). For the reception of the Pan story, see G. A. Gerhard, "Zum Tod des großen Pan," *Wiener Studien: Zeitschrift für klassische Philologie* 37 (1915): 323–52; and his "Nochmals zum Tod des großen Pan," *Wiener Studien: Zeitschrift für klassische Philologie* 38 (1916): 343–76. Further documentation on the Pan-as-Christ controversy is provided by Otto Weinreich, "Zum Tod des großen Pan," *Archiv für Religionswissenschaft* 13 (1910): 467–73. The entire problem is carefully reviewed by Philippe Borgeaud in "La mort du Grand Pan," *Revue de l'Histoire des Religions* 200.1 (1983): 3–39. The history is complicated further by the identification of the conquest of the Aztecs as a version of the death of Pan/paganism; cf. Adriano Prosperi, "New Heaven and New Earth: Prophecy and Propaganda at the Time of the Discovery and Conquest of the Americas," in *Prophetic Rome in the High Renaissance Period: Essays*, ed. Marjorie Reeves (Oxford: Clarendon, 1992), 279–303; here, 294.

[64] Herder, *Sämtliche Werke*, 3:235.

unmöglich, daß Scherasmin gelegentlich von seinem Pfarrer etwas von ihr gehört haben könnte, wiewohl ihm nichts davon im Gedächtnis geblieben, als die isolierte Vorstellung, wie still und tot es auf einmal in der Natur werden müßte, wenn *der große Pan* wirklich zu sterben kommen sollte."[65]

The intrusion of Pan has more than allegorical implications however, since he was often associated with the retinue of Bacchus/Dionysos.[66] The way in which the four companions drink the wine stands in stark opposition to the solemnity of the Liturgy and is reminiscent of bacchanalian revelries. Dedicated entirely to the sensuous, bodily enjoyment of the wine, the four give no thought, show no sign, of any spiritual awakening. The absence of the spiritual dimension is highlighted when we contrast the whole episode with a passage in Rabelais's *Histories of Gargantua and Pantagruel.* I have no doubt that Goethe knew this text and that it needs to be brought into consideration as a source for "Auerbachs Keller in Leipzig."[67] The scene comes at a climax in Rabelais's novel and is vivid,

---

[65] Christoph Martin Wieland, *Werke*, ed. Fritz Martini and Hans Werner Seiffert (Munich: Carl Hanser, 1968), 5:724.

[66] An important source for Goethe on the themes of Pan-Bacchus-Christ is book four of François Rabelais's *The Histories of Gargantua and Pantagruel*, trans. J. M. Cohen (Harmondsworth, UK: Penguin, 1978), 510–13. There is an extensive literature on that passage; see M. A. Screech, "The Death of Pan and the Death of Heroes in the Fourth Book of Rabelais: A Study in Syncretism," *Bibliothèque d'humanisme et renaissance* 17 (1955): 36–55; and A. J. Krailsheimer, "The Significance of the Pan Legend in Rabelais' Thought," *Modern Language Review* 56 (1961): 13–23, and the sources cited there. Once we see the significance of Pan in **Pan**tagruel and **Pan**urge, it will become necessary to consolidate Goethe's frequent recourse to **pan**sophie, **pan**theism, **Pan**dora, **pan**demonium, **pan**tomime and the like. Important in this regard are the comments by William S. Heckscher, "Goethe im Banne der Sinnbilder: Ein Beitrag zur Emblematik," *Jahrbuch der Hamburger Kunstsammlungen* 7 (1962): 35–54; here, 36, on *panourgía*, a term that cropped up in Goethe's conversations and thoughts on 25 December 1776.

[67] Goethe referred to himself as "Panurgo secondo" in the subtitle to "Concerto dramatico" (1773). On Goethe's plans for the Rabelaisian "Reise der Söhne Megaprazons," see Leo Jordan, "Goethe und Rabelais," *Germanisch-Romanische Monatsschrift* 3 (1911): 648–62; and Helmut Praschek, "Goethes Fragmente 'Die Reise der Söhne Megaprazons,'" in *Studien zur Goethezeit: Festschrift für Lieselotte Blumenthal*, ed. Helmut Holtzhauer and Bernhard Zeller, with Hans Henning (Weimar: Hermann Böhlaus Nachfolger, 1968), 330–36. For an analysis of the text in conjunction with Goethe's reaction to the French Revolution, see Gabrielle Bersier, "'Reise der Söhne Megaprazons': Goethe, Rabelais und die Französische Revolution," in *Goethe im Kontext: Kunst und Humanität, Naturwissenschaft und Politik von der Aufklärung bis zur*

unforgettable. An intertextual signal is given by the line that the four companions shout together: "O schöner Brunnen, der uns fließt!" Certainly, the fountain could be simply a metaphor here, but it also links across to the episode in the fifth book of Rabelais, "How the Water of the Fountain tasted of different Wines, according to the imagination of the Drinkers":

> "As a certain Jewish captain of old, a learned and valiant man, was leading his people across the desert in utter famine, he received manna out of the skies, which to their imagination tasted exactly as food had tasted in the past. Similarly here, as you drink of this miraculous liquor you will detect the taste of whatever wine you may imagine."
>
> This we did, and Panurge cried out: "By God, this is the wine of Beaune, and the best that ever I tasted, and may a hundred and six devils run away with me if it isn't! How grand it would be to have a neck six foot long, so as to taste it longer, which was Philoxenus's wish; or as long as a crane's, as Melanthius desired!"
>
> "I swear as a Lanterner," exclaimed Friar John, "that it's Graves wine, gay and sparkling. Pray teach me, lady, the way you make it like this."
>
> "To me," said Pantagruel, "it seems like wine of Mirevaux. For that's what I imagined before I drank. The only think wrong with it is that it is cool. Colder than ice, I should say, colder than Nonacris or Dirce water, colder than the fountain of Cantoporeia in Corinth, which froze the stomach and digestive organs of those who drank it."
>
> " 'Drink,' " said Bacbuc, "once, twice, and three times. And now again, changing your thoughts, and each time you'll find the taste and savour of the liquor just as you imagined it. After this you must confess to God nothing is impossible."
>
> "We never said that anything was," I replied. "We maintain that he is all-powerful."[68]

The parallels of the passage to "Auerbachs Keller" are so striking that they cannot be accidental: the *naming* of the wines, the insistence on the *will* of the drinkers for determining which wine they taste. It may be that Rabelais's

---

*Restauration*, ed. Wolfgang Wittkowski (Tübingen: Max Niemeyer, 1984), 230–40. John R. Williams has identified an allusion to chapter 27 of *Pantagruel* in the "Klassische Walpurgisnacht": "The Flatulence of Seismos: Goethe, Rabelais and the 'Geranomachia,' " *Germanisch-Romanische Monatsschrift* NS 33 (1983): 103–10.

[68] Rabelais, *The Histories of Gargantua and Pantagruel*, 700–701. On the interpretation of this scene, see Florence Weinberg, *The Wine & the Will*, 67–81; George Mallary Masters, "The Hermetic and Platonic Traditions in Rabelais' *Dive Bouteille*," *Studi Francesi* 28 (1966): 15–29; and Quint, *Origin and Originality in Renaissance Literature*, 192–97.

version of this choice of wine and the version in the Faust legends go back to a common source that was circulating in the fifteenth and early sixteenth centuries, but that is beside the point here. Surely when Goethe read Rabelais, he recognized the affinity of this passage to what had been associated with Faust, and amalgamated the versions for his own purposes.

There is a large body of commentary on this passage and the subsequent episode of the "Dive Bouteille," much of which would be relevant to Goethe's concerns, for example, about the theology of wine, but developing the connections goes beyond my present purposes.[69] The most interesting issues arise from the stress laid upon the Biblical context. First, the amazing property of the fountain is identified typologically with the manna, so that the emphasis is upon divine miracles, not just any magic. As a student of theology, Faust should be expected to recognize the contemporary theological overtones, connecting the various tastes of wine with the many flavors of manna, which Erasmus had equated with the variety of interpretations of Scripture.[70] Second, the allusion in Rabelais to what is wine and tastes simultaneously of water restores the possibility of the Miracle at Cana. This is a community of willing believers who are willing to turn their imagination according to the dictates of faith and thereby experience the spiritual via the material. Third, the explicit declaration of faith underscores that these drinkers accept God's omnipotence, unlike those in "Auerbachs Keller," who accept Mephistopheles as their leader and guide. Finally, the syncretism of Christian hermeneutics with Neoplatonism in the ability of the thoughts to alter the flavor of the water-wine indicates a path that Faust could have taken as a participant in the intellectual developments of the fifteenth century. "Magic," properly understood and applied with philosophic wisdom, could yield happy results and ultimately an initiation into sacred mysteries. But Faust has cut himself off from such an integrated worldview and has pinned his hopes on the shortcut through black magic. The drinkers in Rabelais's text will proceed from their fabulous wines to the Temple of Bacchus; Faust goes on to the "Witches' Kitchen," deeper into the realm of superstition and demonic chaos.

---

[69] There was a rich emblematic and devotional literature equating Christ's blood with the wine and with the water/wine of the Fountain of Life. In addition to Weinberg, *The Wine & the Will*, see the discussion of the "fountain of life" in Höltgen, "Arbor, Scala und Fons vitae," 381–89. Höltgen reproduces an emblem from De Montenay's *Emblemes* (1571), which depicts a fountain with Christ as the centerpiece, streams of blood/water flowing from His wounds into two basins, and various lame and crippled people drinking eagerly from the lower one, benefiting from "sa plénitude."

[70] Quint, *Origin and Originality in Renaissance Literature*, 194–95.

# 7: The Epic Encyclopedia

ONE OF THE IMPORTANT ROLES of epic was its didactic function, including teaching about the gods (and then God), imparting ethical ideals, and conveying knowledge of the natural universe. A key figure in the evolution of the epic into a sort of encyclopedic text was Vergil, both as he conceived his own task in relation to Homer[1] and as he was later elevated, first to the status of hermetic philosopher and then in the medieval period to that of a necromancer.[2] By the time Dante came to write the *Divine Comedy*, one of the basic requirements for the epic poem was that it should be a comprehensive guide to all human knowledge. It should be a microcosm, whose carefully constructed designs and patterns would provide an orderly map of the universe, one that would also be elegant, communicating the whole of knowledge in an aesthetically satisfying form.[3] Nor were the rules simply left unstated. The classic digest of the requirements was made by Tasso in his *Discourses on the Heroic Poem*, where he outlined what the epic poet would need to know in order to be successful. It was a daunting prospect, since the poet essentially had to have encyclopedic mastery, demonstrated in the architecture of the text itself:

---

[1] See Philip R. Hardie, *Vergil's* Aeneid: *Cosmos and Imperium* (1986; repr., Oxford: Clarendon, 1989).

[2] On the quest for hermetic knowledge in Vergil, see Pierre Courcelle, "Interprétations néo-platonisantes du livre VI de l'Énéide," in *Entretiens sur l'antiquité classique*, vol. 3: *Recherches sur la tradition platonicienne* (1955): 95–136. The standard work on the medieval reception of Vergil is Domenico Comparetti, *Virgilio nel medio evo* (Firenze: B. Seeber, 1896), available in English as *Vergil in the Middle Ages*, trans. E. F. M. Benecke (1908; repr., London: George Allen & Unwin, 1966; Princeton: Princeton UP, 1997). Useful are H. Theodore Silverstein, "Dante and Vergil the Mystic," *Harvard Studies and Notes in Philology and Literature* 14 (1932): 51–82; and Teresa Hankey, "The Clear and the Obscure: Dante, Virgil and the Role of the Prophet," in *Dante and the Middle Ages: Literary and Historical Essays*, ed. John C. Barnes and Cormac Ó Cuilleanáin (Dublin: Irish Academic P for The Foundation for Italian Studies, University College, Dublin, 1995), 211–29.

[3] On the ideal of the epic poem itself as a microcosm, see Robert M. Durling, *The Figure of the Poet in Renaissance Epic* (Cambridge, MA: Harvard UP, 1965), 123–27. On the encyclopedic comprehensiveness of the epic, see Eberhard Müller-Bochat, "Die Einheit des Wissens und das Epos: Zur Geschichte eines utopischen Gattungsbegriffs," *Romanistisches Jahrbuch* 17 (1966): 58–81.

For just as in this marvellous domain of God called the world we behold the sky scattered over and adorned with such variety of stars, and as we descend from realm to realm, we marvel at the air and the sea full of birds and fish, and the earth host to so many animals wild and tame, with brooks, springs, lakes, meadows, fields, forests, and mountains, here fruits and flowers, there glaciers and snow, here dwellings and ploughed fields, there desert and wilderness; yet for all this, the world that contains in its womb so many diverse things is one, its form and essence one, and one the bond that links its many parts and ties them together in discordant concord, and nothing is missing, yet nothing is there that does not serve for necessity or ornament; just so, I judge, the great poet (who is called divine for no other reason than that as he resembles the supreme Artificer in his workings he comes to participate in his divinity) can form a poem in which, as in a little world, one may read here of armies assembling, here of battles on land or sea, here of conquests of cities, skirmishes and duels, here of jousts, here descriptions of hunger and thirst, here tempests, fires, prodigies, there of celestial and infernal councils, there seditions, there discord, wanderings, adventures, enchantments, deeds of cruelty, daring, courtesy, generosity, there the fortunes of love, now happy, now sad, now joyous, now pitiful. Yet the poem that contains so great a variety of matter none the less should be one, one in form and soul; and all these things should be so combined that each concerns the other necessarily or verisimilarly that removing any one part or changing its place would destroy the whole. And if that is true, the art of composing a poem resembles the plan of the universe, which is composed of contraries, as that of music is. For if it were not multiple it would not be a whole or a plan, as Plotinus says.[4]

The distribution of the passages in which the epic poet conveyed mastery in a knowledge of the natural world, congruent with a knowledge of theology, history, and human nature, was one of the most demanding challenges. How were such nature passages to be introduced without violating the flow and logic of the plot? How were they supposed to be made pleasurable? Chunks lifted from the latest treatise would not be satisfying. How much could the audience be expected to bring as background preparation for reading these visions of nature when difficult concepts were involved? And, by no means least, how was the poet to manage the textual economy, when nature was so vast?[5]

---

[4] Torquato Tasso, *Discourses on the Heroic Poem*, trans. and ed. Marielle Cavalchini and Irene Samuel (Oxford: Clarendon, 1973), 77–78.

[5] For the difficulties that German poets had in linking scientific information with poetic genres, see Walter Schatzberg, *Scientific Themes in the Popular Literature and the Poetry of the German Enlightenment, 1720–1760* (Bern: Herbert Lang, 1973). The so-called "physico-theological poems" became rather tedious catalogues of natural objects and phenomena.

Goethe was well aware of this discussion and of how many epic poets had foundered on the boundlessness of knowledge. Antonio's praise of Tasso in Goethe's play echoes Tasso's catalogue from the above passage on heroic poetry, but we know that Tasso would not achieve the high standards he had set for himself. The *Gerusalemme Liberata* was frequently criticized as being too sprawling and incomplete. With the steady increase in scientific knowledge, the challenge grew more daunting. By the time of Barthold Hinrich Brockes, the epic threatened to collapse under the weight of information that had flowed in to Europe since the sixteenth century. Instead of an ordered landscape, the proliferation of physico-theological poems presented a confused, chaotic universe. It is instructive to compare Tasso's summation of the epic survey with Brockes's "Bewährtes Mittel für die Augen," which begins with the admission of inability. The complexity and richness of the landscape overwhelm the modern eye:

> Wenn wir in einer schönen Landschaft, mit Anmuth rings umgeben, stehn,
> Und, durch die Creatur gerühret, aufmerksamer, als sonst geschehn,
> Den Schmuck derselben zu betrachten und eigentlicher einzusehn,
> Noch einst vernünft'ge Triebe fühlen; so finden wir, daß unsre Augen
> (Durch die Gewohnheit fast verblendet, und gleichsam ungeschickt gemacht)
> Der Vorwürf' Anzahl, Zierlichkeit, der Farben Harmonie und Pracht,
> Indem sie sich zu sehr vertheilen, nicht ordentlich zu sehen taugen.
> Es scheint, als ob sich die Gedanken, so wie der Augen Strahl, zerstreuen,
> Und daß dieß der betrübte Grund, wodurch wir uns der Welt nicht freuen,
> Noch Gott, in Seiner Creatur, mit mehrerm Eifer, ehren können.[6]

In short, the ideal whereby the epic poet perceives and recreates order out of the manifold world has been overwhelmed. The narrator is lost; the readers are overwhelmed; all sense of order seems gone.

In a provocative essay, Gernot Böhme recently challenged the prevailing classification of *Faust* as a drama and suggested that we consider relocating it in the tradition of the long didactic poem ("Lehrgedicht").[7]

---

[6] Barthold Hinrich Brockes, *Irdisches Vergnügen in Gott* (Bern: Herbert Lang, 1970), 7:660–63.

[7] Gernot Böhme, "Kann man Goethes 'Faust' in der Tradition des Lehrgedichts lesen?" *Goethe-Jahrbuch* 117 (2000): 67–77.

Possible precursors would be Hesiod's *Theogony*, Lucretius's *De rerum natura*, Vergil's *Georgics*, and Ovid's *Metamorphoses*, according to Böhme. There are strong indications that Goethe had indeed considered the possibility of writing a "nature poem," perhaps in direct imitation of Lucretius.[8] On 22 January 1799, shortly after he had started working on the *Faust* project again, Goethe wrote to Karl Ludwig von Knebel, who had just done a translation of the first book of *De rerum natura*: "Indem ich es durchlas hat sich manches bey mir geregt, denn seit dem vorigen Sommer habe ich oft über die Möglichkeit eines Naturgedichtes in unsern Tagen gedacht, und seit der kleinen Probe über die Metamorphose der Pflanzen bin ich verschiedentlich aufgemuntert worden."[9] The mention of the "Metamorphosis of the Plants" should perhaps not circumscribe the horizon too narrowly; Goethe might also have had *Faust* in mind.

Rescue from the requirement of encyclopedic inclusiveness came with fundamental shifts in aesthetic theory. A decisive moment is captured in Goethe's report of his encounter with Strasbourg Cathedral. He came prepared, on the basis of classical principles of proportion and harmony, to be repelled by the complexity of Gothic architecture.[10] However, a remarkable aesthetic conversion came about when he did not attempt to grasp the whole structure at once, but began to appreciate the collective impact of the necessary details. This new aesthetic appreciation parallels exactly the hermeneutic methods that Goethe had learned while studying the Bible and then again while reading hermetic texts. The intense involvement with the myriad of details eventually induces an effect of harmony, because the particular features are logically, necessarily related to each other, even if the relationships are not immediately apparent, as the fictional voice of the architect instructs:

> Alle diese Massen waren notwendig, und siehst du sie nicht an allen älteren Kirchen meiner Stadt? Nur ihre willkürliche Größen hab' ich zum stimmenden Verhältnis erhoben. Wie über dem Haupteingang, der zwei kleinere Seiten beherrscht, sich der weite Kreis des Fensters öffnet, der

---

[8] Karl Bapp, "Goethe und Lukrez," *Jahrbuch der Goethe-Gesellschaft* 12 (1926): 47–67; Margarethe Plath, "Der Goethe-Schellingsche Plan eines philosophischen Naturgedichts," *Preussische Jahrbücher* 106 (1901): 44–74; and H. B. Nisbet, "Lucretius in Eighteenth-Century Germany, with a Commentary on Goethe's 'Metamorphose der Tiere,'" *Modern Language Review* 81 (1986): 97–115.

[9] Goethe, *Goethes Briefe*, ed. Karl Robert Mandelkow and Bodo Morawe, 4 vols. (Hamburg: Christian Wegner, 1962), 2:365.

[10] Johann Wolfgang von Goethe, *Werke: Hamburger Ausgabe in 14 Bänden*, ed. Erich Trunz (Munich: C. H. Beck, 1981), 12:10. This "Hamburger Ausgabe" will henceforth be cited as HA.

dem Schiffe der Kirche antwortet und sonst nur Tageloch war, wie hoch
drüber der Glockenplatz die kleineren Fenster forderte! (HA 12:11)

The pleasure of the assemblage no longer depends on how loyal the architect or the author has been to arbitrary principles of form, but comes
instead from the interplay of the parts in the "Raritätenkasten" (curio cabinet).[11] In essence, the breakthrough comes with the realization that if the
shape of the epic were adjusted to that of the "theatre of nature,"[12] then
there would be room for the myriad details of the natural world. The
implications of all this for Goethe's challenges in constructing a modern
epic were enormous. First, he was emancipated from the formal constraints
of imitating the structure of the classical epic without abandoning all order.
But if the poet was no longer required to have a priori the cosmic overview
that Tasso had still heralded in the *Discourses on Heroic Poetry*, then an
entirely different possibility arises: the poet can now concentrate upon pre-
senting in detail episodes or events in which a specific law of nature is
demonstrated. Under the condition that the principle of uniformity holds,
even very limited theatres, such as laboratories, can reveal a partial aspect
of the totality. The microcosm-macrocosm correspondence has not been
abandoned, only modified to deal with the realities of scientific progress,
and in "Auerbachs Keller" we and Faust will be exposed to a series of profound lessons about how the natural universe operates.

## "Auerbachs Keller" as a Theatre of Nature and Theatre of Memory

Writing about Winckelmann in 1805, Goethe reflected upon how difficult
it had become for moderns to penetrate to the essential order of things.
The Greeks had still had the capacity to grasp the totality of the universe,
because their consciousness was whole, not yet fragmented:

> Wenn die gesunde Natur des Menschen als ein Ganzes wirkt, wenn er sich
> in der Welt als in einem großen, schönen, würdigen und werten Ganzen
> fühlt, wenn das harmonische Behagen ihm ein reines, freies Entzücken

---

[11] On the history of the curio cabinet and the museum and their importance
for the development of modern scientific investigation, see Paula Findlen, *Possessing
Nature: Museums, Collecting, and Scientific Culture in Early Modern Italy*
(Berkeley and Los Angeles: U of California P, 1994).

[12] See Ann Blair, *The Theater of Nature: Jean Bodin and Renaissance Science*
(Princeton: Princeton UP, 1997), esp. 153–79. One can never stress enough the
contributions of Frances A. Yates on these topics; on this topic see her *Theatre of
the World* (Chicago: U of Chicago P, 1969).

> gewährt — dann würde das Weltall, wenn es sich selbst empfinden kön-
> nte, als an sein Ziel gelangt aufjauchzen und den Gipfel des eigenen
> Werdens und Wesens bewundern. Denn wozu dient alle der Aufwand von
> Sonnen und Planeten und Monden, von Sternen und Milchstraßen, von
> Kometen und Nebelflecken, von gewordenen und werdenden Welten,
> wenn sich nicht zuletzt ein glücklicher Mensch unbewußt seines Daseins
> erfreut? (HA 12:98)

Behind these reflections is the familiar reciprocal mirroring of the macrocosm and the microcosm, but with an interesting overtone. The remarkable word "Aufwand" brings the connotation that the cosmos has been
assembled with effort, has been staged for the benefit of the individual,
who should be delighted by the spectacle.[13] Someone who is a unified, harmonious microcosm would be able to resonate to the splendor of the
macrocosm. The eloquence of the passage does homage to Winckelmann's
celebrated analysis of the difference between the modes of perception of
the ancients and the moderns. But in the next paragraph Goethe extends
the comparison into unexpected territory, bringing in a theme from the
history of science. The ancients were aided in their concentration because
the frame of their world was fixed; the moderns are confronted by the infinite, open universe:

> Wirft sich der Neuere, wie es uns eben jetzt ergangen, fast bei jeder
> Betrachtung ins Unendliche, um zuletzt, wenn es ihm glückt, auf einen
> beschränkten Punkt wieder zurückzukehren, so fühlten die Alten ohne
> weitern Umweg sogleich ihre einzige Behaglichkeit innerhalb der
> lieblichen Grenzen der schönen Welt. Hieher waren sie gesetzt, hiezu
> berufen, hier fand ihre Tätigkeit Raum, ihre Leidenschaft Gegenstand
> und Nahrung. (HA 12:99)

The problem is epistemological. If the macrocosm is infinite, how can it
represent itself to the individual? And how can the endless panorama be
*represented*, so as to make the totality of complex phenomena immediately
known in particulars and to the individual observer?

The preface to the *Farbenlehre* has an apology for the limitations
inherent in writings about natural science, picking up on the themes in the
Winckelmann essay. A text is deficient in achieving the full effect and might
be compared to the shortcomings of a written play versus a performance.

---

[13] Blair, *The Theater of Nature*, 157, quotes a passage from Linnaeus that shows
the continuity of the topos of the cosmic drama into the eighteenth century.
According to Dorothea Kuhn, in her chapter "Goethe's Relationship to the Theories
of Development of His Time," in *Goethe and the Sciences: A Reappraisal*, ed. Frederick
Amrine, Francis J. Zucker, and Harvey Wheeler (Dordrecht, The Netherlands, and
Boston: D. Reidel, 1987), 3–15, Goethe was fascinated by Linnaeus.

The difficulties of how to represent the natural world are analogous to those of the theatre:

> Denn wie ein gutes Theaterstück eigentlich kaum zur Hälfte gebracht werden kann, vielmehr der größere Teil desselben dem Glanz der Bühne, der Persönlichkeit des Schauspielers, der Kraft seiner Stimme, der Eigentümlichkeit seiner Bewegungen, ja dem Geiste und der guten Laune des Zuschauers anheimgegeben bleibt, so ist es noch viel mehr der Fall mit einem Buche, das von natürlichen Erscheinungen handelt. Wenn es genossen, wenn es genutzt werden soll, so muß dem Leser die Natur entweder wirklich oder in lebhafter Phantasie gegenwärtig sein. Denn eigentlich sollte der Schreibende sprechen und seinen Zuhörern die Phänomene, teils wie sie uns ungesucht entgegenkommen, teils wie sie durch absichtliche Vorrichtungen nach Zweck und Willen dargestellt werden könnnen, als Text erst anschaulich machen; als dann würde jedes Erläutern, Auslegen einer lebendigen Wirkung nicht ermangeln. (HA 13:321)

In short, the scientific processes should be demonstrated so that the mind's eye would have the assistance of the physical eye and would be able to visualize the natural events. What this cluster of quotations elucidates is how the microcosm, the text, and the theatre stage can be thought of as analogues. The analogies are not strange: everyone who has taken basic science courses will remember the "experiments" in a "science theatre," which were demonstrations of some natural principle performed for the audience of students.[14]

But the need to demonstrate, to realize insights into nature theatrically was a fairly recent development in the history of science, and historians have zeroed in on the Renaissance as the period in which science became staged. Not least, the performative nature of alchemy lent itself to discursive intermingling with the practices of the theatre.[15] Wandering alchemists

---

[14] A fascinating overview of the connections between scientific demonstration and entertainment, from Francis Bacon's proposals in the *New Atlantis* to the eighteenth-century fascination with ventriloquism, is Leigh Eric Schmidt's "From Demon Possession to Magic Show: Ventriloquism, Religion, and the Enlightenment," *Church History* 67.2 (1998): 274–304.

[15] Two very different but fascinating analyses of such intermingling are provided from the viewpoint of history of science by Jay Tribby in his article "Cooking (with) Clio and Cleo: Eloquence and Experiment in Seventeenth-Century Florence," *Journal of the History of Ideas* 52.3 (1991): 417–39; and Deborah E. Harkness, "Shows in the Showstone: A Theater of Alchemy and Apocalypse in the Angel Conversations of John Dee (1527–1608/9)," *Renaissance Quarterly* 49 (1996): 707–37.

seeking patronage at a court would of course have a vested interest in demonstrating their skills and thereby legitimating themselves in front of a critical audience.[16] In addition to such "public performances," demonstrations could as often happen in a room set aside specifically for the purpose as a "laboratory," famously depicted in the frontispiece to Heinrich Khunrath's *Amphitheatrum sapientiae aeternae* (1609). Johann Valentin Andreae's description of the ideal "laboratory" makes clear the underlying foundations of the microcosmic construct:

> Hier werden zum menschlichen Gebrauch und zur Beförderung der Gesundheit alle Kräfte der Metalle und Mineralien oder Gewächse, auch der Tiere, untersucht, gereinigt, vermehrt, vereinigt. Hier wird der Himmel der Erde angetraut und die der Erde eingeprägten göttlichen Geheimnisse entdeckt. Hier lernt man das Feuer regieren, die Luft gebrauchen, das Wasser schätzen und die Erde erkennen. Hier hat der Affe der Natur, die Kunst etwas, worin sie spielt, indem sie den ersten Ursprung nachahmt und nach den Fußstapfen des großen Weltgebäudes ein solches im kleinen auf das vortrefflichste nachbildet. Was durch den Fleiß der Alten aus dem Eingeweide der Natur uns ausgegraben und ans Licht gebracht worden ist, wird hier unter die Probe genommen, damit man weiß, ob es uns auch recht redlich entdeckt worden ist.[17]

Evidently enough, the distinctions between a "laboratory" and a "museum" would be collapsed in such a space, and in fact that was often the case.

Before the establishment of state-sponsored laboratories, private individuals frequently established laboratories in their own homes.[18] Goethe himself conducted much of his scientific research in his home and would turn parts of it into a museum. In these spaces, the boundaries between "original experiment" and "demonstration" were blurred. Frequently the science theatre was where the experimenter demonstrated for a public the results that, because they were predictable, confirmed the hypotheses. Thus a demonstrator was a theatre director, who assembled the apparatus and, often with the help of assistants, performed the show and elucidated it for the members of the audience. This is the role that Mephistopheles

---

[16] Pamela H. Smith, "Alchemy as a Language of Mediation at the Habsbourg Court," *Isis* 85.1 (1994): 1–25, cites the examples of alchemical transmutations performed for Leopold I, one by Wenceslas Seiler and one by Johann Joachim Becher.

[17] Johann Valentin Andreae, *Christianopolis* (originally published in 1619), trans. D. S. Georgi, ed. Richard van Dülmen (Stuttgart: Calwer Verlag, 1972), 113.

[18] See especially Steven Shapin, "The House of Experiment in Seventeenth-Century England," *Isis* 79 (1988): 373–404.

assumes in "Auerbachs Keller in Leipzig." A key irony here is that this cellar is located *Auerbach*'s house. The historical Auerbach had been a successful medical doctor and the wine cellar was initially only a by-product of his medical practice. Quite literally, then, the Auerbach house fit the description of the "house of experiment," where the doctor had treated his patients. The space would be ideally suited for a set of demonstrations about the nature and workings of the universe.

Closely linked with the project of distributing knowledge in the space of the "theatre of nature" was the idea of the "memory theatre," with the metaphor of the stage as a crossover.[19] In their practical aspects, such memory theatres were mnemonic devices whose origins go back to the needs of rhetoricians and scholars during what were still predominantly oral cultures. Moving through the memory was like moving through a physical structure, with the topics artfully arranged in their specified, unfixed places. In 1526 an Italian translator of a memory treatise noted at the discussion of the places of Hell that for remembering the places of Hell the works of Vergil and Dante were very helpful. As Yates comments:

---

[19] See the classic studies by Frances A. Yates, *The Art of Memory* (Chicago: U of Chicago P, 1966) and *Theatre of the World*, as well as her articles "The Stage in Robert Fludd's Memory System," *Shakespeare Studies* 3 (1967): 138–66; and "Lodovico da Pirano's Memory Treatise," in *Cultural Aspects of the Italian Renaissance: Essays in Honour of Paul Oskar Kristeller*, ed. Cecil H. Clough (Manchester: Manchester UP and New York: Alfred F. Zambelli, 1976), 111–22. On Fludd, see also Wilhelm Schmidt-Biggemann, "Robert Fludds *Theatrum memoriae*," in *Ars memorativa: Zur kulturgeschichtlichen Bedeutung der Gedächtniskunst, 1400–1750*, ed. Jörg Jochen Berns and Wolfgang Neuber (Tübingen: Max Niemeyer, 1993), 154–69. On the crossover between the theatre of memory and the theatre of the world, see Paolo Rossi, *Clavis Universalis: Arti della memoria e logica combinatoria da Lullo a Leibniz* (Milan and Naples: Ricciardi, 1960; repr., Bologna: Il Mulino, 1983), 103–29; Heinrich F. Plett, "*Topothesia Memorativa*: Imaginäre Architektur in Renaissance und Barock," in *Kunstgriffe: Auskünfte zur Reichweite von Literaturtheorie und Literaturkritik; Festschrift für Herbert Mainusch*, ed. Ulrich Horstmann and Wolfgang Zach (Frankfurt am Main and New York: Peter Lang, 1989), 294–312; and Mary Carruthers, "The Poet as Master Builder: Composition and Locational Memory in the Middle Ages," *New Literary History* 24 (1993): 881–904. On the further connection to the structures of thought, see James Robert Goetsch, Jr., *Vico's Axioms: The Geometry of the Human World* (New Haven: Yale UP, 1995). That the body itself could be a theatre of memory was more than a theoretical possibility, as Horst Wenzel's fascinating work explores: *Hören und Sehen: Schrift und Bild; Kultur und Gedächtnis im Mittelalter* (Munich: C. H. Beck, 1995).

> That Dante's *Inferno* could be regarded as a kind of memory system for memorising Hell and its punishments with striking images on orders of places, will come as a great shock, and I must leave it as a shock. . . . If one thinks of the poem as based on orders of places in Hell, Purgatory, and Paradise, and as a cosmic order of places in which the spheres of Hell are the spheres of Heaven in reverse, it begins to appear as a summa of similitudes and exempla, ranged in order and set out upon the universe.[20]

As Mary Carruthers has pointed out, the analogy between Hell and a physical structure was warranted by the structure of hell in Dante's poem.[21] She explains that what is displayed by architectural design also relates to the work of memory: "The images which Dante encounters in this amphitheater should function for him as mnemonic cues to matters (*res*) that he has in storage and now has the opportunity to use in the new gathering place which the theater images provide for him."[22] Canto 11 of the *Inferno* is especially explicit in reminding Dante the Pilgrim of the need to *remember* the places from relevant texts and to combine them actively:

> "Philosophy, for one who understands it," he said to me, "points out, not in one place alone, how nature takes her course from divine Intellect and from Its art; and if you note well your *Physics*, you will find, after not many pages, that your art, as far as it can, follows her, as the pupil does the master; so that your art is as it were grandchild of God. By these two, if you remember Genesis at the beginning, it behooves man to gain his bread and to prosper." (11.97–108)

The admonition to remember will have to be repeated more than once by Vergil the Guide in the course of the progress through the memory theatre (the text).

In order to present the encompassing vision, Dante had to master the knowledge of his time, had to make his epic a coherent encyclopedia. Although by the eighteenth century the explosion of knowledge was so great that it was virtually impossible for one person to know everything, Goethe made an impressive, valiant effort. In order to convey that knowledge in an epic, he was forced to abandon the regularity of form that had been a defining characteristic of all previous epics. The macrocosm was so complicated that a microcosm with the geometric rigor of the *Aeneid* or the *Divine Comedy* would mislead as a map, giving the false impression of Olympian hegemony over what was a universe that was still unfolding and still being discovered.

---

[20] Yates, *The Art of Memory*, 95.
[21] Carruthers, "The Poet as Master Builder," 882–83.
[22] Carruthers, "The Poet as Master Builder," 84.

For Dante to be able to make his text in the way he did, he had to begin with a scheme that already had a place for all topics. Dante's memory theatre could be so clearly organized because he had already provided places for everything that the individual might need to remember so as to be able to understand the created universe.[23] The theatre could be complete because knowledge was, apparently, finite. But that requires the perspective of an omniscient being whose privileged vantage point had become unavailable by Goethe's time. We are in the situation now of the spectator who enters the theatre from below. The stage, the curtains, the furniture are in place; the actors arrive; the plot unfolds. As spectators, we move through the events being performed and only gradually grasp the plot. The view from below corresponds to a truer concept of the relationship of the microcosm to the macrocosm, for we shall always have access only to the former and must guess at the latter. There can be no omniscience for us, or for the epic poet. We do not recall what there was before the play began, before we entered the cosmic theatre, and do not yet know how the drama will end. The best we can do is to immerse ourselves in the actual performance, hoping to glean from the snippets we observe some understanding of the logic underlying the plot and the events. This is not the counsel of despair, but rather the opening for a new alliance between the scientific method, working with limited experiments yet revealing universal laws, and the aesthetics of the particular as articulated by Goethe. We will not need Dante's thirty-four cantos to depict the world and its principles — one compact scene, shrewdly and vividly made, when thoughtfully and carefully observed, can reveal all that we need to remember about the topic. The universe can be represented in the tight, condensed version of "Auerbachs Keller in Leipzig" if the spectators can observe, collate their observations, and draw the conclusions that can become laws of science.

## Faust between Science and Magic

Goethe was an exemplary scientific investigator and historian of science.[24] The picture here too has been blurred by the persistent misidentification of Goethe as Faust. Unlike Goethe, the historical Faust made no lasting or even transitory contribution to the progress of science. There probably was someone in the sixteenth century who went by the name of "Dr. Faust,"

---

[23] Spencer Pearce, "Dante and the Art of Memory," *The Italianist* 16 (1996): 21–61.

[24] See Karl J. Fink, *Goethe's History of Science* (Cambridge: Cambridge UP, 1991).

but after two centuries of intensive research, neither literary historians nor historians of science have unearthed a single work, whether published or in manuscript, written by him. This is remarkable, all the more so since historians have made immense strides in recovering the "alternative" dimensions of science, counterbalancing the nineteenth-century emphasis on science as rational, technological, and ineluctably progressive. The alchemical, Neoplatonic, and occult discourses have been rehabilitated as subjects for historical investigation, and many interesting figures have come to light,[25] but we have nary a word about the accomplishments of "Faust." What the legends, gossip, and all the bits of evidence indicate is that the historical Faust *was* a charlatan, who operated on the margins of the scholarly community, pretending to have mastered this or that discipline.[26] Goethe could have chosen any of a number of figures from the murky, illusive world of sixteenth-century alchemical and hermetic traditions, all of whom left material traces of their doings, whether published or unpublished.[27] Why then opt for Faust? The answer lies in the range of approaches to scientific problems available in the sixteenth and seventeenth centuries.

---

[25] An overview is available in R. J. W. Evans, *Rudolf II and His World: A Study in Intellectual History, 1576–1612* (Oxford: Clarendon, 1973), especially chapter 6, "Rudolf and the Occult Arts."

[26] The stages of the quest for the historical Faust may be traced via Friedrich Kluge, "Vom geschichtlichen Dr. Faust," orig. "Beilage zur *Allgemeinen Zeitung* Nr. 9 (1896), repr. in Friedrich Kluge, *Bunte Blätter: Kulturgeschichtliche Vorträge und Aufsätze* (Freiburg im Breslau: J. Bielefelds Verlag, 1910), 1–27; Hans Henning, "Faust als historische Gestalt," *Goethe: Neue Folge des Jahrbuchs der Goethe-Gesellschaft* 21 (1959): 107–39.; Jörn Göres, "Dr. Faust in Geschichte und Dichtung," in *Ansichten zu Faust: Karl Theens zum 70. Geburtstag*, ed. Günther Mahal (Stuttgart: W. Kohlhammer, 1973), 9–20; Frank Baron, *Doctor Faustus from History to Legend* (Munich: Fink, 1978); and Baron, "Camerarius and the Historical Doctor Faustus," in *Joachim Camerarius (1500–1574): Beiträge zur Geschichte des Humanismus im Zeitalter der Reformation / Essays on the History of Humanism during the Reformation*, ed. Frank Baron (Munich: Fink, 1978), 200–222.

[27] Some of these have been proposed as the "models" for Faust, e.g. Paracelsus in the work of Agnes Bartscherer, *Paracelsus, Paracelsisten und Goethes Faust: Eine Quellenstudie* (Dortmund: Druck und Verlag von Fr. Wilh. Ruhfus, 1911); or Heinrich Cornelius Agrippa von Nettesheim (1486–1535) nominated by, among others, Frank Möbus, "*Heinrich! Heinrich!* Goethes *Faust*: Genetisches, Genealogisches," *Euphorion* 83 (1989): 337–63. A good candidate would be Johann Joachim Becher (1635–82), whose biography is now available in the excellent study by Pamela H. Smith, *The Business of Alchemy: Science and Culture in the Holy Roman Empire* (Princeton: Princeton UP, 1997).

Broadly speaking, there were three such models. First, there was the traditional position, heavily oriented to textual study and reliant on the standard authorities such as Aristotle. Second, there was the Neoplatonic strain associated with Marsilio Ficino, which came to include the praxis-oriented disciplines such as alchemy, medicine, and astronomy. Although maligned for their inadequate methodological rigor, members of this group played a key role in challenging authority and in turning research to the investigation of natural phenomena. Finally, there were those who engaged in wild speculation, dabbled in "magic," and contributed little useful knowledge (for example, the "Rosicrucians"). Against this background, we see that Faust stands on the threshold demarcating medieval from modern science. He has been trained in the scholastic disciplines, based upon the authoritative texts from which close reasoning should deduce knowledge of the world, but he has found them insufficient in providing answers. His discontent with the canonical teachings does mark him as a modern, a representative of the sixteenth century, who has heard tell of new, more powerful methods of inquiry and has resolved to learn them. However, because he is so desperate for results, Faust does not work his way into the new corpus of learning. Instead, he plunges in without sound preparation and is immediately in trouble as he joins in with the wild, speculative group. Imagining the new science to be a kind of magic alone, without any need to test hypotheses against the world, he resorts to spells, incantations, and demons. He has no inkling of the philosophic underpinnings to the *prisca theologia* (the "ancient theology" thought by Renaissance philosophers such as Marsilio Ficino to be hidden in the sacred texts of all religions) and is baffled by the Erdgeist's attempt to make the connection for him. Faust has succumbed to the superstitious side of the discourse and yields to the temptations of "magic."[28]

The detour into magic, the quest for the words that will give control over demons and elements, leads to a dead end in the history of science. Superstition cannot be equated with reliable knowledge about the world. It is important for our understanding of "Auerbachs Keller in Leipzig" and for the drama as a whole to grasp that Faust has missed a historic opportunity. The paths he might have taken were towards the amalgamation of

---

[28] On "magic" in the Renaissance, see D. P. Walker, *Spiritual and Demonic Magic from Ficino to Campanella* (London: The Warburg Institute, University of London, 1958); and Charles Zika, "Reuchlin's *De Verbo Mirifico* and the Magic Debate of the Late Fifteenth Century," *Journal of the Warburg and Courtauld Institutes* 39 (1976): 104–38. On the *prisca theologia*, see Stephen A. McKnight, *The Modern Age and the Recovery of Ancient Wisdom: A Reconsideration of Historical Consciousness, 1450–1650* (Columbia, MO, and London: U of Missouri P, 1991), esp. 27–59.

Neoplatonic philosophy with the study of nature, but Faust is neither a Paracelsus nor a Newton. Those investigators measured their speculations against evidence, without abandoning the wisdom of Scripture and ancient philosophers. Overall, those figures contributed positively to what came to be known as the "scientific revolution," even if they sometimes harbored ideas that seem bizarre to us today.[29] But the historical Faust made no such contribution, as Goethe knew from having read the evidence of the legends closely. Faust has here been nominated as a representative of those who fail to understand the essence of genuine scientific investigation, who are too impatient or slothful to take the low, rocky road through the evidence in order to discover underlying principles.

Perversely, the one who knows the accomplishments of modern science is Mephistopheles. He has a personal interest in this research, since it might give him an edge in the contest with God. The dramatic logic also requires that he have access to the most up-to-date knowledge of natural laws, since he otherwise would have nothing to offer Faust. Of course, Mephistopheles is duplicitous as a teacher: he provides just enough evidence to enable the pupil to know the truth, but declines to explain principles or teach techniques. Those Faust must deduce for himself, if he will. And if Faust comes to wrong conclusions or fails to comprehend what he sees, such as his rejuvenation? "Well," Mephistopheles could reply smugly, "I've done my best — where is that unerring instinct for truth God supposedly gave these creatures?" In "Auerbachs Keller," Mephistopheles will reveal all the cosmic laws to Faust, but the latter will be totally baffled and none the wiser when the scene is finished.

Goethe was careful to distinguish among the study, the laboratory, and the theatre.[30] Faust begins in his study, which still owes much to the medieval monk's cell. The space seems confining for the modern man, but Faust does not proceed to the space for practical experimentation, the laboratory. That will appear later in the drama as Wagner's space. Instead, Faust moves, or is moved, to "Auerbachs Keller," the theatre where he will only be an observer. Mephistopheles will be doing the demonstration for Faust. But for Mephistopheles, the space is indeed a laboratory, since here he is conducting part of the larger experiment in which Faust has been made a subject through the discussions of the "Prologue in Heaven." The dramatic ironies here are that the audience knows about the experiment being carried out by Mephistopheles and also understands the scientific

---

[29] See Betty Jo Teeter Dobbs, *The Janus Face of Genius: The Role of Alchemy in Newton's Thought* (Cambridge: Cambridge UP, 1991).

[30] Gustav F. Hartlaub discusses the furnishings of Faust's study in "Goethe als Alchemist," *Euphorion* 48 (1954): 19–40; here, 30–31.

principles being demonstrated to Faust, who does not know of his own position and fails to grasp the principles. Two questions arise. How do we know from the text that Faust does not understand the demonstration? How are we supposed to see an order where Faust does not, so as to be able to gauge his success or failure in understanding?

To the first, the evidence is negative: Faust remains passive and indifferent. There are no cries of "Eureka," no gasps of astonishment, no signals of wonder. Yet those are the sorts of reactions that must necessarily follow genuine scientific discovery. As Goethe put it in the passage quoted earlier, there should be a connection between the awareness of the cosmos and a deep emotion: the cosmos should declare the glory of Creation. The impact of a drama, or any work of art, is judged by the responses of the audience. A tragedy without catharsis, a comedy without laughter would indicate either that the drama was poorly made or that the audience has failed to understand what is being shown. The drama here is the whole order of creation, and human beings should be in awe of the spectacle. Passivity in the presence of the spectacle of nature is not sufficient; the scientific mind must actively participate, as Goethe explained in connection with his work on colors:

> Denn das bloße Anblicken einer Sache kann uns nicht fördern. Jedes Ansehen geht über in ein Betrachten, jedes Betrachten in ein Sinnen, jedes Sinnen in ein Verknüpfen, und so kann man sagen, daß wir schon bei jedem aufmerksamen Blick in die Welt theoretisieren. Dieses aber mit Bewußtsein zu bedienen, mit Ironie zu tun und vorzunehmen, eine solche Gewandheit ist nötig, wenn die Abstraktion, vor der wir uns fürchten, unschädlich und das Erfahrungsresultat, das wir hoffen, recht lebendig und nützlich werden soll. (HA 13:317)[31]

There can hardly be a clearer rebuttal from Goethe's pen than this against those who laud Faust's "indifference" in "Auerbachs Keller." If Faust is bored in "Auerbachs Keller," then nothing could quicken him, and subsequent events will tend to confirm that. But he can only be bored because he has missed the point of the demonstration, which reviews the laws of matter so entertainingly.

## Humors and Temperaments

There is nothing in the text that explicitly identifies the four companions as students. The efforts to associate their names with student nicknames or

---

[31] For a subtle and detailed analysis of how Goethe connects perception and theory, see W. Gebhard, " 'Allgemeine Ansicht nach Innen': Ideologiekritische

argot are arbitrary at least and unconvincing at best. More productive were the observations made by Trendlenburg, who noticed that in the revision from the "Urfaust" the four had become less individual and more typical.[32] He also commented on their different characters, one of few critics to do so on the basis of their actions.[33] There are exactly four characters, each of whom represents a unique temperament.[34] Goethe has constructed for each of the four a character corresponding to the old medical system of the humors.[35] In the four different characters, each representing one of the humors, Goethe provided the key for decoding the scientific-medical themes of "Auerbachs Keller in Leipzig."

The usefulness of the system of humors for authors trying to invent fictional characters was immediately obvious to anyone familiar with the system, since each of the types — sanguine, choleric, melancholic, and phlegmatic — comes equipped with a set of responses and attitudes, that is, "characteristics." Basically the medical diagnosis provides an instant description of someone's character. The specific qualities arising from imbalances in the humors was something that doctors strove to correct, whereas writers could exploit the narrative possibilities of an extreme melancholic.[36] Second,

---

Aspekte von Goethes anschauendem Denken," *Philosophia Naturalis* 20.2 (1983): 312–38. Although I concur with the diagnosis, the conclusions reached by Franziska Meier, "Goethes *Faust* als Schiffbrüchiger und Zuschauer: Einige Überlegungen anknüpfend an Hans Blumenbergs Studie zur Daseinsmetapher des Schiffbruchs mit Zuschauer," *Germanisch-Romanische Monatsschrift* NF 49.1 (1999): 55–78, seem at odds with the evidence she adduces. Nowhere does Faust actually *look at* the world; if he did he would have shared the horror of Lynkeus's vision.

[32] Adolf Trendlenburg, *Goethes Faust erklärt* (Berlin and Leipzig: Vereinigung wissenschaftlicher Verleger Walter de Gruyter, 1922), 292.

[33] Trendlenburg, *Goethes Faust erklärt*, 293–94.

[34] On the significance of "four" in Goethe's thinking, see Wolfgang Binder, "Goethes Vierheiten," *Typologia Litterarum: Festschrift für Max Wehrli*, ed. Stefan Sonderegger, Alois M. Haas, and Harald Burger (Zurich: Atlantis, 1969), 311–23. On the symbolic values of four generally, see the overview by S. K. Heninger, Jr., "Some Renaissance Versions of the Pythagorean Tetrad," *Studies in the Renaissance* 8 (1961): 7–33; and Heinz Meyer, *Die Zahlenallegorese im Mittelalter: Methode und Gebrauch* (Munich: Wilhelm Fink, 1975), 123–27.

[35] Friedrich Oberkogler, *Faust 1. Teil von Johann Wolfgang von Goethe: Werkbesprechung und geisteswissenschaftliche Erläuterungen* (Schaffhausen: Novalis Verlag, 1981), 189.

[36] For examples, see John W. Draper, *The Humors & Shakespeare's Characters* (1949; repr., New York: AMS Press, 1970); and James Allen Riddell, *The Evolution*

the appropriation of medical diagnostics for such literary purposes need not seem at all strange today. For instance, the Freudian system has displaced the humoral one so that writers operate with categories derived from clinical practice, such as "oedipal complex," "repression," "schizophrenia," "hysteria," or "inferiority complex." The audience, having a knowledge of at least popularized Freudianism, understands and analyzes these characters accordingly. Even characters produced by writers who did not think in such categories can be retroactively subsumed by this system, so that one gets psychoanalytic readings of Hamlet or Milton's Satan. Finally, we know that Goethe used analogues to chemical-physical processes to construct the characters in *Die Wahlverwandtschaften*.[37] Faust should, as a doctor of medicine, be fully conversant with the system and hence able to recognize what is being demonstrated in "Auerbachs Keller." Although the evidence about Goethe's reliance upon the system of the humors and temperaments will be circumstantial in the case of the four characters in "Auerbachs Keller," there is good indication that he was thinking in such categories at the time. Paralipomenon I to *Faust*, a sketchy outline of a plot, explicitly links temperaments with modalities of knowledge: "Helles kaltes Wissensch. Streben Wagner / Dumpfes warmes — — Schüler."[38] Terms such as "hell," "kalt," "dumpf," and "warm" point unambiguously to the components of the temperaments with which Goethe indexed these two. The contours are consistent, so that for example the student, marked as "moist"[39] and "warm," is sanguine, which corresponds with childhood and naivety.

---

*of the Humours Character in Seventeenth-Century English Comedy* (PhD diss., U of Southern California, 1966), 7–35. Artists were also able to use the humoral system in order to flesh out figures: Hubert Steinke, "Giotto und die Physiognomik," *Zeitschrift für Kunstgeschichte* (1996): 523–47. The intersection of astrology and medicine complicated the system, not only for diagnosis but also for literary production; see Helmut Rehder, "Planetenkinder: Some Problems of Character Portrayal in Literature," *Graduate Journal* (University of Texas) 8 (1968): 69–97.

[37] See Jeremy Adler, *"Eine fast magische Anziehungskraft": Goethes* Wahlverwandtschaften *und die Chemie seiner Zeit* (Munich: C. H. Beck, 1987); Bernhard Buschendorf, *Goethes mythische Denkform: Zur Ikonographie der 'Wahlverwandtschaften'* (Frankfurt am Main: Suhrkamp, 1986); and Waltraud Wiethölter, "Legenden: Zur Mythologie von Goethes *Wahlverwandtschaften*," *Deutsche Vierteljahrsschrift* 56 (1982): 1–64.

[38] Anne Bohnenkamp, *" ... das Hauptgeschäft nicht außer lassend": Die Paralipomena zu Goethes "Faust"* (Frankfurt am Main: Insel, 1994), 221. Compare Hans Mayer, "Der Famulus Wagner und die moderne Wissenschaft," in *Gestaltungsgeschichte und Gesellschaftsgeschichte*, ed. Helmut Kreuzer and Käte Hamburger (Stuttgart: J. B. Metzler, 1969), 176–200.

[39] "Dumpf" is etymologically related to "Dampf" (English "damp") and originally meant "moist, wet," and only later came to mean something like the "dull"

Authors were not the only ones to use the humoral categories in order to develop characters; artists also made extensive use of the same material. The example that comes to mind immediately is Albrecht Dürer's *Melancolia I*, a copy of which Goethe would eventually own,[40] and which has been intensely studied.[41] Less well-known but more interesting for my purposes is another Dürer woodcut, "Männerbad" ("Men's Bathhouse"), which Goethe also owned.[42] That he admired Dürer is already attested in the essay on the Strasbourg Cathedral (HA 12:14). Goethe's early interest in Dürer coincided with his extensive research into the sixteenth century, especially the carnivalesque of Hans Sachs.[43] In the poem "Erklärung eines alten Holzschnittes, vorstellend Hans Sachsens poetische Sendung" ("Explanation of an Old Woodcut, Depicting Hans Sachs"), he praised Dürer:

> Nichts verzierlicht und nichts verkritzelt,
> Nichts verlindert und nichts verwitzelt!
> Sondern die Welt soll vor dir stehn,
> Wie Albrecht Dürer sie hat gesehn:
> Ihr festes Leben und Mannlichkeit,
> Ihr inner Maß und Ständigkeit. (HA 1:136)

These lines suggest that one of the things Goethe admired in Dürer's works was the way in which types were realized as individuals or the temperaments given concrete form.

Dated circa 1496–97, "Männerbad" (see frontispiece) has been given a remarkable interpretation by Edgar Wind, who argued that the picture represents a "Dionysian mystery."[44] Wind describes the scene in terms of the humors and temperaments:

---

of "dulled senses." Cf. Margarete's comment "Es ist so schwül, so dumpfig hie" (2753).

[40] Buschendorf, *Goethes mythische Denkform*, 138–40.

[41] See the massive study by Raymond Klibansky, Erwin Panofsky, and Fritz Saxl, *Saturn and Melancholy: Studies in the History of Natural Philosophy, Religion and Art* (London: Nelson, 1964).

[42] The woodcut is listed as number 149, "Ein Bad mit sechs Männern. gr. fol. B. 128. Guter Abdr.," in Christian Schuchardt, *Goethe's Kunstsammlungen*, 3 vols. in 1 (Hildesheim and New York: Georg Olms Verlag, 1976), 118.

[43] Jens Haustein, "Über Goethes *Erklärung eines alten Holzschnittes vorstellend Hans Sachsens poetische Sendung*," *Archiv für das Studium der neueren Sprachen und Literaturen* 146.1 (1994): 1–21; here, 2–4. On Goethe and Dürer generally, see Johannes Jahn, "Goethe und Dürer," *Goethe* 33 (1971): 75–95.

[44] Edgar Wind, "Dürer's 'Männerbad': A Dionysian Mystery," *Journal of the Warburg and Courtauld Institutes* 2 (1938–39): 269–71.

Within these precincts there are four bathers and two musicians. Each of the bathers is supplied with a particular attribute. The melancholy man on the left leans against a water tap, the fierce-looking fellow in the left foreground has in his hand a scraping knife. He is faced by a man who holds a flower; while the man sitting in the back — a distinctly phlegmatic type drinking from a mug — is the only one of the four whose allegiance to Dionysus is clear at first sight.[45]

The bathhouse is a site of cleansing and of restorative purification. The posture and objects of each are associated with a therapy: "The phlegmatic man takes intoxicating drinks, the sanguine inhales the soothing odour of a flower. The choleric man releases his spleen through rubbing and scratching, and the melancholy one listens to music and hopes for water."[46] The power of visual art over words derives from the simultaneity of the whole scene. Wind's emphasis on the picture as "a broadly humorous travesty of the Dionysian mysteries of inspiration and purification"[47] is countered by other characteristics of the figures. In addition to four distinct attitudes and body types, each of the four has different headgear. Through their symbolism, each of the four represents a different region of the world: the melancholic is a "wild man" of the New World, the phlegmatic's tonsure identifies him as a European, the choleric is an Oriental potentate and the sanguine is an African ("Ethiopian"). Dürer has depicted the temperaments and their underlying medical causes and also displayed a vignette of world history. The two cities in the background, neatly separated by a towering tree trunk to evoke the Tree of Knowledge while the pillars and beams of the bathhouse shape a cross, are the worldly and the heavenly cities. It would be possible to continue, but the point is clear: Dürer has represented the history of the natural and the social worlds.

Various details might lend credence to the possibility that this woodcut should be considered as a source for "Auerbachs Keller in Leipzig." The all-male grouping corresponds to the exclusion of women from "Auerbachs Keller." The composition, with the four humoral bathers and the two non-bathing figures, who are present yet separated, corresponds to the constellation in the drama. The visual pun of the prominent phallic-shaped water tap near the melancholic's crotch, already noted by Wind, would correspond to the genital allusions of "choosing a pope" and of the grape trick. The tension between the figures, especially the opposition between the sanguine and the choleric, hints at the conflicts that will break out in the drama between the four. And, not least, the intrusion of the small figure

---

[45] Wind, "Dürer's 'Männerbad,'" 269.
[46] Wind, "Dürer's 'Männerbad,'" 270.
[47] Wind, "Dürer's 'Männerbad,'" 269.

peering from the background — sometimes assumed to be Dürer's — establishes the whole picture as a double-sided theatre, with the small figure voyeuristically peering in at the bathhouse and thereby mirroring our gazes. We see human beings reduced, nearly naked, to the essentials of their physical, mental, and social being, and it is not a pretty sight. The picture is starkly realistic, showing bodies deformed by their progress through time and individuals largely indifferent to the spiritual powers of the music being played on flute and lyre in the background. Definite proof that Goethe had seen the woodcut by the time he composed "Auerbachs Keller in Leipzig" is lacking, although it is both possible and plausible that he did. Nevertheless, "Männerbad" is useful because it instructs us in ways to look at characters: we should seek the clues and patterns that reveal their temperament and their underlying humors. Each of the four boon companions is precisely sketched according to posture, gesture, and action by Goethe. If we had "Auerbachs Keller in Leipzig" on the stage in front of us, we should be able to identify the melancholic, the sanguine, the choleric, and the phlegmatic just as readily as we can in Dürer's woodcut.

That the temperaments were four in number was due to an ancient and influential tradition sorting things into a quadripartite system.[48] At the basis of the material world were four elements: fire, air, water, and earth, to which corresponded the qualities heat, dryness, moistness, and cold. Combining the qualities produced the four humors blood, phlegm, choler (yellow bile), and black bile and thus the four temperaments. The temperaments were also assigned to the planets of the astrological system, according to the presumed characteristics of the respective gods. Thus the sanguine was under Jupiter, the melancholic under Saturn, the phlegmatic under Venus or the moon, the choleric under Mars or the sun, and a variable temperament under Mercury. Each of the temperaments was also associated with one of the four ages of life, so that it is correct for the melancholic Faust to be mature, around fifty years old.

For ease of reference, the correspondences were usually organized in some sort of table:[49]

---

[48] S. K. Heninger, Jr., *Touches of Sweet Harmony: Pythagorean Cosmology and Renaissance Poetics* (San Marino: The Huntington Library, 1974), 154–55; Draper, *The Humors & Shakespeare's Characters*, 11–15; Jean Seznec, *The Survival of the Pagan Gods: The Mythological Tradition and Its Place in Renaissance Humanism and Art*, trans. Barbara F. Sessions (1972; repr., Princeton: Princeton UP for the Bollingen Foundation, 1995), 44–45; Lawrence Babb, *The Elizabethan Malady: A Study of Melancholia in English Literature from 1580 to 1642* (East Lansing: Michigan State UP, 1951), 9–10.

[49] This is a chart of the basic correspondences only. More extensive tables were published by Heinrich Cornelius Agrippa in his *De occulta philosophia libri III*

| Dominant Humor | Properties | Temperament | Governing Planet | Age of Life |
|---|---|---|---|---|
| Blood | hot + moist | sanguine | Jupiter | childhood |
| Yellow Bile | hot + dry | choleric | Mars / Sun | youth |
| Black Bile | cold + dry | melancholic | Saturn | maturity |
| Phlegm | cold + moist | phlegmatic | Venus / Moon | old age |

Each of the four temperaments was also associated with a body type, as in Dürer's woodcut, and with a set of personal character traits. These were summarized succinctly by Immanuel Kant in his *Anthropologie in pragmatischer Hinsicht* (1798) and are quoted here at length for each of the four companions.[50]

Frosch's temperament is sanguine. The sanguine person is sociable and lively and makes for good company, but also can be unreliable:

> Der Sanguinische . . . ist sorglos und von guter Hoffnung; gibt jedem Dinge für den Augenblick eine große Wichtigkeit, und den folgenden mag er daran nicht weiter denken. Er verspricht ehrlicherweise, aber hält nicht Wort: weil er nicht vorher tief genug nachgedacht hat, ob er es auch zu halten vermögend sein werde. Er ist gutmütig genug, anderen Hülfe zu leisten, ist aber ein schlimmer Schuldner, und verlangt immer Fristen. Er ist ein guter Gesellschafter, scherzhaft, aufgeräumt, mag keinem Dinge gerne große Wichtigkeit geben (Vive la bagatelle!) und hat alle Menschen zu Freunden. Er ist gewöhnlich kein böser Mensch, aber ein schlimm zu bekehrender Sünder, den etwas zwar sehr reut, der aber diese Reue (die nie ein Gram wird) bald vergißt. Er ermüdet unter Geschäften und ist doch rastlos beschäftigt, in dem was bloß Spiel ist; weil dieses Abwechselung bei sich führt und das Beharren seine Sache nicht ist.[51]

---

(Antwerp, 1531) more readily available via the English translation, *Three Books of Occult Philosophy*, trans. John Freake (London, 1651). For a version by Goethe, undated but probably fairly late, see J. W. von Goethe, *Die Schriften zur Naturwissenschaft*, part 2, vol. 3: *Beiträge zur Optik und Anfänge der Farbenlehre, 1790–1808*, ed. Ruprecht Matthaei (Weimar: Hermann Böhlaus Nachfolger, 1951), 507, paralipomenon no. 41. Another version took the form of the "Temperamentenrose" worked out together with Schiller; see Ruprecht Matthaei, "Neue Funde zu Schillers Anteil an Goethes Farbenlehre," *Goethe: Neue Folge des Jahrbuchs der Goethe-Gesellschaft* 20 (1958): 155–77; and his "Die Temperamentenrose aus gemeinsamer Betrachtung Goethes mit Schiller," *Neue Hefte zur Morphologie: Beihefte zur Gesamtausgabe von Goethes Schriften zur Naturwissenschaft* 2 (1956): 33–46.

[50] Similar use of Kant's descriptions is made by Matthaei, "Neue Funde zu Schillers Anteil an Goethes Farbenlehre," 157–58.

[51] Immanuel Kant, *Werke in zehn Bänden*, ed. Wilhelm Weischedel (Darmstadt: Wissenschaftliche Buchgesellschaft, 1983), 10:628–29. On the sanguine type, see

True to his nature, Frosch has the first words in the scene and is the one who wants to get the party going: "Will keiner trinken? keiner lachen? / Ich will euch lehren Gesichter machen!" (2073–74). As the practical joker, he pours the glass of wine over Brander, without taking the prank too seriously. As his name "Frosch" ("Frog") suggests, he springs about from activity to the next, hops from topic to topic. He introduces the political song and then jumps to the love song. His sociability is most apparent when he takes the initiative in speaking to the newcomers, Mephistopheles and Faust. Quick to jump to conclusions, Frosch is the first one to praise Mephistopheles' song with "Bravo! Bravo!" Nothing weighs too heavily upon him, so at the end of the scene his comment "Mir däuchte doch als tränk' ich Wein" (2334) displays no profundity of thought.

The next to appear, Brander, is choleric, under the influence of Mars. His name hints at his "fiery" nature:

> Man sagt von ihm: er ist hitzig; brennt schnell auf, wie Strohfeuer; läßt sich durch Nachgeben des anderen bald besänftigen, zürnt alsdann, ohne zu hassen, und liebt wohl gar den noch desto mehr, der ihm bald nachgegeben hat. Seine Tätigkeit ist rasch, aber nicht anhaltend. Er ist geschäftig, aber unterzieht sich selbst ungern den Geschäften, eben darum weil er es nicht anhaltend ist, und macht also gern den bloßen Befehlshaber, der sie leitet, aber selbst nicht ausführen will. Daher ist seine herrschende Leidenschaft Ehrbegierde; er hat gern mit öffentlichen Geschäften zu tun und will laut gepriesen sein. Er liebt daher den Schein und den Pomp der Formalitäten; nimmt gerne in Schutz und ist dem Scheine nach großmütig, aber nicht aus Liebe, sondern aus Stolz; denn er liebt sich mehr selbst. — Er hält auf Ordnung und scheint deshalb klüger als er ist. Er ist habsüchtig, um nicht filzig zu sein; ist höflich, aber mit Zeremonie, steif und geschroben im Umgange. . . .[52]

Brander's interactions with the others are marked by an aggressiveness to be expected of a martial character. His rhetoric is filled with violence: in his brutal rejoinder to Frosch ("Doppelt Schwein!" [2079]); in the harsh rejection of the political song ("Ein garstig Lied! Pfui! ein politisch Lied / Ein leidig Lied!" [2091–2092]); in his emphasis upon killing after the

---

Draper, *The Humors & Shakespeare's Characters* (New York: AMS Press, 1970), 17–28. On the corresponding dominant influence of Jupiter, see Günther Weydt, *Nachahmung und Schöpfung im Barock: Studien um Grimmelshausen* (Bern and Munich: Francke, 1968), 327, quoting Grimmelshausen's *Ewigwährender Kalender*.

[52] Kant, *Werke in zehn Bänden*, 10:629–30. See also Draper, *The Humors & Shakespeare's Characters*, 44–61; Weydt, *Nachahmung und Schöpfung im Barock*, 328–29; and Carroll Camden, Jr., "Tamburlaine: The Choleric Man," *Modern Language Notes* 44 (1929): 430–35.

"Song of the Flea" ("Spitzt die Finger und packt sie fein!" [2243]); in his outspoken patriotism ("Ein echter deutscher Mann mag keinen Franzen leiden" [2272]); in his threat against Mephistopheles ("Wart nur! Es sollen Schläge regnen!" [2311]). His song about the rat is filled with brutal imagery, and he gains the attention of the others by pounding on the table. The performance reflects both a predilection for pompous ceremony and an obvious vanity. His introduction to the song conforms closely with the characteristics described by Kant:

> Paßt auf! paßt auf! Gehorchet mir!
> Ihr Herrn gesteht, ich weiß zu leben;
> Verliebte Leute sitzen hier,
> Und diesen muß, nach Standsgebühr,
> Zur guten Nacht ich was zum Besten geben.
> Gebt Acht! Ein Lied vom neu'sten Schnitt!
> Und singt den Rundreim kräftig mit! (2119–25)

He knows how to live, he declares, and then stresses the need for a formal procedure. Like a military commander, he orders the others to join in the refrain. Throughout, Brander's preferred mode is the imperative, as he prefers to give orders and dominate the action. An indication of how carefully Goethe constructed his character is the addition of Brander's peremptory demand to Mephistopheles about the wine, missing in the "Urfaust": "Ich will Champagner Wein, / Und recht moussirend soll er sein!" (2268–69).[53] And, as befits his temperament, Brander tries to appear more clever than he is, as when he claims to know something about the guests: "Die kommen eben von der Reise, / Man sieht's an ihrer wunderlichen Weise" (2168–69). Even though he does not know anything about the two, he is rash in jumping to a conclusion: "Marktschreier sind's gewiß, ich wette!" (2178).

It is easy to identify Siebel as melancholic, under the influence of Saturn. With this identification we can also solve the long-standing puzzle of his name, which even the suggestions that these were nicknames from student and fraternity life have never explained satisfactorily. In the premodern astrological system, Saturn was the seventh planet, a fact that SIEBel clearly recalls from the German word for seven, "sieben." The first

---

[53] There may be an etymological connection in the name "Brander" to the verb "branden," a North German word describing the surging or upsurging of water, as when an ocean wave comes in. According to Friedrich Kluge, *Etymologisches Wörterbuch der deutschen Sprache* (Berlin and New York: Walter de Gruyter, 1975), 95, the word entered modern High German use via Klopstock and Voß. This would correspond nicely to the "moussiren" of the champagne when uncorked.

appearance of Siebel on the stage further strengthens the association, for he sings loudly in a deep voice:

SIEBEL.
Zur Tür hinaus wer sich entzweit!
Mit offner Brust sing Runda, sauft und schreit!
ALTMAYER.
    Weh mir, ich bin verloren!
Baumwolle her! Der Kerl sprengt mir die Ohren.
SIEBEL.
Wenn das Gewölbe widerschallt,
Fühlt man erst recht des Basses Grundgewalt. (2081–86)

According to the theory of the "music of the spheres," Saturn, being the slowest of the planets, played the lowest notes,[54] which Siebel obviously echoes. The addition of the specific detail about "the bass" underscores the connection. The mention of "the ceiling" refers quite explicitly to the theoretical background of the "music of the spheres," for it is the vibration of the entire heavenly firmament that is involved. The planetary music should ideally be harmonious, setting an ideal for human beings to imitate. The fact that the music in "Auerbachs Keller in Leipzig" seems to be

---

[54] That Saturn was the deep bass lived on into Kepler's *Harmonice Mundi* (1619), quoted in Spitzer, *Classical and Christian Ideas of World Harmony: Prolegomena to an Interpretation of the Word "Stimmung,"* ed. Ann Granville Hatcher (Baltimore: The Johns Hopkins UP, 1963), 132. Du Bartas listed the voices that corresponded to the humors in his cosmological epic *La Sepmaine* ("The Columns," week 2, day 2, part 3):

> But, brimmer farre then in the Heav'ns, heere
> All these sweet-charming Counter-tunes we heare:
> For *Melancholie, Winter, Earth* below
> Beare aye the *Base*; deepe, hollow, sad, and slow:
> Pale *Phlegme*, moist *Automne, Water* moistly-cold,
> The Plommet-like-smooth-sliding *Tennor* hold:
> Hot-humide *Bloode*, the *Spring*, transparent *Aire*,
> The Maze-like *Meane*, that turnes and wends so faire:
> Curst *Choler, Summer*, and hot-thirsty *Fire*,
> Th'high-warbling *Treble*, loudest in the Quire. (731–40)

Guillaume De Salluste Du Bartas, *The Divine Weeks and Works of Guillaume de Saluste Sieur Du Bartas*, trans. Josuah Sylvester, ed. Susan Snyder (Oxford: Clarendon, 1979), 1:487. On Du Bartas and Goethe, see my "The Double Talk of the Witch's Arithmetic (Hexen-Einmal-Eins) in *Faust I*," *Michigan Germanic Studies* 25.2 (1999 [2001]): 149–66.

strident and discordant reflects the failure of the four companions to recreate the divine harmony; each of them is internally "out of tune" due a humoral imbalance and therefore unable to harmonize externally. Because they are unable to make sweet music together, the four are also unable to provide Faust with one of the possible cures for his melancholy.[55]

Although it seems a contradiction within the system, it is important to maintain the difference between a "normal" temperament as type and one that has become disordered. For example, although someone might be melancholic by nature, an excessive increase in the quantity of black bile or, more commonly, a decrease in one of the other counterbalancing humors could make the individual ill with melancholy. Siebel is such a case; he shows all the signs of the embittered sufferer afflicted with "love melancholy."[56] The moment Frosch begins the love ballad, Siebel interrupts: "Dem Liebchen keinen Gruß! Ich will nichts davon hören!" (2103). When Frosch persists, Siebel pours out his tale of rejection, mingling his disappointment with dire wishes that the woman be violently punished:

> Sie hat mich angeführt, dir wird sie's auch so machen.
> Zum Liebsten sey ein Kobold ihr beschert,
> Der mag mit ihr auf einem Kreuzweg schäkern;
> Ein alter Bock, wenn er vom Blocksberg kehrt,
> Mag im Galopp noch gute Nacht ihr meckern!
> Ein braver Kerl von echtem Fleisch und Blut,
> Ist für die Dirne viel zu gut.

---

[55] On the curative powers of music, especially for those afflicted with melancholy, see Günter Bandmann, *Melancholie und Musik: Ikonographische Studie* (Cologne and Opladen: Westdeutscher Verlag, 1960); Dieter Borchmeyer, "Musik im Zeichen Saturns: Melancholie und Heiterkeit in Thomas Manns *Doktor Faustus*," *Thomas Mann Jahrbuch* 7 (1994): 123–67; Manfred Beetz, "Trost durch Kunst: Zur musikalischen Liebessprache in Christian Weises Gedicht *Auff ein galantes Clavichordium*," in *Die Affekte und ihre Repräsentation in der deutschen Literatur der Frühen Neuzeit*, ed. Jean-Daniel Krebs (Bern and Berlin: Peter Lang, 1996), 137–49; and G. S. Rousseau, "Medicine and the Muses: An Approach to Literature and Medicine," in *Literature and Medicine During the Eighteenth Century*, ed. Marie Mulvey Roberts and Roy Porter (London: Routledge, 1993), 23–57; here, 34–40. The possibility that music could have an immediate and positive impact on Faust's condition can be seen in the way the Easter music — the bells and then the sound of choirs — quickens him and blocks his suicidal impulses.

[56] On this extreme stage of melancholy, see the edition of Jacques Ferrand's *A Treatise on Lovesickness*, trans. and ed. Donald A. Beecher and Massimo Ciavolella (Syracuse, NY: Syracuse UP, 1990) with extensive documentation; Draper, *The Humors & Shakespeare's Characters*, 68–69; and Babb, *The Elizabethan Malady*, 128–74.

> Ich will von keinem Gruße wissen,
> Als ihr die Fenster eingeschmissen! (2110–17)[57]

The outburst has the typical features of the raving to which love melancholy could lead, filled with rage and jealousy. The passage is important within the overall context of the drama because it is the first time that the audience is introduced to the theme that will dominate the rest of *Faust I*, namely the debilitating effects of the affair with Margarete upon Faust's health. Since both Faust and Siebel are melancholic by temperament, they will display similar symptoms when they have fallen deeply into love. Worth noting is the irony that only the audience hears Siebel's tirade; Mephistopheles has not brought Faust into "Auerbachs Keller" early enough for him to observe and perhaps learn from the negative example.

The allusions to the darker realm ("goblin," "witches' Sabbath," and "some old goat") by Siebel are part of a pattern, for he has the strongest affinity among the four companions to Mephistopheles. As discussed earlier, melancholy had long been associated with the influence of the Devil, so that would bring Siebel into his sphere. But there are also ties between Saturn and Satan,[58] and because Siebel has been explicitly placed under planetary influence in the scene, his sympathy for Mephistopheles is heightened. He is the one who first responds politely to Mephistopheles' greeting: "Viel Dank zum Gegengruß" (2184). And it is he who notices the diabolic limp, asking, albeit sotto voce so as not to offend, "Was hinkt der Kerl auf einem Fuß?" (2184).[59] Siebel names their location: "Die Hölle brennt!" (2299). Siebel interacts with Mephistopheles on a familiar basis:

---

[57] The echo of Astolfo's warning to Ruggiero, "ma certo sii di giunger tosto al passo / d'entrar o in fiera o in fonte o in legno o in sasso" (*Orlando Furioso* 6.52.7–8; your time will soon come to be changed into a beast or a fountain, into wood or rock) in Siebel's "dir wird sie's auch so machen" connects this passage to the story of Alcina's enchantments and hence to the story of Circe. It takes on a gruesome quality since Siebel has been disfigured by syphilis, so that the threatened transformation of male lovers into other, less than human, entities becomes a real threat.

[58] Since Saturn was associated in the astrological-humoral scheme with melancholics and because the Devil was a principal cause for melancholy in the theological diagnosis, an equivalence between Saturn and Satan made a certain sense. But the two were connected much earlier; see Samuel L. Macey, *Patriarchs of Time: Dualism in Saturn-Cronus, Father Time, the Watchmaker God, and Father Christmas* (Athens and London: U of Georgia P, 1987), 23–39 and 181–83. One might argue that Satan (Mephistopheles) is also under the influence of Saturn, something most visible in his greed.

[59] In this Siebel anticipates and resembles the witch who also remarks on Mephistopheles' foot in the next scene of the play.

SIEBEL
Was Herr? Er will sich unterstehn,
Und hier sein Hokuspokus treiben?
MEPHISTOPHELES
Still, altes Weinfaß!
SIEBEL
             Besenstiel!
Du willst uns gar noch grob begegnen? (2306–2309)

The address of "sir" echoes his earlier accolade "Ein pfiffiger Patron!" (2195). Mephistopheles puts him back in his place with the brusque insult "old wine barrel," a bizarre epithet which alludes again to Siebel's temperament. The cold and dry qualities of the melancholic frequently manifested themselves physically as a foul odor, such as stinking breath; the dominant taste from Saturn was "sour."[60] Anyone who has encountered old wine barrels would agree that a certain sour smell does emanate from them, so that the epithet is not an arbitrary one. Siebel's final words, "Betrug war alles, Lug und Schein" (2333), conclude on the gloomy note expected of the melancholic.

The phlegmatic temperament can vary, depending upon whether the influence of Venus or the moon predominates. In Altmayer, we have the passivity typical of the lunar influence:

Phlegma, als Schwäche, ist Hang zur Untätigkeit, sich durch selbst starke Triebfedern zu Geschäften nicht bewegen zu lassen. Die Unempfindlichkeit dafür ist willkürliche Unnützlichkeit und die Neigungen gehen nur auf Sättigung und Schlaf.

Phlegma, als Stärke, ist dagegen die Eigenschaft: nicht leicht oder rasch, aber, wenn gleich langsam doch anhaltend bewegt zu werden. Der, welcher eine gute Dosis von Phlegma in seiner Mischung hat, wird langsam warm, aber er behält die Wärme länger. Er gerät nicht leicht in Zorn, sondern bedenkt sich erst, ob er nicht zürnen solle; wenn andrerseits der Cholerische rasend werden möchte, daß er den festen Mann nicht aus seiner Kaltblütigkeit bringen kann.[61]

The name "Altmayer" might be glossed as "the old man (in the moon)," on the basis of the colloquial use of "Meier" for a generic "person" (for example, "Mensch Meier!"). But one might also note the evocation through "maer" (as in the English "nightmare") of the supposed influence

---

[60] Babb, *The Elizabethan Malady*, 27; Weydt, *Nachahmung und Schöpfung im Barock*, 325.

[61] Kant, *Werke in zehn Bänden*, 10:630–31; Draper, *The Humors & Shakespeare's Characters*, 29–43; Weydt, *Nachahmung und Schöpfung im Barock*, 334.

of the moon on dreams. As is evident from counting the lines uttered by him, Altmayer shows the least initiative. He is either passive or merely reacts to others, reflecting what they have said. His first words upon hearing Siebel's "singing" express timidity and softness: "Weh mir, ich bin verloren! / Baumwolle her! der Kerl sprengt mir die Ohren" (2083–84). The gesture is one of retreat and withdrawal. Cotton batting is an apposite material for him, since it is pale in color, soft, and yielding. When not reacting to others, Altmayer's mode is that of hesitant guessing, careful hedging: "Vielleicht!" (2178); "Ihr scheint ein sehr verwöhnter Mann." (2187); "Sie sind vom Rheine, wie ich spüre." (2256). His derivative function is emphasized when he is the last to chime in after the "song of the flea." He echoes Siebel's and Frosch's threat against Mephistopheles, but in a meek subjunctive: "Ich dächt', wir hießen ihn ganz sachte seitwärts gehn" (2304). A main characteristic of the phlegmatic is heaviness — in Dürer's woodcut, he is the only one sitting — and it is found in Altmayer. After the illusion ends, he says "Schafft einen Stuhl, ich sinke nieder" (2325) and again "Es liegt mir bleischwer in den Füßen" (2331).

Not all of the phlegmatic's characteristics are negative. As Kant says, the "cold-blooded" can give the appearance of philosophical insight: "Sein glückliches Temperament vertritt bei ihm die Stelle der Weisheit und man nennt ihn, selbst im gemeinen Leben, oft den Philosophen."[62] The proximity of Altmeyer's temperament to the chill of analytic logic shimmers through when he comments upon the reasons behind Siebel's reaction to the "song of the rat": "Das Unglück macht ihn zahm und mild" (2155). Similarly, there is the undertone of a conclusion in his observations "Da hast du's! Der versteht's!" (2194), after Mephistopheles ripostes Frosch's joke or in his disparaging "Ach das sind Taschenspielersachen" (2267). Altmayer reflects what is happening, but in a cold light, without in turn reflecting upon them with his own inner vision. He observes with some detachment to Frosch "Aha! du fängst schon an die Lippen abzulecken" (2263). With the mirroring function, Altmayer is the one who relates to the others what he has seen near the end: "Ich hab' ihn selbst hinaus zur Kellertüre / Auf einem Fasse reiten sehn — —" (2329–30). Finally, Altmayer's concluding line concentrates upon the problems of vision and reflection: "Nun sag' mir eins, man soll kein Wunder glauben!" (2337).[63]

---

[62] Kant, *Werke in zehn Bänden*, 10:631.

[63] The problem of "Wunder" was not one taken lightly by Goethe. The "grape trick" has connections with Goethe's disagreement about Lavater on just what could constitute a miracle; see the careful discussion by Konrad Rahe, *Cagliostro und Christus: Zu den biblischen Anspielungen in Goethes Komödie "Der Groß-Cophta"* (Hamburg: Verlag Dr. Kovač, 1994), 63–71.

Once the basic temperaments of the four companions have been analyzed, it is necessary to focus upon their choice of wines. Each of them
chooses a different sort of wine. Of course, Frosch is the first to order and
selects "Rhine wine." Brander rudely demands "Champagne," properly
bubbly. Siebel, after some hesitation, confesses that he would prefer a
"really sweet wine" to a "sour wine" and is promised a Tokay. Altmayer,
indecisive as ever, cannot make up his mind and will take "any one"
("jeden"). The significance of their respective selections goes back to the
principles of iatrochemistry. Since each of the humors could be resolved
into a combination of the primary qualities (hot, moist, dry, cold), an
imbalance brought about by too much or too little of one of the humors
could be corrected through diet and medication. As Lawrence Babb
explains:

> Various medicines ('alternatives') are used to change the character of a
> humor by moistening, drying, heating, cooling, thickening, thinning.
> Diet is important. A patient suffering from a hot and dry disease should
> eat cold and moist foods, such as lettuce and cress. In the Renaissance
> dietaries, the various foods are described in terms of heat, cold, moisture,
> and dryness, so that the reader may choose those foods which have a
> nature opposite to that of his complaint.[64]

A key was the principle of opposition, whereby the medication counter-
balanced whatever was excessive or deficient. Thus those who were melancholic (too hot and dry) should avoid food and drink that would heat and
ingest those things that would cool the body. Once we understand the
medical theory that forms the background to "Auerbachs Keller in
Leipzig" and to the whole drama, we are shocked when we realize the per-
version of therapy being shown. Good doctors strive to heal their patients;
Mephistopheles does the opposite, as he skillfully administers whatever will
make people even more ill.

The extreme actions and discordant behavior of the four companions
indicates in each of them the temperament that has become overwhelmed
by the corresponding humor. Instead of prescribing an antidote to correct
the imbalance evident in each of the four companions, Mephistopheles lets
them make their own choice of wine. But it cannot be wise for a doctor to
leave such decisions to patients whose very condition would preclude their
being able to choose judiciously. Instead, each of the patients selects the
wine that will make his condition worse, not better. Siebel, the melancholic, should actually have opted for the "sour wine," since it would have
had a salutary thinning effect upon the black bile. The thick, heavy Tokay

---

[64] Babb, *The Elizabethan Malady*, 7.

is counter-indicated. Marisilio Ficino, one of the medical authorities of the time, was explicit on the sort of wine that prevented melancholy:

> Nothing, however, is better against this pest than wine which is light, clear, pleasant, fragrant — the best adapted to generate spirits clearer than any others. For, as Plato and Aristotle believe, by means of this wine, black bile is softened and grows sweet and clear just as do lupines soaked in water or iron burnt with fire. But just as the use of wine helps the spirits and the intelligence, so the abuse harms them.[65]

Brander, the overactive choleric, should avoid the bubbly champagne, rather than insisting that it be particularly lively. Frosch, already too hot and moist, should not drink any wine at all and certainly not a white wine. Poor Altmayer may or may not be helped, since he has been unable to make up his mind in time and seems content to gamble with his health. None of the four choices would be recommended by a doctor well-versed in humoral medicine, since the conditions of the patients will be worsened.

As always, the motives of Mephistopheles are even more sinister than is apparent at first glance. His laconic "Ich stell' es einem jeden frei" (2261) is suspicious with the reference to "free," ambivalently playing with "at no cost" and "up to each one to decide freely." Mephistopheles never gives anything away for free, so one should be alert and ask what the price might be. The doctor has an ethical responsibility to help the patients; it is absolutely wrong to encourage them to indulge in more of what made them ill. Mephistopheles is clever in cloaking his malpractice and would be able to remonstrate, with some justification, "I did not encourage them, I only let them act out their wishes." The sophistry is required because the rules of the divine game, as God reminded him at the outset, do not allow Mephistopheles to cause direct harm to human beings, although he may through inaction allow them to come to harm. The eagerness with which each of the four gravitates towards the worst choice seems to confirm Mephistopheles' argument that free will for humans was a mistake. These four greedy companions cannot make rational choices, tending rather to speed their own decline. All of this has serious implications for Faust, who also has a severe imbalance of the humors and has been afflicted with melancholy.

---

[65] Marsilio Ficino, *Three Books on Life*, ed. and trans. Carol V. Kaske and John R. Clark (1989; repr., Binghamton, NY: Center for Medieval and Early Renaissance Studies, State University of New York at Binghamton, together with The Renaissance Society of America, 1998), book 1, chapter 10, 135. On Goethe's positive reception of Ficino, see Gaier, *Faust-Dichtungen: Kommentar II*, 114–20 and *passim*.

# Mephistopheles and Modern Science

The theatre of "Auerbachs Keller in Leipzig" has reviewed for Faust and the audience the most ancient principles about the elements and humors and how they determine temperaments. In an entertaining scene, we have seen the sum of Renaissance medical and scientific knowledge displayed for us. "Auerbachs Keller in Leipzig" might be compared to one of those remarkable cosmographic diagrams of a Robert Fludd, where the informed reader can locate all the components of the universe.[66] The advantage of the drama is that the panorama is also dynamic: we see the temperaments interacting, hear the discordant music, are astounded by the chemistry of the wines. All the evidence that Faust needed in order to grasp "was die Welt / Im innersten zusammenhält" (383–84) has been made available in Mephistopheles' cosmic demonstration. There is no "magic" in the scene for those who understand the principles at work, only evidence of the laws of nature as they were understood at the time. The difference between Faust and Mephistopheles is that the former relies upon superstition and guesswork, while the latter uses the powers of reason. Faust has earlier invoked the theory of the elements, but only as part of an incantation, when he tries to control the threatening poodle:

> Erst zu begegnen dem Tiere,
> Brauch' ich den Spruch der Viere:
> > Salamander soll glühen
> > Undene sich winden,
> > Sylphe verschwinden,
> > Kobold sich mühen. (1271–76)

The passage is ironic, beyond the obvious fact that Faust fails to recognize who the poodle really is. With the pronouncement that mastery in magic requires knowing the elements and being able to manipulate them successfully in order to ensorcell, Faust condemns himself. Here he fails utterly in his attempt to control the elements, because he remains on the surface of things, invoking air, earth, fire, and water not through direct techniques but indirectly through the supposed power of magic names. The names he uses for the elements are quoted from speculative alchemy and are basically nonsense. Mumbling a spell is mere necromancy, trying to make use of an incoherent fragment out of the complex system of scientific knowledge as if it were a talisman. In "Auerbachs Keller," on the other hand, we will see how a true adept such as Mephistopheles addresses

---

[66] Some are reproduced in Joscelyn Godwin, *Robert Fludd: Hermetic Philosopher and Surveyor of Two Worlds* (Grand Rapids, MI: Phanes P, 1991).

the elements directly and controls them through his knowledge of their properties. Goethe was especially careful in constructing the scene so that there can be no doubt about the underlying scientific logic. When some of the wine spills, it bursts into flame. The wine, which is essentially hot and moist, releases an excess of heat when the moisture is removed by absorption into the ground. In the "Urfaust," the stage direction referred to the wine flowing on pavement but stones would not have absorbed any moisture. In *Faust*, the mistake is rectified: "der Wein fließt auf die Erde," so that soil ("Erde") can and does absorb the moisture.

One detail in Mephistopheles' manipulation of the elements is striking. When he speaks to the flames, he says "Sei ruhig, freundlich Element!" (2300). Why does he use the epithet "friendly"? And how does his control mesh with the alchemical-humoral system? Pursuing these questions raises some interesting issues. Earlier, Mephistopheles had made a relevant comment about his historical relationship to the elements:

> Der Luft, dem Wasser wie der Erden
> Entwinden tausend Keime sich,
> Im Trocknen, Feuchten, Warmen, Kalten!
> Hätt' ich mir nicht die Flamme vorbehalten,
> Ich hätte nichts Aparts für mich. (1374–78)

Compactly reduced in these lines is a debate that had long been implicit in the confrontation between Christian doctrine and the alchemical-humoral system, but that only broke out in the sixteenth century with the theories of Paracelsus.[67] The crux was the opposition between the *four* elements of the tetrad, going back to the *Timaeus*, and the *three* elements mentioned in Genesis: earth, air, and water. Since three elements had been all that God needed for the work of creation, it could be argued that all natural processes should be replicable with the same number. Paracelsus and his

---

[67] In the wake of Walter Pagel's pioneering research, historians of medicine and of science have taken Paracelsus seriously for his contributions to the advancement of science. See especially Allen G. Debus, *The English Paracelsians* (London: Oldbourne, 1965); Debus, "The Medico-Chemical World of the Paracelsians," in *Changing Perspectives in the History of Science: Essays in Honour of Joseph Needham*, ed. Mikuláš Teich and Robert Young (London: Heinemann, 1973), 86–99; Debus, "Chemists, Physicians, and Changing Perspectives on the Scientific Revolution," *Isis* 89 (1998): 66–81; Charles Webster, "Alchemical and Paracelsian Medicine," in *Health, Medicine and Mortality in the Sixteenth Century*, ed. Charles Webster (Cambridge: Cambridge UP, 1979), 301–34; and Hugh Trevor-Roper, "The Court Physician and Paracelsianism," in *Medicine at the Courts of Europe, 1500–1837*, ed. Vivian Nutton (London and New York: Routledge, 1990), 79–94.

school attempted to rethink the natural order on the basis of a triad, for example sulphur, mercury, and salt. The new system did not immediately supplant the old; the two paradigms competed for authority and made for some confusion;[68] indeed, they contend in the passage just quoted. The four elements are still alluded to by their effects: dryness, moisture, warmth, and cold. But Mephistopheles is no longer an adherent of the older tetrad; he has seized the opportunity proffered by the new theory of the Paracelsians.

Goethe had read and admired Paracelsus and was inspired by the example of his radical critique, no doubt. But this does not mean Faust has been modeled upon Paracelsus: the Paracelsian in the drama is Mephistopheles.[69] Aside from his general tendency to keep up with the latest scientific discoveries, Mephistopheles has been quick to see the advantage for him in the new system. Genesis spoke only of earth, air, and water, as van Helmont pointed out: "Nirgend aber findet man etwas von der Schöpffung des Feuers: Darumb erkenn ich auch nicht / daß dasselbe unter die Elementen gehöre."[70] Well, if fire had not been appropriated by God, then the Devil had an opening and could usurp fire as his element. Again, Mephistopheles has distorted the history ever so slightly, claiming that he was the one who had exercised the privilege of *reserving* fire for himself, when actually he had no role in Genesis and received only what God did not need for creation. God chose first; Mephistopheles got the leavings. But fire suits his purposes and has become his "friend." Fire is entirely negative: it destroys things and cannot be used to build, and hence it is particularly suited to Mephistopheles, the great naysayer.

---

[68] Debus, *The English Paracelsians*, 26–29.

[69] The otherwise exemplary research of Bartscherer, *Paracelsus, Paracelsisten und Goethes Faust* was vitiated by an excessive dedication to showing that Faust was the Paracelsian.

[70] Johann Baptista van Helmont, *Aufgang der Artzney-Kunst*, trans. Christian Knorr von Rosenroth, ed. Walter Pagel and Friedhelm Kemp (Munich: Kösel-Verlag, 1971), 55. Goethe mentions Van Helmont in *Dichtung und Wahrheit* (HA 9:342); the context makes it clear that he must have been quite well informed about him and his reception. See Antonio Clericuzio, "From van Helmont to Boyle: A Study of the Transmission of Helmontian Chemical and Medical Theories in Seventeenth-Century England," *British Journal for the History of Science* 26 (1993): 303–34. Still needing investigation is the extent to which the conflicts around the founding of the College of Physicians in 1665 in London are part of the background to Faust's history of medical ineptitude told on Easter Sunday.

# The Science of the "Wine Trick"

The intersection of theology with the medical-scientific themes of *Faust I* is drastically apparent at the moment when Mephistopheles draws the wine from the table. On the basis of his satire of Christ and of the Eucharist, I argued in the last chapter that the wine is transformed from blood. The means for accomplishing this were made available through the logic of the elements. Wine was closely related to blood in humoral medicine, since it was considered a warming liquid and blood is hot and moist and was often prescribed for fortifying the blood.[71] Mephistopheles' trick is that he has gone one step further and substituted blood for wine. Although the medical use of blood was ethically and morally suspect, there were intimations that some doctors were willing to use blood as a medicine. The cure prescribed in Hartmann von Aue's *Der arme Heinrich* is one fictional example.[72] Closer to the sources with which Goethe would have been familiar, there is Ficino's discussion of the rejuvenating power of blood:

> Good doctors try, with human blood distilled in fire, to restore those whom old age has eaten away. What is wrong with our giving this drink of blood if it will restore people who are almost half-dead with age? It is a common and an ancient opinion that certain women who were fortune-tellers (which we call witches) used to suck the blood of infants and become rejuvenated from it.
>
> Why not then have our own old people — who have no other hope — suck the blood of an adolescent — of a willing adolescent, I mean, who is clean, happy, temperate, and whose blood is excellent but perhaps a little excessive. They could suck it the way leeches do, an ounce or two from a vein on the left arm barely opened.

If someone such as Ficino could seriously propose using blood to regulate the temperaments, then Mephistopheles, the diabolical doctor, will have the way paved for providing the four companions with the gruesome drinks. Remembering the words "Das Blut ist ein ganz besonderer Saft"

---

[71] See Roland Antonioli, "L'éloge du vin dans l'œuvre de Rabelais," in *L'imaginaire du vin: Colloque pluridisciplinaire 15–17 octobre 1981*, ed. Max Milner and Martine Chatelain (Marseille: Éditions Jeanne Laffitte, 1983), 131–40; here, 133.

[72] Hartmann von Aue, *Der arme Heinrich*, ed. Hermann Paul (Tübingen: Max Niemeyer, 1972): "niuwan der maget herzebluot / daz waere vür iuwer suht guot" (lines 231–32; cf. also lines 451–52). On the medical history of "blood transfusions," see the short introduction by Joseph Frank Payne, "Arnold de Villanova on the Therapeutic Use of Human Blood," *Janus* 8 (1903): 477–83.

(1740), we hear in "Der Wein ist saftig" (2286) ("wine is juicy") a literal description of its bloody origins. At the instant when the four imbibe, they are unaware of what they have done, but the hidden truth is revealed in the line "We are as happy as cannibals."

But where does the blood come from? The material economy of the alchemical system was, by definition, closed: matter could be neither created nor destroyed. Not even, or rather especially not, Mephistopheles is permitted to violate the laws of the conservation of matter, for doing so would be tantamount to a new creation. God made all the matter originally and might consume it in time, but during the interim there can be no spontaneous re-creations, no matter what Mephistopheles would have us believe. He cannot perform miracles. The answer to the mystery of whose blood is being transformed is found in canto 13 of Dante's *Inferno*:

> I heard wailings uttered on every side, and saw no one who made them; wherefore, all bewildered, I stopped. I believe that he believed that I believed that all those voices from amid the trunks came from people who were hidden from us. Therefore the master said: "If you break off a little branch from one of these plants, the thoughts you have will all be cut short." Then I stretched my hand a little forward and plucked a twig from a great thornbush, and its stub cried, "Why do you break me?" And when it had become dark with blood, it began again to cry, "Why do you tear me? Have you no spirit of pity? We were men, and now are turned to stocks. Truly your hand ought to be more merciful had we been souls of serpents."
>
> As from a green brand that is burning at one end, and drips from the other, hissing with the escaping air, so from that broken twig came out words and blood together; whereon I let fall the tip, and stood like one who is afraid. (13.22–45)

As Patrick Boyde comments, the comparison of the sap dripping from a tree to the blood seeping from the limbs is "a simile which has won universal admiration."[73] It is an unforgettable image, and imitations of it became de rigueur for epic poets. With the recollection of this scene, the horrible truth about where Mephistopheles gets the raw material is plain: he is using the blood of the damned.

Canto 13 does resemble a sort of scientific experiment. The Poet, not knowing what to make of the sounds he hears, investigates by touching and breaking into the physical reality. The results are unexpected, but do yield more information and some insight. No written or other authority

---

[73] Patrick Boyde, *Dante Philomythes and Philosopher: Man in the Cosmos* (Cambridge: Cambridge UP, 1981), 72.

would have satisfied the Poet as much as the encounter with the material realm. That realm still obeys the laws of Aristotelian science, still reveals the logic of the four elements, as Boccaccio observed in his commentary on the passage.[74] Given Faust's great boast at the beginning of the play that he has mastered so many disciplines of learning, it would seem that he should have had no trouble in remembering canto 13 and decoding its physics. After all Dante's text was a classic. Faust's forgetfulness at this critical juncture serves to block one other possible source of insight that could have helped him understand the phenomena of "Auerbachs Keller in Leipzig." The dire physical economy of blood and wine should have spoken loudly and clearly to a man with his vast learning. The physical events should have turned Faust's thoughts to primary causes and to a recollection of Creation, but he remains disoriented. His forgetfulness is a repetition of the forgetfulness of the Poet in canto 13, who is condemned by his guide Vergil for having had no faith in the authority of the text: " 'If he, O wounded spirit, had been able to believe before,' replied my sage, 'what he had never seen save in my verses, he would not have stretched forth his hand against you; but the incredible thing made me prompt him to a deed that grieves me' " (13.46–49). This applies exactly to Faust's own situation. He too has had no faith, in his case in the authority of Scripture, but requires proof and validation via the material world. Both the Poet and Faust thereby inflict grievous harm on those already consigned to the underworld: the former by tearing the limbs of the bushes and the latter, indirectly, as Mephistopheles converts the blood into wine as part of the entertainment and edification promised earlier. Not satisfied with the consumption of the blood of the dead, Faust will go on to destroy the actual lives of innocent people as well, because he is blind to the laws of the universe. With heavy overtones, one might say that the wine / blood has been spilled in vain in "Auerbachs Keller."

If we try to come to a generalization about the history of medical and scientific thought as it is revealed in the scene, we have to be mindful of Goethe's own position. Faust represents fake science, the sort of quackery that would rouse Goethe's ire when it showed up in the figure of Cagliostro. Unwilling to think back to basic principles, unable to trust sensory data, incapable of synthesizing what is valid from tradition with new discoveries, Faust has only his overweening ambition as a relic of the quest for truth. Mephistopheles, cunning and well-informed, adapts easily to the emergence of modern science, especially as that science veers towards materialism. He appropriates theories that allow him to manipulate matter. Missing from his "experiment" with Faust is any genuine interest in

---

[74] Cf. Patrick Boyde, *Dante Philomythes and Philosopher*, 317, n. 44.

getting at objective truth; going in that direction had to lead to the acceptance of the divine order as well-made. Mephistopheles could have had it in his power to cure and heal, because the means are at his disposal, but his purposes and effects are to sicken and destroy.

## The Science of the "Grape Trick"

A final set of details relating to the history of science serves as a coda to the scene. They are embedded in the "grape trick." How does Mephistopheles accomplish the illusion? The information at the onset is scant:

> MEPHISTOPHELES *mit ernsthafter Gebärde*
> Falsch Gebild und Wort
> Verändern Sinn und Ort!
> Seid hier und dort! (2313–15)

Critics have explained this as a sort of "hypnotism,"[75] and so it actually turns out to be. Taking the reference to hypnotism as a clue does reveal new dimensions to the scene and takes us to the very core of Goethe's personal and intellectual concerns. While the facts that make up the fascinating background history are well-known,[76] they have not been brought to bear upon "Auerbachs Keller."

On 7 September 1774, Lavater wrote somewhat breathlessly and in a state of excitement to Goethe about miraculous doings in the German-speaking part of Switzerland. A faith-healer named Johann Josef Gaßner, an otherwise ordinary Catholic priest, had been curing the sick and lame in droves (later biographers would speak of thousands who had sought his

---

[75] For example, Kuno Fischer, *Die Erklärung des Goetheschen Faust nach der Reihenfolge seiner Szenen, Erster Teil,* vol. 3 of *Goethes Faust,* ed. Victor Michels, 4th ed. (Heidelberg: Carl Winter, 1913), 134.

[76] See above all Hans Grassl, *Aufbruch zur Romantik: Bayerns Beitrag zur deutschen Geistesgeschichte, 1765–1785* (Munich: C. H. Beck, 1968), 131–71. Supplementary details are found in two studies by Ernst Benz, *Franz Anton Mesmer (1734–1815) und seine Ausstrahlung in Europa und Amerika* (Munich: Wilhelm Fink, 1976); and Benz, *Franz Anton Mesmer und die philosophischen Grundlagen des "animalischen Magnetismus"* (Wiesbaden: Franz Steiner, for the Akademie der Wissenschaften und der Literatur, Mainz, 1977). The story has recently been retold by H. C. Erik Midelfort, in his book *Exorcism and Enlightenment: Johann Joseph Gassner and the Demons of Eighteenth-Century Germany* (New Haven: Yale UP, 2005).

help). Lavater's Pietist and mystic background inclined him to believe; further, he had already done some research:

> Es ist in unserm Lande eine Sage, daß ein gewißer catholischer Geistlicher, Nammens Joseph Gaßner von Salmerschweil — täglich im Nammen Jesu entscheidende Wunder, besonders, an Beseßnen, u. Kranken, von dennen er glaube, daß sie vom Satan gekränkt werden — verrichten soll.
>
> Zu dieser allgemeinen Sage, kommen *eigenhändige Briefe von Geheilten,* an ihre Ärzte, die ihnen nicht helfen könnten — die ich gesehen. *Eigenhändige Briefe von Ärzten,* die den Mann Wunder thun, u. Krankheiten, die sie nicht heilen konnten, heilen gesehen.
>
> *Eigenhändige Briefe* des Wunderthäters, die ich ebenfalls gesehen.
>
> Worinn mit der größten Simplicität erzählt wird, daß er 1800. Personen, derren Nammen im Closter Salmerschweilen aufbehalten seyn, in wenigen Minuten geheilet. Daß in diesem Kloster 18. Krüken zurükgelaßen worden, von Leüthen die Jahr u. Tag einen Geist der Schwachheit gehabt hatten, u. plötzlich, gerade, fest u. frisch zum gehen geworden — sobald er den Satan, dem er ihre Übel zuschrieb, in dem Nammen Jesu beschworen.
>
> Nun Bruder, sage mir im Ernste, was soll ich thun?
>
> Wie, soll ich untersuchen? dann daß ich untersuchen soll, wird wol keine Frage seyn — wie fragen? wie schauen u. beobachten? was würdest du thun? wenn du in Salmerschweil wärest?
>
> Mit Beseßnen, das ist, mit solchen, deren Krankheiten ganz vom Satan abhangen, spielt er, wie ein Brief eines Augenzeügen sagt, wie mit einem Hündlein —
>
> Er gebietet den Krankheiten alle Augenblick zukommen, u. wieder zugehen.[77]

Goethe must have asked to see the documentation, since Lavater's next letter in mid-September included the testimonials and also asked Goethe to pass them to their mutual friend, Susanne von Klettenberg. The state of excitement wrought among the Pietist circles can be gauged by her letter of 4 October 1774. We also get there a hint that perhaps Goethe was of a different, more skeptical mind about the credibility of the miracles:

> Hier komen Endlich die Briefe von Gaßener zurück die Goethe so lange Behalten. Was er dazu denckt soll — wird er selbstten Melden, ich bin stille sehe alles an — Bette Herr Dein Reich kome und will nicht gerne zu früh *miracle!* rufen. Bewarheitet sich aber die Sache — hat der Man

---

[77] Heinrich Funck, ed., *Goethe und Lavater: Briefe und Tagebücher,* Schriften der Goethe-Gesellschaft 16 (Weimar: Verlag der Goethe-Gesellschaft, 1901), 36–37.

nur die zwey Krancke Nonnen hergestelt — dann — ja dann vereweigte *Reformatores* der Kirche — dann — Nehmt es mir nicht ungütig wann ich glaube — ihr habt die Kirche nicht nur *Reformirt* sondern auch *retranchirt* — u. wie leicht geschiehet so was! Wie leicht ist mit dem Schutt des Aberglaubens auch der so unansehnliche — Mächtige Kinder Glaube hinaus *Raisonirt* worden — Aber Catholisch werde ich doch nicht — ich werde eigentlich nichts — als immer mehr durch Gottes Gnade das was ich bin.[78]

Doubtless Goethe would have been perturbed by the enthusiasm of his old friend, who seemed to be more than ready to accept the miracles as revealed signs. Lavater mentioned Gaßner once more in a letter of 1 October 1774,[79] but Goethe's subsequent replies avoided the topic and concentrated instead on their joint project on physiognomy. The strains in their relationship were already evident when Goethe chides and scolds Lavater about the slow pace of the project, but the deeper reasons had to do with Goethe's irritation at Lavater's uncritical attitude about religion. When Lavater published letters in the spring of 1775 defending Gaßner, Goethe kept quiet, but he must have been following events closely, not least because he was working on *Faust* during this period.

Despite his silence, Goethe could not have been oblivious to the controversies that Gaßner had provoked. As Susanne von Klettenberg's response showed, the theological stakes were high, especially since Gaßner was Catholic. But even without the confessional dimension, the question of whether he actually could heal people by casting out the Devil, simply by laying on hands and uttering the name "Jesus," aroused widespread interest. In addition to theologians, medical doctors were keen to know if the miracles were legitimate. Repeatedly, they visited Gaßner in his sessions with patients and made careful observations. The evidence seemed incontrovertible: some patients were "healed." For the advocates of Enlightenment rationalism, the claim that the "Devil" existed, possessed people, crippled them, and could be "cast out" through the agency of words alone represented a return to the predominance of superstition. The *Allgemeine Deutsche Bibliothek*, a principal organ of the Enlightenment, inveighed against Gaßner and argued that there had to be a rational explanation based upon natural causes for the phenomena.[80]

The explanation that occurred to both rationalists and critical theologians was — animal magnetism. Gaßner's major Catholic opponent, Don Sterzinger, reported in detail his observations of Gaßner's methods and

---

[78] Funck, *Goethe und Lavater*, 335.

[79] Funck, *Goethe und Lavater*, 42–43.

[80] Grassl, *Aufbruch zur Romantik*, 162–64.

concluded "daß entweder eine Magnetische, Electrische oder Sympathische Kraft die Wirkungen hervorbringe."[81] Sterzinger's equivocation among "magnetism," "electricity," and "sympathetic force" reflects accurately the scientific discussion of the time, which often spoke of the three in tandem, since the relationship between the first two had not yet been made clear. Electricity especially was a "hot topic" of the eighteenth century, for physical scientists, medical doctors, and the general public. What is somewhat surprising today is that these matters were also of acute concern to theologians. It is not so hard to see why: the question of what the life force in human beings really was and how people bonded together spiritually in friendships and communities had immediate implications for religious belief. Was there something akin to a "soul" that animated all things? The idea that bodies were merely objects obeying laws laid down by Newton's theory of gravity was unacceptable to many, and they found solace in the discovery of other "forces" that could explain spiritual affinities.[82] A vivid example of how it was possible to amalgamate theories about electricity and magnetism with mysticism was provided by the Swabian Pietist Friedrich Christoph Oetinger (1702–82), who proposed to refute Newton and who was also among the first to take notice of a theory that

---

[81] Quoted by Grassl, *Aufbruch zur Romantik*, 144.

[82] For an overview of the discussion of attraction and sympathy, see Eric Watkins, "The Development of Physical Influx in Early Eighteenth-Century Germany: Gottsched, Knutzen, and Crusius," *Review of Metaphysics* 49 (December 1995): 295–339. See also Adler, "*Eine fast magische Anziehungskraft.*" On magnetism and theology, see Patricia Fara, *Sympathetic Attractions: Magnetic Practices, Beliefs, and Symbolism in Eighteenth-Century England* (Princeton: Princeton UP, 1996), 146–70; and Anneliese Ego, "Magnetische Auftritte — ideologische Konflikte: Zur Problematik eines medizinischen Konzeptes im Zeitalter der Aufklärung," in *Der ganze Mensch: Anthropologie und Literatur im 18. Jahrhundert: DFG-Symposion 1992*, ed. Hans-Jürgen Schings (Stuttgart and Weimar: J. B. Metzler, 1994), 187–213. On electricity, see Ernst Benz, *Theologie der Elektrizität: Zur Begegnung und Auseinandersetzung von Theologie und Naturwissenschaft im 17. und 18. Jahrhundert* (Mainz: Verlag der Akademie der Wissenschaften und der Literatur, 1971). On the intersection between medicine and electricity, see Roderick W. Home, "Electricity and the Nervous Fluid," *Journal of the History of Biology* 3.2 (1970): 235–51. A stimulating essay on the public display of electrical phenomena is Simon Schaffer's "The Consuming Flame: Electrical Showmen and Tory Mystics in the World of Goods," in *Consumption and the World of Goods*, ed. John Brewer and Roy Porter (London and New York: Routledge, 1993), 489–526.

would support his cause, namely the "animal magnetism" of Franz Anton Mesmer (1734–1815).[83]

Based in Vienna, Mesmer claimed that he had discovered a new vital force that he dubbed "animal magnetism." In his *Schreiben über die Magnetkur* (1775), he advertised the "discovery" and explained how, properly channeled, "animal magnetism" could cure a variety of ailments.[84] As with his colleague Gaßner, news of his "cures" began to circulate.[85] Soon enough, the two wonder-workers confronted each other, for in the spring of 1775, Mesmer was brought in as an "expert" to investigate the validity of Gaßner's methods. Mesmer's conclusions were that there was nothing supernatural about Gaßner's method, that there was no need to talk of "the Devil," and that everything could be explained rationally on the basis of, what else, animal magnetism! As a result, Gaßner was quickly prevented from continuing his "healing," as exorcisms were forbidden in the realm.[86] Mesmer went on to a most interesting career, one which took him to Paris in 1778 where he became enormously popular until he was forced to flee Paris in 1784 after an investigation into the validity of *his* procedures.[87]

---

[83] Benz, *Franz Anton Mesmer und die philosophischen Grundlagen des "animalischen Magnetismus,"* 20.

[84] For the background to Mesmer's ideas, in addition to the studies by Benz, see Rudolf Tischner, *Franz Anton Mesmer: Leben und Wirkungen* (Munich: Verlag der Münchner Drucke, 1928); Bernhard Milt, *Franz Anton Mesmer und seine Beziehungen zur Schweiz: Magie und Heilkunde zu Lavaters Zeit* (Zurich: Druck Leemann, 1953); Johanna Geyer-Kordesch, "Die Nachtseite der Naturwissenschaft: Die 'okkulte' Vorgeschichte zu Franz Anton Mesmer," in *Franz Anton Mesmer und die Geschichte des Mesmerismus: Beiträge zum internationalen wissenschaftlichen Symposion anlässlich des 250. Geburtstages von Mesmer, 10. bis. 13. Mai in Meersburg,* ed. Heinz Schott (Stuttgart: Franz Steiner Verlag, 1985), 13–30; and Ernst Florey, "Franz Anton Mesmers magische Wissenschaft," in *Franz Anton Mesmer und der Mesmerismus: Wissenschaft, Scharlatanerie, Poesie,* ed. Gereon Wolters (Konstanz: Universitätsverlag Konstanz, 1988), 11–40.

[85] Tischner, *Franz Anton Mesmer,* 45–46; Margarethe Hansmann, "Mesmer in Wien," in Schott, *Franz Anton Mesmer und die Geschichte des Mesmerismus,* 51–67.

[86] Benz, *Franz Anton Mesmer und die philosophischen Grundlagen des "animalischen Magnetismus,"* 28–31; Grassl, *Aufbruch zur Romantik,* 154–56.

[87] See Ernst Benz, *Franz Anton Mesmer (1734–1815) und seine Ausstrahlung in Europa und Amerika* (Munich: Wilhelm Fink, 1976). For Mesmer's political impact on the French Revolution, see Robert Darnton, *Mesmerism and the End of the Enlightenment in France* (Cambridge, MA: Harvard UP, 1968). Goethe followed Mesmer's career with considerable and skeptical interest, especially when it

A measure of the lasting impression that these events had made upon Goethe is provided by an almost offhand, yet directly relevant, remark in a letter some forty-five years later.[88] Christian Gottfried Daniel Nees von Esenbeck, a respected medical doctor, botanist, and at the time President of the Leopoldinisch-Carolinische Akademie der Naturforscher, had sent Goethe a treatise on, of all things, magnetism. Goethe tried to find diplomatic language to say why he had not read it and would not involve himself in a dialogue. He wrote on 23 July 1820:

> Da haben Sie mich denn das letzte Mal in ziemlich Versuchung geführt; denn nur an Ihrer treuen Hand konnt ich ein paar Schritten gegen die Nachtseite wagen. Mit meinem besten Willen aber mußt ich bald wieder umkehren: denn ich bin nun einmal dazu nicht berufen. Wo das Auge sich schließt und das Gehirn seine Herrschaft aufgibt, bin ich höchst erquickt, in einen natürlichen Schlaf zu fallen. Wenn ich bedenke, daß, in meinen lebhaftesten Jahren, Gaßner und Mesmer großes Aufsehen machten und lebhafte Wirkung verbreiteten, daß ich Freund von Lavatern war, der auf dieses Naturwunder religiösen Wert legte, so kommt es mir manchmal gar seltsam vor, daß ich nicht angezogen ward, sondern mich gerade verhielt wie einer, der neben einem Flusse hergeht, ohne daß ihn die Lust zu baden ankäme.[89]

The situation of being forced to decline a response elicited from Goethe the admission, couched in the most polite terms, that in his opinion, the topic was nonsense and always had been. It is significant that the mention of magnetism should have brought the events from 1774–75 to mind and that he yoked Gaßner and Mesmer together in one breath, as if they were two of a kind. Goethe had to be circumspect about labeling Nees von Esenbeck's interest a dabbling in magic, but that is the evident meaning of "the night side" as well as of the reference to the shutting of reason's critical eye.

The pseudo-science and pseudo-medicine had left their traces in "Auerbachs Keller." The conjuring done by Mephistopheles reflects both Gaßner's and Mesmer's deception of their patients. The serious gestures

---

touched on the politics of the day. Goethe's suspicions about the reception of Mesmer will have fed into his rejection of the "science" of the Romantics. On the Romantics' theories about magnetism and electricity, see Maria M. Tatar, *Spellbound: Studies on Mesmerism and Literature* (Princeton: Princeton UP, 1978), 45–151.

[88] For the history of Goethe's ongoing interest in problems of magnetism, see Klaus H. Kiefer, "Goethe und der Magnetismus: Grenzphänomene des naturwissenschaftlichen Verständnisses," *Philosophia Naturalis* 20 (1983): 264–311.

[89] Goethe, *Goethes Briefe*, 3:484.

and the incantation with which Mephistopheles casts the spell imitates Gaßner's theatrics, which Goethe would have known from the eyewitness accounts published so widely. The four companions are not actually healed; certainly their temperaments are not adjusted. Their case resembles those of Gaßner's patients: as long as they believed that they had been cured, they acted accordingly, but there was never any real change in their physical condition and so most of them relapsed when the power of suggestion waned. By having Mephistopheles assume the role of Gaßner, Goethe built in an especially sharp satirical barb. Rather than being cast out, the "Devil" has reversed the tables and is now the one deluding the four companions. Mephistopheles also owes a debt to Gaßner, for as a result of the campaign to expel the Devil, he became real and vivid again for thousands of people. The other set of charlatans who had fooled so many were those like Mesmer who pretended to be able to cure with magnetic or electrical forces.[90] Lines added after the "Urfaust" allude to them, when Altmayer says: "Es war ein Schlag, der ging durch alle Glieder! Schafft einen Stuhl, ich sinke nieder!" (2324–25). The word "Schlag" can refer to a jolt of lightning or electricity. But the effect upon Altmayer of the therapy has been counterproductive, since he now feels weak and needs to sit down.

The trick played by Mephistopheles is that no science is involved here at all in order for the illusion to work. Neither Gaßner nor Mesmer was using any genuine physical or material principles whatsoever; both were charlatans who found believers among the gullible populace. Mephistopheles enjoys the opportunity to do likewise, since it also provides another opening to suggest that all faith is merely a deception. Consequently, no magic is needed here, unless we decide to call the power to reinforce self-delusion magical. But once again, the onus should be upon Faust to challenge, to expose, to critique. His non-response is in marked contrast to the inquiring skepticism shown by Goethe towards Gaßner and his ilk, even though the feelings of friends like Lavater or Susanne von Klettenberg might be bruised. Faust's silence represents an abdication of his responsibility to pursue the truth about what he sees. Either he has not penetrated the illusion, or he condones it, in which case he would be the sort of scientist who relies upon fabricated evidence. There is no indication that Mephistopheles believes in or uses "magic": he operates within the framework of scientific principles available to him by the eighteenth century. It is Faust who hopes that magic will give him

---

[90] On the challenge the "scientific" electro-therapies posed for the Enlightenment, see Anneliese Ego, "Magnetische Auftritte — ideologische Konflikte," 197.

direct access to the secrets of the universe and who continues to be self-deluded. Had Faust been able or willing to challenge Mephistopheles, to expose him as a pretender, one whose entire show in "Auerbachs Keller" has been something other than what has been announced, then the play could have been finished. But Faust has squandered the visit to the microcosm and has learned nothing about the universal laws governing the universe and his own physical being.

# Postscript: Lest We Forget

CAN WE REMEMBER THINGS we have never learned? Can we remember the future? Or can we only remember the past, only recover events and knowledge from behind us up to the present, things that are suddenly needed or valuable now? These and similar questions are emerging at the end of the age of modernism with unexpected intensity: keywords such as "memory" and "remembering" are showing up ever more frequently in the bibliographies of critical discourse.[1] Just why this should be happening is a difficult question. Ian Hacking, in his remarkable book on the philosophical problems of repressed memories and multiple personalities, links the phenomenon to the history of the concepts of self and identity in European thought.[2] Other observers have pointed to the sudden collapse of the totalitarian political systems of Eastern Europe, which have unleashed torrents of private and public recollection of everything that oppressive regimes had excluded from collective memory, had banned from the historical narrative.[3] Certainly, one could also point to the symbolic implications of the year 2000, a millennial threshold that touched at a very deep level the relations between history and prophecy in the Christian cultures.

One aspect of the crisis of memory that is specifically modern and has been foregrounded by Goethe in *Faust* arises from the dispersal of topics. The information explosion that began with the discovery of "new worlds" has not abated, and now we are struggling to cope with a situation in which bits of knowledge are scattered over an immense terrain, the mysterious

---

[1] See the profound essay by Michael Borgolte, "Memoria: Zwischenbilanz eines Mittelalterprojekts," *Zeitschrift für Geschichtswissenschaft* 46.3 (1998): 197–210.

[2] Ian Hacking, *Rewriting the Soul: Multiple Personality and the Sciences of Memory* (Princeton: Princeton UP, 1995).

[3] For an overview of the "memory crisis," see Michael Lambek and Paul Antze, "Introduction: Forecasting Memory," in *Tense Past: Cultural Essays in Trauma and Memory*, ed. Paul Antze and Michael Lambek (New York and London: Routledge, 1996), xi–xxxviii. To cite but one discussion of the complexities of the German situation: Claudia Koonz, "Between Memory and Oblivion: Concentration Camps in German Memory," in *Commemorations: The Politics of National Identity*, ed. John R. Gillis (Princeton: Princeton UP, 1994), 258–80.

"Internet," much as the fragments of a bomb, the structures, and the victims are chaotically strewn over the surrounding space in the wake of a ter-
rorist attack. Like the myriads of detectives and analysts attempting to
reconstruct the event after such a blast, looking at the tiniest fragments in
order to locate clues to the hidden identity of the perpetrator, so we in the
world of learning stumble from website to website, are inundated by endless messages mingling noise and information, use "search engines" in
order to find "out there," somewhere, in the epistemological utopia, just
that bit of information that may satisfy us as the answer to our question.
The painstaking work over centuries of building library collections and
developing access devices, such as the Library of Congress cataloguing system, has been demolished and continues to be fragmented as ever more
secondary explosions clutter the bibliographic universe with shards of what
may or may not be information. The loss of systematic information storage and retrieval capacities is nothing less than the collapse of the coherent memory system of the sciences.[4]

We are, once again, where Goethe's Faust stood in the epistemological crisis demarcated by the term "Renaissance."[5] Fuelled by the inrushing
data from the "new" and other worlds "discovered" by "explorers," the
fifteenth and sixteenth centuries also saw the breakdown of the long-standing, stable orders of knowledge represented by the structure of the seven
arts. Only specialists today can imagine the profound anxiety caused for
theology, to give one example, when species never mentioned or imagined
in Scripture were suddenly and all too tangibly presented in Europe.
Questions arose. Not least: where did the aboriginals of the "new" world
fit into the history of the descent from Adam and Eve?[6] Faust's opening

---

[4] That is my pessimistic reading of the developments outlined rather optimisti-
cally by Arnold Sanders, "Hypertext, Learning, and Memory: Some Implications
from Manuscript Tradition," *Text* 8 (1995): 125–43.

[5] On epistemology, memory and the crisis of faith in the sixteenth and seventeenth centuries, see Thomas Leinkauf, "*Scientia universalis, memoria* und *status
corruptionis*: Überlegungen zu philosophischen und theologischen Implikationen
der Universalwissenschaft sowie zum Verhältnis von Universalwissenschaft und
Theorie des Gedächtnisses," in *Ars memorativa: Zur kulturgeschichtlichen
Bedeutung der Gedächtniskunst, 1400–1750*, ed. Jörg Jochen Berns and Wolfgang
Neuber (Tübingen: Max Niemeyer, 1993), 1–34. On the attempts to impose order
through systems, see Timothy J. Reiss, "The Idea of Meaning and the Practice of
Order in Peter Ramus, Henri Estienne, and Others," in *Humanism in Crisis: The
Decline of the French Renaissance*, ed. Philippe Desan (Ann Arbor, MI: U of
Michigan P, 1991), 125–52.

[6] For overviews, see Adriano Prosperi, "New Heaven and New Earth: Prophecy
and Propaganda at the Time of the Discovery and Conquest of the Americas," in

monologue is a vivid testimonial of the sense that the traditional orders of knowledge no longer gave solutions to the important questions. Neither theology nor law nor medicine nor philosophy seemed to be able to bring the questing mind to the origin of answers any more. Without a reliable guide to the stored knowledge of the past, Faust — the modern man — is disoriented, unable to remember the sorts of things that would have satisfied previous generations. Instead of research, which could take him on familiar paths to stored knowledge, Faust is now adrift in an aimless search, hoping to stumble, through trial and error, upon something familiar, useful, comprehensible. Goethe demonstrates this repeatedly, as when Faust is shown casting about for the words with which to translate Scripture, as he tries out various fill-in-the-blank responses, obviously unable to provide the correct translation quickly. Faust can convince himself that his is a plausible translation because he has forgotten the centuries of theological analysis of Scripture. The whole of the drama tells the story of equally hapless, but immediately more damaging, instances of Faust's faulty memory, his repeated errors of comprehension and decision-making associated with his forgetfulness.[7]

The antithesis to Faust is Goethe himself, with a prodigious memory and the capacity to find his way through to the right topic. Consider his account of his walk in the botanical garden of Palermo on 17 April 1787:

> Es ist ein wahres Unglück, wenn man von vielerlei Geistern verfolgt und versucht wird! Heute früh ging ich mit dem festen, ruhigen Vorsatz, meine dichterischen Träume fortzusetzen, nach dem öffentlichen Garten, allein eh' ich mich's versah, erhaschte mich ein anderes Gespenst, das mir schon diese Tage nachgeschlichen. Die vielen Pflanzen, die ich sonst nur in Kübeln und Töpfen, ja die größte Zeit des Jahres nur hinter Glasfenstern zu sehen gewohnt war, stehen hier froh und frisch unter freiem Himmel, und indem sie ihre Bestimmung vollkommen erfüllen, werden sie uns deutlicher. Im Angesicht so vielerlei neuen und erneuten Gebildes fiel mir die alte Grille wieder ein, ob ich nicht unter dieser Schar die Urpflanze entdecken könnte. Eine solche muß es denn doch geben!

---

*Prophetic Rome in the High Renaissance Period: Essays*, ed. Marjorie Reeves (Oxford: Clarendon, 1992), 279–303; and Sabine MacCormack, "Limits of Understanding: Perceptions of Greco-Roman and Amerindian Paganism in Early Modern Europe," in *America in European Consciousness, 1493–1750*, ed. Karen Ordahl Kupperman (Chapel Hill and London: U of North Carolina P, for the Institute of Early American History and Culture, Williamsburg, Virginia, 1995), 79–129.

[7] Notice how many times Mephistopheles twists the knife by reminding Faust of something he had forgotten!

> Woran würde ich sonst erkennen, daß dieses oder jenes Gebilde eine
> Pflanze sei, wenn sie nicht alle nach einem Muster gebildet wären?[8]

The beauties and subtleties of this episode can be appreciated fully only when we become fascinated by the connection between two apparently disparate topics: botany and memory. What does Goethe's famous, some might say notorious, recurrence to the "Urpflanze," have to do with memory? On a surface level, there is Goethe's report that the idea of the original plant has not suddenly come to him for the first time. It is "die alte Grille," "ein anderes Gespenst" — brought to mind unexpectedly. But notice that the memory has not been stimulated by pure accident, for the setting is a botanical garden, a sort of plant museum. One important function of botanical gardens was to present, in some logical sequence, a wide variety of plant specimens so that the observer could learn the identities of the plants, their features and, if possible, their herbal properties and practical uses. The botanic garden is another version of the memory theatre, here transposed to the outdoors. By walking through the garden, Goethe's memory was indeed activated, but rather quirkily. Instead of remembering only the names and properties of the plants actually there, Goethe's mind is moved to recall a plant that he has not yet seen in the world, yet has previously established as an idea. The memory of the ideal plant is not called into doubt. Rather, the fact that he was able to recall that the other entities were plants becomes a confirmation that there must be an original memory of a paradigmatic plant, without which new knowledge could not be founded. Without the memory of *a* plant, no plants could be sorted into the data base.

What seems to be a bizarre inversions of the relationship between topics and topography is utterly consistent with the ancient understanding of how remembering was possible. For, if the peregrination through the memory theatre, the botanic garden, has stimulated a recollection of a previously known idea, then the landscape is actually subordinated to the topic being recalled. That is not to imply such topographies were inconsequential. Well-organized memory theatres should function quickly, efficiently, and accurately. The virtue of the Sicilian botanical garden is precisely that it overwhelms through its tight design the scattered, unconcentrated reverie and forces itself and its order upon the observing consciousness. The setting memorialized, and thereby returned Goethe to, a project of long-standing, considerable significance to him. Goethe is almost compelled to remember something he had, for whatever reason,

---

[8] Johann Wolfgang von Goethe, *Werke: Hamburger Ausgabe in 14 Bänden*, ed. Erich Trunz (Munich: C. H. Beck, 1981), 11:266. This "Hamburger Ausgabe" will henceforth be cited as HA.

forgotten in the interim, just as we might be reminded of a birthday by an entry on the calendar page.

As we zoom in on the garden / memory theatre, it becomes evident that the individual plants are powerful mnemonic devices. Studying them closely, Goethe is compelled to recollections of unity:

> Und ich fand sie immer mehr ähnlich als verschieden, und wollte ich meine botanische Terminologie anbringen, so ging das wohl, aber es fruchtete nicht, es machte mich unruhig, ohne daß es mir weiterhalf. Gestört war mein guter poetischer Vorsatz, der Garten des Alcinous war verschwunden, ein Weltgarten hatte sich aufgetan. (HA 11:267)

The power of the mnemonic signs quite defeats his attempt to repress the memory, to forget the old botanical project and to continue with the plans of the day. Repression does not succeed; the memory has returned with such vehemence that it opens up cosmic vistas. The garden has become a "world garden," and in one rush we suddenly recall an entire history behind this scene, from Adam naming the animals through the language of nature[9] and the doctrine of signatures[10] to the great struggle of eighteenth-century botanists such as Linnaeus to restore order to natural history, so that human beings might again perceive God's divine purpose in Creation.

Not everyone walking through the garden would have had memories such as these. If the memory theatre is to function, the observer must be alert to the signs and signals.[11] In order for there to be scientific progress, searching and remembering must work in tandem. Goethe was no advocate of aimless, uninformed stumbling through the world in the off chance that one might stumble on something useful or valuable. It is for this

---

[9] Hartmut Böhme, *Natur und Subjekt* (Frankfurt am Main: Suhrkamp, 1988), 38–64.

[10] For overviews, see Hennig Brinkmann, "Die 'Zweite Sprache' und die Dichtung des Mittelalters," in *Methoden in Wissenschaft und Kunst des Mittelalters*, ed. Albert Zimmermann with Rudolf Hoffmann (Berlin: Walter de Gruyter, 1970), 155–71; Hans Blumenberg, *Die Lesbarkeit der Welt* (Frankfurt am Main: Suhrkamp, 1993); and Norbert Winkler, "Von der Physiognomie des Weltlabyrinths oder: Das Projekt einer unendlichen Enzyklopädie; Reflexionen zur Signaturenlehre bei Paracelsus," *Deutsche Zeitschrift für Philosophie* 44.1 (1996): 57–74.

[11] On the semiotic aspects of the mnemonic systems, see the work of Renate Lachmann, e.g., "Die Unlöschbarkeit der Zeichen: Das semiotische Unglück des Mnemonisten," in *Gedächtniskunst: Raum — Bild — Schrift; Studien zur Mnemontechnik*, ed. Anselm Haverkamp and Renate Lachmann (Frankfurt am Main: Suhrkamp, 1991), 111–41.

reason that Faust is a negative example of the scientist. Given the crisis of knowledge, Faust reacts irrationally, failing to pay close attention to details and neglecting to use the power of remembering. Nowhere will these shortcomings become as blatantly obvious to the audience as in "Auerbachs Keller in Leipzig." Faust's non-reaction, often praised as the sign of a healthy scepticism, is actually an indictment of someone who stands baffled and unmoved in the presence of extraordinary events. The things Faust observes in the scene should stimulate him to remember important topics in theology, medicine, science, and history, should bring to mind key places in the Bible and in texts by writers such as Tasso, Ariosto, Dante, Vergil, and Homer. But nothing like that happens. The manifold possibilities of the theatre, its topological layerings, make it possible for us, the audience, simultaneously to be in the memory theatre and to observe someone else's reactions to what we see. We can assess Faust's ability to remember against our own capacity to decode the theatre-within-the-theatre, as our memories are stimulated by the allusions to a wide range of important topics.

However, let us not be too harsh or quick in judging and condemning Faust's amnesia. What will ultimately redeem him is that he suffers from melancholy, and melancholic individuals had impaired memories. Faust never becomes healed physically and that sets up the paradox of his salvation, for he cannot be held personally responsible for a physical condition beyond his control. No matter what he *wills*, as long as he cannot *remember*, he cannot be condemned by any reasonable system of justice. Without going into all the complexities, this is what makes Faust radically different from figures such as Aeneas or Adam, who have no one but themselves to blame if they forget something important. The discussion by E. J. Mickel of the medieval *Ordo Representacionis Ade (Jeu d'Adam)* is instructive here:

> Confronted by this unknown Reality, Adam and Eve need reason less than memory. Only in the memory can Adam store Figura's words. And in these words are truth. He need not judge between the truth of Figura's words and those of Diabolus, he need only remember the words.[12]

In that framework, when Adam or Eve forget, that act can be taken straightforwardly as willed disobedience, a crime that can be punished so that order may be restored. That is still very much the situation in Marlowe's *Doctor Faustus*, where the contractual conditions are explicit, albeit updated for the commercial world of the sixteenth century. Faust

---

[12] Emanuel J. Mickel, "Faith, Memory, Treason and Justice in the *Ordo Representacionis Ade (Jeu d'Adam)*," *Romania* 112 (1991): 129–54; here, 42.

cannot be judged so directly, because he is neither the sole agent of his illness nor the solitary culprit. A vacillation between the theological and the
medical interpretations can be seen in the tract *Melancholischer Teufel*
(1572) by the Lutheran theologian Simon Musaeus. Although in the final
instance he returned to positing obedience according to the first commandment as the effective cure, he was well aware of the medical theories,
and willing to prescribe the usual remedies (conversation, wine, music).[13]
Today the prosecution might be inclined not to take "poor memory due
to humoral imbalance" as a valid defense, but Goethe meant it to be
accepted for the case of Faust.

There was fascination, one is tempted to say obsession, with melancholy, in the period from 1500 to 1700. The eclipse of the discourse in
which melancholy could be a major topic of analysis came only towards the
end of the eighteenth century with the rise of empirical physiology and a
concomitant new psychology.[14] Once it receded from the forefront of
awareness, melancholy quickly became a relic in the history of ideas, one
that lingered on in figures of speech but that was no longer productive; it
would be fully displaced by modern categories such as depression.
Shakespeare scholars have difficulty with analyses of Hamlet's melancholic
condition as well. What happens to the ideals and greatness postulated by
Romantic criticism of a tragic hero when that hero turns out to be (merely)
suffering through an illness? We want Hamlet to be hesitating because he
is tormented by philosophical questions about the meaning of life and
death, not because the inability to make up his mind is some sort of symptom. Similarly, when Faust utters the famous lines about "two souls," we
want to hear his torn anguish, not the ravings of a very sick man. The possibility that this inner division, which has seemed so attractive to many,
might be nothing more than a late version of the question raised at the
very beginning of the discourse on melancholy — "Why is it that all those
who have become eminent in philosophy or politics or poetry or the arts

---

[13] Robert Kolb, "God, Faith, and the Devil: Popular Lutheran Treatments of
the First Commandment in the Era of the Book of Concord," *Fides et Historia* 15
(1982): 71–89; here, 82–85.

[14] On the discourse on melancholy in the eighteenth century, see Hans-Jürgen
Schings, *Melancholie und Aufklärung: Melancholiker und ihre Kritiker in
Erfahrungsseelenkunde und Literatur des 18. Jahrhunderts* (Stuttgart: J. B. Metzler,
1977); Mattenklott, *Melancholie in der Dramatik des Sturm und Drang* (Stuttgart:
J. B. Metzler, 1968); and Wolfram Mauser, "Melancholieforschung des 18.
Jahrhunderts zwischen Ikonographie und Ideologiekritik: Auseinandersetzung mit
den bisherigen Ergebnissen und Thesen zu einem Neuansatz," *Lessing Yearbook* 13
(1981): 253–77.

are clearly melancholiacs, and some of them to such an extent as to be affected by diseases caused by black bile?"[15] — flies in the face of established views of Faust's tragedy.

Any trained physician of the sixteenth century would have recognized from the opening scenes of *Faust* that the main character was gravely ill. Up late at night, all alone, rambling in a monologue filled with extreme emotions about excessive ambitions and utter self-contempt, these were all indicators of someone in the grip of serious melancholy. The clinical literature was extensive, but there was broad consensus on the condition of the melancholic, conveniently summarized by J. Michael Richardson:

> The natives of the malevolent Saturn are both unpleasant and unfortunate: they are introspective, gloomy, solitary, pensive, dull-witted, frequently malicious, pale, wan, covetous, taciturn, jealous, stubborn, and sluggish. Saturnians sleep poorly, walk with head down and eyes cast to the ground, neglect their bodies and appearance, complain, mutter, muse or murmur to themselves, and (because they do not know what is good for them) reject the counsel of others. Although hard-working, they do not meet with success in any undertaking, and a troubled mind, in combination with their cold and dry physical constitution, constantly threatens to "accelerate and hasten" their "ruine and decay."[16]

One can hardly imagine a better synopsis of Faust's words and deeds in the opening of the play. One of the dilemmas of the severe melancholic is the inability to diagnose his own affliction (hence the need for the length of Burton's *Anatomy of Melancholy*); they know they are ill but cannot quite say why. When Faust reaches for the deadly vial, it is his body that yearns for an alleviating potion even as his disordered mind is moving towards suicide.

The complex of Faust's melancholy was directly related to Goethe's critique of the political system. Unless the political realm was in good order and at peace, governed wisely for the general well-being, no individual could be wholly free of some internal emotional disorder, which would also manifest itself in physical ailments. The compactness of the allusions within "Auerbachs Keller" made it possible for Goethe to condense a huge amount of the epic tradition within a small space; it remained for

---

[15] The opening of the famous "Problem XXX," attributed to Aristotle, quoted in *Saturn and Melancholy: Studies in the History of Natural Philosophy, Religion and Art*, by Raymond Klibansky, Erwin Panofsky, and Fritz Saxl (London: Nelson, 1964), 18.

[16] J. Michael Richardson, *Astrological Symbolism in Spenser's* The Shepheardes Calender*: The Cultural Background of a Literary Text* (Lewiston, NY and Queenston, ON: Edwin Mellen P, 1989), 77.

us to unpack it. Having worked our way through the scene repeatedly, we can now use it, should we so wish, as a memory theatre of our own. Attached to it is the sequence of passages from epics dealing with trees, and as further evidence about that topic comes to light, it too can be addressed via the scene. One example comes to mind. Because of the trajectory followed by my reading, the primary emphasis has been upon the figural relationships of Faust to a limited cluster of heroes. For practical reasons, the number of those heroes has been curtailed, even at the price of obvious gaps. From the outset, the topic of "Klugheit," of cunning, should have (and indeed did) evoke the figure of Odysseus and his wanderings. The parallels and differences between Odysseus and Faust are as apparent and as fascinating as those between Odysseus and Achilles, and Goethe introduces an allusion to Odysseus in "Auerbachs Keller." Recalling that Goethe had been reading the *Odyssey* just before taking the stroll in the Palermo garden, and that Goethe was contemplating writing "*Ulyß auf Phäa*,"[17] we might remember the famous passage about the signs of memory. Odysseus has returned and is challenged by Laertes to prove that he is indeed the long-missing son. The visible demonstration is the scar, but the truly irrefutable evidence is what Odysseus retrieves from his memory:

"Or come then, let me tell you of the trees in the well-worked
orchard, which you gave me once. I asked you of each one,
when I was a child, following you through the garden. We went
among the trees, and you named them all and told me what each one
was, and you gave me thirteen pear trees, and ten apple trees,
and forty fig trees; and so also you named the fifty
vines you would give. Each of them bore regularly, for there were
grapes at every stage upon them, whenever the seasons
of Zeus came down from the sky upon them, to make them heavy."

He spoke, and Laertes' knees and the heart within him went slack,
As he recognized the clear proofs that Odysseus had given.[18]

---

[17] I refer again to Rüdiger Görner's fine article, "Goethe's Ulysses: On the Meaning of a Project," *Publications of the English Goethe Society* NS 44/45 (1993–95): 21–37, and draw attention in this context to the suggestive piece by Frederick Amrine, "Goethe's Italian Discoveries as a Natural Scientist (The Scientist in the Underworld)," in *Goethe in Italy, 1786–1986: A Bi-Centennial Symposium November 14–16, 1986, University of California, Santa Barbara; Proceedings Volume*, ed. Gerhart Hoffmeister (Amsterdam: Rodopi, 1988), 55–76.

[18] Homer, *The Odyssey of Homer*, trans. Richmond Lattimore (New York: Harper & Row, 1975), lines 335–46.

I must confess that I had entirely forgotten this passage until I read John Henderson's wonderfully informative and suggestive article.[19] But Goethe, fresh from reading the text and walking through a botanical garden, would immediately have made the connection via the poem. And we see what distracted him: it is the catalogue of all the useful fruit trees, so carefully enumerated and recited, that must have brought the whole discourse of the varieties of trees and useful plants to mind. As Henderson says so well: "The fruit-trees can indicate to careful readers that all depends, in gardening, life and narrative, on 'a keen eye for (agri)cultural detail.' Just such detail as this sign, its design and signifying."[20]

What strikes me is the way in which the trees serve as the common sign for the memories of both Odysseus and Laertes. The latter presumably has forgotten the conversation from very long ago, but it was so strongly impressed upon the former that at a critical moment he is able to retrieve and deploy the memory in order to establish his identity. The ability to remember, and to remember so clearly, with such detail, makes the past useful. It is no less than what we would expect of Odysseus's practical cunning, but therein lies the contrast between him and Faust. No matter where he had gone, no matter what trials he had endured, Odysseus had not forgotten the topic of the orchard, had never lost the site / in-sight of his memory, and therefore is able to return home. On the other hand, Faust errs aimlessly because he wants to abandon the sites of memory, wants to forget what *he* learned from *his* father, and therefore will never be able to make productive use of his knowledge, will never arrive at his goal.

Perhaps by now the weary reader wonders if I will ever get to my goal. In a sense, no. The more I have tried to approach "Auerbachs Keller" as a specific place in Goethe's text, the more it has drawn me away from where I thought I was going. I have not found the text I sought. Indeed, if I am correct, then that text, simple and clear, with a straightforward interpretation, is no longer available. Instead, "Auerbachs Keller in Leipzig" is the address where a number of discourses intersect in complicated ways, where key passages from some of the most demanding works of European literature have been afforded a commonplace.[21] This was Goethe's doing. Like Odysseus, he recalled for the view of the audience from the past a constellation of images and figures no less real, no less influential, than the

---

[19] John Henderson, "The Name of the Tree: Recounting *Odyssey* XXIV 340–2," *Journal of Hellenic Studies* 117 (1997): 87–116.

[20] Henderson, "The Name of the Tree," 87. Not to be forgotten is the pruning at the beginning of *Die Wahlverwandtschaften*.

[21] See the evocative article by Aleida Assmann, "Das Gedächtnis der Orte," *Deutsche Vierteljahrsschrift*, Sonderheft (1994): 17*–35*.

"thirteen pear trees, and ten apple trees, and forty fig trees." Laertes was convinced because he shared his son's recollections in common; Faust was not because he chose to forget, was contemptuous of all that was common, including the places of memory.[22] As the audience, we have the choice of whether to let ourselves share with Goethe in the memory of tradition or whether to refuse to recognize ourselves there.

I am well aware that this book could be much longer still, for as it began to develop, new vistas as well as unexpected side roads and intriguing thickets came into view. But restraint seemed advisable, especially since many heads are better than one. If there is any merit to the arguments made here, vistas of entirely new research on *Faust* will have become possible and necessary. And if the arguments provoke someone to trump my conclusions — that would be most welcome. Without dissent, there can be no progress in science; without the risk taken in hypotheses, there would be nothing to dissent against.

And by the way, who *is* Herr Hans, from Rippach?

---

[22] I am thinking here of the analysis by Svetlana Boym, *Common Places: Mythologies of Everyday Life in Russia* (Cambridge, MA: Harvard UP, 1994), esp. 11–20. It would be instructive to scrutinize Faust's contempt for all the everyday things and memories in the lives of ordinary people, in light of Boym's reminder that "clichés often save us from despair and embarrassment by protecting the vulnerability and fragility of our way of life and social communication. . . . One can estrange the common place, but then one has to estrange one's own estrangement" (15).

# Works Cited

Absil, Th. "La Divina Commedia en Faust: Uitreksel uit een overweging." In *Verzamelde Opstellen: Geschreven door oud-Lerlingen von Professor Dr. J. H. Scholte*, edited by Th. C. Van Stockum, H. W. J. Kroes, D. J. C. Zeeman, 110–40. Amsterdam: J. M. Meulenhoff, 1947.

Adler, Jeremy. *"Eine fast magische Anziehungskraft"*: Goethes Wahlverwandtschaften *und die Chemie seiner Zeit*. Munich: C. H. Beck, 1987.

Albrecht, Michael von. *Rom: Spiegel Europas; Texte und Themen*. Heidelberg: Verlag Lambert Schneider, 1988.

Alewyn, Richard. *Das große Welttheater: Die Epoche der höfischen Feste*. Munich: C. H. Beck, 1989.

Alighieri, Dante. *The Divine Comedy*. Translation and commentary by Charles S. Singleton. 6 vols. Princeton: Princeton UP, 1989.

Allen, A. W. "The Dullest Book of the *Aeneid*." *The Classical Journal* 47 (1951–52): 119–23.

Amrine, Frederick. "Goethe's Italian Discoveries as a Natural Scientist (The Scientist in the Underworld)." In *Goethe in Italy, 1786–1986: A Bi-centennial Symposium November 14–16, 1986, University of California, Santa Barbara: Proceedings Volume*, edited by Gerhart Hoffmeister, 55–76. Amsterdam: Rodopi, 1988.

Anderegg, Johannes, and Edith Anna Kunz, eds. *Goethe und die Bibel*. Stuttgart: Deutsche Bibelgesellschaft, 2005.

Andreae, Johann Valentin. *Christianopolis*. First published 1619. Translated by D. S. Georgi, 1741. Edited by Richard van Dülmen. Stuttgart: Calwer Verlag, 1972.

Antonioli, Roland. "L'éloge du vin dans l'œuvre de Rabelais." In *L'imaginaire du vin: Colloque pluridisciplinaire 15–17 octobre 1981*, edited by Max Milner and Martine Chatelain, 131–40. Marseille: Éditions Jeanne Laffitte, 1983.

Apollodorus. *The Library*. Translated by James George Frazer. Loeb Classical Library. London: William Heinemann, and Cambridge, MA: Harvard UP, 1967.

Appleby, Joyce Oldham. *Economic Thought and Ideology in Seventeenth-Century England*. Princeton: Princeton UP, 1978.

Arbesmann, Rudolph. "The Concept of 'Christus Medicus' in St. Augustine." *Traditio* 10 (1954): 1–28.

Arens, Hans. *Kommentar zu Goethes Faust I*. Heidelberg: Winter, 1982.

Ariosto, Ludovico. *Orlando Furioso*. Translated by Guido Waldman. Oxford: Oxford UP, 1983.

Aristotle. *Poetics*. Translated by Gerald F. Else. Ann Arbor, MI: U of Michigan P, 1973.

Armour, Peter. *Dante's Griffin and the History of the World: A Study of the Earthly Paradise (Purgatorio, cantos xxix–xxxiii)*. Oxford: Clarendon, 1989.

Ascoli, Albert Russell. *Ariosto's Bitter Harmony: Crisis and Evasion in the Italian Renaissance*. Princeton: Princeton UP, 1987.

Assmann, Aleida. "Das Gedächtnis der Orte." *Deutsche Vierteljahrsschrift* Sonderheft (1994): 17*–35*.

Astell, Ann W. *The Song of Songs in the Middle Ages*. Ithaca and London: Cornell UP, 1990.

Atherton, Geoffrey. Disiciendi membra poetae: *Vergil and the Germans in the Eighteenth Century*. PhD diss., Yale U, 1996.

Atkins, Stuart. "Goethe und die Renaissancelyrik." In *Goethe und die Tradition*, edited by Hans Reiss, 102–29. Frankfurt am Main: Athenäum, 1972. In English, "Goethe and the Poetry of the Renaissance." Translated by Jane K. Brown. In Stuart Atkins, *Essays on Goethe*, edited by Jane K. Brown and Thomas P. Saine, 92–117. Columbia, SC: Camden House, 1995.

———. *Goethe's Faust: A Literary Analysis*. Cambridge, MA: Harvard UP, 1958.

Avetisyan, Vladimir A. *Gete i Dante*. Izhevsk: Isdatel'stvo Udmurtskovo Universiteta, 1998.

Babb, Lawrence. *The Elizabethan Malady: A Study of Melancholia in English Literature from 1580 to 1642*. East Lansing: Michigan State UP, 1951.

Badt, Benno. "Goethe als Übersetzer des Hohenliedes." *Neue Jahrbücher für Philologie und Paedagogik* 51 (1881): 346–57.

Baildam, John. *Paradisal Love: Johann Gottfried Herder and the Song of Songs*. Sheffield: Sheffield Academic P, 1999.

Baillet, R. "L'Arioste et les Princes d'Este: Poésie et politique." In *Le pouvoir et la plume: Incitation, contrôle et répression: Actes du colloque internationale organisé par le Centre interuniversitaire de recherche sur la renaissance italienne et l'Institut culturel italien de Marseille, Aix-en-Provence, Marseille, 14–16 Mai 1981*, 85–95. Paris: Université de La Sorbonne Nouvelle, 1982.

Bakhtin, Mikhail. *Rabelais and His World*. Translated by Hélène Iswolsky. Bloomington: Indiana UP, 1984.

Bandmann, Günter. *Melancholie und Musik: Ikonographische Studien*. Cologne and Opladen: Westdeutscher Verlag, 1960.

Bapp, Karl. "Goethe und Lukrez," *Jahrbuch der Goethe-Gesellschaft* 12 (1926): 47–67.

Barkan, Leonard. *Nature's Work of Art: The Human Body as Image of the World*. New Haven and London: Yale UP, 1975.

Barnes, J. C. "Inferno XIII." In *Dante Soundings: Eight Literary and Historical Essays*, edited by David Nolan, 28–58. Dublin: Irish Academic P and Totowa, NJ: Rowman and Littlefield, for The Foundation for Italian Studies, University College, Dublin, 1981.

Baron, Frank. "Camerarius and the Historical Doctor Faustus." In *Joachim Camerarius (1500–1574): Beiträge zur Geschichte des Humanismus im Zeitalter der Reformation / Essays on the History of Humanism during the Reformation*, edited by Frank Baron, 200–222. Munich: Fink, 1978.

———. *Doctor Faustus from History to Legend*. Munich: Fink, 1978.

Bartscherer, Agnes. *Paracelsus, Paracelsisten und Goethes Faust: Eine Quellenstudie*. Dortmund: Druck und Verlag von Fr. Wilh. Ruhfus, 1911.

Bassermann, Alfred. "Nachlese zu dem Kapitel 'Goethe und Dante.'" *Euphorion* 24 (1922): 166–71.

Bate, Walter Jackson. *John Keats*. Cambridge, MA: Belknap Press of Harvard UP, 1963.

Bauer, Markus. "Melancholie und Memoria: Zur Theorie von Gedächtnisschwund und fixer Idee im 17. Jahrhundert." In *Ars memorativa: Zur kulturgeschichtlichen Bedeutung der Gedächtniskunst, 1400–1750*, edited by Jörg Jochen Berns and Wolfgang Neuber, 313–30. Tübingen: Max Niemeyer, 1993.

Becker-Cantarino, Baerbel. "Die 'Schwarze Legende': Zum Spanienbild in der deutschen Literatur des 18. Jahrhunderts." *Zeitschrift für deutsche Philologie* 94.2 (1975): 183–203.

Beetz, Manfred. "Trost durch Kunst: Zur musikalischen Liebessprache in Christian Weises Gedicht *Auff ein galantes Clavichordium*." In *Die Affekte und ihre Repräsentation in der deutschen Literatur der Frühen Neuzeit*, edited by Jean-Daniel Krebs, 137–49. Bern and Berlin: Peter Lang, 1996.

Bellamy, Elizabeth J. "From Virgil to Tasso: The Epic Topos as an Uncanny Return." In *Desire in the Renaissance: Psychoanalysis and Literature*, edited by Valeria Finucci and Regina Schwartz, 207–32. Princeton: Princeton UP, 1994.

Benedict, Barbara M. *Curiosity: A Cultural History of Early Modern Inquiry*. Chicago and London: U of Chicago P, 2001.

Bennett, Benjamin. *Goethe's Theory of Poetry:* Faust *and the Regeneration of Language*. Ithaca and London: Cornell UP, 1986.

Benz, Ernst. *Franz Anton Mesmer und die philosophischen Grundlagen des "animalischen Magnetismus."* Wiesbaden: Franz Steiner, for the Akademie der Wissenschaften und der Literatur, Mainz, 1977.

———. *Franz Anton Mesmer (1734–1815) und seine Ausstrahlung in Europa und Amerika*. Munich: Wilhelm Fink, 1976.

———. *Theologie der Elektrizität: Zur Begegnung und Auseinandersetzung von Theologie und Naturwissenschaft im 17. und 18. Jahrhundert*. Mainz: Verlag der Akademie der Wissenschaften und der Literatur, 1971.

Bersier, Gabrielle. "'Reise der Söhne Megaprazons': Goethe, Rabelais und die Französische Revolution." In *Goethe im Kontext: Kunst und Humanität, Naturwissenschaft und Politik von der Aufklärung bis zur Restauration*, edited by Wolfgang Wittkowski, 230–40. Tübingen: Max Niemeyer, 1984.

Binder, Wolfgang. "Goethes Vierheiten." In *Typologia Litterarum: Festschrift für Max Wehrli*, edited by Stefan Sonderegger, Alois M. Haas, and Harald Burger, 311–23. Zurich: Atlantis, 1969.

Binswanger, Hans Christoph. *Money and Magic: A Critique of the Modern Economy in the Light of Goethe's* Faust. Translated by J. E. Harrison. Chicago and London: U of Chicago P, 1994. Originally published in German as *Geld und Magie: Deutung und Kritik der modern Wirtschaft anhand von Goethes* Faust. Stuttgart: Weitbrecht Verlag in K. Thienemanns Verlag, 1985.

Biow, Douglas. "From Ignorance to Knowledge: The Marvelous in *Inferno* 13." In *The Poetry of Allusion: Virgil and Ovid in Dante's* Commedia, edited by Rachel Jacoff and Jeffrey T. Schnapp, 45–61; 261–64. Stanford: Stanford UP, 1991.

Blair, Ann. *The Theater of Nature: Jean Bodin and Renaissance Science.* Princeton: Princeton UP, 1997.

Blissett, William. "Caesar and Satan." *Journal of the History of Ideas* 18 (1957): 221–32.

Blumenberg, Hans. *Die Lesbarkeit der Welt*. Frankfurt am Main: Suhrkamp, 1993.

———. "Neugierde und Wissenstrieb: Supplemente zu *Curiositas*." *Archiv für Begriffsgeschichte* 14.1 (1970): 7–40.

Blumenthal, Lieselotte. "Arkadien in Goethes 'Tasso.'" *Goethe: Jahrbuch der Goethe-Gesellschaft* NS 21 (1959): 1–24.

Boas, George. *Vox Populi: Essays in the History of an Idea.* Baltimore: The Johns Hopkins UP, 1969.

Boethius. *The Consolation of Philosophy.* Translated by V. W. Watts. Harmondsworth, UK: Penguin, 1969.

Bohm, Arnd. "An Allusion to Tasso in "The Thorn." *The Wordsworth Circle* 33.2 (2002): 77–79.

———. "The Double Talk of the Witch's Arithmetic (Hexen-Einmal-Eins) in *Faust I*." *Michigan Germanic Studies* 25.2 (1999 [2001]): 149–66.

———. "Epic and the History of *Faust*." *Modern Language Studies* 31.1 (2001): 79–97.

———. "Gretchen am Spinnrad." Unpublished paper presented at the Goethe Museum Düsseldorf, 13 June 2001.

———. "Margarete's Innocence and the Guilt of Faust." *Deutsche Vierteljahrsschrift* 75.2 (June 2001): 216–50.

———. "Naming Goethe's Faust: A Matter of Signficance." Forthcoming in *Deutsche Vierteljahrsschrift*.

———. "Narratives for a Post-Heroic Age: Peter Bichsel's Short Prose." *The University of Dayton Review* 19.2 (Summer 1988–89): 55–68.

———. "The Tell-Tale Chalice: 'Es war ein König in Thule' and *Orlando Furioso.*" *Monatshefte* 92.1 (2000): 20–34.

———. "Typology and History in the 'Rattenlied' (*Faust I*)." *Goethe Yearbook* 10 (2001): 65–83.

Böhme, Gernot. "Kann man Goethes 'Faust' in der Tradition des Lehrgedichts lesen?" *Goethe-Jahrbuch* 117 (2000): 67–77.

Böhme, Hartmut. "Lebendige Natur — Wissenschaftskritik, Naturforschung und allegorische Hermetik." *Deutsche Vierteljahrsschrift* 60.2 (1986): 249–72.

———. *Natur und Subjekt.* Frankfurt am Main: Suhrkamp, 1988.

Bohnenkamp, Anne. "*. . . das Hauptgeschäft nicht außer lassend*": *Die Paralipomena zu Goethes "Faust."* Frankfurt am Main: Insel, 1994.

Boitani, Piero. *The Shadow of Ulysses: Figures of a Myth.* Translated by Anita Weston. Oxford: Clarendon, 1994.

Bonadeo, Alfredo. "Note sulla Pazzia di Orlando." *Forum Italicum* 4 (1970): 39–57.

Bonfatti, Emilio. *La "Civil Conversazione" in Germania: Letteratura del compartamento de Stefano Guazzo a Adolph Knigge, 1574–1788.* Verona: Del Bianco Editore, 1979.

Bono, Barbara J. *Literary Transvaluation: From Vergilian Epic to Shakespearean Tragicomedy.* Berkeley and Los Angeles: U of California P, 1984.

Borchardt, Frank L. *German Antiquity in Renaissance Myth.* Baltimore and London: The Johns Hopkins UP, 1971.

Borchmeyer, Dieter. "Musik im Zeichen Saturns: Melancholie und Heiterkeit in Thomas Manns *Doktor Faustus.*" *Thomas Mann Jahrbuch* 7 (1994): 123–67.

Borgeaud, Philippe. "La Mort du Grand Pan." *Revue de l'Histoire des Religions* 200.1 (1983): 3–39.

Borgolte, Michael. "Memoria: Zwischenbilanz eines Mittelalterprojekts." *Zeitschrift für Geschichtswissenschaft* 46.3 (1998): 197–210.

Bornkamm, Fritz. "Goethe, Johann Wolfgang." In *Enciclopedia Virgiliana*, edited by Francesco Corte et al. Rome: Instituto della Enciclopedia Italiana, 1985, 2:776–78.

Bowers, A. Joan. "The Tree of Charity in *Piers Plowman*: Its Allegorical and Structural Significance." In *Literary Monographs*, vol. 6, *Medieval and Renaissance Literature*, edited by Erich Rothstein and Joseph Anthony Wittreich, Jr., 3–34; 157–60. Madison and London: U of Wisconsin P, for the Department of English, U of Wisconsin, 1975.

Bowra, C. M. *From Virgil to Milton.* London: MacMillan and New York: St Martin's P, 1967.

Boyd, James. *Goethe's Knowledge of English Literature*. Oxford: Clarendon, 1932.

Boyde, Patrick. *Dante Philomythes and Philosopher: Man in the Cosmos*. Cambridge: Cambridge UP, 1981.

———. "*Inferno* XIII." In *Cambridge Readings in Dante's* Comedy, edited by Kenelm Foster and Patrick Boyde, 1–22. Cambridge and London: Cambridge UP, 1981.

Boyle, A. J. "The Meaning of the Aeneid: A Critical Inquiry, Part II: *Homo Immemor*: Book VI and its Thematic Ramifications." *Ramus: Critical Studies in Greek and Roman Literature* 1.2 (1972): 113–52.

Boym, Svetlana. *Common Places: Mythologies of Everyday Life in Russia*. Cambridge, MA: Harvard UP, 1994.

Bradish, Joseph A. von. "Auerbachs Keller: Geschichte und Legende." *Jahrbuch des Wiener Goethe-Vereins* NS 64 (1960): 106–16.

———. "Geschichte und Legende um Auerbachs Keller." *The German Quarterly* 16 (1943): 76–89.

Brand, C. P. "Ludovico Ariosto — Poet and Poem in the Italian Renaissance." *Forum for Modern Language Studies* 4 (1968): 87–101.

Brandi, Karl. "Dantes Monarchia und die Italienpolitik Mercurino Gattinaras." *Deutsches Dante-Jahrbuch* 24 (1942): 1–19.

Braudy, Leo. *The Frenzy of Renown: Fame and Its History*. New York and Oxford: Oxford UP, 1986.

Braungart, Georg. "Mythos und Herrschaft: Maximilian I. als Hercules Germanicus." In *Traditionswandel und Traditionsverhalten*, edited by Walter Haug und Burghart Wachinger, 77–95. Tübingen: Niemeyer, 1991.

Breuer, Dieter. "Bergschluchten: Die Schlußszene von Goethes *Faust*." *Ernst Meister Gesellschaft Jahrbuch* 2002 [2003]: 75–101.

———. "Mephisto als Theologe." *Goethe Jahrbuch* 109 (1992): 91–100.

———. "Origenes im 18. Jahrhundert in Deutschland." *Seminar: A Journal of Germanic Studies* 21.1 (1985): 1–30.

Breuer, Ulrich. *Melancholie und Reise: Studien zur Archäologie des Individuellen im deutschen Roman des 16.-18. Jahrhunderts*. Hamburg: Lit Verlag Münster-Hamburg, 1994.

Brinkmann, Hennig. "Die 'Zweite Sprache' und die Dichtung des Mittelalters." In *Methoden in Wissenschaft und Kunst des Mittelalters*, edited by Albert Zimmermann, with Rudolf Hoffmann, 155–71. Berlin: Walter de Gruyter, 1970.

Brockes, Barthold Hinrich. *Irdisches Vergnügen in Gott*. Bern: Herbert Lang, 1970.

Brown, Jane K. *Goethe's Faust: The German Tragedy*. Ithaca and London: Cornell UP, 1986.

———. "Mephistopheles the Nature Spirit." *Studies in Romanticism* 24 (1985): 475–90.

Browning, Robert M. "On the Structure of the *Urfaust.*" *PMLA* 68 (1953): 458–95.

Brumble, H. David. "John Donne's 'The Flea': Some Implications of the Encyclopedic and Poetic Flea Traditions." *Critical Quarterly* 15.2 (1973): 147–54.

Bulloch, Anthony. "Jason's Cloak." *Hermes* 134.1 (2006): 44–68.

Burkert, Walter. *Griechische Religion der archaischen und klassischen Epoche.* Stuttgart: W. Kohlhammer, 1997.

———. "Offerings in Perspective: Surrender, Distribution, Exchange." In *Gifts to the Gods: Proceedings of the Uppsala Symposium 1985*, edited by Tullia Lunders and Gullög Nordquist, 43–50. Uppsala: Acta Universitatis Upsaliensis, 1987.

Burns, Marjorie Jean, and Laureen K. Nussbaum. " 'Das Flohlied' in Goethe's *Faust*: Mephistopheles' Parable of the Politics of Heaven." *Papers on Language and Literature* 16.1 (1980): 81–89.

Burrow, Colin. *Epic Romance: Homer to Milton.* Oxford: Clarendon, 1993.

Buschendorf, Bernhard. *Goethes mythische Denkform: Zur Ikonographie der "Wahlverwandtschaften."* Frankfurt am Main: Suhrkamp, 1986.

Butler, E. M. *The Tyranny of Greece over Germany.* 1935. Repr., Boston: Beacon P, 1958.

Camden, Carroll, Jr. "Tamburlaine: The Choleric Man." *Modern Language Notes* 44 (1929): 430–35.

Carne-Ross, D. S. "The One and the Many: A Reading of Orlando Furioso, Cantos 1 and 8." *Arion* 5 (1966): 195–234.

Carruthers, Mary J. *The Book of Memory: A Study of Memory in Medieval Culture.* Cambridge: Cambridge UP, 1990.

———. "The Poet as Master Builder: Composition and Locational Memory in the Middle Ages." *New Literary History* 24 (1993): 881–904.

Cassell, Anthony K. *Dante's Fearful Art of Justice.* Toronto and Buffalo: U of Toronto P, 1984.

———. "Pier della Vigna's Metamorphosis: Iconography and History." In *Dante, Petrarch, Boccaccio: Studies in the Italian Trecento In Honor of Charles S. Singleton*, edited by Aldo S. Bernardo and Anthony L. Pellegrini, 31–76. Binghamton, NY: Center for Medieval and Renaissance Texts and Studies, SUNY Binghamton, 1983.

Casteen, John. "*Andreas*: Mermedonian Cannibalism and Figural Narration." *Neuphilologische Mitteilungen* 75 (1974): 74–78.

Caviglia, Franco. "Polidoro." *Enciclopedia Virgiliana*, edited by Francesco Corte et. al. Rome: Instituto della Enciclopedia Italiana, 1998, 4:162–64.

Céard, Jean, ed. *La curiosité à la Renaissance.* Paris: Société d'Édition d'Enseignement Supérieur, 1986.

Cellini, Benvenuto. *The Life of Benvenuto Cellini, Written by Himself,* translated by John Addington Symonds. London: Phaidon, 1960.

Chamberlain, David. "The Music of the Spheres and *The Parlement of Foules*." *The Chaucer Review* 5 (1970–71): 32–56.

Chiampi, James Thomas. "Between Voice and Writing: Ariosto's Irony according to Saint John." *Italica* 60 (1983): 340–50.

———. "*Consequentia Rerum*: Dante's Pier della Vigna and the Vine of Israel." *Romanic Review* 75 (1984): 162–75.

Clairmont, Heinrich. "Der ewige Jude." In Otto and Witte, *Gedichte*, 540–46.

Clericuzio, Antonio. "From van Helmont to Boyle: A Study of the Transmission of Helmontian Chemical and Medical Theories in Seventeenth-Century England." *British Journal for the History of Science* 26 (1993): 303–34.

Cochrane, Eric. *Florence in the Forgotten Centuries, 1527–1800: A History of Florence and the Florentines in the Age of the Grand Dukes.* Chicago and London: U of Chicago P, 1973.

Cohn, Norman. *The Pursuit of the Millennium: Revolutionary Millenarians and Mystical Anarchists of the Middle Ages.* 1957. Reprint, London: Paladin, 1970.

Collard, Christopher. "Medea and Dido." *Prometheus* 1 (1975): 131–51.

Collatz, Christian-Friedrich. "Achilleis." In Otto and Witte, *Gedichte,* 537–40.

Comparetti, Domenico. *Vergil in the Middle Ages.* Translated by E. F. M. Benecke. 1908; Reprint, London: George Allen & Unwin, 1966; Princeton: Princeton UP, 1997.

Conger, George Perrigo. *Theories of Macrocosms and Microcosms in the History of Philosophy.* 1922. Reprint, New York: Russell & Russell, 1967.

Constantine, David. "*Achilleis* and *Nausikaa*: Goethe in Homer's World." *Oxford German Studies* 15 (1984): 95–111.

Cook, Patrick J. "The Epic Chronotype from Ariosto to Spenser." *Annali d'italianistica* 12 (1994): 115–41.

Costa, Dennis. "Domesticating the Divine Economy: Humanist Theology in Erasmus's *Convivia.*" In *Creative Imitation: New Essays on Renaissance Literature in Honor of Thomas M. Greene,* edited by David Quint, Margaret W. Ferguson, G. W. Pigman III, and Wayne A. Rebhorn, 11–29. Binghamton, NY: Medieval and Renaissance Texts and Studies, 1992.

Courcelle, Pierre. "Interprétations néo-platonisantes du livre VI de l'Énéide." *Entretiens sur l'Antiquité Classique, Tome III: Recherches sur la Tradition Platonicienne* (1955): 95–136.

Courtney, Edward, "Vergil's Military Catalogues and Their Antecedents." *Vergilius* 34 (1988): 3–8.

Curran, Stuart. *Poetic Form and British Romanticism.* New York and Oxford: Oxford UP, 1986.

Curtius, Ernst Robert. *European Literature and the Latin Middle Ages.* Translated by Willard R. Trask. Princeton: Princeton UP for the Bollingen Foundation, 1973.

Dahnke, Hans-Dietrich. "Die Geheimnisse." In Otto and Witte, *Gedichte*, 546–52.

Daiches, David, and Anthony Thorlby, eds. *Literature and Western Civilization*. Vol. 3, *The Old World: Discovery and Rebirth*. London: Aldus Books, 1974.

Daraki, Maria. "ΟΙΝΟΨΙΙΟΝΤΟΣ: La mer dionysiaque." *Revue de l'Histoire des Religions* 199.1 (1982): 3–22.

Darnton, Robert. *Mesmerism and the End of the Enlightenment in France*. Cambridge, MA: Harvard UP, 1968.

Davis, Charles T. "Rome and Babylon in Dante." In *Rome in the Renaissance: The City and the Myth; Papers of the Thirteenth Annual Conference of the Center for Medieval and Early Renaissance Studies*, edited by Paul A. Ramsey, 19–40. Binghamton, NY: Center for Medieval and Early Renaissance Studies, 1982.

De Santillana, Giorgio, and Hertha von Dechend. *Hamlet's Mill: An Essay on Myth and the Frame of Time*. 1969. Reprint, Boston: David R. Godine, 1977.

Debus, Allen G. "Chemists, Physicians, and Changing Perspectives on the Scientific Revolution." *Isis* 89 (1998): 66–81.

———. *The English Paracelsians*. London: Oldbourne, 1965.

———. "The Medico-Chemical World of the Paracelsians." In *Changing Perspectives in the History of Science: Essays in Honour of Joseph Needham*, edited by Mikuláš Teich and Robert Young, 86–99. London: Heinemann, 1973.

Di Cesare, Mario A. *The Altar and the City: A Reading of Vergil's* Aeneid. New York and London: Columbia UP, 1974.

Di Tommaso, Andrea. "*Insania* and *Furor*: A Diagnostic Note on Orlando's Malady." *Romance Notes* 14.3 (1973): 583–88.

DiPasquale, Theresa M. "'Heav'n's last best gift': Eve and Wisdom in *Paradise Lost*." *Modern Philology* 95.1 (1997): 44–67.

Dobbs, Betty Jo Teeter. *The Janus Face of Genius: The Role of Alchemy in Newton's Thought*. Cambridge: Cambridge UP, 1991.

Donato, Eugenio. "'*Per selve e boscherecci labirinti*': Desire and Narrative Structure in Ariosto's *Orlando Furioso*." *Barroco* 4 (1972): 17–34.

Draper, John W. *The Humors & Shakespeare's Characters*. 1949. Reprint, New York: AMS Press, 1970.

Dreisbach, Elke. *Goethes "Achilleis."* Heidelberg: Universitätsverlag C. Winter, 1994.

Du Bartas, Guillaume De Salluste. *The Divine Weeks and Works of Guillaume de Salluste Sieur Du Bartas*. Translated by Josuah Sylvester. Edited by Susan Snyder. 2 vols. Oxford: Clarendon, 1979.

Dubois, Page. *History, Rhetorical Description and the Epic: From Homer to Spenser*. Cambridge: D. S. Brewer, and Totowa, NJ: Biblio Distribution Services, 1982.

Dummer, E. Heyse. "Goethe's Literary Clubs." *The German Quarterly* 22.4 (1949): 195–201.

Durling, Robert M. "The Epic Ideal." In Daiches and Thorlby, *Literature and Western Civilization*, vol. 3, *The Old World*, 105–46.

———. *The Figure of the Poet in Renaissance Epic*. Cambridge, MA: Harvard UP, 1965.

Durrani, Osman. *Faust and the Bible: A Study of Goethe's Use of Scriptural Allusions and Christian Religious Motifs in Faust I and II*. Bern and Frankfurt am Main: Peter Lang, 1977.

Eckermann, Johann Peter. *Gespräche mit Goethe in den letzten Jahren seines Lebens*. Edited by Ernst Beutler. Vol. 24 of the *Gedenkausgabe*. Zurich: Artemis, 1949.

Ego, Anneliese. "Magnetische Auftritte — ideologische Konflikte: Zur Problematik eines medizinischen Konzeptes im Zeitalter der Aufklärung." In *Der ganze Mensch: Anthropologie und Literatur im 18. Jahrhundert; DFG-Symposion 1992*, edited by Hans-Jürgen Schings, 187–213. Stuttgart and Weimar: J. B. Metzler, 1994.

Elsaghe, Yahya A. "Hermann und Dorothea." In Otto and Witte, *Gedichte*, 519–37.

Emrich, Wilhelm. *Die Symbolik von Faust II: Sinn und Vorformen*. 1957. Reprint, Frankfurt am Main: Athenäum, 1964.

Ergang, Robert. *Europe from the Renaissance to Waterloo*. Boston and New York: D. C. Heath, 1954.

Erler, Michael. "Der Zorn des Helden: Philodems 'De Ira' und Vergils Konzept des Zorns in der 'Aeneis.'" *Grazer Beiträge: Zeitschrift für die klassische Altertumswissenschaft* 18 (1992): 103–26.

Euripides. *Hecuba*. Translated and edited by Christopher Collard. Warminster, UK: Aris + Phillips, 1991.

Evans, R. J. W. *Rudolf II and His World: A Study in Intellectual History, 1576–1612*. Oxford: Clarendon, 1973.

Fara, Patricia. *Sympathetic Attractions: Magnetic Practices, Beliefs, and Symbolism in Eighteenth-Century England*. Princeton: Princeton UP, 1996.

Farrell, Joseph. "Walcott's *Omeros*: The Classical Epic in a Postmodern World." *The South Atlantic Quarterly* 96.2 (1997): 247–73.

Fasolt, Constantin. "Visions of Order in the Canonists and Civilians." In *Handbook of European History, 1400–1600: Late Middle Ages, Renaissance and Reformation*. Vol. 2, *Visions, Programs and Outcomes*, edited by Thomas A. Brady, Jr., Heiko A. Oberman, and James D. Tracey, 31–59. Leiden and New York: E. J. Brill, 1995.

Feeney, D. C. "History and Revelation in Vergil's Underworld." *Proceedings of the Cambridge Philological Society* NS No. 31 (1985): 1–24.

Ferguson, Margaret W. *Trials of Desire: Renaissance Defenses of Poetry*. New Haven and London: Yale UP, 1983.

Ferrand, Jacques. *A Treatise on Lovesickness*. Translated and edited by Donald A. Beecher and Massimo Ciavolella. Syracuse, NY: Syracuse UP, 1990.

Ferrante, Joan M. *The Political Vision of the* Divine Comedy. Princeton: Princeton UP, 1984.

Février, P.-A. "Les quatre fleuves du Paradis." *Rivista di Archeologia Cristiana* 32 (1956): 179–88.

Fichter, Andrew. *Poets Historical: Dynastic Epic in the Renaissance*. New Haven and London: Yale UP, 1982.

Ficino, Marsilio. *Three Books on Life*. Edited and translated by Carol V. Kaske and John R. Clark. 1989. Reprint, Binghamton, NY: Center for Medieval and Early Renaissance Studies, State U of New York at Binghamton, together with The Renaissance Society of America, 1998.

Findlen, Paula. *Possessing Nature: Museums, Collecting, and Scientific Culture in Early Modern Italy*. Berkeley and Los Angeles: U of California P, 1994.

Fink, Karl J. *Goethe's History of Science*. Cambridge: Cambridge UP, 1991.

Fischer, Kuno. *Goethes Faust*. Edited by Victor Michels. Vol. 3, *Die Erklärung des Goetheschen Faust nach der Reihenfolge seiner Szenen: Erster Teil*. 4th edition. Heidelberg: Carl Winter, 1913.

Fischer-Lamberg, Hanna. "Das Bibelzitat beim jungen Goethe." In *Gedenkschrift für Ferdinand Josef Schneider (1879–1954)*, edited by Karl Bischoff, 201–21. Weimar: Hermann Böhlaus Nachfolger, 1956.

———. "Zur Datierung der ältesten Szenen des Urfaust." *Zeitschrift für deutsche Philologie* 76 (1957): 379–406.

Flaherty, M. G. "Money, Gold, and the Golden Age in Germany." In Daiches and Thorlby, *Literature and Western Civilization*, vol. 3, *The Old World*, 363–411.

Florey, Ernst. "Franz Anton Mesmers magische Wissenschaft." In *Franz Anton Mesmer und der Mesmerismus: Wissenschaft, Scharlatanerie, Poesie*, edited by Gereon Wolters, 11–40. Constance: Universitätsverlag Konstanz, 1988.

Fontenelle, Bernard Le Bovier de. *Histoire des oracles*. Edited by Louis Maigron. Paris: Librairie Droz, 1934.

Forster, Leonard. "Faust and the Sin of Sloth, Mephistopheles and the Sin of Pride." In *The Discontinuous Tradition: Studies in German Literature in Honour of Ernest Ludwig Stahl*, edited by P. F. Ganz, 54–66. Oxford: Clarendon, 1971.

———. "Faust und die *acedia*: Mephisto und die *superbia*." In *Dichtung, Sprache, Gesellschaft: Akten des IV. Internationalen Germanisten-Kongresses 1970 in Princeton*, edited by Victor Lange and Hans-Gert Roloff, 307–19. Frankfurt am Main: Athenäum, 1971.

———. *The Man Who Wanted to Know Everything*. The 1980 Bithell Memorial Lecture. London: Institute of Germanic Studies, University of London, 1981.

Forsyth, Neil. *The Satanic Epic*. Princeton and Oxford: Princeton UP, 2003.

Forti, Fiorenzo. " 'Curiositas' o 'Fol Hardement'?" In *Magnanimitade: Studi su un tema dantesco*, 161–206. Bologna: Pàtron Editore, 1977.

Françon, Marcel. "Un motif de la poésie amoureuse au XVI$^c$ siècle." *PMLA* 56.2 (1941): 307–36.

Frankel, Margherita. "Biblical Figuration in Dante's Reading of the *Aeneid*." *Dante Studies* 100 (1982): 11–23.

Franz, Erich. "Die verlorene Hades-Szene in Goethes Faust II." *Germanisch-Romanische Monatsschrift* 38 (1957): 343–49.

Freeman, James A. *Milton and the Martial Muse*: Paradise Lost *and European Traditions of War*. Princeton: Princeton UP, 1980.

Frenzel, Elisabeth. *Stoffe der Weltliteratur: Ein Lexikon dichtungsgeschichtlicher Längsschnitte*. Stuttgart: Alfred Kröner, 1988.

Frenzel, Herbert. "Der Stammbaum der Este: Ein Beitrag zur genealogischen Trojalegende." In *Wort und Text: Festschrift für Fritz Schalk*, edited by Harri Meier and Hans Sckommodau, 187–99. Frankfurt am Main: Vittorio Klostermann, 1963.

Friedrich, Theodor, and Lothar J. Scheithauer. *Kommentar zu Goethes Faust: Mit einem Faust-Wörterbuch und einer Faust-Bibliographie*. Stuttgart: Reclam, 1994.

Fuchs, Albert. *Le* Faust *de Goethe: Mystère — document humain — confession personnelle*. Paris: Éditions Klincksieck, 1973.

Funck, Heinrich, ed. *Goethe und Lavater: Briefe und Tagebücher*. Weimar: Verlag der Goethe-Gesellschaft, 1901.

Gaier, Ulrich. "Goethes *Faust* als Neu- und Fortschreibung der *Ilias*." In *Europäische Mythen von Liebe, Leidenschaft, Untergang und Tod im (Musik-) Theater: Der Trojanische Krieg; Vorträge und Gespräche des Salzburger Symposions 2000*, edited by Peter Csobadi, 307–18. Salzburg: Verlag Mueller-Speiser, 2002.

———. *Kommentar I*. Vol. 2 of Goethe, *Faust-Dichtungen*, edited by Ulrich Gaier,

———. *Kommentar II*. Vol. 3 of Goethe, *Faust-Dichtungen*, edited by Ulrich Gaier,

Galinsky, Karl. "The Anger of Aeneas." *American Journal of Philology* 109 (1988): 321–48.

Garber, Jörn. "Trojaner — Römer — Franken — Deutsche: 'Nationale' Abstammungstheorien im Vorfeld der Nationalstaatsbildung." In *Nation und Literatur in der Frühen Neuzeit: Akten des 1. Internationalen Osnabrücker Kongresses zur Kulturgeschichte der Frühen Neuzeit*, edited by Klaus Garber, 108–63. Tübingen: Niemeyer, 1989.

Gardner, Edmund G. *The Arthurian Legend in Italian Literature*. London: J. M. Dent; New York: E. P. Dutton, 1930.

Garnett, Richard. *A History of Italian Literature*. New York: D. Appleton & Co., 1898.

Garrison, James D. *Pietas from Vergil to Dryden*. University Park: Pennsylvania State UP, 1992.

Gebhard, W. "'Allgemeine Ansicht nach Innen': Ideologiekritische Aspekte von Goethes anschauendem Denken." *Philosophia Naturalis* 20.2 (1983): 312–38.

Gelzer, Thomas. "Helena im Faust: Ein Beispiel für Goethes Umgang mit der antiken Mythologie." In *Mythographie der frühen Neuzeit: Ihre Anwendung in den Künsten*, edited by Walter Killy, 223–53. Wiesbaden: Otto Harrassowitz for the Herzog August Bibliothek Wolfenbüttel, 1984.

Gerhard, G. A. "Nochmals zum Tod des großen Pan." *Wiener Studien: Zeitschrift für klassische Philologie* 38 (1916): 343–76.

———. "Zum Tod des großen Pan." *Wiener Studien: Zeitschrift für klassische Philologie* 37 (1915): 323–52.

Gerhard, Melitta. "Götter-Kosmos und Gesetzes-Suche: Zu Goethes Versuch seines Achilleis-Epos." *Monatshefte* 56.4 (1964): 145–59.

Geyer-Kordesch, Johanna. "Die Nachtseite der Naturwissenschaft: Die 'okkulte' Vorgeschichte zu Franz Anton Mesmer." In *Franz Anton Mesmer und die Geschichte des Mesmerismus: Beiträge zum internationalen wissenschaftlichen Symposion anlässlich des 250. Geburtstages von Mesmer, 10. bis. 13. Mai in Meersburg*, edited by Heinz Schott, 13–30. Stuttgart: Franz Steiner Verlag, 1985.

Giamatti, A. Bartlett. *The Earthly Paradise and the Renaissance Epic*. Princeton: Princeton UP, 1966.

———. "Introduction." In Ludovico Ariosto, *Orlando Furioso*, translated by William Stewart Rose, edited by Stewart A. Baker and A. Bartlett Giamatti, xiii–xliv. Indianapolis, IN and New York: Bobbs-Merrill, 1968.

Gill, Christopher. "Passion as Madness in Roman Poetry." In *The Passions in Roman Thought and Literature*, edited by Susanna Morton Braund and Christopher Gill, 213–41. Cambridge: Cambridge UP, 1997.

Giustiniani, Vito R. "Goethes Übersetzungen aus dem Italienischen." In *"Italien in Germanien": Deutsche Italien Rezeption von 1750–1850; Akten des Symposiums der Stiftung Weimarer Klassik, Herzogin Anna Amalia Bibliothek, Schiller-Museum, 24.-26. März 1994*, edited by Frank-Rutger Hausmann, with Michael Knoche and Harro Stammerjohann, 275–99. Tübingen: Gunter Narr, 1996.

Godwin, Joscelyn. *Robert Fludd: Hermetic Philosopher and Surveyor of Two Worlds*. Grand Rapids, MI: Phanes P, 1991.

Goedeke, Karl. "[Review]: *Faust: Eine Tragödie von Goethe*, mit Einleitung und erläuternden Anmerkungen von G. von Loeper. Berlin. Gustav Hempel. 1870. LXIV und 173, und LXXX und 272 S. 8°." *Göttingsche gelehrte Anzeigen* Nr. 10 (6 March 1872): 361–77.

Goethe, Johann Wolfgang von. *Faust: Texte* and *Faust: Kommentare*. 2 vols. Edited by Albrecht Schöne. Darmstadt: Wissenschaftliche Buchgesellschaft, 1999. [Identical with the fourth, revised edition of vols. 7.1 and 7.2 of

*Sämtliche Werke*, edited by Dieter Bouchmeyer et al., Frankfurt am Main: Deutscher Klassiker Verlag, 1985–1999]. "Deutsche Klassiker-Ausgabe."

———. *Faust: Eine Tragödie*. Edited by Franz Carl Endres. Basel: Benno Schwabe, 1949.

———. *Faust-Dichtungen*. Edited by Ulrich Gaier. 3 vols. Stuttgart: Philipp Reclam jun., 1999.

———. *Goethes Briefe*. Edited by Karl Robert Mandelkow and Bodo Morawe. 4 vols. Hamburg: Christian Wegner, 1962.

———. *Goethes Werke*. Commissioned by the Grand Duchess Sophie of Saxony. 4 pts., 133 vols. in 143. Weimar: Böhlau, 1887–1919.

———. *Der junge Goethe: Neu bearbeitete Ausgabe in fünf Bänden*. Edited by Hanna Fischer-Lamberg. Berlin and New York: Walter de Gruyter, 1973.

———. *Sämtliche Werke nach Epochen seines Schaffens: Münchner Ausgabe*. Edited by Karl Richter, with Herbert G. Göpfert, Norbert Miller, Gerhard Sauder, and Edith Zehm. Munich: Carl Hanser, 1985–98. "Münchener Ausgabe."

———. *Die Schriften zur Naturwissenschaft*. Part 2, vol. 3, *Beiträge zur Optik und Anfänge der Farbenlehre, 1790–1808*. Edited by Ruprecht Matthaei. Weimar: Hermann Böhlaus Nachfolger, 1951.

———. *Werke: Hamburger Ausgabe in 14 Bänden*. Edited by Erich Trunz. Munich: C. H. Beck, 1981. "Hamburger Ausgabe."

Goetsch, James Robert, Jr. *Vico's Axioms: The Geometry of the Human World*. New Haven and London: Yale UP, 1995.

Goldsmith, Elizabeth C. *"Exclusive Conversations": The Art of Interaction in Seventeenth-Century France*. Philadelphia: U of Pennsylvania P, 1988.

Goodman, Dena. *The Republic of Letters: A Cultural History of the French Enlightenment*. Ithaca and London: Cornell UP, 1994.

Göres, Jörn. "Dr. Faust in Geschichte und Dichtung." In *Ansichten zu Faust: Karl Theens zum 70. Geburtstag*, edited by Günther Mahal, 9–20. Stuttgart: W. Kohlhammer, 1973.

Görner, Rüdiger. "Goethe's Ulysses: On the Meaning of a Project." *Publications of the English Goethe Society* NS 44/45 (1993–95): 21–37.

Gössmann, Elisabeth. "Die 'Päpstin Johanna': Zur vor- und nachreformatorischen Rezeption ihrer Gestalt." In *Eva — Verführerin oder Gottes Meisterwerk? Philosophie- und theologiegeschichtliche Frauenforschung*, edited by Dieter R. Bauer and Elisabeth Gössmann, 143–66. Stuttgart: Akademie der Diözese Rottenburg-Stuttgart, 1987.

Götting, Franz. "Die Bibliothek von Goethes Vater." *Nassauische Annalen: Jahrbuch des Vereins für Nassauischen Altertumskunde und Geschichtsforschung* 64 (1953): 23–69.

Gould, Robert. "Problems of Reception and Autobiographical Method in the 'Zweiter römischer Aufenthalt' of Goethe's *Italienische Reise*." *Carleton Germanic Papers* 22 (1994): 71–85.

Graevenitz, Gerhart von. "Gewendete Allegorie: Das Ende der 'Erlebnislyrik' und die Vorbereitung einer Poetik der modernen Lyrik in Goethes Sonett-Zyklus von 1815/1827." In *Allegorie: Konfigurationen von Text, Bild und Lektüre,* edited by Evan Horn and Manfred Weinberg, 97–117. Opladen: Westdeutscher Verlag, 1998.

Gransden, K. W. "The *Aeneid* and *Paradise Lost.*" In *Virgil and His Influence: Bimillennial Studies,* edited by Charles Martindale, 95–116. Bristol: Bristol Classical P, 1984.

Grassl, Hans. *Aufbruch zur Romantik: Bayerns Beitrag zur deutschen Geistesgeschichte, 1765–1785.* Munich: C. H. Beck, 1968.

Gray, Thomas, and William Collins. *Gray and Collins: Poetical Works.* Edited by Austin Lane Poole. London: Oxford UP, 1974.

Greene, Thomas. *The Descent from Heaven: A Study in Epic Continuity.* New Haven and London: Yale UP, 1963.

Greenhill, Eleanor Simmons. "The Child in the Tree: A Study of the Cosmological Tree in Christian Tradition." *Traditio* 10 (1954): 323–71.

Gregerson, Linda. *The Reformation of the Subject: Spenser, Milton, and the English Protestant Epic.* Cambridge: Cambridge UP, 1995.

Grendler, Paul F. "Chivalric Romances in the Italian Renaissance." *Studies in Medieval and Renaissance History* NS 10 (1988): 59–102.

Grimmelshausen, Hans Jacob Christoffel von. *Werke.* Edited by Dieter Breuer. Frankfurt am Main: Deutscher Klassiker Verlag, 1989.

Groos, Arthur. *Romancing the Grail: Genre, Science, and Quest in Wolfram's Parzival.* Ithaca and London: Cornell UP, 1995.

Grumach, Ernst. *Goethe und die Antike: Eine Sammlung.* Potsdam: Verlag Eduard Stichnote, 1949.

———. "Prolog und Epilog im Faustplan von 1797." *Goethe* 14/15 (1952–53): 63–107.

Gwynne, Paul. " 'Tu alter Caesar eris': Maximilian I, Vladislav II, Johannes Michael Nagonius and the *renovatio Imperii.*" *Renaissance Studies* 10.1 (1996): 56–71.

Hacking, Ian. *Rewriting the Soul: Multiple Personality and the Sciences of Memory.* Princeton: Princeton UP, 1995.

Hagen, Fred, and Ursula Mahlendorf. "Commitment, Concern and Memory in Goethe's Faust." *Journal of Aesthetics and Art Criticism* 21 (1962–63): 473–84.

Hale, David George. *The Body Politic: A Political Metaphor in Renaissance English Literature.* The Hague and Paris: Mouton, 1971.

Hale, J. R. "Gunpowder and the Renaissance: An Essay in the History of Ideas." In *From the Renaissance to the Counter-Reformation: Essays in Honor of Garrett Mattingly,* edited by Charles H. Carter, 113–44. New York: Random House, 1965.

Hamacher, Werner. "Faust, Geld." *Athenäum: Jahrbuch für Romantik* 4 (1994): 131–87.

Hamlin, Cyrus. "Tracking the Eternal-Feminine in Goethe's *Faust II*." In *Interpreting Goethes* Faust *Today*, edited by Jane K. Brown, Meredith Lee, and Thomas P. Saine, in collaboration with Paul Hernadi and Cyrus Hamlin, 142–55. Columbia, SC: Camden House, 1994.

Hammerstein, Reinhold. *Diabolus in Musica: Studien zur Ikonographie der Musik im Mittelalter*. Bern and Munich: Francke, 1974.

Hankey, Teresa. "The Clear and the Obscure: Dante, Virgil and the Role of the Prophet." In *Dante and the Middle Ages: Literary and Historical Essays*, edited by John C. Barnes and Cormac Ó Culleanáin, 211–29. Dublin: Irish Academic P for The Foundation for Italian Studies, University College, Dublin, 1995.

Hansmann, Margarethe. "Mesmer in Wien." In *Franz Anton Mesmer und die Geschichte des Mesmerismus: Beiträge zum internationalen wissenschaftlichen Symposion anlässlich des 250. Geburtstages von Mesmer, 10. bis. 13. Mai in Meersburg*, edited by Heinz Schott, 51–67. Stuttgart: Franz Steiner Verlag, 1985.

Häntzschel, Günter. "Die Ausbildung der deutschen Literatursprache des 18. Jahrhunderts durch Übersetzungen: Homer-Verdeutschungen als produktive Kraft." In *Mehrsprachigkeit in der deutschen Aufklärung*, edited by Dieter Kimpel, 117–32. Hamburg: Felix Meiner, 1985.

Hardie, Philip. "After Rome: Renaissance Epic." In *Roman Epic*, edited by A. J. Boyle, 294–313. London and New York: Routledge, 1993.

———. *The Epic Successors of Virgil: A Study in the Dynamics of a Tradition*. Cambridge: Cambridge UP, 1993.

———. *Vergil's* Aeneid*: Cosmos and Imperium*. 1986. Reprint, Oxford: Clarendon, 1989.

Harkness, Deborah E. "Shows in the Showstone: A Theater of Alchemy and Apocalypse in the Angel Conversations of John Dee (1527–1608/9)." *Renaissance Quarterly* 49 (1996): 707–37.

Harrison, E. L. "Foundation Prodigies in the *Aeneid*." *Papers of the Liverpool Latin Seminar* 5 (1985): 131–64.

Hartlaub, Gustav F. "Goethe als Alchemist." *Euphorion* 48 (1954): 19–40.

Hartmann von Aue. *Der arme Heinrich*. Edited by Hermann Paul. Tübingen: Max Niemeyer, 1972.

Haustein, Jens. "Über Goethes *Erklärung eines alten Holzschnittes vorstellend Hans Sachsens poetische Sendung*." *Archiv für das Studium der neueren Sprachen und Literaturen* 146.1 (1994): 1–21.

Hayn, Hugo, and Alfred N. Gotendorf. *Floh-Litteratur (de pulicibus) des In- und Auslandes, vom XVI. Jahrhundert bis zur Neuzeit*. Berlin, 1913.

Headley, John M. "The Habsburg World Empire and the Revival of Ghibellinism." *Medieval and Renaissance Studies* 7 (1978): 93–127.

Heckscher, William S. "Goethe im Banne der Sinnbilder: Ein Beitrag zur Emblematik." *Jahrbuch der Hamburger Kunstsammlungen* 7 (1962): 35–54.

Hederich, Benjamin. *Gründliches mythologisches Lexikon*. Edited by Johann Joachim Schwabe. 1770. Reprint, Darmstadt: Wissenschaftliche Buchgesellschaft, 1967.

Hegel, Georg Wilhelm Friedrich. *Sämtliche Werke: Jubiläumsausgabe in zwanzig Bänden*, edited by Hermann Glockner. Vol. 14, *Vorlesungen über die Aesthetik*. Edited by Heinrich Gustav Hotho. Stuttgart-Bad Cannstatt: Friedrich Frommann Verlag, 1964.

Heinze, Richard. *Virgils epische Technik*. 1915. Reprint, Leipzig and Berlin: B. G. Teubner, 1928.

Helgerson, Richard. *Self-Crowned Laureates: Spenser Jonson Milton and the Literary System*. Berkeley and Los Angeles: U of California P, 1983.

Heller, Otto. *Faust and Faustus: A Study of Goethe's Relation to Marlowe*. 1931. Reprint, New York: Cooper Square, 1972.

Henderson, John. "The Name of the Tree: Recounting *Odyssey* XXIV 340-2." *Journal of Hellenic Studies* 117 (1997): 87–116.

Heninger, S. K., Jr. "Some Renaissance Versions of the Pythagorean Tetrad." *Studies in the Renaissance* 8 (1961): 7–35.

———. *Touches of Sweet Harmony: Pythagorean Cosmology and Renaissance Poetics*. San Marino: The Huntington Library, 1974.

Henkel, Arthur. "Das Ärgernis Faust." In *Versuche zu Goethe: Festschrift für Erich Heller; Zum 65. Geburtstag am 27.3.1976*, edited by Volker Dürr and Géza von Molnár, 282–304. Heidelberg: Lothar Stiehm, 1976.

Hennig, John. "Goethes Kenntnis der schönen Literatur Italiens. In *Goethes Europakunde: Goethes Kenntnisse des nichtdeutschsprachigen Europas: Ausgewählte Aufsätze*, 128–50. Amsterdam: Rodopi, 1987. Orig. published in *Literaturwissenschaftliches Jahrbuch* 21 (1980): 363–83.

Henning, Hans. "Faust als historische Gestalt." *Goethe: Neue Folge des Jahrbuchs der Goethe-Gesellschaft* 21 (1959): 107–39.

Henn-Schmölders, Claudia. "Ars conversationis: Zur Geschichte des sprachlichen Umgangs." *arcadia* 10 (1975): 16–33.

Henrichs, Albert. "Der rasende Gott: Zur Psychologie des Dionysos und des Dionysischen in Mythos und Literatur." *Antike und Abendland* 40 (1994): 31–58.

Herbers, Klaus. "Die Päpstin Johanna: Ein kritischer Forschungsbericht." *Historisches Jahrbuch der Görres-Gesellschaft* 108 (1988): 174–94.

Herder, Johann Gottfried. *Sämtliche Werke*. Edited by Bernhard Suphan. 1880. Reprint, Hildesheim: Georg Olms, 1967.

Hering, Carl Joseph. "Das Welttheater als religions- und rechtsdidaktisches Gleichnis." In *Aequitas und Toleranz: Gesammelte Schriften von Carl Joseph Hering*, edited by Erich Fechner, Ernst von Hippel, and Herbert Frost, 199–221. Bonn: Bouvier Verlag Herbert Grundmann, 1971.

Hermann, Hans Peter. "'Ich bin fürs Vaterland zu sterben auch bereit': Patriotismus oder Nationalismus im 18. Jahrhundert? Lesenotizen zu den deutschen Arminiusdramen 1740–1808." In *Machtphantasie Deutschland:*

*Nationalismus, Männlichkeit und Fremdenhaß im Vaterlandsdiskurs deutscher Schriftsteller des 18. Jahrhunderts*, edited by Hans Peter Herrmann, Hans-Martin Blitz, and Susanna Moßmann, 32–65. Frankfurt am Main: Suhrkamp, 1996.

Herwig, Wolfgang, ed. *Goethes Gespräche: Eine Sammlung zeitgenössischer Berichte aus seinem Umgang auf Grund der Ausgabe und des Nachlasses von Flodoard Freiherrn von Biedermann*. Vol. 2, *1805–1817*. Zurich and Stuttgart: Artemis, 1969.

Herzman, Ronald B. "Cannibalism and Communion in *Inferno* XXXIII." *Dante Studies* 98 (1980): 53–78.

Herzog, Reinhart. "Aeneas' epische Vergessen: Zur Poetik der memoria." In *Memoria: Vergessen und Erinnern*, edited by Anselm Haverkamp and Renate Lachmann, with Reinhard Herzog, 81–116. Munich: Wilhelm Fink, 1993.

Higgins, David H. "Cicero, Aquinas, and St. Matthew in *Inferno* XIII." *Dante Studies* 93 (1975): 61–94.

Hilliard, K. F. "Goethe and the Cure for Melancholy: 'Mahomets Gesang,' Orientalism and the Medical Psychology of the 18th Century." *Oxford German Studies* 23 (1994): 71–103.

Hinderer, Walter. "Torquato Tasso." In *Goethes Dramen: Neue Interpretationen*, edited by Walter Hinderer. Stuttgart: Reclam, 1980.

Hinz, Manfred. *Rhetorische Strategien des Hofmannes: Studien zu den italienischen Hofmannstraktaten des 16. und 17. Jahrhunderts*. Stuttgart: J. B. Metzler, 1992.

Hirdt, Willi. "Goethe e Dante." *Studi Danteschi* 62 (1990): 97–115.

———. "Goethe und Dante." *Deutsches Dante-Jahrbuch* 68–69 (1993–94): 31–80.

Hirschman, Albert O. *The Passions and the Interests: Political Arguments for Capitalism before Its Triumph*. Princeton: Princeton UP, 1977.

Hofmann, Heinz. "*Adveniat tandem Typhis qui detegat orbes*: COLUMBUS in Neo-Latin Epic Poetry (16th–18th Centuries)." In *The Classical Tradition and the Americas*, vol. 1, *European Images of the Americas and the Classical Tradition*, edited by Wolfgang Haase and Meyer Reinhold, 421–656. New York: Walter de Gruyter, 1994.

———. "Aeneas in Amerika: Komplikationen des Weltbildwandels im Humanismus am Beispiel neulateinischer Columbusepen." *Philologus* 129 (1995): 39–61.

———. "The Discovery of America and Its Refashioning as Epic." *Allegorica* 15 (1994): 31–40.

Hollander, John. *The Untuning of the Sky: Ideas of Music in English Poetry, 1500–1700*. New York: W. W. Norton, 1970.

Hollister, C. Warren. *Medieval Europe: A Short History*. New York: John Wiley & Sons, 1964.

Holmes, T. M. "Homage and Revolt in Goethe's 'Torquato Tasso.'" *Modern Language Review* 65 (1970): 813–19.

Hölscher-Lohmeyer, Dorothea. "Natur und Gedächtnis: Reflexionen über die Klassische Walpurgisnacht." *Jahrbuch des Freien Deutschen Hochstifts* (1987): 85–113.

Höltgen, Karl Josef. "Arbor, Scala und Fons vitae: Vorformen devotionaler Embleme in einer mittelenglischen Handschrift (B.M. Add. MS 37049)." In *Chaucer und seine Zeit: Symposion für Walter F. Schirmer*, edited by Arno Esch, 355–91. Tübingen: Max Niemeyer, 1968.

Home, Roderick W. "Electricity and the Nervous Fluid." *Journal of the History of Biology* 3.2 (1970): 235–51.

Homer. *The Iliad of Homer*. Translated by Richmond Lattimore. 1951. Reprint, Chicago and London: U of Chicago P, 1961.

———. *The Odyssey of Homer*. Translated by Richmond Lattimore. New York: Harper & Row, 1975.

Hübner, Wolfgang. "Poesie der Antipoesie: Überlegungen zum dritten Buch der *Aeneis*." *Grazer Beiträge: Zeitschrift für die klassische Altertumswissenschaft* 21 (1995): 95–120.

Hucke, Karl-Heinz. *Figuren der Unruhe: Faustdichtungen*. Tübingen: Niemeyer, 1992.

Hughes, Merritt Y. "The Christ of *Paradise Regained* and the Renaissance Heroic Tradition." *Studies in Philology* 35 (1938): 254–77.

Imbach, Ruedi. "experiens Ulixes: Hinweise zur Figur des Odysseus im Denken der Patristik, des Mittelalters und bei Dante." In *Lange Irrfahrt — Grosse Heimkehr: Odysseus als Archetyp — zur Aktualität des Mythos*, edited by Gotthard Fuchs, 59–80. Frankfurt am Main: Verlag Josef Knecht, 1994.

Jacoff, Rachel. "The Hermeneutics of Hunger." In *Speaking Images: Essays in Honor of V. A. Kolve*, edited by Robert F. Yeager and Charlotte C. Morse, 95–110. Asheville, NC: Pegasus P, 2004.

Jacquot, Jean. "Le théâtre du monde." *Revue de Littérature Comparée* 31 (1957): 341–72.

Jäger, Hans-Wolf. "Reineke Fuchs." In Otto and Witte, *Gedichte*, 508–18.

Jahn, Johannes. "Goethe und Dürer." *Goethe* 33 (1971): 75–95.

Jantz, Harold. *The Mothers in* Faust: *The Myth of Time and Creativity*. Baltimore: The Johns Hopkins UP, 1969.

Javitch, Daniel. "The Imitation of Imitations in *Orlando Furioso*." *Renaissance Quarterly* 38 (1985): 215–39.

———. *Proclaiming a Classic: The Canonization of* Orlando Furioso. Princeton: Princeton UP, 1991.

Jones, Ann Rosalind. "Contentious Readings: Urban Humanism and Gender Difference in *La Puce de Madame Des-Roches* (1582)." *Renaissance Quarterly* 48 (1995): 109–28.

Jones, R. O. "Renaissance Butterfly, Mannerist Flea: Tradition and Change in Renaissance Poetry." *Modern Language Notes* 80 (1965): 166–84.

Jordan, Leo. "Goethe und Rabelais." *Germanisch-Romanische Monatsschrift* 3 (1911): 648–62.

Kallendorf, Craig. "Virgil, Dante, and Empire in Italian Thought, 1300–1500." *Vergilius* 34 (1988): 44–69.

Kamen, Henry. *The Spanish Inquisition*. London and Toronto: White Lion Publishers, 1976.

Kanduth, Erika. "Bemerkungen zu Dante-Reminiszenzen im 'Orlando furioso.' " In *Studien zu Dante und zu anderen Themen der romanischen Literaturen: Festschrift für Rudolf Palgen zu seinem 75. Geburtstag*, edited by Klaus Lichem and Hans Joachim Simon, 59–70. Graz: Universitäts-Buchdruckerei Styria for the Hugo Schuchardtsche Malwinenstiftung Graz, 1971.

Kant, Immanuel. *Werke in zehn Bänden*. Edited by Wilhelm Weischedel. Darmstadt: Wissenschaftliche Buchgesellschaft, 1983.

Kantorowicz, Ernst. *Frederick the Second, 1194–1250*. Translated by. E. O. Lorimer. New York: Frederick Ungar, 1957.

Kaske, R. E. "Dante's *Purgatorio* XXXII and XXXIII: A Survey of Christian History." *University of Toronto Quarterly* 43.3 (1974): 193–214.

Kay, Richard. "Two Pairs of Tricks: Ulysses and Guido in Dante's *Inferno* XXVI–XXVII." *Quaderni d'italianistica* 1.2 (1980): 107–24.

Keller, Werner. "*Faust: Eine Tragödie* (1808)." In *Goethes Dramen: Neue Interpretationen*, edited by Walter Hinderer, 244–80. Stuttgart: Reclam, 1980.

Kennedy, William J. "Ariosto's Ironic Allegory." *Modern Language Notes* 88.1 (1973): 44–67.

———. "Irony Allegoresis, and Allegory in Virgil, Ovid and Dante." *arcadia* 7 (1972): 115–34.

———. "The Problem of Allegory in Tasso's *Gerusalemme Liberata*." *Italian Quarterly* 15 (1972): 27–51.

Kenny, Neil. " 'Curiosité' and Philosophical Poetry in the French Renaissance." *Renaissance Studies* 5.1 (1991): 263–76.

Kiefer, Klaus H. "Goethe und der Magnetismus: Grenzphänomene des naturwissenschaftlichen Verständnisses." *Philosophia Naturalis* 20 (1983): 264–311.

Kirkpatrick, Robin. *Dante's* Inferno: *Difficulty and Dead Poetry*. Cambridge: Cambridge UP, 1987.

Kirsch, J. P. "Joan, Popess." In *The Catholic Encyclopedia*, edited by Charles G. Herbermann et al., 8:407–9. New York: Robert Appleton, 1910.

Klecker, Elisabeth. "Kaiser Maximilians Homer." *Wiener Studien: Zeitschrift für Klassische Philologie und Patristik* 107/108 (1994–95): 613–37.

Kleinhenz, Christopher. "Dante and the Bible: Biblical Citation in the *Divine Comedy*." In *Dante: Contemporary Perspectives*, edited by Amilcare A. Iannucci, 74–93. Toronto and Buffalo: U of Toronto P, 1997.

Klibansky, Raymond, Erwin Panofsky, and Fritz Saxl. *Saturn and Melancholy: Studies in the History of Natural Philosophy, Religion and Art*. London: Nelson, 1964.

Klopstock, Friedrich Gottlieb. *Werke in einem Band*. Edited by Karl August Schleiden. Munich and Vienna: Carl Hanser, 1969.

Klostermann, Wolf-Günther. "Acedia und Schwarze Galle: Bemerkungen zu Dante, *Inferno* VII, 115ff." *Romanische Forschungen* 74 (1964): 183–93.

Kluge, Friedrich. *Bunte Blätter: Kulturgeschichtliche Vorträge und Aufsätze*. Freiburg im Breisgau: J. Bielefelds Verlag, 1910.

———. *Etymologisches Wörterbuch der deutschen Sprache*. Berlin and New York: Walter de Gruyter, 1975.

———. "Vom geschichtlichen Dr. Faust." Beilage zur *Allgemeinen Zeitung* Nr. 9 (1896). Reprinted in Kluge, *Bunte Blätter*, 1–27.

———. "Wir wollen einen Papst erwählen (Goethes Faust I V. 2098)." In Kluge, *Bunte Blätter*, 101–8.

Knapp, Lothar. "Ariosts 'Orlando Furioso': Die Kritik der Waffen und der Triumph der Liebe." In *Das Epos in der Romania: Festschrift für Dieter Kremers zum 65. Geburtstag*, edited by Susanne Knaller and Edith Mara, 177–92. Tübingen: Gunter Narr, 1986.

Knecht, R. J. *Renaissance Warrior and Patron: The Reign of Francis I*. Cambridge: Cambridge UP, 1994.

Knieger, Bernard. "The Purchase-Sale: Patterns of Business Imagery in the Poetry of George Herbert." *Studies in English Literature* 6 (1966): 111–24.

Knoll, Renate. "Zu Goethes erster Erwähnung des Origenes." In *Geist und Zeichen: Festschrift für Arthur Henkel, zu seinem sechzigsten Geburtstag dargebracht von Freunden und Schülern*, edited by Herbert Anton, Bernhard Gajek, and Peter Pfaff, 192–207. Heidelberg: Carl Winter Universitätsverlag, 1977.

Knust, Herbert. "Columbiads in Eighteenth Century European and American Literature." *European Contributions to American Studies* 34 (1996): 33–48.

Koenigsberger, Dorothy. "*Leben des Benvenuto Cellini*: Goethe, Cellini and Transformation." *European History Quarterly* 22 (1992): 7–37.

Kolb, Robert. "God, Faith, and the Devil: Popular Lutheran Treatments of the First Commandment in the Era of the Book of Concord." *Fides et Historia* 15 (1982): 71–89.

Koonz, Claudia. "Between Memory and Oblivion: Concentration Camps in German Memory." In *Commemorations: The Politics of National Identity*, edited by John R. Gillis, 258–80. Princeton: Princeton UP, 1994.

Krailsheimer, A. J. "The Significance of the Pan Legend in Rabelais' Thought." *Modern Language Review* 56 (1961): 13–23.

Kreutzer, Hans Joachim. "'Der edelste der Triebe': Über die Wißbegierde in der Literatur am Beginn der Neuzeit." In *Das neuzeitliche Ich in der Literatur des 18. und 19. Jahrhunderts: Zur Dialektik der Moderne; Ein internationales Symposion*, edited by Ulrich Fülleborn and Manfred Engel, 59–70. Munich: Wilhelm Fink, 1988.

Kroeber, Karl. *Romantic Narrative Art*. Madison, WI: U of Wisconsin P, 1960.

Kroes, Gabriele. "Zur Geschichte der deutschen Übersetzungen von Ariosts *Orlando furioso*." In *Italienische Literatur in deutscher Sprache: Bilanz und Perspektiven*, edited by Reinhard Klescewzki and Bernhard König, 11–26. Tübingen: Gunter Narr, 1990.

Kroker, Ernst. *Doktor Faust und Auerbachs Keller*. Leipzig: Dieterich'sche Verlagsbuchhandlung, 1903.

Kuehnemund, Richard. *Arminius or the Rise of National Symbol in Literature*. Chapel Hill, NC: U of North Carolina P, 1953.

Kuhn, Dorothea. "Goethe's Relationship to the Theories of Development of His Time." In *Goethe and the Sciences: A Reappraisal*, edited by Frederick Amrine, Francis J. Zucker, and Harvey Wheeler, 3–15. Dordrecht, The Netherlands, and Boston: D. Reidel, 1987.

Kühne, August. ed, *Das älteste Faustbuch: Wortgetreuer Abdruck der editio princeps des Spies'schen Faustbuchs vom Jahr 1587.* 1868. Reprint, Amsterdam: Rodopi, 1970.

Kühnel, Harry. "Die Fliege — Symbol des Teufels und der Sündhaftigkeit." In *Aspekte der Germanistik: Festschrift für Hans-Heinrich Rosenfeld zum 90. Geburtstag*, edited by Walter Tauber, 285–305. Göppingen: Kümmerle Verlag, 1989.

Kurze, Dietrich. "Nationale Regungen in der spätmittelalterlichen Prophetie." *Historische Zeitschrift* 202 (1966): 1–23.

Labhardt, André. "Curiositas: Notes sur l'histoire d'un mot et d'une notion." *Museum Helveticum* 17 (1960): 206–24.

Lachmann, Renate. "Die Unlöschbarkeit der Zeichen: Das semiotische Unglück des Mnemonisten." In *Gedächtniskunst: Raum — Bild — Schrift: Studien zur Mnemontechnik*, edited by Anselm Haverkamp and Renate Lachmann, 111–41. Frankfurt am Main: Suhrkamp, 1991.

Lambek, Michael, and Paul Antze. "Introduction: Forecasting Memory." In *Tense Past: Cultural Essays in Trauma and Memory*, edited by Paul Antze and Michael Lambek, xi–xxxviii. New York and London: Routledge, 1996.

Landolt, Stephan. "Goethes 'Faust': Das Verhältnis von Grablegungs- und Bergschluchtenszene zur Kirchen-Lehre." *Sprachkunst* 21 (1990): 155–94.

Langer, Ulrich. "Boring Epic in Early Modern France." In *Epic and Epoch: Essays on the Interpretation and History of a Genre*, edited by Steven M. Oberhelman, Van Kelly, and Richard J. Goslan, 208–29. Lubbock: Texas Tech UP, 1994.

Lee, Meredith. *Displacing Authority: Goethe's Poetic Reception of Klopstock*. Heidelberg: Universitätsverlag C. Winter, 1999.

Lee, Rensselaer W. *Names on Trees: Ariosto into Art*. Princeton: Princeton UP, 1977.

Lefèvre, Eckard. "Goethe als Schüler der alten Sprachen, oder vom Sinn der Tradition." *Gymnasium* 92 (1985): 288–98.

Leinkauf, Thomas. "*Scientia universalis, memoria* und *status corruptionis*: Überlegungen zu philosophischen und theologischen Implikationen der

Universalwissenschaft sowie zum Verhältnis von Universalwissenschaft und Theorie des Gedächtnisses." In *Ars memorativa: Zur kulturgeschichtlichen Bedeutung der Gedächtniskunst, 1400–1750*, edited by Jörg Jochen Berns and Wolfgang Neuber, 1–34. Tübingen: Max Niemeyer, 1993.

Lenz, Jakob Michael Reinhold. *Werke: Dramen Prosa Gedichte*. Edited by Karen Lauer. Munich: Deutscher Taschenbuch Verlag, 1992.

Lessing, Gotthold Ephraim. *Werke und Briefe*. Edited by Wilfried Barner et al. Vol. 11.1, *Briefe von und an Lessing, 1743–1770*. Edited by Helmuth Kiesel with Georg Braungart and Klaus Fischer. Frankfurt am Main: Deutscher Klassiker Verlag, 1987.

Lestringant, Frank. "Le cannibale et ses paradoxes: images du cannibalisme au temps des Guerres de Religion." *Mentalities / Mentalités* 1.2 (1983): 4–19.

Levenson, Jon D. "The Grundworte of Pier Delle Vigne." *Forum Italicum* 5 (1971): 499–513.

Lewalski, Barbara Kiefer. *Milton's Brief Epic: The Genre, Meaning, and Art of Paradise Regained*. Providence, RI: Brown UP and London: Methuen, 1966.

———. *Protestant Poetics and the Seventeenth-Century Religious Lyric*. Princeton: Princeton UP, 1979.

Lewy, Hans. *Sobria Ebrietas: Untersuchungen zur Geschichte der antiken Mystik*. Gießen: Verlag von Alfred Töpelmann, 1929.

Ley, Klaus. " 'sii grand'uomo e sii infelice': Zur Umwertung des Tasso-Bildes am Beginn des Ottocento: Voraussetzungen und Hintergründe im europäischen Rahmen (La Harpe/Gilbert — Goethe — Foscolo." *Germanisch-Romanische Monatsschrift* NS 46.2 (1996): 131–73.

Lievsay, John L. *Stefano Guazzo and the English Renaissance, 1575–1675*. Chapel Hill: U of North Carolina P, 1961.

Lind, L. R. "The Great American Epic." *Classical and Modern Literature* 17.1 (1996): 7–29.

Lipking, Lawrence. *Abandoned Women and the Poetic Tradition*. Chicago and London: U of Chicago P, 1988.

———. *The Life of the Poet: Beginning and Ending Poetic Careers*. Chicago and London: U of Chicago P, 1981.

Littlejohns, Richard. "The Discussion between Goethe and Schiller on the Epic and Dramatic and Its Relevance to *Faust*." *Neophilologus* 71 (1987): 388–401.

Llewellyn, Nigel. "Virgil and the Visual Arts." In *Virgil and His Influence: Bimillennial Studies*, edited by Charles Martindale, 117–40. Bristol: Bristol Classical P, 1984.

Loen, Johann Michael. *Gesammelte kleine Schriften (1749–1752)*. Edited by J. C. Schneider. Frankfurt am Main: Athenäum, 1972.

Lohse, Gerhard. "Die Homerrezeption im 'Sturm und Drang' und deutscher Nationalismus im 18. Jahrhundert." *International Journal of the Classical Tradition* 4.2 (1997): 195–231.

Lorenz, Otto. "Verschwiegenheit: Zum Geheimnis-Motiv der 'Römischen Elegien.'" In *Text + Kritik*, Sonderband: *Johann Wolfgang von Goethe*, 130–52. Munich: text + kritik, 1982.

Luther, Martin. "An den christlichen Adel deutscher Nation von des christlichen Standes Besserung." In *Studienausgabe*, 2:96–167 (1982).

———. "Auch wider die räuberischen und mörderischen Rotten der anderen Bauern." In *Studienausgabe*, 3:140–47 (1983).

———. *Studienausgabe*. Edited by Hans-Ulrich Delius, with Helmar Junghans, Joachim Rogge, and Günther Wartenberg. Berlin: Evangelische Verlagsanstalt, 1979–92.

———. *Tischreden oder* Colloqvia Doct. *Mart. Luthers / So er in in vielen Jaren / gegen gelarten Leuten / auch frembden Gesten / und seinen Tischgesellen gefüret / nach den Heubtstücken unserer Christlichen Lere / zusammen getragen*. 1566. Reprint, Berlin: Nationales Druckhaus Berlin for Friedrich Bahn Verlag Konstanz, 1967.

Lyons, Bridget Gellert. *Voices of Melancholy: Studies in Literary Treatments of Melancholy in Renaissance England*. 1971. Reprint, New York: Norton, 1975.

MacCormack, Sabine. "Limits of Understanding: Perceptions of Greco-Roman and Amerindian Paganism in Early Modern Europe." In *America in European Consciousness, 1493–1750*, edited by Karen Ordahl Kupperman, 79–129. Chapel Hill, NC, and London: U of North Carolina P, for the Institute of Early American History and Culture, Williamsburg, Virginia, 1995.

Macdonald, Ronald R. *The Burial-Places of Memory: Epic Underworlds in Vergil, Dante, and Milton*. Amherst, MA: U of Massachusetts P, 1987.

Macey, Samuel L. *Patriarchs of Time: Dualism in Saturn-Cronus, Father Time, the Watchmaker God, and Father Christmas*. Athens, GA, and London: U of Georgia P, 1987.

Macpherson, C. B. *The Political Theory of Possessive Individualism: Hobbes to Locke*. 1962. Reprint, Oxford: Oxford UP, 1977.

Maltby, William S. *The Black Legend in England: The Development of Anti-Spanish Sentiment, 1558–1660*. Durham, NC: Duke UP, 1971.

Marlowe, Christopher. *Doctor Faustus: A 1604-Version Edition*. Edited by Michael Keefer. Peterborough, ON and Lewiston, NY: Broadview P, 1991.

Martin, Dieter. *Das deutsche Versepos im 18. Jahrhundert: Studien und kommentierte Gattungsbibliographie*. Berlin and New York: de Gruyter, 1993.

Maskell, David. *The Historical Epic in France, 1500–1700*. Oxford: Oxford UP, 1973.

Masters, George Mallary. "The Hermetic and Platonic Traditions in Rabelais' *Dive Bouteille*." *Studi Francesi* 28 (1966): 15–29.

Mattenklott, Gert. *Melancholie in der Dramatik des Sturm und Drang*. Stuttgart: J. B. Metzler, 1968.

Matthaei, Ruprecht. "Neue Funde zu Schillers Anteil an Goethes Farbenlehre." *Goethe: Neue Folge des Jahrbuchs der Goethe-Gesellschaft* 20 (1958): 155–77.

———. "Die Temperamentenrose aus gemeinsamer Betrachtung Goethes mit Schiller." *Neue Hefte zur Morphologie: Beihefte zur Gesamtausgabe von Goethes Schriften zur Naturwissenschaft* 2 (1956): 33–46.

Mauser, Wolfram. "Melancholieforschung des 18. Jahrhunderts zwischen Ikonographie und Ideologiekritik: Auseinandersetzung mit den bisherigen Ergebnissen und Thesen zu einem Neuansatz." *Lessing Yearbook* 13 (1981): 253–77.

Mayer, Hans. "Der Famulus Wagner und die moderne Wissenschaft." In *Gestaltungsgeschichte und Gesellschaftsgeschichte*, edited by Helmut Kreutzer and Käte Hamburger, 176–200. Stuttgart: J. B. Metzler, 1969.

Mazzotta, Giuseppe. *Dante, Poet of the Desert: History and Allegory in the Divine Comedy*. Princeton: Princeton UP, 1979.

McClain, William H. "The Arcadian Fiction in Goethe's Torquato Tasso." In *Vistas and Vectors: Essays Honoring the Memory of Helmut Rehder*, edited by Lee B. Jennings and George Schulz-Berend, 104–13. Austin, TX: Department of Germanic Languages, The University of Texas at Austin, 1979.

McGinty, Park. "Dionysos's Revenge and the Validation of the Hellenic World-View." *The Harvard Theological Review* 71 (1978): 77–94.

McKnight, Stephen A. *The Modern Age and the Recovery of Ancient Wisdom: A Reconsideration of Historical Consciousness, 1450–1650*. Columbia, MO and London: U of Missouri P, 1991.

McNair, Philip. "The Madness of Orlando." In *Renaissance and Other Studies: Essays Presented to Peter M. Brown*, edited by. Eileen A. Millar, 144–59. Glasgow: University of Glasgow, Department of Italian, 1988.

Meier, Albert. " 'Und so war sein Leben selbst Roman und Poesie': Tasso-Biographien in Deutschland." In *Torquato Tasso in Deutschland: Seine Wirkung in Literatur, Kunst und Musik seit der Mitte des 18. Jahrhunderts*, edited by Achim Aurnhammer, 11–32. Berlin and New York: Walter de Gruyter, 1995.

Meier, Franziska. "Goethes *Faust* als Schiffbrüchiger und Zuschauer: Einige Überlegungen anknüpfend an Hans Blumenbergs Studie zur Daseinsmetapher des Schiffbruchs mit Zuschauer." *Germanisch-Romanische Monatsschrift* NF 49.1 (1999): 55–78.

Meilaender, Gilbert G. *The Theory and Practice of Virtue*. Notre Dame, IN: U of Notre Dame P, 1984.

Meinhold, Peter. *Goethe zur Geschichte des Christentums*. Freiburg im Breslau and Munich: Verlag Karl Alber, 1958.

Mette, Hans Joachim. "Curiositas." In *Festschrift for Bruno Snell zum 60. Geburtstag am 18. Juni 1956, von Freunden und Schülern überreicht*, 227–35. Munich: C. H. Beck, 1961.

Meyer, Heinz. *Die Zahlenallegorese im Mittelalter: Methode und Gebrauch*. Munich: Wilhelm Fink, 1975.

Mickel, Emanuel J. "Faith, Memory, Treason and Justice in the *Ordo Representacionis Ade (Jeu d'Adam)*." *Romania* 112 (1991): 129–54.

Midelfort, H. C. Erik. *Exorcism and Enlightenment: Johann Joseph Gassner and the Demons of Eighteenth-Century Germany*. New Haven: Yale UP, 2005.

Miller, Dean A. *The Epic Hero*. Baltimore and London: The Johns Hopkins UP, 2000.

Milt, Bernhard. *Franz Anton Mesmer und seine Beziehungen zur Schweiz: Magie und Heilkunde zu Lavaters Zeit*. Zurich: Druck Leemann, 1953.

Milton, John. *The Poems of John Milton*. Edited by John Carey and Alastair Fowler. London: Longmans, 1968.

Möbus, Frank. "*Heinrich! Heinrich!* Goethes *Faust*: Genetisches, Genealogisches." *Euphorion* 83 (1989): 337–63.

———. "Des Plutus zwiefache Rede: Eine kryptische Bibelanspielung in der Mummenschanz des Faust II." *Zeitschrift für deutsche Philologie* 107: *Sonderheft* (1988): *71–*84.

Mommsen, Momme. "Zur Entstehung und Datierung einiger Faust-Szenen um 1800." *Euphorion* 47 (1953): 295–330.

Moog-Grünewald, Maria. "Tassos Leid: Zum Ursprung moderner Dichtung." *arcadia* 21 (1986): 113–32.

———. "Torquato Tasso in den poetologischen Kontroversen des 18. Jahrhunderts." In *Torquato Tasso in Deutschland: Seine Wirkung in Literatur, Kunst und Musik seit der Mitte des 18. Jahrhunderts*, edited by Achim Aurnhammer, 382–97. Berlin and New York: Walter de Gruyter, 1995.

Moore, Leslie. " 'Instructive Trees': Swift's *Broom-Stick*, Boyle's *Reflections*, and Satiric Figuration." *Eighteenth-Century Studies* 19.3 (1986): 313–32.

Moreau, Alain. *Le Mythe de Jason et Médée: Le va-nu-pied et la sorcière*. Paris: Les Belles Lettres, 1994.

Moretti, Franco. *Modern Epic: The World-System from Goethe to García Márquez*. Translated by Quintin Hoare. London and New York: Verso, 1996.

Mori, Masaki. *Epic Grandeur: Toward a Comparative Poetics of the Epic*. Albany: SUNY P, 1997.

Most, Glenn. "The 'Virgilian' *Culex*." In *Homo Viator: Classical Essays for John Bramble*, edited by Michael Whitby, Philip Hardie, and Mary Whitby, 199–209. Bristol: Bristol Classical P, and Oak Park, IL: Bochazy-Carducci Publishers, 1987.

Mülder-Bach, Inka. " 'Schlangenwandelnd': Geschichten vom Fall bei Milton und Goethe." In *Von der Natur zur Kunst zurück: Neue Beiträge zur Goethe-Forschung; Gotthart Wunberg zum 65. Geburtstag*, edited by Moritz Baßler, Christoph Brecht, and Dirk Niefanger, 79–94. Tübingen: Max Niemeyer, 1997.

Müller, Jan-Dirk. "*Curiositas* und *erfarung* der Welt im frühen deutschen Prosaroman." In *Literatur und Laienbildung im Spätmittelalter und in der*

*Reformationszeit: Symposion Wolfenbüttel 1981,* edited by Ludger Grenzmann and Karl Stackmann, 252–71. Stuttgart: J. B. Metzler, 1984.

Müller, Maria E. "Der andere Faust: Melancholie und Individualität in der Historia von D. Johann Fausten." *Deutsche Vierteljahrsschrift* 60 (1986): 572–608.

Müller-Bochat, Eberhard. "Die Einheit des Wissens und das Epos: Zur Geschichte eines utopischen Gattungsbegriffs." *Romanistisches Jahrbuch* 17 (1966): 58–81.

Münster, Arnold. *Über Goethes Verhältnis zu Dante.* Frankfurt am Main: R. G. Fischer, 1990.

Murrin, Michael. *The Allegorical Epic: Essays in Its Rise and Decline.* Chicago and London: U of Chicago P, 1980.

———. *History and Warfare in Renaissance Epic.* Chicago and London: U of Chicago P, 1994.

Nelson, Benjamin. "The Medieval Canon Law of Contracts, Renaissance 'Spirit of Capitalism,' and the Reformation 'Conscience': A Vote For Max Weber." In *Philomathes: Studies and Essays in the Humanities in Memory of Philip Merlan,* edited by Robert B. Palmer and Robert Hamerton-Kelly, 525–48. The Hague: Martinus Nijhoff, 1971.

Neuse, Richard. *Chaucer's Dante: Allegory and Epic Theater in The Canterbury Tales.* Berkeley and Los Angeles: U of California P, 1991.

Newhauser, Richard. "Towards a History of Human Curiosity: A Prolegomenon to Its Medieval Phase." *Deutsche Vierteljahrsschrift* 56 (1982): 559–73.

Nicholls, David. "Heresy and Protestantism, 1520–1542: Questions of Perception and Communication." *French History* 10.2 (1996): 182–205.

Nisbet, H. B. "Lucretius in Eighteenth-Century Germany, with a Commentary on Goethe's 'Metamorphose der Tiere.'" *Modern Language Review* 81 (1986): 97–115.

Nollendorfs, Valters. *Der Streit um den Urfaust.* The Hague and Paris: Mouton, 1967.

Noyer-Weidner, Alfred. *Umgang mit Texten.* Vol. 2, *Von der Aufklärung bis zur Moderne.* Edited by Gerhard Regn. Stuttgart: Franz Steiner, 1986.

Oberkogler, Friedrich. *Faust 1. Teil von Johann Wolfgang von Goethe: Werkbesprechung und geisteswissenschaftliche Erläuterungen.* Schaffhausen: Novalis Verlag, 1981.

O'Flaherty, James C. *The Quarrel of Reason with Itself: Essays on Hamann, Michaelis, Lessing, Nietzsche.* Columbia, SC: Camden House, 1988.

O'Hara, James J. *Death and the Optimistic Prophecy in Vergil's Aeneid.* Princeton: Princeton UP, 1990.

Olschki, Leonard. "Dante and Peter de Vinea." *Romanic Review* 31 (1940): 105–11.

Oppenheimer, Ernst M. *Goethe's Poetry for Occasions.* Toronto: U of Toronto P, 1974.

Origenes. *The Song of Songs: Commentary and Homilies.* Translated by R. P. Lawson. Westminster, MD: Newman P, and London: Longman, Greens, 1957.

Ortner, Hanspeter. "Syntaktisch hervorgehobene Konnektoren im Deutschen." *Deutsche Sprache* 11 (1983): 97–121.

Otis, Brooks. *Virgil: A Study in Civilized Poetry.* Oxford: Clarendon, 1963.

Otto, Regine, and Bernd Witte, eds. *Gedichte.* Stuttgart and Weimar: J. B. Metzler, 1996. Vol. 1 of *Goethe Handbuch in vier Bänden,* edited by Bernd Witte, Theo Buck, Hans-Dietrich Dahnke, Regine Otto and Peter Schmidt.

Ovid. *Metamorphoses.* Translated by A. D. Melville. Oxford: Oxford UP, 1998.

Padoan, Giorgio. "Un'eco della 'Divina Commedia' nell' 'Agathon' di Wieland." In *Miscellanea di studi offerta a Armando Balduino e Bianca Bianchi per le Loro Nozze, Vicenza — 30 giugno 1962,* 67–69. Padova: Presso Il Seminario di Filologia Moderna dell'Universita, 1962.

Parel, Anthony J. *The Machiavellian Cosmos.* New Haven and London: Yale UP, 1992.

Parry, Hugh. "The *Apologos* of Odysseus: Lies, All Lies?" *Phoenix* 48 (1994): 1–20.

Pausch, Alfons, and Jutta Pausch. *Goethes Juristenlaufbahn: Rechtsstudent Advokat Staatsdiener; Eine Fachbiographie.* Cologne: Verlag Dr. Otto Schmidt, 1996.

Payne, Joseph Frank. "Arnold de Villanova on the Therapeutic Use of Human Blood." *Janus* 8 (1903): 477–83.

Pearce, Howard D. "A Phenomenological Approach to the *Theatrum Mundi* Metaphor." *PMLA* 95.1 (1980): 42–57.

Pearce, Spencer. "Dante and the Art of Memory." *The Italianist* 16 (1996): 21–61.

Pelikan, Jaroslav. *Faust the Theologian.* New Haven: Yale UP, 1995.

Peterfreund, Stuart. "*The Prelude*: Wordsworth's Metamorphic Epic." *Genre* 14 (1981): 441–72.

Peters, Edward. "The Voyage of Ulysses and the Wisdom of Solomon: Dante and the *vitium curiositatis.*" *Majestas* 7 (1999): 75–87.

Petersen, Uwe. *Goethe und Euripides: Untersuchungen zur Euripides-Rezeption in der Goethezeit.* Heidelberg: Carl Winter, 1974.

Plath, Margarethe. "Der Goethe-Schellingsche Plan eines philosophischen Naturgedichts." *Preussische Jahrbücher* 106 (1901): 44–74.

Plett, Heinrich F. "*Topothesia Memorativa*: Imaginäre Architektur in Renaissance und Barock." In *Kunstgriffe: Auskünfte zur Reichweite von Literaturtheorie und Literaturkritik; Festschrift für Herbert Mainusch,* edited by Ulrich Horstmann and Wolfgang Zach, 294–312. Frankfurt am Main and New York: Peter Lang, 1989.

Pniower, Otto. "Goethes Faust und das Hohe Lied." *Goethe-Jahrbuch* 13 (1892): 181–98.

Poeschke, J. "Paradiesflüsse." In *Lexikon der christlichen Ikonographie*, edited by Engelbert Kirschbaum, SJ, with Günter Bandmann, Wolfgang Braunfels, Johannes Kollwitz, Wilhelm Mrazek, Alfred A. Schmid, and Hugo Schnell, 3: cols. 382–84. Freiburg im Breisgau: Herder, 1971.

Potz, Erich. "Pius furor und der Tod des Turnus." *Gymnasium* 99 (1991): 248–62.

Powell, Hugh. "A Neglected Faustian Drama and its Cultural Roots in Seventeenth-Century Germany." In *Faust through Four Centuries: Retrospect and Analysis / Vierhundert Jahre Faust: Rückblick und Analyse*, edited by Peter Boerner and Sidney Johnson, 65–77. Tübingen: Niemeyer, 1989.

Praschek, Helmut. "Goethes Fragmente 'Die Reise der Söhne Megaprazons.'" In *Studien zur Goethezeit: Festschrift für Lieselotte Blumenthal*, edited by Helmut Holtzhauer and Bernhard Zeller, with Hans Henning, 330–56. Weimar: Hermann Böhlaus Nachfolger, 1968.

Praz, Mario. *The Romantic Agony*. Translated by Angus Davidson. Oxford: Oxford UP, 1951.

Priest, Paul. "Dante and the 'Song of Songs.'" *Studi Danteschi* 49 (1972): 79–115.

Prosperi, Adriano. "New Heaven and New Earth: Prophecy and Propaganda at the Time of the Discovery and Conquest of the Americas." In *Prophetic Rome in the High Renaissance Period: Essays*, edited by Marjorie Reeves, 279–303. Oxford: Clarendon, 1992.

Putnam, Michael C. J. *Virgil's Aeneid: Interpretation and Influence*. Chapel Hill and London: U of North Carolina P, 1995.

Quint, David. *Epic and Empire: Politics and Generic Form from Virgil to Milton*. Princeton: Princeton UP, 1993.

———. *Origin and Originality in Renaissance Literature: Versions of the Source*. New Haven and London: Yale UP, 1983.

Rabelais, François. *The Histories of Gargantua and Pantagruel*. Translated by J. M. Cohen. Harmondsworth, UK: Penguin, 1978.

———. *Oeuvres Complètes*. Edited by Guy Demerson. Paris: Éditions du Seuil, 1973.

Rahe, Konrad. *Cagliostro und Christus: Zu den biblischen Anspielungen in Goethes Komödie 'Der Groß-Cophta.'* Hamburg: Verlag Dr. Kovač, 1994.

Raybin, David. "Translation, Theft, and *Li Jeus de Saint Nicolai*." *Romanic Review* 85.1 (1994): 27–48.

Reckford, Kenneth J. "Some Trees in Virgil and Tolkien." In *Perspectives of Roman Poetry: A Classics Symposium*, edited by G. Karl Galinsky, 57–91. Austin and London: U of Texas P for the College of Humanities and the College of Fine Arts of The University of Texas at Austin, 1974.

Reeves, Marjorie. *The Influence of Prophecy in the Later Middle Ages: A Study in Joachimism*. Oxford: Clarendon, 1969.

———. "A Note on Prophecy and the Sack of Rome (1527)." In *Prophetic Rome in the High Renaissance Period: Essays*, edited by Marjorie Reeves, 271–78. Oxford: Clarendon P, 1992.

Rehder, Helmut. "Planetenkinder: Some Problems of Character Portrayal in Literature." *Graduate Journal* (University of Texas) 8 (1968): 69–97.

Reichenberger, Kurt. "Das epische Proömium bei Ronsard, Scève, Du Bartas: Stilkritische Betrachtungen zum Problem von 'klassischer' und 'manieristischer' Dichtung in der 2. Hälfte des 16. Jahrhunderts." *Zeitschrift für romanische Philologie* 78 (1962): 1–31.

Reiman, Donald H. "*Don Juan* in Epic Context." *Studies in Romanticism* 16 (1977): 587–94.

Reiss, Timothy J. "The Idea of Meaning and the Practice of Order in Peter Ramus, Henri Estienne, and Others." In *Humanism in Crisis: The Decline of the French Renaissance*, edited by Philippe Desan, 125–52. Ann Arbor: U of Michigan P, 1991.

Revard, Stella Purce. *The War in Heaven:* Paradise Lost *and the Tradition of Satan's Rebellion*. Ithaca and London: Cornell UP, 1980.

Reybekiel, W. von. "Der 'Fons vitae' in der christlichen Kunst." *Niederdeutsche Zeitschrift für Volkskunde* 12 (1934): 87–136.

Richardson, J. Michael. *Astrological Symbolism in Spenser's* The Shepheardes Calender: *The Cultural Background of a Literary Text*. Lewiston, NY and Queenston, ON: Edwin Mellen P, 1989.

Riddell, James Allen. *The Evolution of the Humours Character in Seventeenth-Century English Comedy*. PhD diss., U of Southern California, 1966.

Riesz, János. "Goethe's 'Canon' of Contemporary Italian Literature in his *Italienische Reise*." In *Goethe in Italy, 1786–1986: A Bi-Centennial Symposium November 14–16, 1986, University of California, Santa Barbara; Proceedings Volume*, edited by Gerhart Hoffmeister, 133–46. Amsterdam: Rodopi, 1988.

Robertson, D. W., Jr. *A Preface to Chaucer: Studies in Medieval Perspectives*. 1962. Reprint, Princeton: Princeton UP, 1970.

Rogers, John. *The Matter of Revolution: Science, Poetry, and Politics in the Age of Milton*. Ithaca and London: Cornell UP, 1996.

Roscher, W. H. *Ausführliches Lexikon der griechischen und römischen Mythologie*. Hildesheim: Georg Olms, 1965.

Ross, Werner. "Der Held in der Hölle: Ein Versuch über den Odysseus-Gesang des Inferno." *Deutsches Dante-Jahrbuch* 64 (1989): 61–74.

Rossi, Paolo. *Clavis Universalis: Arti della memoria e logica combinatoria da Lullo a Leibniz*. Milan and Naples: Ricciardi, 1960. Reprint, Bologna: Il Mulino, 1983.

Rousseau, G. S. "Medicine and the Muses: An Approach to Literature and Medicine." In *Literature and Medicine During the Eighteenth Century*, edited by Marie Mulvey Roberts and Roy Porter, 23–57. London: Routledge, 1993.

Rüdiger, Horst. "*Curiositas* und Magie: Apuleius und Lucius als literarische Archetypen der Faust-Gestalt." In *Goethe und Europa: Essays und Aufsätze,*

*1944–1983*, edited by Willy R. Berger and Erwin Koppen, 66–88. Berlin and New York: de Gruyter, 1990.

———. "Dante als Erwecker geistiger Kräfte in der deutschen Literatur." In *Festschrift für Richard Alewyn*, edited by Herbert Singer and Benno von Wiese, 17–45. Cologne and Graz: Böhlau, 1967.

Salomon, Richard G. "The Grape Trick." In *Culture in History: Essays in Honor of Paul Radin*, edited by Stanley Diamond, 531–40. New York: Columbia UP for Brandeis University, 1960.

Sanders, Arnold. "Hypertext, Learning, and Memory: Some Implications from Manuscript Tradition." *Text* 8 (1995): 125–43.

Saße, Günter. "Wilhelm Meister als Leser Tassos." In *Torquato Tasso in Deutschland: Seine Wirkung in Literatur, Kunst und Musik seit der Mitte des 18. Jahrhunderts*, edited by Achim Aurnhammer, 370–81. Berlin and New York: Walter de Gruyter, 1995.

Savoia, Francesca. "Notes on the Metaphor of the Body in the *Gerusalemme liberata*." In *Western Gerusalem: University of California Studies on Tasso*, edited by Luisa Del Giudice, 57–70. New York: Out of London P, 1984.

Scaglione, Aldo. "XIII." *Lectura Dantis. No. 6: Supplement*, edited by Tibor Wlassics (Spring 1990): 163–72.

Schadewaldt, Wolfgang. "Fausts Ende und die Achilleis." In *Weltbewohner und Weimaraner: Ernst Beutler zugedacht 1960*, edited by Benno Reifenberg and Emil Staiger, 243–60. Zurich and Stuttgart: Artemis, 1960.

Schaffer, Simon. "The Consuming Flame: Electrical Showmen and Tory Mystics in the World of Goods." In *Consumption and the World of Goods*, edited by John Brewer and Roy Porter, 489–526. London and New York: Routledge, 1993.

Schaller, Dieter. "Das mittelalterliche Epos im Gattungsystem." In *Kontinuität und Transformation der Antike im Mittelalter: Veröffentlichung der Kongreßakten zum Freiburgr Symposion des Mediävistenverbandes*, edited by Willi Erzgräber. Sigmaringen: Jan Thorbecke, 1989. 355–71.

Schatzberg, Walter. *Scientific Themes in the Popular Literature and the Poetry of the German Enlightenment, 1720–1760*. Bern: Herbert Lang, 1973.

Scheller, Robert W. "Imperial Themes in Art and Literature of the Early French Renaissance: The Period of Charles VIII." Translated by Michael Hoyle. *Simiolus* 12.1 (1981–82): 5–69.

Schieder, Theodor. "'Der junge Goethe im alten Reich': Historische Fragmente aus 'Dichtung und Wahrheit.'" In *Staat und Gesellschaft im Zeitalter Goethes: Festschrift für Hans Tümmler zu seinem 70. Geburtstag*, edited by Peter Berglar, 131–45 Cologne and Vienna: Böhlau, 1977.

Schings, Hans-Jürgen. *Melancholie und Aufklärung: Melancholiker und ihre Kritiker in Erfahrungsseelenkunde und Literatur des 18. Jahrhunderts*. Stuttgart: J. B. Metzler, 1977.

Schlee, Ernst. *Die Ikonographie der Paradiesflüsse.* Leipzig: Dieterich'sche Verlagsbuchhandlung, 1937.

Schleiner, Winfried. *The Imagery of John Donne's Sermons.* Providence, RI: Brown UP, 1970.

———. *Melancholy, Genius, and Utopia in the Renaissance.* Wiesbaden: Otto Harrassowitz, 1991.

Schmidt, Erich. "Danteskes in Faust." *Archiv für das Studium der neueren Sprachen und Litteraturen* 107 (1901): 241–52.

Schmidt, Jochen. "Faust als Melancholiker und Melancholie als struktur-bildendes Element bis zum Teufelspakt." *Jahrbuch der Deutschen Schillergesellschaft* 41 (1997): 125–39.

———. "Gesellschaftliche Unvernunft und Französische Revolution in Goethes '*Faust*': Zu den Szenen 'Auerbachs Keller' und 'Hexenküche.'" In *Gesellige Vernunft: Zur Kultur der literarischen Aufklärung; Festschrift für Wolfram Mauser zum 65. Geburtstag,* edited by Ortrud Gutjahr, Wilhelm Kühlmann, and Wolf Wucherpfennig, 297–310. Würzburg: Königshausen + Neumann, 1993.

Schmidt, Leigh Eric. "From Demon Possession to Magic Show: Ventriloquism, Religion, and the Enlightenment." *Church History* 67.2 (1998): 274–304.

Schmidt-Biggemann, Wilhelm. "Robert Fludds *Theatrum memoriae.*" In *Ars memorativa: Zur kulturgeschichtlichen Bedeutung der Gedächtniskunst, 1400–1750,* edited by Jörg Jochen Berns and Wolfgang Neuber, 154–69. Tübingen: Max Niemeyer, 1993.

Schmitz, Hans-Günter. "Das Melancholieproblem in Wissenschaft und Kunst der frühen Neuzeit." *Sudhoffs Archiv für die Geschichte der Medizin und Naturwissenschaft* 60.2 (1976): 135–62.

———. *Physiologie des Scherzes: Bedeutung und Rechtfertigung der Ars Iocandi im 16. Jahrhundert.* Hildesheim and New York: Georg Olms, 1972.

Schnapp, Jeffrey T. *The Transfiguration of History at the Center of Dante's Paradise.* Princeton: Princeton UP, 1986.

Schöffler, Herbert. "Der junge Goethe und das englische Bibelwerk." In *Deutscher Geist im 18. Jahrhundert: Essays zur Geistes- und Religionsgeschichte,* 97–113; 309. Göttingen: Vandenhoeck + Ruprecht, 1967.

Schott, Heinz, ed. *Franz Anton Mesmer und die Geschichte des Mesmerismus: Beiträge zum internationalen wissenschaftlichen Symposion anlässlich des 250. Geburtstages von Mesmer, 10. bis. 13. Mai in Meersburg.* Stuttgart: Franz Steiner Verlag, 1985.

Schottroff, Willy. "Goethe als Bibelwissenschaftler." *Evangelische Theologie* 44 (1984): 463–85.

Schuchardt, Christina. *Goethe's Kunstsammlungen.* 3 vols. in 1. Hildesheim and New York: Georg Olms Verlag, 1976.

Schueler, H. J. *The German Verse Epic in the Nineteenth and Twentieth Centuries.* The Hague: Martinus Nijhoff, 1967.

Schulze, Winfried. *Deutsche Geschichte im 16. Jahrhundert, 1500–1618.* 1987. Reprint, Darmstadt: Wissenschaftliche Buchgesellschaft, 1997.

Schwab, Lothar. *Vom Sünder zum Schelmen: Goethes Bearbeitung des Reineke Fuchs.* Frankfurt am Main: Athenäum, 1971.

Schwindt, Jürgen Paul. "Dido, Klopstock und Charlotte Buff: Vergilreminiszenz(en) in Goethes 'Werther'?" *Antike und Abendland* 42 (1996): 103–18.

Schwinge, Ernst-Richard. *Goethe und die Poesie der Griechen.* Mainz: Akademie der Wissenschaften und der Literatur, and Stuttgart: Franz Steiner Verlag Wiesbaden, 1986.

Scott, John A. "Inferno XXVI: Dante's Ulysses." *Lettere Italiane* 23.2 (1971): 145–86.

Scott, Shirley Clay. "From Polydorus to Fradubio: The History of a *Topos.*" *Spenser Studies: A Renaissance Poetry Annual* 7 (1987): 27–57.

Screech, M. A. "The Death of Pan and the Death of Heroes in the Fourth Book of Rabelais: A Study in Syncretism." *Bibliothèque d'Humanisme et Renaissance* 17 (1955): 36–55.

———. *Montaigne and Melancholy: The Wisdom of the* Essays. London: Duckworth, 1983.

Scribner, R. W. "Ritual and Popular Religion in Catholic Germany at the Time of the Reformation." *Journal of Ecclesiastical History* 35.1 (1984): 47–77.

Scully, Stephen. "Reading the Shield of Achilles: Terror, Anger, Delight." *Harvard Studies in Classical Philology* 101 (2003): 29–47.

Seeberg, Erich. *Gottfried Arnold: Die Wissenschaft und die Mystik seiner Zeit: Studien zur Historiographie und zur Mystik.* 1923. Reprint, Darmstadt: Wissenschaftliche Buchgesellschaft, 1964.

Segal, Charles. *Euripides and the Poetics of Sorrow: Art, Gender and Commemoration in* Alcestis, Hippolytus *and* Hecuba. Durham, NC: Duke UP, 1993.

Semrau, Eberhard. *Dido in der deutschen Dichtung.* Berlin and Leipzig: Walter de Gruyter, 1930.

Sena, John F. *A Bibliography of Melancholy, 1660–1800.* London: The Nether P, 1970.

Sengle, Friedrich. *Neues zu Goethe: Essays und Vorträge.* Stuttgart: J. B. Metzler, 1989.

Seznec, Jean. *The Survival of the Pagan Gods: The Mythological Tradition and Its Place in Renaissance Humanism and Art.* Translated by Barbara F. Sessions. 1972. Reprint, Princeton: Princeton UP for the Bollingen Foundation, 1995.

Shapin, Steven. "The House of Experiment in Seventeenth-Century England." *Isis* 79 (1988): 373–404.

———. *A Social History of Truth: Civility and Science in Seventeenth-Century England.* Chicago and London: U of Chicago P, 1994.

Shell, Marc. *Money, Language, and Thought: Literary and Philosophical Economies from the Medieval to the Modern Era*. Berkeley and Los Angeles and London: U of California P, 1982.

Shelley, Percy Bysshe. *Poetical Works*. Edited by Thomas Hutchinson. 1943. Reprint, London and New York: Oxford UP, 1967.

Shields, David S. *Civil Tongues & Polite Letters in British America*. Chapel Hill, NC, and London: U of North Carolina P, for the Institute of Early American History and Culture, 1997.

Shoaf, R. A. " 'Dante in ynglyssh': The *Prologue* to the *Legend of Good Women* and *Inf.* 13 (Chaucer and Pier della Vigna)." *Annali d'Italianistica* 8 (1990): 384–94.

———. *Milton, Poet of Duality*. New Haven and London: Yale UP, 1985.

Silverstein, H. Theodore. "Dante and Vergil the Mystic." *Harvard Studies and Notes in Philology and Literature* 14 (1932): 51–82.

Simpson, James. *Goethe and Patriarchy: Faust and the Fates of Desire* (Oxford: European Humanities Research Centre, University of Oxford, 1998.

Simpson, James. *Sciences and the Self in Medieval Poetry: Alan of Lille's* Anticlaudianus *and John Gower's* Confessio amantis. Cambridge: Cambridge UP, 1995.

Singleton, Charles S. Commentary to Dante Alighieri, *The Divine Comedy: Inferno. 2. Commentary*. Translation and commentary by Charles S. Singleton. 6 vols. Princeton: Princeton UP, 1989.

Skinner, Quentin. *The Foundations of Modern Political Thought*. Vol. 1, *The Renaissance*. Cambridge: Cambridge UP, 1978.

Skrine, Peter N. *The Baroque: Literature and Culture in Seventeenth-Century Europe*. London: Methuen, 1978.

Smith, Pamela H. "Alchemy as a Language of Mediation at the Habsbourg Court." *Isis* 85.1 (1994): 1–25.

———. *The Business of Alchemy: Science and Culture in the Holy Roman Empire*. Princeton: Princeton UP, 1997.

Soave-Bowe, Clotilde. "Dante and the Hohenstaufen: From Chronicle to Poetry." In *Dante and the Middle Ages: Literary and Historical Essays*, edited by John C. Barnes and Cormac Ó Culleanáin, 181–210. Dublin: Irish Academic P for The Foundation for Italian Studies, University College, Dublin, 1995.

Sommerhalder, Hugo. *Johann Fischarts Werk: Eine Einführung*. Berlin: de Gruyter, 1960.

Sparn, Walter. "Vernünftiges Christentum: Über die geschichtliche Aufgabe der theologischen Aufklärung im 18. Jahrhundert in Deutschland." In *Wissenschaften im Zeitalter der Aufklärung: Aus Anlaß des 250 jährigen Bestehens des Verlages Vandenhoeck & Ruprecht*, edited by Rudolf Vierhaus, 18–57. Göttingen: Vandenhoeck & Ruprecht, 1985.

Speroni, Charles. "The Motif of the Bleeding and Speaking Trees of Dante's Suicides." *Italian Quarterly* 9 (1965): 44–55.

Spitzer, Leo. "Speech and Language in 'Inferno' XIII." In *Representative Essays*, edited by Alban K. Forcione, Herbert Lindenberger, and Madeline Sutherland, 143–71; 461–63. Stanford: Stanford UP, 1998.

———. *Classical and Christian ideas of World Harmony: Prolegomena to an Interpretation of the Word 'Stimmung.'* Edited by Ann Granville Hatcher. Baltimore: The Johns Hopkins UP, 1963.

Stadler, Ulrich. "Der Augenblick am Hofe: Allgemeines und Besonderes in Goethes Schauspiel *Torquato Tasso*." In *Wahrheit und Wort: Festschrift für Rolf Tarot zum 65. Geburtstag*, edited by Gabriela Scherer and Beatrice Wehrli, 463–81. Bern: Lang, 1996.

Stahl, E. L. "Schiller and the Composition of Goethe's *Faust*." *Germanic Review* 34 (1959): 185–99.

Steadman, John M. *Milton and the Paradoxes of Renaissance Heroism*. Baton Rouge and London: Louisiana State UP, 1987.

———. *Milton and the Renaissance Hero*. Oxford: Clarendon, 1967.

———. *Milton's Epic Characters: Image and Idol*. Chapel Hill, NC: U of North Carolina P, 1968.

———. "Two Theological Epics: Reconsiderations of the Dante-Milton Parallel." *Cithara* 35.1 (1995): 5–21.

Steiger, Johann Anselm. *Melancholie, Diätetik und Trost: Konzepte der Melancholie-Therapie im 16. und 17. Jahrhundert*. Heidelberg: Manutius Verlag, 1996.

Stein, Arnold. "Milton's War in Heaven — An Extended Metaphor." In *Milton: Modern Essays in Criticism*, edited by Arthur E. Barker, 264–83. Oxford: Oxford UP, 1965.

Steinke, Hubert. "Giotto und die Physiognomik." *Zeitschrift für Kunstgeschichte* (1996): 523–47.

Stephany, William A. "Pier della Vigna's Self-Fulfilling Prophecies: The 'Eulogy' of Frederick II and 'Inferno' 13." *Traditio* 38 (1982): 193–212.

Stephens, Walter. "Tasso and the Witches." *Annali d'italianistica* 12 (1994): 181–202.

Stevens, Paul. "*Paradise Lost* and the Colonial Empire." *Milton Studies* 34 (1996): 3–21.

Stierle, Karlheinz. "Odysseus und Aeneas: Eine typologische Konfiguration in Dantes *Divina Commedia*." In *Das fremde Wort: Studien zur Interdependenz von Texten; Festschrift für Karl Maurer zum 60. Geburtstag*, edited by Ilse Nolting-Hauff and Joachim Schulze, 111–54. Amsterdam: Verlag B. R. Grüner, 1988.

Strack, Friedrich. *Im Schatten der Neugier: Christliche Tradition und kritische Philosophie im Werk Friedrichs von Hardenberg*. Tübingen: Niemeyer, 1982.

Strich, Fritz. *Goethe und die Weltliteratur*. Bern: A. Francke, 1946.

Suerbaum, Werner. "Die Ich-Erzählungen des Odysseus: Überlegungen zur epischen Technik der Odysee." *Poetica* 2 (1968): 150–77.

Sulger-Gebing, Emil. *Goethe und Dante: Studien zur vergleichenden Literaturgeschichte.* Berlin: Verlag von Alexander Duncker, 1907.

Suzuki, Mihoko. *Metamorphoses of Helen: Authority, Difference, and the Epic.* Ithaca and London: Cornell UP, 1989.

Tanner, Marie. *The Last Descendant of Aeneas: The Hapsburgs and the Mythic Image of the Emperor.* New Haven and London: Yale UP, 1993.

Tasso, Torquato. *Discourses on the Heroic Poem.* Translated and edited by Marielle Cavalchini and Irene Samuel. Oxford: Clarendon, 1973.

———. *Jerusalem Delivered.* Translated and edited by Ralph Nash. Detroit: Wayne State UP, 1987.

Tatar, Maria M. *Spellbound: Studies on Mesmerism and Literature.* Princeton: Princeton UP, 1978.

Tawney, R. H. *Religion and the Rise of Capitalism: A Historical Study.* 1926. Reprint, Harmondsworth, UK: Penguin, 1990.

Teskey, Gordon. " 'And therefore as a stranger give it welcome': Courtesy and Thinking." *Spenser Studies* 18 (2003): 343–59.

———. "Milton's Choice of Subject in the Context of Renaissance Critical Theory." *ELH* 53 (1986): 53–72.

Thomas, Alois. "Christus in der Kelter." In *Reallexikon zur deutschen Kunstgeschichte*, edited by Ernst Gall and L. H. Heydenreich, 3: cols. 673–87. Stuttgart: Alfred Druckenmüller, 1954.

———. *Die Darstellung Christi in der Kelter: Eine theologische und kulturhistorische Studie, zugleich ein Beitrag zur Geschichte und Volkskunde des Weinbaus.* 1936. Reprint, Düsseldorf: Pädagogischer Verlag Schwann, 1981.

Tillyard, E. M. W. *The English Epic and Its Background.* London: Chatto and Windus, 1954.

Timm, Eitel. *Ketzer und Dichter: Lessing, Goethe, Thomas Mann und die Postmoderne in der Tradition des Häresiegedankens.* Heidelberg: Carl Winter, 1989.

Tischner, Rudolf. *Franz Anton Mesmer: Leben, Werk und Wirkungen.* Munich: Verlag der Münchner Drucke, 1928.

Toohey, Peter. "Some Ancient Histories of Literary Melancholy." *Illinois Classical Studies* 15 (1990): 143–61.

Treip, Mindele Anne. *Allegorical Poetics & the Epic: The Renaissance Tradition to Paradise Lost.* Lexington, KY: U of Kentucky P, 1994.

Trendlenburg, Adolf. *Goethes Faust erklärt.* Berlin and Leipzig: Vereinigung wissenschaftlicher Verleger Walter de Gruyter, 1922.

Trevelyan, Humphry. *Goethe and the Greeks.* Cambridge: Cambridge UP, 1941. Reprint, New York: Octagon Books, 1972.

Trevor-Roper, Hugh. "The Court Physician and Paracelsianism." In *Medicine at the Courts of Europe, 1500–1837*, edited by Vivian Nutton, 79–94. London and New York: Routledge, 1990.

Tribby, Jay. "Cooking (with) Clio and Cleo: Eloquence and Experiment in Seventeenth-Century Florence." *Journal of the History of Ideas* 52.3 (1991): 417–39.

Tupet, A.-M. "Didon magicienne." *Revue des Études Latines* 48 (1970): 229–58.

Tuveson, Ernest Lee. *The Imagination as a Means of Grace: Locke and the Aesthetics of Romanticism.* Berkeley and Los Angeles: U of California P, 1960.

Tylus, Jane. "Tasso's Trees: Epic and Local Culture." In *Epic Traditions in the Contemporary World: The Poetics of Community,* edited by Margaret Beissinger, Jane Tylus, and Susanne Wofford, 108–30. Berkeley and Los Angeles: U of California P, 1999.

Ullmann, Walter. "Dante's 'Monarchia' as an Illustration of a Politico-Religious 'Renovatio.'" In *Traditio — Krisis — Renovatio aus theologischer Sicht: Festschrift Winfried Zeller zum 65. Geburtstag,* edited by Bernd Jaspert and Rudolf Mohr, 101–13. Marburg: N. G. Elwert, 1976.

Underwood, Paul. "The Fountain of Life in Manuscripts of the Gospels." *Dumbarton Oaks Papers* 5 (1950): 43–138.

Utley, Francis Lee. "The Prose *Salomon and Saturn* and the Tree Called Chy." *Medieval Studies* 19 (1957): 55–78.

Valesio, Paolo. "The Language of Madness in the Renaissance." *Yearbook of Italian Studies* 1 (1971): 199–234.

Valk, Thorsten. *Melancholie im Werk Goethes: Genese, Symptomatik, Therapie.* Tübingen: Niemeyer, 2002.

Van Cleve, Thomas Curtis. *The Emperor Frederick II of Hohenstaufen: Immutator Mundi.* Oxford: Clarendon, 1972.

Van Helmont, Johann Baptista von. *Aufgang der Artzney-Kunst.* Translated by Christian Knorr von Rosenroth. Edited by Walter Pagel and Friedhelm Kemp. Munich: Kösel-Verlag, 1971.

Van Ingen, Ferdinand. "Faust — *homo melancholicus.*" In *Wissen aus Erfahrungen: Werkbegriff und Interpretation heute; Festschrift für Herman Meyer zum 65. Geburtstag,* edited by Alexander von Bormann, 256–81. Tübingen: Niemeyer, 1976.

Vergil. *The Aeneid.* Translated by C. Day Lewis. Oxford: Oxford UP, 1998.

———. *Aenidos liber tertius.* Edited by R. D. Williams. Oxford: Clarendon, 1962.

Vonessen, Franz. "Das Opfer der Götter." In *Dialektik und Dynamik der Person: Festschrift für Robert Heiss zum 60. Geburtstag am 22. Januar 1963,* edited by Hildegard Hiltmann and Franz Vonessen, 265–85. Cologne and Berlin: Kiepenheuer + Witsch, 1963.

Wais, Kurt. "Die *Divina Commedia* als dichterisches Vorbild im XIX. und XX. Jahrhundert." *arcadia* 3 (1968): 27–47.

Walker, D. P. *Spiritual and Demonic Magic from Ficino to Campanella.* London: Warburg Institute, University of London, 1958.

Walters, Alice N. "Conversation Pieces: Science and Politeness in Eighteenth-Century England." *History of Science* 30 (1997): 121–54.

Wandel, Lee Palmer. "Setting the Lutheran Eucharist." *Journal of Early Modern History* 2.2 (1998): 124–55.

Warnke, Frank J. "The World as Theatre: Baroque Variations on a Traditional Topos." In *Festschrift für Edgar Mertner*, edited by Bernhard Fabian and Ulrich Suerbaum, 185–200. Munich: Wilhelm Fink, 1969.

Watkins, Eric. "The Development of Physical Influx in Early Eighteenth-Century Germany: Gottsched, Knutzen, and Crusius." *Review of Metaphysics* 49 (December 1995): 295–339.

Watt, Jeffrey R. "Calvin on Suicide." *Church History* 66.3 (1997): 468–76.

Weber, Max. *The Protestant Ethic and the Spirit of Capitalism.* Translated by Talcott Parsons. New York: Charles Scribner's Sons, 1958.

Webster, Charles. "Alchemical and Paracelsian Medicine." In *Health, Medicine and Mortality in the Sixteenth Century*, edited by Charles Webster, 301–34. Cambridge: Cambridge UP, 1979.

Wehrli, Max. *Johann Jakob Bodmer und die Geschichte der Literatur.* Frauenfeld and Leipzig: Huber, 1936.

Weinberg, Bernhard. *A History of Literary Criticism in the Italian Renaissance.* 2 vols. Chicago: Uof Chicago P, 1961.

Weinberg, Florence M. *The Wine & the Will: Rabelais's Bacchic Christianity.* Detroit: Wayne State UP, 1972.

Weinreich, Otto. "Zum Tod des großen Pan." *Archiv für Religionswissenschaft* 13 (1910): 467–73.

Weinrich, Harald. "Der zivilisierte Teufel." In *Interpreting Goethe's* Faust *Today*, edited by Jane K. Brown, Meredith Lee, and Thomas P. Saine, 61–67. Columbia, SC: Camden House, 1994.

Weisberg, David. "Rule, Self, Subject: The Problem of Power in *Paradise Lost*." *Milton Studies* 30 (1993): 85–107.

Wenzel, Horst. *Hören und Sehen: Schrift und Bild; Kultur und Gedächtnis im Mittelalter.* Munich: C. H. Beck, 1995.

West, William N. "The Idea of a Theater: Humanist Ideology and the Imaginary Stage in Early Modern Europe." *Renaissance Drama* NS 28 (1999): 245–87.

Weydt, Günther. *Nachahmung und Schöpfung im Barock: Studien um Grimmelshausen.* Bern and Munich: Francke, 1968.

Wiedemann, Conrad. "Zwischen Nationalgeist und Kosmopolitismus: Über die Schwierigkeiten der deutschen Klassiker, einen Nationalhelden zu finden." *Aufklärung* 4.2 (1989): 75–101.

Wieland, Christoph Martin. *Wielands gesammelte Schriften: Erste Abteilung; Werke.* Edited by Deutsche Kommission der Königlich Preußischen Akademie der Wissenschaften. Berlin: Weidmannsche Buchhandlung, 1909–.

———. *Werke.* Edited by Fritz Martini and Hans Werner Seiffert. Munich: Carl Hanser, 1968.

Wiesflecker, Hermann. "Der Kaiser in Goethes Faust: Beobachtung über Goethes Verhältnis zur Geschichte." In *Tradition und Entwicklung: Festschrift Eugen Thurnher zum 60. Geburtstag*, edited by Werner M. Bauer, Achim Masser, and Guntram P. Plangg, 271–82. Innsbruck: Institut für Germanistik der Universität Innsbruck, 1982.

Wiethölter, Waltraud. "Legenden: Zur Mythologie von Goethes *Wahlverwandtschaften*." *Deutsche Vierteljahrsschrift* 56 (1982): 1–64.

Wilkie, Brian. *Romantic Poets and Epic Tradition*. Madison and Milwaukee: U of Wisconsin P, 1965.

Wilkinson, Elizabeth M. "The Theological Basis of Faust's *Credo*." *German Life and Letters* NS 10 (1947): 229–39.

Williams, Gordon. *Technique and Idea in the* Aeneid. New Haven and London: Yale UP, 1983.

Williams, John R. "The Flatulence of Seismos: Goethe, Rabelais and the 'Geranomachia.' " *Germanisch-Romanische Monatsschrift* NS 33 (1983): 103–10.

———. *Goethe's Faust*. London: Allen + Unwin, 1987.

———. "Mephisto's Magical Mystery Tour: Goethe, Cagliostro, and the Mothers in *Faust, Part Two*." *Publications of the English Goethe Society* NS 58 (1989): 84–102.

Williams, R. D., commentary, in Vergil, *Aeneidos liber Tertius*.

Willoughby, Leonard A. " 'Wine that maketh glad . . . ': The Interplay of Reality and Symbol in Goethe's Life and Work." *Publications of the English Goethe Society* 47 (1976–77): 68–133.

Wind, Edgar. "Dürer's 'Männerbad': A Dionysian Mystery." *Journal of the Warburg and Courtauld Institutes* 2 (1938–39): 269–71.

Winkler, Norbert. "Von der Physiognomie des Weltlabyrinths oder: Das Projekt einer unendlichen Enzyklopädie; Reflexionen zur Signaturenlehre bei Paracelsus." *Deutsche Zeitschrift für Philosophie* 44.1 (1996): 57–74.

Witkowski, Georg, ed. *Goethes Faust*. Vol. 2, *Kommentar und Erläuterungen*. 1910. Reprint, Leiden: E. J. Brill, 1950.

Wohlleben, Joachim. "Goethe and the Homeric Question." *Germanic Review* 42 (1967): 251–75.

Wolf, Gunther. "Universales Kaisertum und nationales Königtum im Zeitalter Kaiser Friedrichs II. (Ansprüche und Wirklichkeit)." In *Universalismus und Partikularismus im Mittelalter*, edited by Paul Wilpert, 243–69. Berlin: de Gruyter, 1968.

Wolfrum, Edgar. "Die Kultur des (Un-)Friedens vom 17. bis zum 19. Jahrhundert: Dimensionen einer Gesamtsicht." *Zeitschrift für Geschichtswissenschaft* 48 (2000): 894–908.

Woodmansee, Martha. *The Author, Art, and the Market: Rereading the History of Aesthetics*. New York: Columbia UP, 1994.

Wordsworth, William. *The Five-Book Prelude*. Edited by Duncan Wu. Oxford: Blackwell, 1997.

Wustmann, Gustav. *Der Wirt von Auerbachs Keller: Dr. Heinrich Stromer von Auerbach, 1482–1542.* Leipzig: Hermann Seemann Nachfolger, 1902.

Yandell, Cathy. "Of Lice and Women: Rhetoric and Gender in *La Puce de Madame des Roches.*" *Journal of Medieval and Renaissance Studies* 20 (1990): 123–35.

Yates, Frances A. *The Art of Memory.* Chicago: U of Chicago P, 1966.

———. "Lodovico da Pirano's Memory Treatise." In *Cultural Aspects of the Italian Renaissance: Essays in Honour of Paul Oskar Kristeller,* edited by Cecil H. Clough, 111–22. Manchester: Manchester UP, and New York: Alfred F. Zambelli, 1976.

———. "The Stage in Robert Fludd's Memory System." *Shakespeare Studies* 3 (1967): 138–66.

———. *Theatre of the World.* Chicago: U of Chicago P, 1969.

Zacher, Christian K. *Curiosity and Pilgrimage: The Literature of Discovery in Fourteenth-Century England.* Baltimore and London: The Johns Hopkins UP, 1976.

Zagari, Luciano. "Natur und Geschichte: Metamorphisches und Archetypisches in der *Klassischen Walpurgisnacht.*" In *Bausteine zu einem neuen Goethe,* edited by Paolo Chiarini, 148–85. Frankfurt am Main: Athenäum, 1987.

Zika, Charles. "Reuchlin's *De Verbo Mirifico* and the Magic Debate of the Late Fifteenth Century." *Journal of the Warburg and Courtauld Institutes* 39 (1976): 104–38.

Zimmermann, Harro. *Freiheit und Geschichte: F. G. Klopstock als historischer Dichter und Denker.* Heidelberg: Carl Winter, 1987.

Zimmermann, Rolf Christian. "Goethes 'Faust' und die 'Wiederbringung aller Dinge': Kritische Bemerkungen zu einem unkritisch aufgenommenen Interpretationsversuch." *Goethe-Jahrbuch* 111 (1994): 171–85.

Ziolkowski, Theodore. *Virgil and the Moderns.* Princeton: Princeton UP, 1993.

# Index

WITHDRAWN